Advance Praise for *Becoming One With the World: A Guide to Neohumanist Education*

What a wonderful book! Packed into its pages are decades of experience as a meditator, yogi, parent, educator, and Neohumanist. This latter is the crux of this text, designed to lay out in clear accessible language the fundamentals of this rich and inspiring philosophy and to touch on ways it can find its way into the daily flow of the classroom and school. A philosophy worth its salt is one that actually makes a difference in the day to day lives of people. In Kathleen Kesson and her comprehensive book, we find just this: practical, pragmatic insights into a philosophy both new and ancient! It is a gift to educators and anyone committed to wholesome futures for children, society and of course, the planet.

—Dr. Marcus Bussey
Senior Lecturer in History and Futures, School of Law and Society
University of the Sunshine Coast, Australia

Becoming One With the World is an extraordinary book. While its primary aims are explaining the philosophy of Neohumanism and detailing a Neohumanistic approach to education, it is simultaneously a comprehensive summary and synthesis of scholarly literature in the field of holistic education. Unifying knowledge and methods from many curricula areas, including spirituality, ecology, aesthetics, literacy, cultural diversity and ethics, it offers a clear orientation to a way of educating young people that seems key to human surviving and thriving.

—Dr. Aostre Johnson
Professor Emeritus of Education
Saint Michael's College in Vermont

This book by Dr. Kathleen Kesson is beautiful, wonderful, and powerful. I am sheerly impressed by the spectrum of Kathleen's mindset and the depth of her spiritual wisdom that reaches into all dimensions of learning, teaching, being, and the "cosmic mystery" including human and non-human lives. Kathleen is a visionary educator and a leader for a New Era of Neohumanism. Her immense mind, incredibly deep scholarship, unfathomable wisdom, master level of writing and analytical abilities, and her ability to integrate many disciplines and incorporate new sciences and knowledge, makes her a rare modern-day polymath. Anyone who has read this book will feel elevated, intrigued, cleansed, broadened, enriched, and better equipped to bring positive changes to the world.

—Dr. Jing Lin
Professor, International Education Policy
University of Maryland

Dr. Kathleen Kesson is a senior educational consultant and a long time Professor of Education. She has won the hearts of students around the globe through her introductory course on Neohumanist Education that she has

delivered at The Neohumanist College of Asheville. *Becoming One With the World* is a superb introduction to this subject, a perfect entry to understand the philosophy, pedagogic principles and methods of Neohumanist Education. It is a long awaited book and we are pleased to see it finally made available to a larger audience.

—**Dr. Acharya Shambhushivananda**
Chancellor, A.M. Gurukula, Anandanagar, India

Kathleen Kesson has written a book that presents a path to building an education based on the interdependency of life on the planet through a Neohumanist lens. I am not a scholar of Neohumanism, but this is a book that I have been longing for. The writing is clear and compelling, easing the reader into comfort with unfamiliar concepts. Kesson makes a strong case for the necessity of making a shift away from the standpoint of human exceptionalism in every academic discipline. As a former scientist and science teacher, I am most impressed by her ability to hold open the value of the traditions of scientific study at the same time she challenges the largely positivist and materialist approaches in the sciences that have so often led to our alienation from non-human nature.

—**Dr. Susan Huddleston Edgerton**
Professor Emeritus, Massachusetts College of Liberal Arts

Kesson has put together a remarkably engaging and superbly practical educational blueprint for our returning to Oneness. A must read for teachers, coaches, yogis, parents, children and corporate leaders who recognize the plight our separation from the rest of Nature has caused.

—**Four Arrows**
co-author of *Restoring the Kinship Worldview*
and of *Teaching Truly: A Curriculum to Indigenize Mainstream Education.*

Kesson's *Becoming One with the World* is a timely book in this planetary transition. The transition is from a world created through patriarchy, capitalism, and the nation-state—a dominator world—to a world of gender partnership, cooperative economics and global governance/bio regions. The transition cannot be accomplished without a shift in worldview, a shift to Neohumanism. Kesson takes us on a brilliant tour of this new framework—her work is theoretically edgy, practical, beautifully written, and much needed.

—**Dr. Sohail Inayatullah**
UNESCO Chair in Futures Studies
Sejahtera Centre for Sustainability and Humanity, IIUM
Professor of Futures Studies, Tamkang University
Researcher, Metafuture.org

In *Becoming One with the World* by Kathleen Kesson we are introduced to Neohumanist education in a powerful and engaging manner. This book guides us through the theory and practices of Neohumanist education. In these difficult times educators around the world can benefit greatly from this book.

—**John (Jack) Miller**
Professor, University of Toronto
and author of *The Holistic Curriculum*

Becoming One With the World by Professor Kathleen Kesson is simply outstanding. It is the kind of book that is epoch changing with ideas whose time has come. The book is an answer to a long dream of humanity. Education, as said by Nelson Mandela, is still the most potent weapon for social and global transformation. I commend this book to all well-wishers of humanity and deeply thank the author for having put together what may be the best work to date on Humanistic and Holistic education. Like her, I believe that it is up to us human beings where we lead the planet. I am deeply convinced that humanity will prevail and bring forth a sustainable planet in all aspects. This book is a great guide in that direction.

—**Acharya Jinanananda**
Yogic monk serving in Brazil

Dr. Kesson's newest contribution to the field of pedagogy, *Becoming One with the World: A Guide to Neohumanist Education* offers a window into both the theory and practice of a critically important approach to education. The first part of the book reminds us of many principles of holistic education, updated with a powerful analysis of colonization and what is needed to decolonize our work in this field. Kesson then brings these ideas to life with many nuanced and richly textured examples of integrating specific practices of yoga, music, art, story, and a reconceptualized STEAM and how these disciplines support a Neohumanist education. This book offers its readers a hopeful and coherent vision for a pedagogy for today, and well into a beautiful future.

—**Paul Freedman**
Senior Editor, *Holistic Education Review*

Dr. Kathleen Kesson's *Becoming One With the World* offers a profound vision for a new, different education based on Neohumanist principles, which include social, ecological, and spiritual values, and promises to lay a foundation for the development of our society as a whole. Her vast personal and professional experience has led to the production of knowledge from multiple perspectives which are seamlessly woven together in a fashion that echoes a significant theme which guides her pioneering work in the field—"unity in diversity"—while at the same time reflecting the (trans)modern spirit of the ancient dictum *Sá vidyá yá vimuktaye*—"Education is that which liberates."

—**Dr. Marco Oliveira**
Instructor in Liberating Humanities & Arts
Neohumanist College of Asheville, United States of America

Becoming One With the World

A volume in
Transforming Education for the Future
Jing Lin, Rebecca L. Oxford, Vachel W. Miller,
and Amanda Jane Fiore, *Series Editors*

Transforming Education for the Future

Jing Lin, Rebecca L. Oxford, Vachel W. Miller,
and Amanda Jane Fiore, *Series Editors*

Fallow Lands of Plenty: Public Schools as Leaders in Rural Food System Relocalization (2023)
    Eric Klein

Hope for the Embattled Language Classroom: Pedagogies for Well-Being and Trauma Healing (2023)
    Olivia Kanna

The Wisdom Way of Teaching: Educating for Social Conscience and Inner Awakening in the High School Classroom (2022)
    Martin E. Schmidt

Contemplative Pedagogies for Transformative Teaching, Learning, and Being (2019)
    Jing Lin, Tom E. Culham, and Sachi Edwards

Apocalyptic Leadership in Education: Facing an Unsustainable World from Where We Stand (2017)
    Vachel W. Miller

Critical Conversations about Religion: Promises and Pitfalls of a Social Justice Approach to Interfaith Dialogue (2016)
    Sachi Edwards

Toward a Spiritual Research Paradigm: Exploring New Ways of Knowing, Researching and Being (2016)
    Jing Lin, Rebecca L. Oxford, and Tom E. Culham

Re-Envisioning Higher Education: Embodied Pathways to Wisdom and Social Transformation (2013)
    Jing Lin, Rebecca L. Oxford, and Edward J. Brantmeier

Ethics Education of Business Leaders: Emotional Intelligence, Virtues, and Contemplative Learning (2013)
    Tom E. Culham

Transformative Eco-Education for Human and Planetary Survival (2011)
    Jing Lin and Rebecca L. Oxford

Becoming One With the World

A Guide to Neohumanist Education

Kathleen Kesson
LIU–Brooklyn

INFORMATION AGE PUBLISHING, INC.
Charlotte, NC • www.infoagepub.com

Library of Congress Cataloging-in-Publication Data

A CIP record for this book is available from the Library of Congress
http://www.loc.gov

ISBN: 979-8-88730-750-3 (Paperback)
      979-8-88730-751-0 (Hardcover)
      979-8-88730-752-7 (E-Book)

Copyright © 2024 Information Age Publishing Inc.

All rights reserved. No part of this publication may be reproduced, stored in a retrieval system, or transmitted, in any form or by any means, electronic, mechanical, photocopying, microfilming, recording or otherwise, without written permission from the publisher.

Printed in the United States of America

Contents

Epigraph ix
Preface xi
Foreword xvii
Introduction xxiii
Acknowledgments xli

SECTION I

The Foundations of Neohumanist Education

1 **Neohumanism: A Philosophy of Education for Our Time** 3
   Four Major Philosophical Categories 5
   Thinking Philosophically 12
   Building on Historical Philosophies 17
   Key Aspects of an Education for "Liberation" 18
   Conclusion 19
   References 20

2 **The Development of a Neohumanist Educator** 23
   What Teachers Need to Know 24
   Self Knowledge and Self Development 25
   Care of the Self 28

v

Teacher Development and Neohumanist Philosophy
     of Education 32
  Becoming Wise.. 33
  References 34

3 Reconceptualizing Child Development 37
  Why Study Child Development? 39
  Foundations of Neohumanist Child Development Theory 40
  The Social Construction of Childhood 42
  Some Limitations of Conventional Child
     Development Theory 43
  A Neohumanist Theory of Development 50
  References 53

4 The Science of Learning.. 55
  What Is Intelligence? What Is Learning? 55
  What Is Learning Theory? 56
  The Theory of Multiple Intelligences... 60
  Philosophy and Learning Theory... 62
  A Neohumanist Theory of Learning 66
  Core Principles of a Neohumanist Learning Theory 69
  Cultivating Wisdom 72
  References 74

5 Healing the World: Decolonizing Education 77
  A Neohumanist Perspective on Decolonization 79
  A Pedagogy of Decolonization.. 81
  References 88

6 Contemplative Inquiry: The Art of Knowing the Child.................91
  Descriptive Inquiry 94
  Seeing the Whole Child 99
  Cultivating Intuition 105
  Making Inquiry Central to a School.. 106
  References 108

SECTION II

Pedagogy and Practices of Neohumanist Education

- **7 Curriculum Theory and Design for a Neohumanist Future 113**
  - Who Controls the Curriculum? 114
  - Sources of Curriculum 116
  - Curriculum Design 117
  - The Future of Curriculum 131
  - Appendix A: Learning Skills 137
  - Appendix B: Arts-Based Literacy Curriculum Unit Plan Template 138
  - Appendix C: Sample Curriculum Unit Plan 139
  - References 143

- **8 The Art of Teaching 145**
  - Philosophies of Teaching 147
  - Neohumanist Teaching 148
  - Alternative Metaphors for Schooling 150
  - Overview of Instructional Methods 152
  - Cultivating *Presence* 161
  - References 162

- **9 Arts-Based Learning at the Center 165**
  - What Is Art For? 165
  - Neohumanist Education and the Arts 168
  - Spiritual Development and the Arts 176
  - References 178

- **10 Multiple Literacies: The Role of Language and Story in Neohumanist Education 179**
  - What Does It Mean To Be "Literate?" 180
  - Literacy Pedagogy in the Early Years 192
  - References 201

- **11 Visual Art and Emergence: Bringing Worlds Into Being 203**
  with Alieta Belle and Leeza Stratford
  - Elements of Drawing and Painting 207
  - Art and Development 210

viii ▪ Contents

    Facilitating Creative Process 213
    Modeling and Sculpture.. 214
    Viewing and Responding to Art 216
    The Spiritual Dimension of Art-Making.. 218
    Becoming One With The World Through Art 223
    Connection to Country 225
    References 228

12 The Superpower of Music...231
    Music and the Human Brain 232
    Elements of Music 234
    Benefits of Music in Education 234
    Music and Culture 237
    Bringing Music Into the Classroom 239
    Music and Spirituality... 241
    References 246

13 Neohumanist Education and the "Lively Arts": Integrating Creative Movement Across the Curriculum 249
    What Is "Creative Movement?" 250
    The Creative Movement Program 251
    Elements of Creative Movement 253
    Starting Points for Movement 254
    Curricular Applications.. 262
    Academic Learning and Creative Movement 265
    Conclusion.. 266
    References 268
    Additional Resources.. 268

14 Neohumanist Education and the "Lively Arts": Integrating Creative Drama Across the Curriculum 269
    Fantasy Play and Storymaking: The Early Roots of Creative Drama.. 270
    Preparing the Way: The Importance of Warm-Ups 272
    Moving Beyond the Warm-ups: Creative Drama Enactments ... 274
    Creating Dramas From Simple Stories.. 276
    The Many Uses of Creative Drama... 281
    Cultivating Neohumanism Through Drama 282
    References 284

Contents ▪ ix

15 Teaching Ashtanga Yoga to Children 287
with MahaJyoti Glassman

    A Yoga Origin Story 290
    The Eight Limbs of Yoga 291
    Yoga Ethics 292
    Yoga Postures—Asana 302
    Breath—Pranayama 306
    Deep Relaxation—Pratyahara 308
    Meditation—Dharana, Dhyana, and Samadhi 311
    References 315

16 Studying the Social World: Towards a Neohumanist Future 317

    Knowledge Wars 319
    Philosophies and Perspectives in the Social Studies 319
    Neohumanism and the Holistic Paradigm 320
    A Just, Peaceful, and Sustainable Vision for the Future 321
    Neohumanist Principles and Practices in the Social Studies 324
    Engaging Students in the Study of the Social World 335
    Appendix 339
    References 341

17 Rethinking STEAM for the Anthropocene—Part I: Science and the Modern World 343

    The Power and the Limits of Science 346
    Beyond Science 349
    Cultivating the New Story of Science 352
    References 356

18 Rethinking STEAM for the Anthropocene—Part II: Towards a Neohumanist STEAM Pedagogy 357

    STEAM Themes 358
    Integrating the STEAM Curriculum 363
    The Spiral Curriculum 372
    Ritual, Ceremony, and Festival 376
    Bringing It All Together 377
    References 379

19	**Conclusion: Education for a Bright Future**................................381	
	November 2023 381	
	References 386	
	Further Resources **389**	
	Publications... 389	
	About the Author **391**	
	About the Contributors..**393**	
	Index...**395**	

Epigraph

ONLY LOVE

And so I imagine the entire earth
as one beating heart held in the space
of this universe, inside a larger body
we can't fathom, filling with enough
love to lead each of us out of the cave
of our personal pain and into the light—
enough love to lead all humans as one
out of collective fear, rage, and hate
into a place of peace that is found only
within our own hearts, beating in sync
with the pulse of this planet we were
born to inhabit, despite the daily storms
which overtake us and make us forget
we are the lifeblood pumped into these
veins, every particle of love we generate
running into rivers, lakes, and creeks,
evaporating into the air we breathe,
give back, and breathe again.

—James Crews
from *The Path to Kindness: Poems of Connection & Joy,*
2022, Storey Publishing

Preface

In the mid-1960s, I was working as a dancer on a movie set at the old Allied Arts Studio on Sunset Boulevard in Hollywood. The leading actors in the film were reading to each other from a very thick book with a picture of a long-haired Yogi dressed in orange on the cover. I was intrigued, as I had bought a paperback book on Hatha Yoga and been practicing the Yoga poses (asanas) in my studio apartment in Hollywood for some time. The actors invited me to lunch at a vegetarian restaurant that was associated with the Self-Realization Fellowship next door to the movie studio, and I experienced my first soybean pattie, brown rice, and herbal tea. I was hooked. I bought the book, *Autobiography of a Yogi* by Paramahansa Yogananda (1998), and thus commenced my lifelong study of Yoga.

For the next few years, as I danced professionally and traveled abroad in between jobs, I studied the work of many spiritual teachers: Yoganananda, Master Subramuniya, Jiddu Krishnamurti, Meher Baba, Ramakrishna Paramahansa, Swami Vivekananda, Sri Aurobindo, and others. I had a successful career as a dancer, working in opera, musical theater, large Nevada showrooms, television, and movies. But I felt empty inside—none of the glamor, parties, or excitement was enough to bring me contentment and the Hollywood lifestyle was eating away at my soul, with its competitiveness, its disappointments, its shallowness, and the drugs and alcohol that fueled so much of the "scene."

I spent every spare penny of my measly dancer salaries on books at the local Pickwick Book Shop on Hollywood Boulevard and devoured them in between shows in my various dressing rooms. I read widely in classic literature and across the spectrum of social and psychological theory, and in comparative religion and philosophy, resonating with the message of the Yogis about the essential unity of all religions, and the idea that all spiritual paths lead to the same ultimate goal of self-realization. When I could no longer handle the contradictions between my lifestyle and what I was learning, I left "show business," which had constituted my entire life experience since my early days as a child performer. I was a bit lost as to what to do with my life—a self-educated philosopher and highly trained professional dancer with no skills in anything that might get me a job in the real world. So, I did what many of my peers did at the time, hooked up with the counterculture and its exhilarating social, spiritual, and political experiments.

I worked with the University Without Walls to establish a free university in partnership with Native American activists in Oklahoma. It was here that my ideas about education began to be shaped. I read Paulo Freire, John Dewey, Miles Horton and other great thinkers in education. I immersed myself in Native American history and current Indian politics. I met the man who was to become the father of my four sons, a fellow of Chickamauga Cherokee, Shawnee, Scotch, and Abenaki descent. Earl happened to have been initiated into Kriya Yoga by Roy Eugene Davis, a spiritual teacher who had been ordained by Paramahansa Yogananda in 1951.

When we met, Earl was emerging from a 6-month stay in an ashram where he practiced Yoga, following a couple of years engaged in the anti-war politics of Berkeley, California and a sojourn on the beaches of Maui. During his lengthy and solitary period of Yoga practice and reflection, he had decided to become a history teacher. We met outside the University Without Walls Center where I had found work that I enjoyed in education and community organizing.

Given our many common interests—Yoga, organic food and gardening, food cooperatives, free schools, environmental activism, and radical politics, we became a couple.

Together we discovered a group of Yogis living near Tulsa, Oklahoma. They farmed 65 acres, supplied natural food stores and co-ops all over Oklahoma, and held weekly meditations (dharmacakras) at their farmhouse. They welcomed us into their community. It was here that I encountered the teachings of Prabhat Ranjan Sarkar (1921–1990). I was drawn to the teachings; it was the first teacher I found who integrated deep spiritual guidance and a well-developed, practical social/economic theory that was aligned with my own beliefs and commitments. I became a lifelong student of Shrii Sarkar's ideas.

This book is not a memoir, and I must ask forgiveness for going on so long about personal history. But I do believe that readers have a right to know how an author's ideas are shaped, and by the cultural influences that have played a part. My educational perspectives have been formed by my counter cultural experiences in the free/alternative school movement, as well as by many years in graduate school where I had the good fortune to have wonderful professors who gave me scope to design my own learning path. My theories have been challenged and tempered by my hundreds of students and colleagues since beginning my academic career as a lecturer and teaching assistant and through many years as a professor and researcher. But I must credit my four children with the best of my learning; watching them grow and develop, and teaching and being taught by them, has provided me with more understanding than any book or course has given me, and I am grateful for the good fortune to have raised them.

Shrii Sarkar's (1982) ideas about education, part of his more general theory of neohumanism, resonated with me when I first read his book *The Liberation of Intellect: Neohumanism*. As a curriculum theorist and philosopher of education, my aim has long been the integration of a spiritual and aesthetic perspective with a critical social theory, worldviews that seem contradictory for many people, but which are perfectly compatible from my own perspective. I have spent much of the past five decades working out the details of this paradigm, and I offer it in these pages, with some important caveats.

First, thinking does not happen in isolation; it is a result of reading multiple books and having conversations with many scholars and practitioners. Thus, I truly consider this book a collaborative effort. Second, my cultural perspective is limited, given that most of my life and educational background has been in the United States, and so my ideas are likely to contain preconceptions that I fail to recognize. I have spent many years excavating (through conversation and study) the personal biases and perspectives accrued as a white, mostly middle class, cis-gendered woman of European descent, but am constantly reminded of how much remains to be learned. Neohumanist education is a global movement, and I cannot possibly know the many nuances and particularities that may apply to education, human development, and social life in cultures other than my own. I believe that the next few years will see a proliferation of books and articles from the many places in the world where neohumanist education is taking place, and it will be a stronger movement for its differences.

Last, I have been something of a futures thinker for most of my career, meaning that I try to account for the trajectories of the present and imagine where they might lead. My educational perspective is based on the idea, laid out in more detail in the Introduction, that we have reached an evolutionary bifurcation, and that the pathways of the modern world, with its environmental degradation, cultural conflicts, materialism, and capitalist production, consumption, and unlimited growth, is no longer serving life. I do not believe that technical fixes and the greenwashing of corporate business will get us to where we need to be in order to survive and thrive.

I believe that we need to educate young people in ways that provide them with the insights and the practical wisdom to change course, to choose the evolutionary pathway towards a more just, peaceful, and sustainable world. A more gentle world, a partnership model rather than a dominator model (Eisler, 2000). I believe that we need to cultivate the "new human," beings who care deeply about all life and feel the connection with all of creation; that's the simple version of neohumanism.

I know that many people share this viewpoint. I can sense it in the global social movements for justice...in the advocates for gender equity...in the anti-racist activists...in the emerging economic models that center universal well-being...in the eco-warriors who risk much to save the planet...and in the awakening of spiritual sentiments across boundaries of doctrine and ideology. I am aware that there are those who believe that artificial intelligence and space travel are the way of the future, and that it matters little that we ravage the Planet Earth. It is possible that human evolution is destined to transform into a digitized artificial reality and maybe that is even a step towards a total psychic reality. Like all humans, I have limited vision and may not be seeing the future accurately. I may be lost in the past, hoping for a holistic, regenerative, luminous and enchanted world that never was and never will be. But for now, I believe it is our best hope.

It is my sincere desire that this book finds a use in the hands of folks who will engage with the ideas, challenge them, adapt them, and apply them. It has been designed as a textbook, with ideas for group discussion, individual reflection, and practical application at the end of each chapter, so that it might be used in courses and study groups in different cultural contexts. The book provides a recurring comparative overview of a few major educational philosophies for those readers who want to know more about how neohumanist education fits into the larger context of educational history. There is a debate in this history about whether schools can influence social change, or if they are destined to merely reflect the status quo. George Counts, in 1932, outlined this debate in a little book called *Dare the School Build a New Social Order*, in which he argued that teachers should serve as leaders in social change. The context and the content of the ideas in his book have changed since the early 20th century, but the essence of the question remains: what is the role of education in the transformation of society? Neohumanist education challenges the very foundations of conventional thinking in education, and is aligned with a radical re-visioning of the nature of the human, the purpose of life, what knowledge is of most worth, and the values we need to guide us through this volatile and dangerous present into a bright new future. It dares to create a new social order.

References

Counts, G. S. (1932/1978). *Dare the school build a new social order?* Southern Illinois University Press.

Eisler, R. (2000). *Tomorrow's children: A blueprint for partnership education in the 21st century.* Westview Press.

Sarkar, P. R. (1982). *The liberation of intellect: Neo-Humanism.* A'nanda Márga Pracáraka Samgha.

Yogananda, P. (1998). *Autobiography of a Yogi.* Self-Realization Fellowship.

Foreword

The philosophy of neohumanism is almost entirely unknown in the academic world and the mainstream education profession in my country, the United States, because American culture generally does not draw from the deep wellspring of yogic wisdom. Insightful Indian philosophers like Prabhat Ranjan Sarkar have virtually no influence outside a small subculture that appreciates and applies their thinking in obscure communities and personal lifestyles. This neglect is a great loss to our society, for the yogic tradition offers paths out of the deadly morass in which modern Western culture is trapped. Kathleen Kesson tells us that "the love for all created beings is at the core of neohumanist thought, and at the center of neohumanist educational theory." It seems to me that love for all created beings is exactly what industrial, capitalist society lacks, and that this deficiency is at the root of our urgent crises of social justice, mental health, and degradation of the natural world. A few small subcultures in Western society have tried to bring forth this cardinal ethical principle, but the yogic tradition, as Dr. Kesson explains, has honed it into a practical science.

May I drop the usage of academic formality and refer here to my longtime colleague and friend as Kathleen? We became acquainted in 1988—nearly 36 years ago—when she submitted a superb paper to my new journal, *Holistic Education Review*. Her topic was none other than neohumanist education. She has been thinking about this approach and refining her understanding of it during all the decades since. You, dear reader, are in the hands of a writer who knows this philosophy backward and forward.

Becoming One With the World, pages xix–xxiii
Copyright © 2024 by Information Age Publishing
www.infoagepub.com
All rights of reproduction in any form reserved.

Moreover, she is a nimble, voracious scholar who has deeply scoured the extensive and complicated literatures of educational theory and postmodern thought. She explains, better than anyone I have read, how the yogic tradition can speak to the concerns of our culture and our time. I cannot imagine a better introduction to neohumanist education for Western scholars, students and teachers than this book.

One of the small Western subcultures I have in mind above is the pedagogical movement known as "holistic education." Without the benefit of deep exposure to Indian (or other non-modern/Western) thinking, several generations of dissident educators and educational thinkers have explored pedagogical approaches that challenge the industrial-capitalist worldview. Since the Romantic period, when Rousseau, Pestalozzi, and Froebel in Europe and Transcendentalists in the United States expressed faith in the latent powers of the young human mind, through the sophisticated models of Montessori and Steiner developed early in the twentieth century, and into the "human potential" movement that followed the cultural upheaval of the 1960s, these educators adopted a holistic understanding of teaching and learning, grounded in an expanded view of the human being's place in the cosmos. The term *holistic education* was first used by a group of humanistic psychologists and educators at a conference in 1979; it was nine years later that I established the journal bearing this name while simultaneously, a Canadian scholar, John P. (Jack) Miller (no relation), came out with his landmark book *The Holistic Curriculum*.

Kathleen immediately recognized the affinity between this countercultural Western pedagogy and the principles of neohumanism. She joined us at conferences in 1990 and 1991 where we sought to forge a coherent and effective educational reform movement. This effort never quite got off the ground, largely because our society (particularly its educational system) had by then entered a period of reaction and regression that was hostile to critical alternatives. Still, individual schools and pockets of scholarship on holistic education (especially in Canada thanks to Jack's influence) have remained active through the years. A new generation of activist educators has recently revived *Holistic Education Review* online (see https://her.journals.publicknowledgeproject.org/index.php/her/index). Currently, then, there exist parallel communities of educators and schools pursuing holistic alternatives to mainstream schooling: those that explicitly identify as "holistic," the quiet network of neohumanist schools that Kathleen mentions and addresses in this book, the Montessori and Waldorf (Steiner) movements that for the most part remain independent and self-contained, and a scattering of others inspired by particular traditions or teachers (e.g., Friends [Quaker] schools).

Kathleen's work—this book in particular—is uniquely positioned to introduce neohumanist philosophy to this wider community of alternative educators and to the educational world at large. She clearly demonstrates how practices grounded in yogic spirituality are philosophically similar to those arising from more secular or Euro-American spiritual paths. "A teacher who accepts the idea," she writes, "that each young person in their care is on a unique and soulful evolutionary journey seeks to understand the interests and motivations of each child, in order to help them find meaning and purpose and discover their unique gifts." This idea is at the heart of any holistic approach, regardless of which spiritual tradition or countercultural philosophy has led a teacher to practice it. The terminology used by the yogic tradition ("*yamas*" and "*niyamas*," "*koshas*," "*Brahmacakra*," "*Svádhyáya*," and so on) will sound foreign and exotic to modern ears, reflecting an ancient, nonwestern worldview wholly different from ours. But the meanings conveyed by such terms have analogues in remote corners of our heritage, too, and Kathleen skillfully describes their correspondence.

P. R. Sarkar was apparently a multidisciplinary genius, with a panoramic perspective on the problems of the modern world. It takes a scholar of Kathleen's caliber, with a similarly expansive perspective, to fully appreciate the extraordinary relevance of his thinking to our current predicament. Her explication of the historical meaning of "humanism," showing both its powerful impacts and its limitations, helps us understand why *neo*humanism is a timely and necessary corrective, a logical next step in expanding our worldview to meet the critical needs of this age. Because it is rooted in "an ontology of relationality" (I'll let Kathleen explain what this means), Sarkar's philosophy goes to the source of the widespread alienation, loneliness, and existential despair that so many of us experience in these unsettling times. We should not shy away from neohumanist education because it comes from an unfamiliar intellectual and spiritual heritage; rather, we should embrace it because it supplies what is most desperately missing from our familiar worldview. It reinforces what holistic thinkers and educators have been trying to get across for many years.

Of course, many readers of this book will already be immersed in the practice of neohumanist education or involved in personal spiritual practice. It may not be as important to you, as it is to the uninitiated, to grasp the connections to other holistic approaches. Kathleen's insights and explanations will surely help you become a more aware and effective teacher within your tradition, and that is a valuable contribution in itself. Still, I invite you to follow the expert guidance she provides to understanding the larger historical and societal dimensions of your work as an educator. She will help you realize that your work with children is related to a massive cultural project of "decolonization," which is a healing of multigenerational trauma and injustice. Know that you have allies who are not themselves practitioners of Ashtanga Yoga; you are part of a larger movement seeking to change the suicidal trajectory of modern civilization. You share a hopeful, inspiring vision of a more humane and ecologically sensible culture.

This book lays out a clear, logically organized path for developing skill as a neohumanist/holistic educator. Holding a holistic perspective is not easily done! You need to be comfortable with the complexity of the world and of human nature. You need to cultivate inner qualities and virtues and strive to attain genuine wisdom. There are no simple recipes for becoming an effective neohumanist teacher, and Kathleen does not pretend that there are. But she is exceptionally adept at presenting complex, challenging ideas in straightforward and graspable ways. This book is an invitation to go deep, to wrestle with wholeness and complexity—and yet the text itself does not require strenuous wrestling. You need not be an academic savant to understand the language or the concepts contained herein.

One of the more important concepts Kathleen introduces is what she calls "*radically diversified universalism.*" At a time when our culture is polarized into hostile political and ideological factions that cannot even agree on a shared reality, this seeming paradox of "diversified universalism" is a refreshing antidote. Holism teaches unity through diversity; it honors our multiple differences and distinctions but also insists that we are all in this together, that there is a common good, a higher good, that unites us as human beings. Kathleen explains what this looks like in practice: "Neohumanist schools, while promoting the universal sentiments of care, equality, and rights, and recognizing that the problems facing humanity are global in scope and thus require global solutions, also acknowledges the importance of local cultural expressions, languages, and the specificities of context." Here is a prime example of the complexity that we must learn to accept. Phenomena in the world, even in the social world, can rarely be understood in either/or terms; they require us to accept *both/and* descriptions. We need to learn how to hold the tension between different perspectives, different aspects of complex realities.

Even so, there is little tension in the pages that follow. Unlike most activists and radical thinkers today (and she is both), Kathleen writes in a gentle, patient, coaxing voice. She does not demand that you adopt her point of view or risk the downfall of civilization (a common either/or scare tactic). Instead, she calmly and carefully describes the challenges we are facing and invites us to try on a way of thinking that just might address them effectively. I admit my bias, because I have been advocating a version of this way of thinking myself for the past forty years, but I do believe that Kathleen makes the case very persuasively.

Finally, I want to observe that this book is impressively comprehensive. Kathleen explores every aspect of educational theory and practice that has concerned holistic educators over the years, from broad philosophical questions to nitty-gritty details about organizing a classroom and responding to children's needs. She introduces readers to a wide range of theorists, educators, psychologists and other researchers whose work has inspired or informed our field over the years, without being a partisan devotee of any one body of work. Even her presentation of Sarkar's philosophy is modest, treating his work—as original and central to neohumanism as it is—within a rich intellectual context. Indeed, this is not only the premier textbook on neohumanist education: It is the most complete depiction of holistic education generally in all our literature. If you are not affiliated with the yogic path or Indian philosophy and the Sanskrit terminology confuses or distances you, just glide over it and substitute "holistic" for "neohumanist," and you will still have an extremely useful and insightful guide to the practice of an alternative educational approach powerful enough to meet the pressing needs of our time.

I am sure that this book will enable numerous educators to fashion better classrooms and schools, making a positive if not transformational difference in the lives of children and their communities, and ultimately in our struggling civilization.

— **Ron Miller**

Ron Miller founded the journal *Holistic Education Review* in 1988 and was publisher/editor of other periodicals and books, and author or editor of nine of his own books, on the history and philosophy of educational alternatives. He has been a teacher from Montessori preschool through adult education.

Introduction

As of this writing, it is no longer possible to deny that we live in calamitous times. Stories of disasters reach our ears daily, attuned as much of humanity now is to a global flow of news. The megatrends are more than visible for any with the desire and the means to see. The majority of the world's scientists agree that we are entering a volatile global era that is already bringing treacherous heat waves, sea level rise, disastrous flooding, unpredictable weather patterns, increasing droughts, sand and dust storms, intensifying forest fires, species extinction, crop failure, food insecurity, and increasing inequality as the poor and vulnerable suffer the greater part of the burden of global warming.

Many scholars, including the authors of numerous United Nations reports on climate change, believe that human impacts on the environment related to energy use and other factors are shifting the world out of the Holocene period into a new geological era, often termed the Anthropocene (Greek: ánthrōpos, "man, human" + *cene*, "an epoch or geologic period"). The Holocene, the most recent epoch of the Cenozoic Era, begun well over 10,000 years ago, has been characterized by relatively stable climate patterns that enabled the flourishing of complex human cultures. In the Anthropocene, thought by some scholars to commence with the "Age of Discovery" (1492) and by others with the industrial revolution, humans have impacted geological and environmental systems dramatically, culminating in the "great acceleration" (a term coined by environmental historian John McNeill) from the mid-twentieth century onwards, during which the loss

Becoming One With the World, pages xxv–xli
Copyright © 2024 by Information Age Publishing
www.infoagepub.com
All rights of reproduction in any form reserved.

of ecosystems due to temperature overshoot, pollution, and other factors may be irreversible. Our generation—those of us born in the mid-twentieth century and forward—may be responsible for the elimination of life as we know it on our planet.

There is, according to some scholars (Moore, 2015; Wilke, 2013) a fundamental error in attributing the current ravages on our planet to humans in general, disregarding the reality that it is a specific civilization that has driven these processes of resource extraction, labor exploitation, capital accumulation and what some are calling *ecocide*. European civilization (and its most powerful former colony, the United States), with its roots in the Enlightenment philosophy of humanism and its centuries-long narrative of conquest, colonialism, genocide, plunder, and slave labor:

> The term "Anthropocene" actually disguises the fact that a small part of the world's population is single-handedly responsible for depositing that thin carbon layer in the Earth's crust around 1800 and that the values, economic paradigms, and consumption patterns of that one civilization among many now constitute the dominant framework in this new age that we call the Anthropocene. (Wilke, 2013, p. 70)

While global warming may be the most urgent of the issues that we face, there are other serious problems; many of these are centrally or peripherally related to climate change and ecological crisis, but not all. Numerous armed conflicts are going on across the world, with tragic collateral effects—famine, disease, loss of homes, involuntary migrations, ecological destruction. These are wars over ideology, territory, religious dogma, language, ethnic rivalries, drugs, and many other factors. Humanity has not yet learned to solve its problems non-violently, nor has it developed truly effective international structures to resolve major conflicts.

Smaller wars, no less virulent to the people who experience them include gender violence, racism, hate crimes, domestic crime, and police brutality. Gross income inequality persists despite global lip service to eradicate poverty, and over a billion children on the planet are deprived of the food and basic services they need to survive and thrive (World Bank, n.d.). Signs of despair infect modern industrial cultures, and most tragically, our youth: drugs, alcoholism, mental illness, suicide (Cohen, 2022).

Humanism and Its Failings

The roots of Western Humanism are deep, tracing back to early Greek and Roman cultures, but we concern ourselves here with the version that (re) surfaced in 13th century Italy, spread throughout Europe, and has continued, albeit in changing forms, to the present day. The philosophy of humanism is a constellation of ideas that released the Western world from the grip of medieval dogma and superstition and began to replace prevailing religious ideologies with a new view of the individual and its social potential. Renaissance Humanism, in concert with an emerging Enlightenment science, ushered in a new era of human inquiry and self-reflection, scientific and technological development, and human rights, and has had a lasting impact on the field of education.

The Enlightenment philosophy of humanism and its practical handmaidens, science and technology, brought us incredible control over the natural world through the application of empiricism and reason, harnessing the energies of nature to bring portions of the world to its current peak of technological development. It also influenced social structures, bringing in its wake tolerance for diversity, the ideals of democratic governance, and the universal recognition of human rights, all promises yet to be fully realized.

In addition to the advancement of knowledge and understanding of the world we live in, humanism has had contradictory social and political effects, paralleling (and supporting) a global system of empire-building, colonialism, and capitalism. Capitalism, the economic system that developed alongside the Enlightenment and the industrial revolution, and which promised to mobilize material resources for the benefit of humanity, is now revealed to serve the interests of the few at the expense of the many, and its commitment to unlimited growth is proving to be a danger to life itself. And communism, the great hope of the oppressed masses, crumbled under the weight of its repressions, exterminations, crimes against humanity, environmental degradation, and misguided attempts at social engineering.

The (unfinished) liberation of humans from superstitious dogmas, coupled with the advance of Enlightenment science, has had profound consequences, as Max Weber proposed over 100 years ago: the advent of a world that benefitted in many ways from rationally derived explanations, but a world no longer rich with the mysteries and wonder of creation—a disenchanted, alienating place devoid of spiritual and transcendent dimensions of experience (Labaree, 2019). And compounding the long term effects of this emergent worldview, the new empowerment of the individual resulted in the centering of the human species and an emphasis on the mastery, domination, and control of nature, rather than an acknowledgement of our entanglement with all of creation.

The Post-Humanist Turn

In the wake of humanism's failure to bring about universal justice, well-being, widespread happiness, an ecologically stable bio-system, and world peace, a new set of "posthuman" discourses arose in the late 20th century that challenge some of the central premises of humanism. Variously termed antihumanism, dehumanism, transhumanism, voluntary human extinction, and neohumanism, there are consistencies as well as variations among them. All suggest the possibility of a "new form of human," and of decentering the traditional humanist subject, with its individual ego and the premise that humans could and should exert mastery over the rest of nature. The intersecting discourses on posthumanism all, to varying degrees, consider the triadic formulation of human/animal/machine. Many of the posthuman discourses focus on the historical violence enacted in the name of defining some people as human and some as "subhuman." Some posthumanist discourses explore the new forms of being generated by novel human/machinic connections: the impact on cognition through digitized information technology, including AI and virtual realities; enhanced physicality through prosthetics, pacemakers, and the like; increased awareness of microworlds and macroworlds through equipment that enhances our senses, such as the electron microscope and telescopes. Some scholars are focusing on new understandings of the human/animal connections, including, but not limited to studies of animal behavior and interspecies communication.

Of these visions of the future of humanity, one offers a potentially optimistic vision of the future; not a rejection of humanity as hopelessly flawed, but a vision of humanity that is intimately linked to all other life forms and places creativity and love at the center of all of our endeavors. Neohumanism does not abandon the main organizing principles of humanism; rather it believes the philosophy needs to be revised in terms of new understandings that place humanity not at the center, but as a unique and essential part of the ontological whole of creation. And it demands the full realization of the promises of humanism: the celebration of diversity, the implementation of democratic governance, and the universal recognition of human rights. Crucially, it extends these rights beyond the human realm to embrace other-than-human species, animate and inanimate, with whom we share the planet.

Neohumanism

The philosophy of neohumanism was articulated by Prabhat Ranjan Sarkar (1921–1990), also known by the spiritual name of Shrii Shrii

Ánandamúrti—Indian philosopher, guru, social reformer, linguist, author, and composer—in *The Liberation of Intellect: Neohumanism* (1982). In this book, Shrii Sarkar reconceptualized the centuries-old philosophy of humanism, retaining its utopian vision of a humanity united in its quest for peace and global justice, but challenging the multiple forms of domination, subordination, discrimination, materialism, exploitation, and the imposition of "pseudo-culture" (i.e., capitalist cultural products)—the whole range of "power-over" tactics that characterize the era of modernity/coloniality founded on humanism.

He extended the critique of human domination over other humans to the rest of the world as well: plants, animals, and other animate and inanimate systems. In some ways, his ideas are aligned with deep ecology but without the anti-human baggage of some thinkers in this area (Bookchin, 1995; Devall & Sessions, 1985). In the neohumanist paradigm, humans are the most developed species as defined by cognitive function, language, and collective intelligence; they therefore hold great responsibility for the well-being of all, an "all" in which humans, animals, plants and the rest of the natural world are deeply interconnected and mutually interdependent.

From a neohumanist standpoint, "the 'baby' of spirituality has been thrown out with the 'bathwater' of organized religion" (Vedaprajinananda, 2006, p. 28), and the time has come to cultivate a non-dogmatic, ecumenical spirituality based on contemplative practices and authentic morality in order to truly realize the high ideals promoted by the humanists. And furthermore, the attribution of moral standing and rights must be extended to all creation in order to overcome the anthropocentrism fostered by classical humanism: "The recognition of the existential value of plants and animals," and even more recently, of bodies of water and land, "adds an ecological dimension to Humanism" (Vedaprajinananda, 2006, p. 29).. Only with such a "deepening of humanism with a psycho-spiritual approach and the widening of Humanism, with an ecological component" (Vedaprajinananda, 2006, p. 29) might we finally have the effective tools we need for tackling the enormous social, ecological and socio-economic problems facing our global society.

Among Shrii Sarkar's many contributions to the world was the formation of an international Yoga society (A'nanda Márga Pracáraka Samgha) set up to propagate the ancient Indic teachings of Ashtanga Yoga (the Eightfold Path of Yoga), which he updated for modern times. While traditional Yoga practitioners focused on individual liberation (the transcendence of the limitations of the ego), Sarkar expanded the understanding of Yoga spiritual practice to include the welfare of the collective as well, with his discourses on economic, political, social, ecological, and educational theory. Numerous disciples were charged with the task of bringing Yoga out of the mountains and forests where the *sannyasis* (religious ascetics who renounce the world) had traditionally dwelled and into the world, with the aim of bringing about a societal transformation towards greater peace, justice, equality, and what we are now calling "sustainability"—living in harmony with the multitudes of more-than-human others (Abram, 1996) with whom we homo sapiens share the planet. The phrase "more-than-human others" signifies a conceptual shift away from the idea of human exceptionalism to a recognition that humans are but part of a greater assemblage of beings, an intelligent and interpenetrated web of life that shapes the events of the world.

In 1990, Shrii Sarkar created *Gurukula* which was to become the Board of Education for all neohumanist schools. The etymology of the Sanskrit word is *Gu*: "darkness"; *ru*: "dispeller"; *kula*: "an institution." Gurukula, thus, is an institution designed to help students dispel the "darkness of ignorance" and to lead to the emancipation of the individual and society at large. In the next section, we take a look at the fundamental principles at the heart of neohumanist education.

Neohumanist Education

While Shrii Sarkar spoke on a multitude of subjects, including wide-ranging prescriptions for social change and justice in the spheres of politics, economics, and culture, the philosophy of neohumanism finds one of its most developed expressions in educational theory and practice, at the heart of which is an ontology (Greek: ōn, *ont-*, "being" + -*logy*, "study of") of *relationality*. Deeper and more connected ways of knowing, thinking, doing, and being are at the heart of neohumanist pedagogy, supported by the understanding of the roots of conflict and domination in limiting geographic and social sentiments such as the rigid attachments to nation, class, caste, race, religion, or species that divide the beings of the Earth. Overcoming destructive cognitive and affective sentiments is a significant task of neohumanist education, a pedagogy that integrates and synthesizes critical pedagogy, decolonization, academic learning, and spirituality in ways profoundly relevant to the present world-historical moment.

Two approaches capture the essence of this task. The first is the cultivation of an awakened rationality capable of discerning limiting sentiments when they arise, even when they are well-disguised. In place of the limiting sentiments is the *principle of social equality*, the cornerstone of building a genuinely just global society. In Sanskrit, this movement of humanity is termed *Sama Samaj Tattva*. This disposition to develop what Sarkar (1982) terms a "rationalistic mentality" (p. 74) is not merely the adoption of a set of beliefs, however. In neohumanism, the process of cultivating such a mindset depends on the second approach: a psycho-spiritual practice, that is, the conscious mental effort to expand the radius of one's care outward from the limiting sentiments to a universal love for all and a concern for the common welfare. This process involves developing awareness of one's inner world, and expanding the heart through meditation and empathy.

Shrii Sarkar's lectures on education and other social topics were aimed at a larger audience than his circle of devotees. He recognized that humanity faces a critical evolutionary juncture, and that conventional education has failed to cultivate the "new human" equipped with the knowledge, skills, and dispositions necessary to radically reimagine and enact a paradigm shift in our conceptions of what it means to be human, and how to live respectfully and humbly on a damaged planet and in a pluriverse of equality. In that, his mid-twentieth century discourses are consistent with principles that are only now emerging at the very highest level of policy making.

In 2020, the United Nations Educational, Scientific, and Cultural Organization (UNESCO) published a report on educational futures by the Common Worlds Research Collective (CWRC), an interdisciplinary network of researchers "concerned with our relations with the more-than-human world" (CWRC, 2020, n.p.). In that visionary document, a number of declarations are put forth that call upon educators to challenge and fundamentally reconfigure the role of education and schooling in order to radically reimagine and relearn our place and agency in the world:

- We must preserve the best of humanism—justice—but extend it beyond the human.
- We must acknowledge that we are ecological—not just social—beings.
- We need to cease promoting human "exceptionalism," while also accepting responsibility for the differential positioning and treatment of other species.
- We need to discard conventional individual and social developmental frameworks in favor of fostering collective dispositions and convivial, reparative human and more-than-human relations.
- We must learn to become *with* the world, not stand apart from it.
- The spirit of universalism must embrace multiple and diverse human worlds, as well as the multiplicity of our entanglements in multispecies ecologies.
- We need to adopt an ethics that is collective, more-than-human, and reparative.

Neohumanist education shares the essence of these educational aims, but takes us further down the road with its focus not just on transformational theories, but the pedagogical practices that might enable us to attain these ideals.

The Spiritual Dimensions of Neohumanist Education

It is one thing to have lofty aspirations, and even to create academic content that teaches about our relationships with the more-than-human others with whom we share the planet. The field of environmental education has been around since at least the 1970s, more than 50 years, but it has not had the impact on human behavior that its founders hoped for. Though it is a rich area of study, its focus on knowledge *about* the environment, inquiry, and critical thinking, with a dominant focus on human management and stewardship of resources, lacks an important dimension.

Establishing deep connections with all of creation, animate and inanimate, and awakening to the realization of the self-organizing intelligence of the universe, lie in the *imaginal realm*—what some scholars describe as the "metaphysical background" of the world (Buhner, 2014). Developing these "suprasensory" capacities (sensing that lies beyond thought and language) is the pathway to what the UNESCO report alludes to when they state that we must become *with* the world, not merely stand apart from it. We must aim for *interspecies intersubjectivity,* or what Thich Nhat Hanh calls *interbeing* (2017) not merely *subject/object* relations if we are to become the "new humans" with the perception, knowledge, understanding, skills, and dispositions to help our damaged planet to recuperate.

It is possible that this inherent relationality is the blissful ontological state that humans are born into, but that the dominant paradigm of materialism (the belief that all that exists is matter and its movements and modifications) and conventional schooling with its limited focus on learning about the external world, not to mention the consumerist addictions fostered by a capitalist economy, effectively close the advanced sensory gateways that must remain open to subtle phenomena in order to *decenter* the human and reconnect with more-than-human others. Sensory gating refers to the brain's skill at filtering out unnecessary sensory stimuli in order to function in the world (Buhner, 2014). We have all been conditioned since birth, our sensory gateways well established, by the institutions of our culture: families, school, church, and media. Jiddu Krishnamurti (1994) says this about habitual thinking:

> Our problem is the mind, the mind which is conditioned, which is shaped, which is the plaything of every influence, every culture, the mind which is

the result of the past, burdened with innumerable memories, experiences. How is such a mind to free itself from all this? (p. 1)

To address this problem of social conditioning and cultivate the human capacity to access the imaginal realm, Neohumanist education strives for a balance between *extroversial* and *introversial* learning: learning about the external world through the application of observation, inquiry, logic, reason and critical thinking, and learning about the inner world and the subtle energies of emotion, intuition, values, aesthetics, and interspecies communion through meditation, somatic awareness, contemplation, and opening the heart to overcome the limiting sentiments of our social conditioning.

The holistic education movement (Miller, 1997) has long proclaimed the spiritual dimension of the child, but educational policy debates consistently get hung up on the entanglement of spirituality and religion. Shrii Sarkar was a vociferous critic of religion, decrying the bloody battles and indoctrination, the superstition, gender and caste discrimination, and the blind, irrational devotion to dogma by followers of religions, criticisms that did not earn him any points among the elites of his society (he was equally critical of economic and social dogmas). He consistently called for an "awakened consciousness"—the integration of rationality, intuitive discernment, and ethics.

Ashtanga Yoga (the traditional "eightfold path" of Yoga) is an ancient, Indigenous tradition of India, clarified and revitalized for the modern era by Shrii Sarkar, who encouraged its global spread. It is featured as a centerpiece of neohumanist education in this book; that said, it is one of many contemplative approaches to spirituality that might be found in a neohumanist school. Contemplative paths aligned with the purposes of neohumanism share an understanding of the various dimensions of the self—body, mind, and spirit—as an integrated whole. At the level of the body and the individual ego, there is a sense of separation, isolation, and a false sense of permanence. The entire constellation of personal memories, experiences, reactions, mental habits, and desires constitute this enclosed self. By utilizing specific practices and disciplines (meditation, concentration, mindful attentiveness, visualization, etc.), one comes to understand the illusion of this isolate self and begins to move beyond such limitation into a genuinely somatic awareness of the interconnectedness and the dynamism of all creation (Kesson, 2001). This exquisitely subtle form of understanding, the elimination of the subject/object dichotomy, is "the diamond that cuts through illusion" (Thich Nhat Hanh, 2006), and is the basis for becoming *with* the world, rather than *apart* from it.

Yoga in the Western world, specifically the United States, is both extremely popular and also divisive, especially when it comes to teaching Yoga to children. The latter part of the twentieth century saw a number of lawsuits over the "moment of silence" in schools, usually involving Buddhist-derived "mindfulness" practices or Transcendental Meditation. The defense of Yoga generally cites the secular aspects of the practices that most people in the West are familiar with and supportive of—the physical exercises (asanas), relaxation, and breath control. Indeed, there is a growing body of research on the health effects, both mental and physical, of practicing posture-based Yoga as well as meditation: emotional regulation, improved attention span, and the reduction of stress and anxiety (Goleman & Davidson, 2017).

The case against Yoga often boils down to claims that its roots in Eastern religions, specifically Hinduism and Buddhism, cause it to violate constitutional separations between Church and State. In fact, the conservative legal groups most active in bringing cases "are actually designed to maintain the dominance of Christianity in the United States" (Helderman, 2019). Yoga, then, is caught in the crossfire of the culture wars, at least in the United States. People fear what they do not understand, and people in the grip of limiting socio-sentiments such as caste, race, nationality, religion, or creed, often fear new ideas that threaten their secure beliefs. Though Yoga and mindfulness practices are often found in public schools now, neohumanist schools are likely to be independent rather than state-sponsored schools, unless situated in countries or cultures that do not perceive Yoga as a threat.

The Yoga taught to children in neohumanist schools has been carefully designed over the past few decades to be developmentally appropriate for different age groups, and teachers are highly trained in these practices. Young children are not necessarily taught formal meditation (though this is welcomed in some cultures), but neohumanist schools feature a "quiet time" in which teachers may use creative visualizations or affirmations to generate feelings of love and safety. Yoga is taught in a playful way, often using puppets, storytelling, creative movement, and songs. Reflective and imaginative techniques that align with neohumanist principles are sometimes invoked during other teaching and learning activities; for example, in a unit about space, students might be encouraged to close their eyes and visualize the planets circling in our solar system or in a unit about trees, students might imagine how a tree might feel to be chopped down.

Neohumanist education does not conceal the fact that it is a character-based education, with an ethical foundation in the ancient traditions of Yama and Niyama, the first two limbs of the eightfold path of Ashtanga Yoga, refined and adapted by Shrii Sarkar so that ordinary people can put them into practice in different contexts. The "Yamas" are considered to be guidelines that regulate behavior with the external world, the "Niyamas" are considered guidelines that relate to one's inner world. They are much simplified in neohumanist education, interpreted differently by people in differing cultural contexts, and include virtues such as kindness, honesty, responsibility, simple living, respect for self and others, contentment, service, self-reflection, and empathy, virtues that are for the most part, universal across cultures. The cultivation of morality is not prescriptively rule-based in neohumanism, but behavior is governed by an overarching and dynamic principle of seeking the welfare of all, the common good.

It is often claimed that Yoga is a "spiritual science," and this is true in the sense that one can practice it and observe the results objectively in one's own life. The insight and intuition gained from contemplative practice are intended to foster the ability to make wise judgments about the choices we make. And though there will always be those who adopt beliefs dogmatically, practitioners of Ashtanga Yoga are encouraged to question and explore.

Though considered a spiritual science, Yoga practices do share with religions the "transcendent impulse," the yearning to experience a more expansive state of *being* beyond the small "I"—called by various names depending on how one conceptualizes this: God, The Creator, Pure Consciousness, the Collective Unconscious (Jung, 1916), the Witnessing Entity (Towsey, 1986), the Noosphere (de Chardin, 1959), the Planetary Mind, the Supreme Being, the Ocean of Being, the Implicate Order (Bohm, 1980), the Tao, Emptiness, Cosmic Consciousness. In contrast to the notion in most religions that this state is a realm separate from creation, Yoga-inspired neohumanism understands this "cosmic consciousness" to be immanent and non-dualistic, in that it does not categorize mind and spirit as "holy" and matter as "unholy," but sees all of creation as divine, and as emanating from a common source. So while neohumanism is designed to be free of doctrine and dogma, the ethical foundation does hold to a principled spiritual purpose: extending the sense of love and connection beyond one's small self and immediate circle and experiencing the "Oneness" of all creation.

James Moffett (1994), a well-known and revered teacher of language arts, was one of the earliest mainstream education scholars in the West to take seriously the idea of a universal spiritual principle that must be attended to in the growth, development, and education of youth. Eschewing both religious dogma and the dogma of a secular society that acknowledges only a materialistic version of humanity, he defined spirituality in this way:

> Spirituality is totally cosmopolitan, because only the cosmic framework is all-inclusive. To be spiritual is to perceive our oneness with everybody and everything and to act on this perception. It is to be whole within oneself and with the world. Morality ensues. (p. xix)

Moffett was a serious student of Yoga, both the embodied practices and its deep philosophical meanings. He spent the latter part of his life drawing out the connections between his growing understanding of how the spirit works through human life and what we need to do in education to cultivate wise, compassionate human beings. Like Shrii Sarkar and Jiddu Krishnamurti, he understood how profoundly conditioned our minds are by the cultural messages we have received, and how persistent negative mental programming can be in determining our actions, even when such actions are so obviously against our best interests. Moffett saw the "deconditioning" of the human mind as essential to an education that might liberate the human spirit from its personal and social conditioning.

For Moffett, meditation is the primary method by which we learn to "witness" our mental functioning in ways that allow us to understand the origins of our habitual thinking and desires, and ultimately to transcend these. He also understood that spirituality is not merely an individual pursuit, but that we have a responsibility, through service, to bring others along with us on the path of liberation. The commitment to service is a hallmark of a neohumanist education. Throughout their school careers, students are encouraged to apply what they have learned for the benefit of others, including more-than-human others. In this way, spirituality, ethics, and social commitment are given concrete expression in a multitude of ways to develop care, compassion, and the expansion of love to all creation.

Neohumanist Schools

Since Shrii Sarkar put forth the ideas of neohumanism, many people have been inspired to create neohumanist schools in over fifty countries with hundreds of kindergartens, primary schools, secondary schools, colleges, and children's homes established over the past 50 years. Some are exemplary models that have been recognized for their excellence; others are located in environments such as refugee camps, impoverished urban settlements, or poor villages where teachers, parents, and children struggle to find the simplest of materials and equipment. The quality of the schools varies widely depending on a number of factors: available resources, governmental influence, teacher professionalism, and engrained local/cultural beliefs about education. Shrii Sarkar provided some guidance on the pedagogies and practices of neohumanist education, but it has been through the grassroots, collaborative efforts of neohumanist teachers sharing ideas in informal peer workshops, contributions by neohumanist scholars (e.g., Inayatullah et al., 2006) and a newsletter (see Gurukula Network, https://gurukul.edu/newsletter/about-amgk-newsletter/) that the model has taken shape.

This book was inspired by a request for some formalizing of the practices and a more systematic approach that might equalize the quality of the schools as well as the preparation of neohumanist teachers. There have been attempts to create a teacher education program in the past, but the global nature of the neohumanist network proved to be a substantial hurdle to bringing people together for shared learning. It has only been with the rapid expansion of digital teaching and learning technology, greatly accelerated during the COVID pandemic that began in 2019, that it has become feasible to offer courses to students in many different countries simultaneously.

It's important to note that "systematic" does not imply "standardized." A key feature of neohumanist education is its rootedness in local culture, and its deep commitment to a sense of place. Sarkar was a proponent of a universalism which he defined as the love for all created beings—an outlook that refutes discrimination based on caste, creed, color, race, and gender, and rejects all sentiments which impose limitations on human development. He often spoke of the ways that colonizing cultures, whether those of the older European colonizers or those of the newer neo-liberal economic imperialists, inject feelings of inferiority into people which then makes it possible to exploit them, socially or economically. In hundreds of citations, we read him pointing out the injustices wrought by these imposed inferiority and superiority complexes.   Neohumanist education is devoted to decolonization, understanding that this is a long term process that involves removing not just the political, but the intellectual and emotional shackles of the oppressor who has brought about the systematic destruction of so many of the world's languages, local ecosystems, and self-sustaining and appropriately scaled economies. Sarkar's universalism, then, is a *radically diversified universalism* (Kesson & de Oliviera, 2023), not the universalized Western standards that identify some people as "more human" than others and some social models as inherently superior to others. Neohumanist schools, while promoting the universal sentiments of care, equality, and rights, and recognizing that the problems facing humanity are global in scope and thus require global solutions, also acknowledges the importance of local cultural expressions, languages, and the specificities of context. Therefore, while neohumanist schools are subject to guiding principles, they are not carbon copies of each other, but as diverse as the cultures in which they are situated.

The first iteration of the book project was a series of interactive webinars offered to a number of neohumanist educators in 2019 that resulted in the initial chapters of the book being written. Following these webinars, the author was invited to design a program for teacher preparation that would be offered under the auspices of India-based Gurukula, through the newly formed Neohumanist College of Asheville (NHCA) in North Carolina. New book chapters were written to align with the classes offered in the program, and NHCA graduated its first cohort of certified neohumanist educators in the Summer of 2023.

The idea that we can design an education that intentionally integrates critical thinking, rationality, and contemplative practice may seem like an impossible dream. However, we truly are at the dawn of a new era in that science itself is pointing us in a transcendent direction, awakening us to the deeper mysteries of the universe even as it answers many of the questions that have been with humans for centuries. The great discovery of contemporary science, say authors Swimme and Tucker (2011), "is that the universe is not simply a place, but a story—a story in which we are immersed, to which we belong, and out of which we arose" (p. 2). Swimme and his colleagues (Griffin, 1988) who consider themselves "postmodern cosmologists" articulate a new story emerging from science itself, drawn from the descriptions of matter generated by quantum physics, from the power of cosmological observations enabled by advanced telescopes, and from the intricacies of the plant world revealed by the electron microscope and time lapse photography. It is a moment in time when East and West may be meeting in a new synthesis.

Shrii Sarkar elucidated a philosophy of creation—*Brahmacakra*—that closely parallels this new story coming to us from Western science. In this narrative, pure consciousness exists in a state of equilibrium, before time, containing within it an infinite, immanent creative power. When the creative force manifests itself, the cosmic cycle is initiated, and everything—"galaxies, stars, planets, rocks, bacteria, plants, animals, and human beings" (Ratnesh, 1989, p. 21)—evolves and exists in various states of vibrational frequency as a thought projection of (and within) the cosmic mind. Not only does this particular mythos embrace the modern evolutionary synthesis, it is consistent with emergent explanations of the universe as a self-organizing, intelligent system (or system of systems).

This book poses an essential question: "How might this vitalized 'new story' of the universe, a cosmology that integrates both rational and contemplative ways of knowing, Eastern and Western ways of understanding, find its way into education?" We must begin with ontology, and a shift from perceiving the human being as an isolated individual, separate from the rest of creation whose destiny is to manipulate and control nature solely for human benefit to one who is deeply connected with the "pluriverse" of beings—plants, animals, and animate and inanimate matter. From this sense of connection springs a radical empathy, and with it the capacity to discern meaning and purpose, for meaning is fundamentally relational. Neohumanist education fosters the bonds and relations formed in everyday life, but also nurtures the "transcendent impulse"—the relationship with the ultimate context of our lives.

At the center of the educational principles that flow from this neohumanist perspective is the notion of "epistemological pluralism," which requires that we look beyond the contributions of modern Western-trained scientists to Indigenous people and others who have lived in harmony with their biosystems, for forms of knowledge such as traditional ecological knowledge, intergenerational knowledge, ancestral wisdom and mythic insights, narrative knowing, embodied and intuitional knowing, a spectrum of the ways of knowing that have been marginalized under the regime of a modernity governed by capitalism and colonialism.

With the new ontology of relationship, deepened appreciation of the existential value of humans and more-than-humans, and an appreciation of the multiple ways of knowing by which we construct knowledge, arises the need for a new ethics, a way of navigating the complex waters of this emerging world. It is with the humble awareness of the necessary ontological, epistemological, and ethical shifts, and their extraordinary implications for basically everything we think we know about the education of young people, that we invite you into this book in the hope that you will find ideas that resonate with our deepest feelings about the kind of future we desire, the kind of world we wish for our children and our grandchildren, and for those generations of humans (and more-than-humans) yet to come.

References

Abram, D. (1997). *The spell of the sensuous.* Vintage Books.
Bohm, D. (1980). *Wholeness and the implicate order.* Routledge.
Bookchin, M. (1995). *Reenchanting humanity: A defense of the human spirit against anti-humanism, misanthropy, mysticism, and primitivism.* Cassell Books.
Buhner, S. H. (2014). *Plant intelligence and the imaginal realm: Into the dreaming of earth.* Bear and Company.

Common Worlds Research Collective. (2020). Learning to become with the world: Education for future survival. *Education Research and Foresight Working Paper, 28*. UNESCO.

Cohen, S. (2022, March). *Suicide rates highest among teens and young adults*. UCLA health. https://www.uclahealth.org/news/suicide-rate-highest-among-teens-and-young-adults

De Chardin, T. (1959). *The phenomenon of man*. Harper and Row.

Devall, B., & Sessions, G. (1985). *Deep ecology: Living as if nature mattered*. Gibbs Smith.

Goleman, D., & Davidson, R. J. (2017). *Altered traits: Science reveals how meditation changes your mind, brain, and body*. Random House.

Griffin, D. R. (1988). *The reenchantment of science*. SUNY Press.

Helderman, I. (2019). The crusade against mindfulness. *Psychology Today*. https://www.psychologytoday.com/us/blog/therapy-and-buddhist-traditions/201909/the-crusade-against-mindfulness

Inayatullah, S., Bussey, M., & Milojević, I. (2006). *Neohumanist educational futures: Liberating the pedagogical intellect*. Tamkang University Press.

Jung, C. G. (1916). The structure of the unconscious. In *The collected works of C. G. Jung, Vol. 7: Two essays on analytical psychology*. Princeton University Press.

Kesson, K. (2001). Contemplative spirituality, currere, and social transformation: Finding our "way." *Journal of Curriculum Theorizing, 17*(4), 67–88.

Kesson, K., & Oliveira, M. (2023). Diversifying universalism: Neohumanism, internationalism, and interculturalism in education. *Práxis Educativa, 18*, 1–14. https://doi.org/10.5212/PraxEduc.v.18.21481.049

Krishnamurti, J. (1994). *On learning and knowledge*. Harpers.

Labaree, D. (2019). Max Weber's "science as a vocation." https://davidlabaree.com/2019/07/29/max-webers-science-as-a-vocation/

Miller, R. (1997). *What are schools for? Holistic education in American culture* (3rd ed.). Holistic Education Press.

Moffett, J. (1994). *The universal schoolhouse: Awakening spirituality through education*. Jossey-Bass.

Moore, Jason. (2015). *Capitalism in the web of life: Ecology and the accumulation of capital*. Verso Books.

Ratnesh, A. (1989). *Microvita: Cosmic seeds of life*. Dharma Verlag.

Sarkar, P. R. (1982). *The liberation of intellect: Neo-Humanism*. A'nanda Márga Pracáraka Samgha.

Swimme, B. T., & Tucker, M. E. (2011). *Journey of the universe*. Yale University Press.

Thich Nhat Hanh. (2017). The insight of interbeing. *The Garrison Institute*. https://www.garrisoninstitute.org/blog/insight-of-interbeing/

Thich Nhat Hanh. (2006). *The diamond that cuts through illusion*. Parallax Press.

Towsey, M. (1986). *Eternal dance of macrocosm*. Proutist Publications.

Vedaprajinananda, A. (2006). Neohumanism, globalisation and world futures. In S. Inayatullah, M. Bussey, & I. Milojević (Eds.), *Neohumanist educational futures: Liberating the pedagogical intellect* (pp. 25–35). Tamkang University Press.

Wilke, S. (2013). Anthropocenic poetics: Ethics and aesthetics in a new geological age. In H. Trischler (Ed.), *Anthropocene: Exploring the future of the age of humans.* RCC Perspectives 3, 67–74.

World Bank. (n.d.). *Global trends in child monetary poverty according to international poverty lines.* https://www.worldbank.org/en/topic/poverty/publication/global-trends-in-child-monetary-poverty-according-to-international-poverty-lines#:~:text=Approximately%20333%20million%20children%20globally,than%20US%246.85%20a%20day

Acknowledgments

First my deep appreciation to Shrii P. R. Sarkar (1921–1990) for bringing to the world the immense scope of his thought. On a personal level, I can truly say that the Yoga and meditation I learned from him turned the direction of my life towards a sense of meaning, purpose and fulfilment, and I am forever grateful for that.

To my editor from Information Age Publishing, Jing Lin, for her enthusiasm for the book as well as her insights that prodded me to further exploration. Thank you for all of your help, and for introducing me to new areas of inquiry in language and spirituality.

To Shaman Hatley, for his advice on the finer points of Sanskrit philosophy and language. Any errors in this are mine alone.

To my many intellectual mentors who helped me find my footing in academia, beginning with my Oklahoma State University doctoral advisors Russell Dobson and Randall Koetting, who created such an open space for my graduate studies, and Doren Recker, who taught me much about the philosophy of science.

To my mentors Donald Oliver of Harvard University, Chet Bowers of the University of Oregon and Portland State University, and William Doll of Louisiana State University, who all, in wonderfully different ways, confirmed my intuitive thinking and provided the conceptual tools to challenge prevailing educational orthodoxies. They have passed from this world now, but their intellectual legacies live on, and I can only hope to have carried their ideas forward in respectful ways.

To my many colleagues in the field of curriculum studies, an amazing home for the speculative and the experimental in thought and in practice—you know who you are, and I appreciate all I have learned from you.

To my wonderful Goddard College colleagues for a decade, fellow travellers in the world of student-directed learning who sought to create space for meaningful, purpose driven inquiry.

To my LIU-Brooklyn colleagues during the opening decades of the new millennium, who were committed to keeping humanistic and holistic pedagogies alive in the midst of a challenging urban educational environment.

To my current travelling companions at the Neohumanist College of Asheville (NHCA) with whom I have worked to shape a teacher preparation program designed to help the ideas in the book find their way into the world of schools and communities, and to the staff and board at Gurukula, India for their on-going support of this work.

To my many students over the years, from Goddard College to the urban campus of LIU-Brooklyn, to the NHCA, who have challenged, shaped, and sustained my commitment to education.

To my colleagues in the Great Transition Initiative, a global group of scholars committed to the shaping of a just and sustainable future—you have broadened and deepened my thinking in so many ways.

To the many scholars and writers I have only met in your books—thank you for committing yourselves to a life of study and sharing what you have learned. In a world composed largely of sound bites and tweets, this work is of vital importance.

To the artists, teachers, musicians, imagination activists, parents, monks, poets, nuns, community organizers, scholars, environmental warriors, farmers, scientists, and especially young people—all of you who are giving selflessly of your time and energy to create a brighter future—keep up the good work.

And finally, to my wonderful four sons, Steven, Shaman, Räm, and Chris, who have been my most important teachers in this life and my inspiration to carry on.

SECTION I

The Foundations of Neohumanist Education

1

Neohumanism

A Philosophy of Education for Our Time

Philosophy (Greek: *philo-* 'loving' + *sophia* 'knowledge, wisdom') is at the heart of all theories of education. The love of wisdom may seem like an old-fashioned idea in modern cultures, with their emphases on getting a good job, gaining status, and accumulating wealth. But we live in challenging times: We have entered a new era in human history that scholars call the Anthropocene, a phase of planetary development in which human impacts on the earth may cause or have caused irreversible damage. The challenging problems faced by humanity now and in the near future require more than instrumental solutions; we need to bring ethics, imagination, intuition, and compassion into the mix. If we are to survive and thrive, we need wisdom now more than ever. To cultivate wisdom in the new generation of human beings requires a radical rethinking of the aims, purposes, and practices of modern education.

Every decision made by a teacher (and they make hundreds of decisions a day) is grounded in a set of beliefs, whether these are held consciously or unconsciously. These beliefs are concerned with the Big Questions:

Becoming One With the World, pages 3–21
Copyright © 2024 by Information Age Publishing
www.infoagepub.com
All rights of reproduction in any form reserved.

- What does it mean to be human?
- What is the purpose of life?
- What is knowledge and how do we come to know?
- What do we value? How should we live?

Underneath these Big Questions are inquiries specific to education:

- What should be the aim of education?
- What is the role of culture in the educational process?
- How do children learn best?
- What is the appropriate role of the teacher?
- What is worth knowing, and how does a teacher decide what to teach?

In the "Introduction" to this book, we compared and contrasted the main ideas of humanism and neohumanism as articulated by Prabhat Ranjan Sarkar (1982) in his book *The Liberation of Intellect: Neohumanism*. We noted the power of the philosophy of humanism and its importance in the creation of modern forms of education. With the expansion of educational opportunity to more and more people came increasing rights to many (not all). The ideas of democracy took hold in Europe, though its monarchies would survive into the present day. Scientists accelerated the exploration of the world with new tools of observation, measurement, and the application of reason and logic. Truth became something discovered, not something revealed from a divine source. Discoveries and inventions made life easier and more comfortable for many people.

We also noted some of the consequences of humanism that have brought us to the brink of global disaster. An economy based on unlimited growth, increasing consumption, and the acquisition of capital requires the extraction of ever greater quantities of the Earth's resources. Humans have poisoned the planet with the waste products of industrialism. Technology has brought not just comfort and ease for a few, but ever greater weapons of destruction, some capable of wiping out all life on the planet. People are engaged in a competitive struggle for survival, and with the dissolution of the traditional bonds of family, tribe, and community, an epidemic of mental illness, substance abuse, and despair has swept many societies.

Humanism can be said to have contained the seeds of its own demolition. In order to overcome these negative developments in human society, human consciousness must *evolve* to a more advanced level. Humanist philosophy and its educational offspring are inadequate to this evolutionary task. We need to cultivate new ways of thinking aligned with pedagogical practices that will help us bring up a new generation of souls capable of surviving and thriving in these extraordinary times.

The love for all created beings is at the core of neohumanist thought, and at the center of neohumanist educational theory. This reconceptualization of what it means to be human and the deepening of our relationships with each other and with all creatures, and of learning to live in life-sustaining and planet-sustaining ways—this is the evolutionary task before us, and one to which neohumanist education is profoundly well-suited. What follows is an overview of four of the main categories of thought that philosophers address, and a brief contrast of the ideas of humanism and neohumanism as these relate to the education of young people.

Four Major Philosophical Categories

Cosmology/Metaphysics

Cosmology and metaphysics ask fundamental questions about the origin and nature of the universe, such as:

- Is there a Creator?
- Why was the universe (or the pluriverse/multiverse) created?
- How did life come about?
- How do human beings fit into the plan?
- What is the relation between mind and matter?

Throughout all time, humans have told themselves *cosmic creation stories*, explanations for the mystery of existence. At the core of all human societies with their rituals, customs, folkways, traditions, and ethics is their creation story. Whether our story features a giant turtle or a big bang, they are all attempts to provide meaning and purpose to human life. We are at an evolutionary crossroads now, and the story we tell ourselves may determine the future of life on Earth. Scientists and religionists alike say we need a new story—one that is consistent with all we know from our scientific endeavors, but one that embraces the great mystery that science has yet to penetrate (Swimme, 1988).

Neohumanism is such a story—one that posits the existence of a supreme guiding intelligence, *and* honors the rationality and wonder at the root of scientific investigation. It adopts the premise that all matter is generated from this cosmic consciousness and mind evolves from matter as described in the Yogic cycle of creation (Brahmacakra). In this model of creation, the "unit mind" (what many call the "soul") experiences evolution similar to the scientific understandings of evolution, but with a fundamental difference: the ultimate unification of the unit mind with the supreme consciousness from which it was created (*Yoga,* from the Sanskrit root *yug*: to yoke, attach, join). This core idea—the ultimate union of the human with the Infinite—is an idea shared by the many different historic and contemporary schools of Yogic thought.

Yogis believe that this inherent divinity is the motivation guiding humans to learn, expand their minds, and develop their full potential. A teacher who accepts the idea that each young person in their care is on a unique and soulful evolutionary journey seeks to understand the interests and motivations of each child, in order to help them find meaning and purpose and discover their unique gifts. Understanding the nature of *samskaras* (the cause and effect actions and reactions activated as the soul progresses towards its destiny), the thoughtful teacher pays close attention to the psychic bondages and limitations in each child and provides support to overcome them. In this way, the neohumanist educator works with the child in the construction of the young person's personal story, a story that is embedded in the larger narratives of their culture and of all creation. The ultimate aim of such an education is that a young person will grow to expand their circle of love, connect in meaningful ways with all beings, and embrace a benevolent universal outlook to guide their journey in the world.

What differentiates this spiritual approach from other religion-based pedagogies is the rejection of dogma. Neohumanist education is concerned with overcoming the bondages and limitations in the mind—limitations such as biases, false ideas, complexes, neuroses, and so on, as well as the inclination to favor one's own race, religion, nation, or social class above others. It accomplishes this by pairing the development of the intellect through rational thinking with the development of the spirit through contemplation, insight, and the awakening of conscience.

Ontology

Ontology (Greek ōn, *ont-* 'being' + *-logy* 'study of') is the study of what it means to be human. Related to metaphysics and cosmology, but focused more explicitly on the nature of *being*, it asks fundamental questions about personal meaning and purpose:

- Why was I born?
- What does it mean to be human?
- What is my purpose in life?
- Do I have a soul?
- How should I relate to other beings?

We have learned that neohumanism is a philosophy that encompasses the mundane and the cosmic, which understands the known universe as dynamic and evolving, and that defines the human as a multi-dimensional being engaged in a quest for realization and spiritual understanding.

One main idea that profoundly shaped humanist thinking about *being* is the idea of the individual, the "I" as a bounded entity, surrounded by stable substances and objects in space that constitute separate "others" to manipulate, utilize, and transact with. This sense of separation, mastery, and control in concert with an economic system predicated on resource extraction, endless growth, and needless consumption has led us to the ecological tipping point at which we find ourselves. Neohumanism requires the cultivation of an ontology that is *relational*, that understands there is no separation of self and other, of knower and known, of subject and object, but rather endless flows of being and becoming in which we are deeply entangled with everything in creation, visible and invisible, material and molecular, objective and subjective.

Here is what one of our great Western scientists had to say about the nature of ontological *being*:

> A human being is a spatially and temporally limited piece of the whole, what we call the "Universe." He experiences himself and his feelings as separate from the rest, an optical illusion of his consciousness. The quest for liberation from this bondage [or illusion] is the only object of true religion. (Einstein, 1950, in Haymond [n/d.], para. 14)

How to facilitate the growth of young people in this "quest for liberation" from the limited sense of "I-ness" to an expanding circle of connection? In the first phase of existence, there is the small self, the ego and its identification with the body and its needs and the growing awareness of the surrounding world. The individual's sense of identity expands to the family, their sense of place (geo-sentiment) and ever outwards to include one's social groups, clan, social class, race and ethnicity, religion, and so on (socio-sentiment), and ideally, to all of humanity (humanism). Neohumanism transcends even this species-centric sentiment to embrace all of creation with love. This is not a linear process and it is not a "stage theory" (an inevitable progression through identifiable stages of growth).

None of these phases of identity are problematic in themselves: One can hold a great love for the land on which they live, or one's social identity can be a source of strength. Problems can arise when a person gets stuck on this identity "chain"—when they come to feel that their race is superior or that their religion is the only correct one. Their expansive flow is then blocked, or reversed. Neohumanism teaches that it is our destiny to remove all such limiting labels and continue to expand our consciousness into an identity of interconnectedness, of integral unity, rather than separation and superiority. When we remove all the labels we have affixed to ourselves, we find something that precedes all labels, and with that existential awareness lies the connection with the consciousness of everything in the universe. This is the ontological task of neohumanist educators, to facilitate the movement of young people through this ever-expanding circle of connection.

In the context of *relational being and becoming*, neohumanist education challenges everything from our notions of individual achievement to our valuing of independence and autonomy, from our theories of human development and cognition to theories of experience and academic subject matter. If everything is in process, or relational, then we must awaken to the profound interdependence between the human organism and the environment, the life histories and trajectories of "objects" and our own implication in these, as well as the human connection to transcendent levels of mind. A neohumanist curriculum embraces this multidimensionality, the whole of ontological experience. The tangible implications of this central idea will be more fully articulated in upcoming chapters.

Epistemology

Epistemology (Greek *epistēmē* 'knowledge'+ -*logy* 'study of') asks fundamental questions about the nature of knowing:

- What is knowledge?
- How is knowledge constructed?
- What are the sources of knowledge?
- How do we come to know anything?
- How can we know what is true?

Conventional education concerns itself primarily with knowledge about the external world, what Shrii Sarkar calls "extroversial knowledge." Neohumanist education approaches extroversial knowledge through the application of current systematic principles of investigation, inquiry, documentation, analysis, logic, and critical thinking. Neohumanist education also recognizes the validity of "introversial knowledge," gaining knowledge about one's Self through the practice of meditation and intuition. This careful balancing of the pursuits of external and internal knowledge aims to awaken the capacities of insight, imagination, intuition, empathy, compassion, and discernment in order to ensure that knowledge gained through study of material phenomena is applied in ethical and conscientious ways, for the welfare of all.

Throughout our humanist history, conventional Western models of education have spread across the planet, resulting in the loss of language, tradition, culture, and Indigenous ecological knowledge. Some scholars have aptly called this *epistemicide* (de Sousa Santos, 2014). In the process of valuing a particular version of scientific investigation and reason over all other forms of knowledge creation, and in the context of conquest, colonization, patriarchy, and economic imperialism, ways of knowing that exist outside these contours have been marginalized or suppressed: embodied knowing, contemplative knowing, intuitional knowing, narrative knowing, aesthetic knowing, mythic knowing, and ancestral/intergenerational knowing. Neohumanist educators work to cultivate an *epistemological pluralism*, while understanding that all ways of knowing are not necessarily equal, and that different epistemologies are suited to different tasks and purposes.

The quest for truth is the epistemological task, a task now made more urgent by the contemporary global infrastructure of misinformation and disinformation. Digital technologies and popular media, for all of their potential worth, have brought about a flourishing ecosystem of alternate realities that make it possible to mislead masses of people, spread false ideas, and gain power over the lives of human beings.

To be a neohumanist educator is to engage with some challenging epistemological contradictions:

- How do you navigate the tensions between reason and intuition, the spiritual and the rational, the material and the ideal, the internal and the external, skepticism and inner knowing?
- How do you teach in a way that is deeply rooted in the language and culture of specific people and places, while cultivating a sense of universalism (love for all creation)?

One Western scholar states the challenge of our time this way, when he notes that this younger generation

> may be the last who can still reverse the negative megatrends converging today. In order for these children to learn the needed new ways of thinking, the present generation in charge of society must begin to set up for them *a kind of education it never had and arrange to educate itself further at the same* time [emphasis added]. (Moffett, 1994, p. xii)

These new ways of thinking must cultivate a sense of universal love for all creation, an understanding of the deep interconnectedness of all life, and an appreciation for the multiple ways of knowing available to humanity. They must strive to free the mind from any and all discrimination and bias on the basis of race, class, caste, gender, and so on. They must nurture the capacity to penetrate the lies and misinformation that permeate the mental sphere, and foster the courage to "speak truth to power"—to challenge corruption, authoritarianism, oppression, and violence wherever it threatens the collective welfare. They must *liberate the intellect*, and cultivate the wisdom to see humanity through the spiritual, psychic, intellectual, and physical challenges of this era.

Axiology

Axiology (GR: *axia* 'value' *or* 'worth' + *-logy* 'study of') includes the study of both ethics and of aesthetics. It asks fundamental questions of value:

- What do we consider to be of worth?
- What constitutes the good, the true, the beautiful?
- What is progress?
- How should we live?
- What are my values?

Neohumanist education is an inherently value-oriented philosophy and character-based pedagogy, adhering to concepts of universalism, love for all creation, social equality and all-around benevolence. The German word *Bildung*, meaning both education and formation, is an apt term for it, referring as it does to the harmonization of a person's mind, heart, character, and identity, a process of "becoming" that signifies development over the span of human life.

Ethics

Along with the necessary new ways of thinking that need to be nurtured, new ways of *being* are required for the new era. We are currently living in a time of cultural pluralism, a fine idea at its core, but one which has had consequences. It has brought about a sense of ethical relativism, and there is uncertainty about what if anything, can be considered a cardinal value. In our late-humanist society, in which "man is the measure of all things," self-interest often supersedes nobler intentions such as altruism and service. As well, capitalist ethics have become the dominant social value, and the market is an ultimate arbiter of ethical questions. Should we endanger fragile habitat in order to drill for oil? Of course, if profit is the main value.

Humanism measures *progress* in terms of increasing material abundance, personal comfort, and convenience (for some) and scientific and technological achievements (with little regard for their consequences). While not ignoring economic well-being nor downplaying the importance of scientific knowledge, neohumanism applies other measures to progress: how a society treats *all* of its people, how it relates to other species and the environment, and in terms of non-material factors such as happiness and fulfillment. In neohumanism, progress means growing our circle of love, making our society reflect that love, and ultimately moving away from the exclusive focus on materialism towards the mysterious source of existence (divinity). The movement towards these goals, in neohumanism, represents authentic progress.

In the relational, process philosophy of neohumanism, in which the inherent value of all living things is acknowledged, ethics are the principles we must use to regulate these many and varied relationships. Shrii Sarkar rejects the kind of simple rule-based morality encoded in many traditions, yet subscribes to the notion of overarching ethical principles under the broad umbrella of the question: *Does this contribute to the welfare of all?* The curriculum can no longer be constructed to serve dominant economic and political interests, as it does currently, but must address the deep interconnections that we are coming to understand between and amongst humans and all "other" life forms.

In a neohumanist education, ethics is infused throughout the curriculum; every subject from biology to history is approached through an ethical study framework. Social-emotional learning is essential in developing empathy, compassion, and understanding of the "other." In the study of ethical dilemmas (and we face countless of them in this new era), it is important to cultivate the arts of reflection, deliberation, and discerning judgment, to invoke, as Sarkar suggests, both reason and intuition. In these ways, ethics can become a facilitator of personal and social transformation—a tool for expansion.

Aesthetics

Since the beginning of recorded human history, people have engaged in painting, design, song, music, storytelling and movement. Such activities are literally how we create our worlds. In modern Western societies, the arts are commodities, with ascribed value based on notions of uniqueness and scarcity. In many other societies, especially those that have lived in a simpler harmony with their environments, aesthetic practices are so embedded in culture that their languages literally have no word for "art."

The arts are essential to neohumanist educational practice, both on their own individual merits, and as entry points and expressive possibilities for all subject matter. In neohumanist education the arts serve ancient and life-preserving functions, involving young people in participatory aesthetic experiences that create and recreate the fundamental stories of our existence—our human bonds, our relationships with plants, animals, sea and sky, and the mythic stories that carry forth and transmit the blueprints of a moral universe (Kesson, 2019). In these ways, the arts are both catalysts and facilitators of the metaphysical, ontological, epistemological, and ethical foundations of education. For neohumanist educators, ethics and aesthetics are essential to determining what is worth knowing, what should be taught, how should subjects be organized and what are essential guiding questions. Both of these topics will be addressed in more depth in subsequent chapters.

Thinking Philosophically

A philosophy is not much use if it cannot guide our actions. Neohumanist education has not emerged in a vacuum. In the same way that neohumanism has retained much of worth from earlier philosophies of humanism, so neohumanist educational philosophy draws some things of value from earlier philosophical traditions of education. Educational philosophy has very practical implications for how teachers go about all that is involved in teaching and learning: how they conceive of the learner, how knowledge is constructed, what is worth knowing and doing, what and how they choose to teach, how they make decisions, and how they can cultivate the kind of character in young people that will enable them to survive and thrive in these extraordinary times.

In many ways, neohumanist education represents a creative synthesis of the most important ideas in education to date, in particular, those ideas designed to equip young people with the mindsets, knowledge, skills, and dispositions to work towards the creation of a world characterized by peace, justice, creativity, joy, and the long term well-being of the Earth itself and all its creatures. Here we take a look at six historical educational traditions with an eye to what is worth saving in older traditions, and what is unique to the emergent tradition of neohumanist education.

Perennialism

Perennialists believe that the important ideas put forth by major thinkers in human history need to be passed down from generation to generation through the study of classic texts. It is a conservative philosophy that is teacher-centered, subject matter centered, and focused on intellectual development and the preservation of culture.

Behaviorism

Behaviorism, a philosophy that has dominated Western educational thought and practice, concerns itself with the outward presentation of a child (their *behaviors*), not their inner life. In this model, children are born with minds considered "blank slates," which can be written upon with any ideas valued by the culture. Young people's behavior is conditioned with precise stimuli, rewards, reinforcements and punishments; this model proves particularly useful for social engineering.

Romanticism

The Romantics, in the late 18th and early 19th centuries, reacted against mechanistic materialism, science, new technologies, and the emerging bureaucratic society. They rejected the idea of the human being as a blank slate, and believed us to be born with innate powers, or a divine spark. They embraced the deep feelings of the individual soul and its emotional, spiritual, poetic, and artistic nature. The Romantics believed that the Enlightenment period had "disenchanted" the Earth, and they sought to reestablish the magic, mystery, mysticism, and myth that had characterized most of human history. Teaching methods in this framework foster personal freedom, awe, wonder, and the cultivation of imagination.

Pragmatism

Pragmatists believe that learning is a transaction between the inner world and the outer world, and that people construct knowledge through having experiences and reflecting on them. They advocate inquiry-based learning, practical activities, analysis, reason, and logic. Pragmatists value democracy and democratic ways of living, so teaching methods in this framework are characterized by cooperative group learning, real world problem-solving, and discussion.

Critical Pedagogy

Challenges to these earlier philosophies of education came in the later 20th century with the advent of critical pedagogy, a philosophy of education that takes a hard look at the social structures that construct our worlds. Drawing upon a Marxist conceptual foundation, critical pedagogy insists that we acknowledge the ways that capitalist relations, racism, sexism, ableism, and other forms of oppression have limited the full development of human powers. It supports forms of education grounded in the development of critical thinking and social analysis in order to understand and overthrow these limitations.

The above traditions of education may seem radically different from each other. For example, on knowledge: The perennialists believe that knowledge resides in texts and is best transmitted that way from generation to generation. The behaviorists believe that knowledge only matters if it results in observable behavioral change, and that such change can be conditioned through rewards and punishments. The Romantics believe that each soul is born with innate knowledge, and they seek to "draw out" (Latin: ēducēre) the potential of the child. The pragmatists believe that knowledge resides in the interaction between the external world and the mind of the child. The critical pedagogues would assert that without critical thinking about received knowledge, we would just continue being brainwashed by the dominant culture.

Other significant differences concern the role of the teacher: For the perennialists, the teacher is an authority figure, the holder of cultural knowledge, and the students are the receivers of this knowledge. For the behaviorists, the role of the teacher is to provide conditioning stimuli, and ensure the correct response. For the Romantics, the teacher is a "gardener," nurturing the plant (the child) but allowing the child to grow freely. For the pragmatists, the teacher is the "guide on the side"—a facilitator of knowledge, setting up the environment, and organizing activity. And for the critical pedagogues, the teacher is a sort of consciousness raiser, posing critical questions and helping students learn to "read the world," and understand how power operates in the lives of people (Freire, 1970/2018).

Despite these major differences, and with the partial exception of Romanticism, all of these ways of thinking about education share a common root: the Enlightenment philosophy of humanism, a philosophy with a number of key (mostly unexamined) assumptions:

- Humans are the masters of creation, separate, and disconnected from nature.

- Nature exists to be measured, controlled, and utilized for human benefit
- The individual is the primary unit in society, and self-interest should govern our behavior.
- Reason and logic are the most valuable ways of knowing.
- Progress is equated with unfettered technological development and unlimited economic growth.

One philosophy with ancient roots but newly conceived in relation to 20th century science attempted to address the shortcomings of the five traditions noted above. This was the philosophy of *holism*, and its associated tradition, holistic education.

Holism

In 1926, Afrikaner statesman and philosopher Jan Smuts (1926/2017) coined the term "holism" in a book titled *Holism and Evolution*, advancing a challenge to the prevailing reductionist paradigm with the idea that nothing can be understood in isolation. He claimed that reality can only be discerned by considering its components systemically, as parts of a dynamic whole, a whole which is greater than the sum of its parts. His ideas would come to influence many branches of science and human affairs, including physics, biology, ecology, and systems theory as well as theories of human development, psychology, education, and political science (including aspirations of global governance). Though his primary focus was scientific, he believed that holism was purposeful: "A cosmic process of individuation that produced individuals progressively complex in structure" (van Wyk, 2016, p. 3) and in the "gradual development and stratification of a progressive series of wholes stretching from the inorganic beginnings to the higher levels of spiritual creation" (in van Wyk, p. 1). He linked human evolution to the creation of an ideal realm of values, where could be found truth, beauty, and goodness.

Smuts was an internationalist who promoted early forms of global organization, such as the League of Nations, the United Nations, and the Commonwealth of Nations. He was also a white supremacist who supported racial segregation. It's important to note that holism does not preclude hierarchy, either in the natural sciences nor in social theory. Thus, holistic ways of thinking must be tempered by critical pedagogy if the aims of neohumanism are to be realized.

Some early "alternative educators" (Montessori, Pestalozzi, Steiner, etc.) claimed a spiritual dimension to child development, and designed educational models to enhance this aspect of learning and growth. It was only in the 1980s however, that a "holistic education paradigm" began to take its place as a recognizable way of thinking about modern education. James Macdonald (1995), a revered curriculum theorist, challenged the conventional set of paradigms of the field (which he named the Romantic, the Cultural Transmission, the Developmental and the Radical) claiming that they were useful, but only partial accounts of what it means to be human and how we come to know the world. Drawing on the ideas of such diverse 20th century thinkers as Michael Polyani, Carl Jung, William James, Mary Caroline Richards, and others, he proposed a *dual dialectic* that would expand the individual/social dialectic into the deeper reaches of the self variously termed the "unconscious," the "void," the "ground of being," or in the religious sense, "God." He called this dual dialectic a *transcendental/developmental paradigm*, and thus opened the academic field of curriculum studies to a larger discussion of spirituality, values and human purposes.

Alongside this interest from scholars, holistic education, with its ancient roots, developed as a field of practice focused on cultivating dimensions of human experience largely ignored by modern schooling with its priorities of learning facts, mastering the basics (reading, writing, and math) and doing well on exams. Influenced by various academic movements including humanistic psychology, transpersonal psychology, systems theory, holism, ecology, and the "new sciences" of complexity, holistic education aimed to cultivate the subtle human faculties of aesthetics, intuition, imagination, emotional intelligence, and spirituality, as well as a progressive social and ecological sense of responsibility. Holistic educators focused on the *interconnectedness* of experience and reality, the relationships between the whole and the part, the student as an active, participatory and critical learner, and respect and reverence for the inner life of the child (see Mahmoudi et al., 2012). Many holistic thinkers subscribed to the notion of "ultimacy"—the idea that inherent to human development is a drive toward wholeness and the capacity to attain a "peak state" of realization, with resultant attainment of primary human values such as compassion and integrity, accompanied by an overarching state of well-being (Forbes, 2003).

While the major strands of holistic thought were concerned with the individual and their spiritual development, one group of scholars advanced a more explicit commitment to social justice within this paradigm: "Holism, then, is the recognition that spiritual enlightenment, ecological awareness, and the quest for social justice must be brought together in order to adequately confront the crisis of our time" (Miller, 1993, p. 21).

Building on Historical Philosophies

The philosophical foundations of neohumanist education draw something of value from each of the earlier philosophical traditions. From the perennialists comes the idea that knowledge, to be of worth, need not necessarily be *new*. There is wisdom to be found in the past, and the knowledge embedded in cultural traditions, such as the knowledge that has been passed down by Indigenous people about how to live in ecological balance with their environments, is valuable.

From the behaviorists comes the idea that in order for any learning to be internalized, there must be reinforcement from the environment. We can decry the social engineering aspect of this philosophy, while retaining the notion of positive reinforcement, and the importance of providing authentic feedback and celebrating the accomplishments of young people.

From the Romantics comes the essential idea of the inner life of the child, and how vital it is to value the motivations and interests of each learner. They also remind us of the magic and mystery at the heart of existence, and of the importance of nurturing the imagination.

From the pragmatists comes the very key idea that *experience*—real life engagement with the "stuff" of the world—should be at the center of education. Learning needs to be active, with a rich and stimulating environment that engages the child in doing, playing, experimenting, making, feeling, and thinking. Inquiry, collaboration, cooperation, and problem-solving are key elements of neohumanist education.

Critical pedagogy addresses the vital importance of learning to question what is given, to examine texts (written, spoken, visual, etc.) for the ways that they shape and limit our thinking, to learn to "read the world," and to be alert for manifestations of power and oppression.

It is only the holistic paradigm of education that attempts a synthesis of the most vital aspects of these earlier philosophies, with its "deep concern for connection, relatedness, and integration in human experience" (Miller, 1993, p. 20), and, as noted above, by at least one strand of its thinkers an equivalent commitment to social justice (Kesson, 1993; Purpel, 1993). Shrii Sarkar's discourses place neohumanist education in this philosophical camp, a perspective that integrates spiritual purpose with a commitment to justice. Neohumanist education draws upon important ideas from other philosophies, especially Romanticism, pragmatism and critical pedagogy, but adds important new concepts and practices, while deepening and extending these important ideas in particular ways.

Key Aspects of an Education for "Liberation"

Sá vidyá yá vimuktaye—*"Education is that which liberates."*

> The real meaning of education is trilateral development—simultaneous development in the physical, mental and spiritual realms of human existence. This development should enhance the integration of the human personality. By this, dormant human potentialities will be awakened and put to proper use. (Shrii Sarkar, 1998, p. 111)

In order to "awaken dormant human potentialities" Neohumanist educators seek to integrate the following principles into their philosophy and practice:

- Focus on the *wholeness* of reality (understanding the interconnections between humans and rest of natural world, the systemic nature of all creation, the importance of relationships—between humans, plants, animals, soil, sea and sky—and the subtle ways that changes in anything affect everything else at some level).
- Focus on *wholeness* of the individual (balanced attention to physical, intellectual, emotional, social, aesthetic, and spiritual dimensions of the child).
- Character development grounded in universal moral values (in attunement with local cultural values)
- Overcoming limiting sentiments (geo-sentiment, socio-sentiment, species-sentiment) and the extension of identity, love, and connection to all humanity as well as non-human species
- Commitment to "decolonizing pedagogies" (more about this in upcoming chapters), recognition of the fundamental equality of all people, and responsibility to repair and heal the social wounds of the past and present
- Explicit cultivation of a deep ecological sensibility, with an emphasis on caring for land, water, plants, and animals
- Fostering scientific learning and contemplative learning, aiming to reconcile humanity's commitment to rational thought and a just society with its hunger for "ultimacy" (balancing introversial and extroversial knowledge)
- Valuing the specifics of culture and place, and cultivating a universal sentiment as well
- Emphasis on spiritual growth, service, and social activism in the causes of universal welfare (subjective approach/objective adjustment).

Neohumanism offers a dynamic educational vision, in contrast to older educational alternatives, capable of adapting to changing times, places, worldly circumstances, and new knowledge. It is this point that may protect neohumanist education from *reification*, a process that too often turns innovative educational ideas into stale dogma.

Conclusion

The centuries old philosophy of humanism brought us an educational model premised on individual achievement, competition, the acquisition of increasingly abstract forms of knowledge, the myth of meritocracy, and the sifting and sorting of humankind according to narrow definitions of ability. This model has spread across the planet, and conventional wisdom states that the more educated one is, the better, and the more people who have access to this form of education, the better off we will all be. There are very real achievements that have been brought about by modern, Western ways of knowing. But we must acknowledge that much of the damage being inflicted upon the planet in the forms of chemical pollution, climate change, species extinction, and sophisticated weaponry has been implemented by highly educated people (Orr, 1993/1998). And this doesn't even address the collateral damage of competitive forms of education: suicide, an epidemic of depression and anxiety among the young, increasing rates of school dropouts, the loss of languages, cultures, and accelerating inequality.

The old vision of reality is a fragmented one, one in which relationships have been fractured—relations between people, between people and animals, between people and the plant world, between people and their labor, and between people and the mysterious energies of the cosmos that sustain the coming into being, the sustaining, and the perishing of life. Neohumanism asks us to reconsider the fundamental purposes of education. It strives for a harmonious balance between inner development and engagement with the world, in the belief that meditation and inner work foster an awakened conscience, which translates into transcending differences and creating a sense of unity with all beings. Its principles lie in three main areas:

1. Expanding the circle of love to include everyone and everything
2. Freeing the mind from dogma and limitations, cultivating a broad-minded and compassionate rationality that serves as a gateway to realizing our full individual and collective potential.
3. Awakening the desire for social and environmental justice through the practice of selfless service; translating values into action to achieve a sense of purpose and connection

Rather than educate so that a tiny sliver of people rise to the top of the global income chain, neohumanism aims to educate all people for the art of living well on a fragile and sacred planet. With this in mind, it emphasizes not just academic achievement and high test scores, but highlights the importance of cultivating compassion, community, empathy, imagination, insight, friendship, creativity, communication, justice, practicality, pleasure, courage, humor, wisdom, introspection, transcendence, ethics, service, and the ability to live well within the carrying capacity of our ecosystems.

In upcoming sections, we will take a deeper dive into topics that have been touched on in this chapter: the role of culture in the educational process, how children learn and the most effective ways to teach, reaching all learners, the importance of family and community in the educational process, the various roles that a teacher plays, arts-based learning, place-based learning, and how curriculum is developed and organized. The philosophy of neohumanist education as presented here will be woven throughout all of the more practical dimensions of teaching and learning, so we can begin to understand the coherence and integration of all aspects of neohumanist education.

FOR CONTINUING STUDY

> *Discussion/Reflection:* It is said that an image is worth a thousand words. What might be your image/metaphor for each of the philosophies (perennialism, etc.) in this chapter?
>
> *Discussion/Reflection:* Choose a common curricular topic (creating communities; discovering America; the solar system). Choose different ways of knowing from the section on epistemological pluralism, and discuss how the topic might be approached from each.
>
> *Application:* Our ideas about education are formed early by our own experiences. Write your own "educational autobiography" and discuss how you were shaped by your education. Can you identify what philosophies might have been operative in your own schooling? (You may need to do a bit of research online to learn more about the different philosophies). Aim for 250–500 words.
>
> *Application:* Write a "letter to prospective families" in a new neohumanist school. Describe the school's philosophy of education, addressing all of the major philosophical categories, in language easily understood by a parent interested in enrolling their child.

References

de Sousa Santos, B. (2014). *Epistemologies of the south: Justice against epistemicide.* Routledge.

Forbes, S. H. (2003). *Holistic education: An analysis of its ideas and nature*. Resource Center for Redesigning.

Freire, P. (2018). *Pedagogy of the oppressed*. Bloomsbury Publishing. (Original published 1970)

Haymond, B. (n.d.) Einstein's misquote on the illusion of being separate from the whole. https://www.thymindoman.com/einsteins-misquote-on-the-illusion-of-feeling-separate-from-the-whole/

Kesson, K. (1993). Critical theory and holistic education: Carrying on the conversation. In R. Miller (Ed.), *The renewal of meaning in education: Responses to the cultural and ecological crisis of our time* (pp. 92–110). Holistic Education Press.

Kesson, K. (January, 2019). Cultivating ecological wisdom through the arts. *Gurukula Network*, 47.

Macdonald, J. B., & Macdonald, B. J. (Ed.). (1995). *Theory as a prayerful act: The collected essays of James B. Macdonald*. Peter Lang.

Mahmoudi, S., Jafari, E., Nasrabadi, H. A., & Liaghatdar, M. J. (2012). Holistic education: An approach for 21 century. *International Education Studies*, 5(2), 178–186. http://dx.doi.org/10.5539/ies.v5n3p178

Miller, R. (1993). *The renewal of meaning in education: Responses to the cultural and ecological crisis of our time*. Holistic Education Press.

Moffett, J. (1994). *The universal schoolhouse: Spiritual awakening through education*. Jossey-Bass.

Orr, D. (1993/1998). The dangers of education. In R. Miller (Ed.), *The renewal of meaning in education: Responses to the cultural and ecological crisis of our time* (pp. 25–37). Holistic Education Press.

Purpel, D. (1993). Holistic education in a prophetic voice. In R. Miller (Ed.), *The renewal of meaning in education: Responses to the cultural and ecological crisis of our time* (pp. 68–91). Holistic Education Press.

Sarkar, P. R. (1998). *Discourses on neohumanist education*. Ananda Marga Publications.

Sarkar, P. R. (1982). *The liberation of intellect: Neo-Humanism*. A'nanda Márga Pracáraka Samgha.

Smuts, J. (2017). *Holism and evolution*. Andesite Press. (Original work published 1926) https://openlibrary.org/search?q=holism+and+evolution&mode=everything

Swimme, B. (1988). The cosmic creation story. In D. R. Griffin (Ed.), *The reenchantment of science* (pp. 47–56). SUNY Press.

van Wyk, C. (2016). *Holism and evolution by Jan Christian Smuts—A re-evaluation after 90 years*. https://www.academia.edu/21995931/Holism_and_Evolution_by_Jan_Christian_Smuts_a_re_evaluation_after_90_years

2

The Development of a Neohumanist Educator

> *To teach is the central expression of our humanity. Schooling has formalised* [sic] *this process but it has not altered the fact that people teach people and that children look to their elders to be guided into life. The source of inspiration in teaching is the teacher's joy in living. We cannot teach what we do not feel, and the more we explore ourselves, our world and our relationships the more we come to feel. It is in this joyous self-development that the teacher finds the requisite source of inspiration for others.*
>
> —Marcus Bussey, personal correspondence

In Chapter 1, "Neohumanism: A Philosophy of Education for Our Time," we explored the outline of a comprehensive philosophy of education that pointed to new understandings of what it means to be human, how we come to know, what constitutes the good, the true, and the beautiful, and how we need a more eco-centric ethics to guide us into a very uncertain, and in many ways dangerous, future. We noted that conventional approaches to education are no longer adequate to prepare a new generation of leaders and global citizens to meet the challenges of the Anthropocene, an emergent epoch in which it has become clear that humanity has come to a crossroads in terms of its own survival. We noted that "information" or even "knowledge" alone are no longer what is needed, but that we must cultivate *wisdom* to see us through these times and into the future. In this chapter we ask two important questions: "What are the qualities that constitute a wise teacher?" and "What kind of development helps to cultivate this teacher wisdom?"

What Teachers Need to Know

Academic Content

It goes without saying that anyone who claims the mantle of "teacher" must have knowledge of specific subject matter (the academic disciplines of history, mathematics, language arts, science, etc.) that has evolved to explain how the world works. They also need to understand how these different forms of knowledge relate to each other—their *interdisciplinarity*. It is important that they understand how knowledge is created and how specialists in their fields think. Mathematicians have specific ways of problem-solving, and historians engage in their own unique forms of inquiry. Understanding how knowledge is *made* and the political, social, and epistemological foundations of knowledge construction will help the neohumanist educator discern the truth, perspective, and value of the content they are teaching.

Pedagogical Arts

Teachers must also have a grasp of the "pedagogical arts"—how to connect subject matter to the needs and interests of young people in meaningful, integrated ways, present knowledge to students at different levels of age and development, orchestrate the dynamics of a classroom, support experiential and community-based learning, and balance structured learning with choice and self-direction. Most importantly, they need a keen awareness of how to awaken the thirst for knowledge: "Society will gain no lasting benefit if teachers force students to swallow knowledge like quinine pills instead of awakening the thirst for knowledge in the minds of young children, or for that matter in the mind of any student" (Sarkar, 1959, para. 30).

Knowing the Learner

The knowledge of young people—their physical development, cognitive development, emotional development, social development, and moral development—provides a crucial foundation for teaching. Understanding how young people grow and learn at different stages of their lives is essential to making sound choices about curriculum and instruction. The neohumanist educator can also critically analyze conventional development theories, and construct their own knowledge of the learner based on careful observation, reflection, and intuition.

Social Context

To really understand the individual learner, the teacher must have a broad, holistic understanding of the multiple and interpenetrating systems in which children are born and raised. How do their families interact with each other? What challenges have they faced? What beliefs and practices have they grown up with? How have they been disciplined? What is their ancestral history and cultural worldview? What language(s) do they understand and speak?

Self-Knowledge and Self-Development

It is not enough, however, to have knowledge of the world, academic subject matter, a sense of how to teach different learners, and the social contexts of schooling. Long after your students have forgotten what you taught them, they will remember WHO you were: "Part of what a student experiences in education is what the teacher actually *is*, not what the teacher pretends or intends to be" (Forbes, 1999, p. 151).

C. G. Jung, the Swiss psychologist, believed that the relationship between teacher and student was of primary importance to teaching and learning. Because of the subtle but important effects of the unconscious mind of the teacher on the student, he felt that the teacher should be engaged in the process of self-discovery and healing: "No principles, however sound, no clever technique or mechanical aids can replace the influence of a well-developed personality" (Fordham, 1966, p. 112). Shrii Sarkar emphasized the importance of balanced development in three spheres—physical, psychic and spiritual—in order to bring about the integration of personality. Self-knowledge is the foundation of a truly wise teacher.

Self Knowledge and Self Development

Teachers must possess such qualities as personal integrity, strength of character, righteousness, a feeling for social service, unselfishness, an inspiring personality and leadership ability.

—Sarkar, 1959, para. 5

The Call to Teach

The "call to teach" is more than a career choice—it is a vocation. The Latin root of vocation, *vocare,* means "to call," and "it denotes a summons or bidding to be of service" (Hansen, 1995, p. 1). It is a calling of the very highest order. One scholar notes:

> The Latin *educare* means to lead out—specifically to lead from darkness into light. The Sanskrit word for teacher, *guru,* means the one who shows the way from darkness into light. (Jagla, 1992, p. 62)

There are many ways to think about showing the way from darkness into light. A teacher may awaken a student to a concept that they never knew before, such as the existence of a force called gravity. Or they may lead them in learning a skill they did not possess (how to calculate a percentage or how to mix colors yellow and red to get orange). A teacher can lead students to question a given reality (understanding different economic systems), become enlightened as to how their thinking has been shaped (media literacy), or open up new possibilities for their lives (career education).

While all of these pedagogical tasks are important, the mission of a neohumanist educator is even broader: to awaken both the intellect and the intuition, to lead people into a deep appreciation for the oneness of all creation, and to awaken the spirit of benevolence and service to humanity. In order to rise to this challenge, neohumanist educators need to cultivate a deep knowledge of the self, and an understanding of how *who they are* affects *how they teach*. This involves being in touch with their emotions and where these originate, understanding their motivations and desires, developing their relationship skills and communicative competencies, and striving to live an ethical life. Neohumanist educators must be engaged in their own all around, balanced development in order to guide and facilitate the balanced development of the young people in their care.

The Dimensions of the Self

If self-knowledge is a central part of teacher development, it begs the question: "What is this 'self' that we are referring to?" There are many ways of thinking about what constitutes a self. In the last chapter, we noted that the Yogic model of the self conceives of a "multi-dimensional being" constituted of layers of expression ranging from the most dense material structure (the body) into the most subtle abstract layers of the causal mind. The Yogis have names for these layers, which they term "koshas." The koshas are defined thusly:

- Annamaya kosha (the physical body)
- Ka'mamaya kosha (senses and instincts)
- Manomaya kosha (thinking and remembering)
- Atima'nasa kosha (aesthetics, imagination, creativity)
- Vijina'amaya kosha (intuition, discernment, non-attachment)
- Hiran'yama kosha (spiritual longing and universal love)

While most classical Western models conceive of body, mind, and spirit as separate realms, more current thinking in quantum mechanics, transpersonal psychology, and mind/body studies suggest a more integrated model, akin to the Yogic model. Even classic Western psychology refers to different "levels" of mind, such as the conscious mind and the subconscious mind, and scholars are coming to recognize the important ways that experiences at various levels of the continuum influence and penetrate each other. For the purposes of our discussion of teacher development, we will refer to "levels" or "layers" of the mind/body continuum, with the caution that 'levels and layers' do not exist as actual spaces or as discrete units, but more as concepts to help us understand the different human capacities that need to be developed. These spheres are not *separate*—they are related in multiple ways (e.g., emotions affect physical well-being and vice versa), and in reality, all of the capacities operate somewhat like a hologram, in which each sphere is part of an ever expanding, ever enlarging whole. And just as the whole contains all the parts, each part contains within it the whole.

Scholars who study clinical aspects of Yoga are making important contributions to the emerging field of biopsychology, and many of the ideas that Yogis have arrived at through centuries of intuitional science are now being validated by empirical studies. A full discussion of this topic is beyond the scope of this chapter; suffice it to say that the Yoga concept of biopsychology is a point where biology, psychology and spirituality meet. What is important for our purposes is to note that unlike most forms of conventional Western education, which primarily aims to develop the intellect, a neohumanist education seeks the balanced development of all of the spheres of human existence. And so, the neohumanist teacher is similarly engaged in the all-around development of their personality.

Self-reflection, self-inquiry, and self-discipline are at the heart of Yoga practices. Ironically, *self-surrender* lives alongside this, in the sense that the "separate self" is an illusion of modernity and the philosophy of humanism. In neohumanism, we understand that what we think of as a separate self, is in fact an ever-changing, dynamic locus of experience, a center that is deeply interconnected with and dependent upon, the rest of creation. Letting go of the separate self (the ego) and connecting with the ground of our being (the universal Love that pervades the universe) is a key aspect of Yogic development. That said, such a "subjective approach" must be coupled with a disciplined "objective adjustment" in order to live a balanced life in the world!

Care of the Self

> Teachers have the power to transform their students by their own example and loving guidance and to nurture the highest aspirations of the human spirit; therefore their personal, moral, and spiritual development is very important. (Ananda Rama & Brim, 2010, p. 62)

In order to progress towards wisdom, to overcome our personal limitations, complexes, and misunderstandings, it is important to engage in a daily spiritual practice. Contemplative activities can include meditation, spiritual study, enjoying solitude, exploring nature, or listening to uplifting music. Spiritual development is the heart and soul of the neohumanist teacher's personality, yet it depends on all other aspects of development such as the physical care of the body, emotional, interpersonal and social development, the cultivation of the intellect, and the nurturing of creativity. Without a balanced biopsychological functioning of the body and mind, spiritual development would not have a sound foundation.

Spiritual development furthermore involves the teacher's psychological attitude toward themselves and their life, how they view themselves as part of the environment, and how they relate to others. It includes how the teacher is being shaped by their philosophy and experiences of life and how these experiences affect their understanding of, and their desire to improve both themselves and the world. So, although the nurturing of the soul or the spirit leads the person to an integral, holistic way of being, the other aspects of *being* need to be well cared for as well.

Care of the Body

Yogis recognize the body as the foundation of all development. A healthy body helps to develop a strong mind and a discerning intuition. Neohumanist educators are role models for their students in terms of care for the body, so they are sure to eat healthy and life sustaining foods, practice asanas (Yoga physical culture), engage in physical exercise, and get adequate rest. The physical practices of Yoga—the asanas, or Yoga postures—are probably the most familiar form of Yoga to most Westerners. However, this "Hatha Yoga" is but one aspect of a more comprehensive approach that includes mind, spirit, and action in the world as well.

Balanced Emotions

Working with children requires that a teacher be well balanced emotionally, and be in touch with the ways in which their subconscious or unconscious mind influences their thinking and behavior. Below the surface of consciousness lie repressed memories, trauma, and assimilation of information from nonverbal cues, including images, and so on. Teachers need to be reflective about the challenges and events that have happened in their own community/culture and family systems and have some cognitive distance from and resolution of those, so that they do not impact their interactions with students. According to some psychologists, meditation, much like the psychological technique of free association, can bring unconscious elements to the conscious surface of the mind so that they can be processed and dealt with (Ahmed, 2023). Other activities people engage in for emotional well-being include recalling dreams, keeping a journal, therapeutic conversations, improvisational arts, and interpreting personal symbols.

Social Competence

Conventional ideas about social competence highlight the ability to communicate clearly and well, to be able to take another's perspective, to know how to listen, and to interpret social cues. All of these skills are required to successfully cultivate relationships. To teach is to engage in relationship. But this requires more than mere skill in social transactions. As one scholar puts it, to teach is "to 'see' one's self and the other in relation to our centers of being; to touch and be touched by another in terms of something fundamental to our shared existence" (Macdonald, 1995, p. 95). This level of relationship requires *authenticity,* which can only come about when a person has engaged in a deep quest for self-knowledge. Many new teachers adopt a teacher "persona"—a defensive professional mask. But young people are highly skilled at detecting pretense. What they really want is to know the authentic *person* behind the teacher mask, keeping in mind the importance of observing professional boundaries.

Inspiring the Intellect

One of the most wonderful things about being a teacher is the opportunity to be a lifelong learner. It is a role that requires continued study and inquiry. The very best teachers bring their own intellectual passions to teaching. Many young people, when asked what they liked most in their teachers, say that enthusiasm for subject matter was one of the most important qualities in a great teacher. There are many activities that foster intellectual development: reading and writing, of course, but also seeking out new experiences, travel, and attending conferences and lectures.

There are many ways to be intelligent, and given that "epistemological pluralism" is a key ingredient of neohumanist education, teachers should expand their epistemological boundaries: make friends with someone from a cultural background different from your own, try on a new "intelligence"—musical, kinesthetic, or visual—or interview an elder in your community to find out what life was life a half-century ago. Importantly, when you are busy expanding your horizons, practice "meta-cognition"—that is watching how your brain works when you are learning something new. It will help you remain sensitive to the many challenges young people experience when learning new things, and perhaps give you more patience and understanding with their struggles.

Cultivating Creativity

The creative layer of the mind is where the mental capacities of imagination, visualization, divergent thinking, experimentation, and the capacity to reorder phenomena in original ways lie. To engage in creative pursuits such as music-making, movement, painting, drawing, poetic writing, sculpture, or craft, especially 'improvisational' forms of art-making (art "from-the-inside-out" that allows expression to come forth from the less conscious levels of mind) is an important aspect of teacher development.

Creativity, however, is not just about the expressive arts. Creativity is a disposition that includes a number of habits of mind that are important in general learning and problem-solving: the ability to generate possibilities (thinking-outside-the-box); the awareness of one's process (choice making, self-assessing, failing effectively); experimentation (risk-taking, combining and mixing, synthesizing); engaging multiple perspectives (considering differing points of view, refocusing attention from big picture to details). Cultivating creativity is an essential element of all learning.

Moral Development

All teachers are role models for young people in their care, and their values, beliefs and behaviors are influential in the development of children. Yoga practitioners observe an ethical guide to living encapsulated in ten principles termed, in Sanskrit *Yamas* (observances) and *Niyamas* (restraints). Simply defined, the Yamas include:

- Ahim'sá—Non-Harming
- Satya—Benevolent Truthfulness
- Asteya—Non-Stealing
- Brahmacarya—Universal Love
- Aparigraha—Moderation

The Niyamas refer to a spiritual aspirant's inner discipline, and include:

- Shaoca—Purity
- Santos'a—Contentment
- Tapah—Service
- Svádhyáya—Wisdom Study
- Ishvara Pran'idhána—Taking Cosmic Shelter

These are not rigid doctrines of behavior, and their application differs according to one's role in life as well as one's culture. Interpretation varies according to different Yoga traditions. Shrii Sarkar rejects the kind of rule-based morality encoded in many monotheistic traditions, recognizing that "proscriptive ethical frameworks, expressed as absolutes yet applied within relative frameworks of time, space and person, have the potential to become institutions of exploitation and dogma" (Fitzgerald, 1999, p. 62). Yet, he does subscribe to the notion of overarching ethical principles under the broad umbrella of the question: "Does this contribute to the welfare of all?" and "Is this the essence of neohumanism, the cultivation of love for all created beings of the universe?"

Developing Intuition

Intuition is the capacity to acquire insight or knowledge while bypassing the conscious mind and analytic reasoning. It can utilize many aspects of the unconscious mind (pattern retrieval, inner sensing, calling up of visual images, preconscious perception, etc.) and can result in hunches and/or the feeling of "rightness" or "wrongness." Not to be confused with mere instinct, or feeling, the intuitive faculties are sharpened and put to proper use when balanced with the disciplines of discernment and judgment. Intuition is developed through spiritual practice, and is honed in daily life. Intuition helps to develop the capacity for "indwelling"—the deep empathy that is required to lead a young person on their soul's journey, that capacity, as Macdonald says, "to touch and be touched by another in terms of something fundamental to our shared existence" (1995, p. 95).

Neohumanist educators are exploring multiple approaches to engaging all of the *koshas* in the educational process. These experiments form the foundation of curricular thinking in neohumanist education, and will be explored further in upcoming chapters. In order to teach holistically, all of the attributes we have looked at need to be developed or *developing* in the teacher.

Teacher Development and Neohumanist Philosophy of Education

In this section, we revisit the philosophical categories that were illustrated in Chapter 1, and connect the development of a teacher as outlined above to the foundational philosophical principles of a neohumanist education.

Cosmology

The neohumanist educator is a guide on an evolutionary journey in which they aid the child in discovering who they are and in creating their personal narrative of purpose and meaning. Without self-knowledge, awareness and insight, the teacher may "project" their unresolved psychic conflicts onto their students (examples include re-enacting harsh forms of discipline that connect to their own childhood, implicit bias unconsciously assimilated from family or culture, or unreflective models of achievement and success) that create blockages or limitations in a young person's development.

Ontology

In order to cultivate "new humans" with a love for all creation, the teacher needs to have cultivated this deep sense of relationality and connectedness in him or herself. The teacher is a role model for this way of being, and their actions need to demonstrate, in concrete ways, how to live these neohumanist principles.

Epistemology

Balancing academic study with creative and intuitional practice helps the teacher cultivate "epistemological pluralism"—the awareness that there are many ways of knowing, that all have value, and that different approaches are suitable in different circumstances. If possible, immersing oneself in a culture other than one's birth culture can be very illuminating, in terms of really understanding the variations in how people come to know the world. Open-mindedness is an important habit of mind, especially when one encounters "epistemological variation."

Axiology

Through the internalization of the principles of Yama and Niyama, the teacher models an ethical approach to life. Neohumanism requires a new approach to ethics, one that encompasses many aspects of life: ethics of non-harm, of love for all creatures, of relationship with all beings, of radical egalitarianism, of conscious consumption, of gratitude, of service, of peace, and of social justice. These ethics are the basis for a balanced individual, and by extension, a harmonious society.

Becoming Wise

> *Wisdom is not something that you get and then have. It is not a thing, but a process; not static, but dynamic; not a technique, but a way of living.*
> —Henderson & Kesson, 2004, p. 6

Wisdom is defined in the *Oxford English Dictionary* as "the capacity of judging rightly in matters relating to life and conduct; soundness of judgment in the choice of means and ends, sometimes, less strictly, sound sense, especially in practical affairs." Many people call this era we live in the "information age." But as we noted above, information, even knowledge, is not adequate to guide us into the future. We need wisdom.

There are many wisdom traditions in the world, and most of them are oriented towards cultivating a state of mind that is receptive to inner wisdom, or the truth of the spirit. All of them are embedded in specific cultural frameworks and their languages, histories, origin stories, and so on. While all wisdom traditions are rooted in specific cultures, neohumanism suggests that there are kernels of wisdom that are universally shared. Yoga practices are intended to lead one to an awakened spirituality, but this is a spirituality that is "ecumenical" in that the practices are compatible with many belief systems. The main requirement is that one is involved in a sincere quest for wisdom and self-development. While wisdom is a lofty concept, it has a very worldly dimension: it "denotes a soulful and holistic practical artistry directed toward personal and social goods" (Henderson & Kesson, 2004, p. 4).

In conclusion, neohumanist educators must have broad knowledge of the world they are educating young people for. They must be actively cultivating deep self-knowledge. As well they must embody a number of critical dispositions: visionary and contemplative thinking, aesthetic appreciation, discerning intellect, practical skills, perspective taking, appreciation for differences, sound judgment, and the ability to identify and challenge oppression and injustice. All of this requires a sincere commitment to on-going study and contemplative practice, a quest to connect with the source of all existence via the doorway of one's spiritual heart. Neohumanist teachers need to be fully alive to the moment and deeply connected to the purpose of their teaching, which is also central to their own learning and wisdom. It is a tall order, but our young people deserve no less than the wisest guides to lead them into a future that is undoubtedly filled with challenges, but also with enormous possibilities for the expansion of human potential.

FOR CONTINUING STUDY

Discussion/Reflection: Who are the teachers that stand out when you think about your educational autobiography? How did they influence you (for better or worse!) Try to identify the qualities that make these teachers memorable.

Application: Choose one or more areas of development important to teachers (cultivating creativity, balanced emotions, care of the body, etc.) and keep a journal on your activities and thoughts/feelings for at least a month. If you wish to do this with a colleague, you can meet regularly to discuss your experiences.

Application: If you have experienced the "call to teach," explore the most important reasons why you wish to make this your work. Perhaps you genuinely enjoy spending time with children, or are passionate about a particular subject. Maybe you hope to have your summers free, or you have a strong desire to change the world! This exercise is to give you the opportunity to examine your purposes and intentions in becoming a teacher.

References

Ahmed, D. R. (2023). The perspective of psychological action mechanism of mindfulness meditation: Mindfulness meditation blurs the transparent boundary between the unconscious and the conscious mind. *Psychiatry Investigation, 20*(5), 393–394. https://doi.org/10.30773/pi.2023.0032

Ananda Rama, D., & Brim, A. (2010). *Foundations of neohumanist education: Philosophy, principles, practice.* Ananda Marga Gurukula Publications.

Fitzgerald, J. (1999). Rekindling the wisdom tradition. In S. Inayatullah & J. Fitzgerald (Eds.), *Transcending boundaries: Prabhat Rainjan Sarkar's theories of individual and social transformation* (pp. 61–77). Gurukula Press.

Forbes, S. H. (1999). *Holistic education: An analysis of its intellectual precedents and nature* [Unpublished doctoral dissertation]. Green College.

Fordham, F. (1966). An *introduction to Jung's psychology.* Penguin Books.

Hansen, D. T. (1995). *The call to teach.* Teachers College Press.

Henderson, J., & Kesson, K. (2004). *Curriculum wisdom: Educational decisions in democratic societies.* Merrill Prentice-Hall.

Jagla, V. M. (1992). Teachers' everyday imagination and intuition. In W. H. Schubert & W. C. Ayers (Eds.), *Teacher lore: Learning from our own experience* (pp. 61–79). Longman Publishing Group.

Macdonald, J. B., & Macdonald, B. J. (Ed.). (1995). *Theory as a prayerful act: The collected essays of James B. Macdonald.* Peter Lang.

Sarkar P. R. (1959). Education. In *Human Society Part 1.* A'nanda Ma'rga Proca'raka Sam'gha.

3

Reconceptualizing Child Development

> *The child becoming incarnate is a spiritual embryo which needs its own special environment... the spiritual embryo needs to be protected by an external environment that is warm with love and rich with nourishment, where everything is disposed to welcome, and nothing to harm it.*
> — Maria Montessori, *The Secret of Childhood*, 1982

Neohumanism envisions spiritual awakening, the unification of the "small I" with the cosmic mind, or infinite consciousness, as the ultimate human destiny. This form of spirituality, drawn from the classic practices of Ashtanga Yoga that were systematized in the ancient Yoga Sutras, differs from religious awakening in that it adheres to no particular dogma or doctrine, but promotes a universalistic outlook, valuing the many diverse ways that people seek to align themselves with spirit. The "Eight Limbs" of Ashtanga Yoga include "physical health, mental well-being, moral education, and concentration practices that help to focus and still the mind" (Ananda Rama & Brim, 2010, p. 69). If it can be said to have an ideology, it might be best summarized by the aim to cultivate love for all creation, and to act in accordance with this value.

As we noted in the last chapter on the development of the teacher, theories of bio-psychology informed by Yoga philosophy conceive of the human being as a multi-dimensional creature composed of "layers" of mind (in Sanskrit, *koshas*). Sometimes likened to the many strata of an onion, or a banana flower, which peel away to reveal yet new layers, the koshas encompass the physical body (and senses), the cognitive mind and the intellect, intuition, imagination, higher states of consciousness, and ultimately, the realization of the interconnectedness of all life—the divine.

A neohumanist conception of development across the lifespan hence is an expansive one ultimately aimed toward the cultivation of this mystical sense of oneness with all creation. In Western philosophies of humanism, with some exceptions, matter and spirit are seen as occupying separate realms, mostly irreconcilable. In the Ashtanga Yoga tradition of human development as promulgated by Shrii Sarkar, these realms of human experience are deeply interrelated, differentiated by their relative *density*. Spirituality in this context is an embodied experience, with transcendent possibilities.

In order to facilitate this holistic development, children in neohumanist schools are introduced, in developmentally appropriate ways, to the practices of Ashtanga Yoga, including postures and exercises, mindful breathing, healthy diet, and quiet time. The practices are not rigidly imposed, but rather introduced through songs and games and physical movement. Western science has identified a broad range of positive effects of basic Yoga practices: strengthening of bone and muscle structure, improved posture, increasing flexibility, reduction of stress, and creating an overall sense of well-being. Neohumanist educators who have included Yoga in their curricula for decades note that the practices also improve concentration and focus, resulting in improved academic performance. What is essential to the neohumanist theory of development is understanding how Yoga practices create a foundation for attunement to the subtle human capacities of imagination, insight, intuition, and mental peace. The theories behind these processes are beyond the scope of this chapter, indeed this book. Suffice it to say that ordinary mental states are extra busy—the mind, according to Yoga wisdom, jumps around like a monkey, flitting to and from worries, self-doubt, planning, needs, desires, anticipation, regrets, and other cognitive chatter that keeps us from fully engaging in the present moment. Yoga practices are designed to relieve stress, cultivate a calm mind, deepen personal insight into how one's mind works, and to foster a sense of well-being. The process of human evolution towards greater clarity, meaning, insight and purpose spans a lifetime, but the developmental seeds can be planted in childhood.

Why Study Child Development?

While conventional education focuses almost exclusively on learning about the external world, neohumanist education aims for the balanced integration of the many levels of human experience—inner and outer. In order to accomplish this, the teacher must have holistic insight into the child and their potential. Understanding child development has long been an essential part of becoming a teacher, and at least one course in most teacher preparation programs is devoted to the study of how children learn and grow. People develop from birth to adulthood in many dimensions: physical, cognitive, emotional, social, and moral, to mention just a few of the major domains, or subsets of the field. The growing child masters a number of developmental tasks on their journey, including:

- *Physical Tasks* (gross and fine motor development, crawling, sitting, standing, walking, coordination, grasping, climbing, manipulating objects)
- *Speech and Language Tasks* (babbling, word formation, sentences, self-talk, communication)
- *Cognitive Tasks* (perception, memory, classification, exploration, creating schema (mental models), mental operations, connection-making, choices, imagination, logic)

Important questions are addressed by the study of childhood development:

- How do children develop their identity?
- What do we know about how children relate to each other and construct friendships?
- What are some sources of conflict among children and between children and adults and how can conflict best be resolved?
- What kind of adult authority do children benefit most from?
- How do children construct their knowledge about the world?
- When do children begin to exercise moral judgment and how can we nurture this?

An overarching question in the development world is *How do experiences in childhood shape later life?* (Belsky et al., 2020).

Neohumanist child development theory concerns itself with these practical questions, but poses additional ones that this and subsequent chapters will address:

- How can education nourish a "love for all species" that encourages young people to care for the Earth and all its creatures?
- How can education foster a sense of "radical equality" that encourages young people to value all people equally?
- How can educators help maintain the sense of wonder and awe that children are born with?
- How can education serve to form a healthy functional ego while also supporting growth toward a "higher" (post-egoic) self?
- What educational experiences foster true happiness?

Neohumanist schools span the globe, with students who live in modern technological/industrial countries, students raised in tribal villages, children from disadvantaged urban centers, orphans and children who have experienced trauma, and children who are refugees fleeing from war, famine, or natural disasters. Children develop differently in every culture and every situation, and while we can identify certain experiences that are more or less universal, there is more variation that we have acknowledged. A neohumanist theory of child development takes all of these variations into account, understanding that teachers must cultivate nuanced judgment according to differences in time, place and circumstances. What is universal in neohumanism, across cultures, is the aim of education to build a strong foundation from which the developing human can realize their spiritual potential, and "recognize their 'interconnectedness of being' with the natural world and Planet Earth" (Towsey, 2019, p. 8).

Foundations of Neohumanist Child Development Theory

Conventional materialist thinking tells us that human birth results from a random collision of particles, that the human being is born with a blank slate for a mind, and that growth and development are a combination of nature (genetics) and nurture (the effect of the environment, including human relations). In contrast with this purely materialist point of view, religious thinkers from a variety of traditions offer doctrinal versions of a non-material human soul and its earthly journey. Within these traditions, the concept of the soul evolves and changes through time. Much of what we believe about the nature of the soul comes to us from revealed knowledge (knowledge passed down from on high). Because the nature of the soul is intangible, it does not lend itself to empirical study, though that has not deterred scientists and pseudo-scientists from pursuing investigations into paranormal psychology, psychic phenomena, transmigration, morphogenetic fields, or transpersonal awareness.

Many Asian religions, some ancient Middle Eastern traditions, peripheral Christian traditions such as gnosticism, and some more modern religious movements such as theosophy believe that the soul persists in the energy fields of the universe (or the "multiverse") after bodily death and takes rebirth, according to its *reactive momenta*, known in Sanskrit as *saṁskáras*. In the popular imagination this is commonly understood as karma, or the universal law of cause and effect, which implies that one's actions continue to reverberate through time and space causing reactions. Eastern and Western thinkers alike, including Walt Whitman, Henry Ford, Thomas Edison, Gandhi, and Leo Tolstoy expressed a belief in rebirth. Though physicists and Yogis do agree that the entirety of the universe consists of energy waves and frequencies, the scientific jury is most definitely out on whether the energy of thought waves, or consciousness, survives the death of the body. This book on neohumanist education does not propose to resolve the mysteries of quantum mechanics and theology. It does, however, accept some basic principles as foundational to human birth and development that have pedagogical implications.

1. Shrii Sarkar (1979), in one of his spoken discourses on childhood, noted that "From the beginning, every created being is situated in bliss... Not only a human child, every newborn being feels this certain type of bliss from the start" (para. 1). Embodied in this quote is the compelling notion that true happiness is the birthright of every created being.
2. Whether talking about this one precious lifetime, or multiple lifetimes, the soul is on an evolutionary journey.
3. Enormous potential lies dormant within every child that is born, waiting to be awakened.
4. Teaching or parenting is a sacred responsibility.

Children arrive on planet Earth in a state of wholeness, their perception, says William James (1890; American philosopher, 1842–1910) "one great blooming, buzzing confusion" (p. 488) not yet shaped by the culture of their birth with its categories and divisions, its distortions and diversions, its limitations and its boundaries: self/other; nature/culture; animate/inanimate; inside/outside; me/not me; enemy/friend; good/bad. They are possessed, suggests one child psychologist, with "a porous, permeable, sensitive essence intertwined with all other essences, affecting and affected by them with its every breath" (Barrows, 1995, p. 101). Much adult effort is expended on moving children out of this animistic state where everything is alive, conscious, and enchanted into an adult version of maturity, a state characterized by the humanist conception of the rational, autonomous adult male self as the normative ideal. But what if our efforts and our theories have been misdirected, misguided, and are in fact, essential drivers of the dysfunctional state we now find the world in? What if the psychologist mentioned above, Anita Barrows, is correct, that in order to "shift the paradigm of a bounded, individual self toward a vision of a self that is permeable, interconnected not only with other human selves but with all living beings and processes, *a new theory of child development must be evolved* [emphasis added]" (p. 103)? Some researchers, asserting that our theories have failed to adequately understand the child as deeply embedded in nature, have come up with a new term to signify this interconnectedness—*childhoodnature* (Murris, 2018).

The overarching question we ask in this chapter is: "How can we facilitate conventional developmental tasks, especially those that center around the consolidation of memory and experience into a sense of self—an identity—while maintaining the deep sense of interconnection and ecological resonance that is at the heart of young children's primary experience of the world?" We outline the contours of a theory of child development, informed by a neohumanist understanding of human development across the lifespan. It does not profess to be the "final word" on neohumanist child development for a number of reasons: posthumanist research in the areas of culture, language, and development is on-going and should inform a dynamic, evolving theoretical perspective; empirical research on the development of subtle mental states is in its early stages and will necessarily inform the theory in the future; the insights of neohumanist educators are important components of the development of the theory. Neohumanist education is a dynamic process, in continuous evolution, and will necessarily be informed by new ideas that prove useful and are collaboratively agreed upon. This will help to ensure its on-going relevance.

The Social Construction of Childhood

In its formative years, child development research was focused on children growing up in WEIRD (Western-Educated-Industrialized-Rich-Democratic) societies, and the principles discovered were thought to be *universal*—that is, applicable to all children, everywhere. Only in the latter part of the 20th century did some scholars begin to acknowledge development theory as a culturally specific, *socially constructed* artifact of human thinking. Along with this, it is now understood as an historical construct, one that changes over time and context.

As with other social constructs, most people tend to think their ideas about the raising of children are natural, disregarding the ways that the society we live in conditions us to certain conceptions that align with dominant visions of the good society. For example, in most WEIRD societies, we think of childhood as a time of preparation for launching into life as an autonomous individual. Western parenting practices often emphasize the cultivation of self-reliance and personal choice. In more traditional societies that have been less influenced by Western ideas, and even in Western social classes less predisposed to conventional ideals of success and upward mobility, more emphasis may be placed on kinship, belonging, duty, and/or empathy.

Education practices are closely related to ideas about child development. In the above case, for example, pedagogical strategies can be loosely categorized as promoting either autonomy or interdependence. Self-directed learning, individual assignments, competitive grading, testing, and nurturing self-esteem can be seen as fostering *independence* and autonomy. In contrast, practices such as cooperative learning, social learning, service learning, and shared goals and rewards can be said to foster *interdependence.*

All of this is to say that the topic of child development and its influence on pedagogy is very complex, with vast cultural differences. This is an important reason why teachers need to be engaged in self-examination, which includes unpacking one's own cultural biases and perspectives. An example often cited in the United States is that non-Native teachers, when working with Indigenous children, misinterpret a lack of eye contact and a failure to respond enthusiastically to teacher questioning as disinterest or aberrant behavior. In many Native cultures, however, eye contact may be considered rude and disrespectful, while eagerness to show off individual knowledge may be seen as an undesirable form of self-promotion.

Neohumanist educators need to be astute observers, well attuned to the society in which they teach, and find the sweet spot between honoring the child rearing practices of the local culture and shaping their pedagogy around neohumanist educational ideals. If teaching in a cultural setting that uses authoritative, even corporal punishment in raising children, for example, a neohumanist teacher who values benevolent non-violence needs to skillfully navigate the terrain of cultural differences in beliefs about how children should be disciplined.

Some Limitations of Conventional Child Development Theory

The Ends-in-View

The commonly accepted focus of developmental theory and practice is to cultivate adults who can function successfully in their society. This focus on goals, or outcomes, while seemingly obvious, has made it hard for people to value childhood on its own terms. As one scholar puts it:

> Immaturity has become an umbrella term for a period in a human's life that is lacking: lacking cognitive ability, moral responsibility, emotional independency [*sic*] and rationality. (Murris, 2018, p. 7)

It is thought that the immature child needs the guidance of adults to become fully human, the wild "natural" child needs to be tamed, the disobedient child requires discipline and punishment, and the uncivilized child requires socialization into society's norms. But what might it mean, instead, to value the child on their own terms, and by extension, to "cease conceiving of education as mere preparation for later life, and make it the full meaning of the present life" (Dewey, 1893, p. 660)?

Yes, the child is on a journey that culminates in adulthood, and yes, educators are responsible for helping to design experiences that will facilitate positive outcomes. But we need to consider carefully the "ends" we are attempting to shape the child to, and what model of adulthood is best suited to this new era we find ourselves in. We need to unpack the ideas of what it means to be fully human, what it is in the natural child that we seek to tame, the possibility that what the adult sees as disobedience might be better framed as *creative maladjustment*, a term coined by Martin Luther King Jr. and applied to children and learning by Herbert Kohl (1994), suggesting that socialization into a dysfunctional society may not be in the best interests of human survival.

Stage Theories

Child development theories abound with speculation about the various stages and sub stages of development that children go through. Stage theory proposes that children progress through identifiable periods of growth which prepare the way for later growth, that there are developmental milestones to watch for, that there are educational experiences appropriate to each stage of growth, and that a mismatch between developmental readiness and instruction may prove ineffective, or even harmful. There are also suggestions that later forms of desired learning may be thwarted if the proper groundwork has not been laid at an earlier stage (e.g., one theory suggests that difficulty with mathematical reasoning suffers if children have not had opportunities to manipulate various concrete materials such as blocks, Cuisenaire rods, etc.).

Jean Piaget (Swiss psychologist, 1896–1980) focused on how children's mental, or cognitive abilities develop, and posited four main stages: the sensorimotor (birth–2 years), preoperational (2–7 years), concrete operational (7–11 years), and formal operational (12+). His ideas have been extremely influential in the field of education, and contributed to what is known as "constructivist theory," the idea that knowledge acquisition is an active process in which new information hooks onto existing mental schema, resulting in new schema, behavior changes, and more developed views of reality. For educators, perhaps his most relevant idea is that of *readiness*: according to Piaget, each stage produces the conditions necessary to learn new concepts or behaviors; if a parent or teacher ignores readiness, then the learning will not take hold. The idea of developmental readiness, for example, supports the importance of play in a young child's development, and thus, best practices in early childhood education have tended to eschew inappropriately early academic instruction.

Maria Montessori (Italian physician and educator, 1870–1952) proposed her own theory of development, suggesting that the child from birth to 6 has an *absorbent mind*, from 6–12 makes a transition from this absorbent mind to more formal reasoning, and from 12–18 develops their personalities and social consciousness. Montessori education puts a great emphasis on having the proper tools and materials in the environment, which, along with structured, stage-specific activities, stimulate cognitive development.

Rudolph Steiner (Austrian esoteric philosopher, 1861–1925) created a somewhat arcane development theory to guide the Waldorf schools which relies on 7-year cycles and is connected to astrology. He posited that from birth to 7, the child is descending from the ethereal realms into a physical body, from 7–14 is developing the imagination, and from 14–21 is able to engage in logical thinking and connect with academic subject matter. Waldorf education emphasizes the cultivation of aesthetics and the imagination as foundational to spiritual development.

The above examples are just a small sample of the enormous number of development theories, and are necessarily oversimplified. We note them only to hint at the range of ideas about how children develop and the significant differences between theorists. A study of these theories can be bewildering. There have been many thoughtful critiques of stage theory, and it has largely fallen out of favor, though it is still taught in many schools of education. The problems with stage theories include:

- There are many exceptions to the rules that govern development from one stage to another.
- Children can make wildly uneven, non-linear developmental leaps.

- Development levels can vary widely even within one individual child.
- Ideas about stages fail to grasp the incredible variation that exists between and amongst children.
- Stages of development are affected by numerous environmental and cultural factors.

Despite these criticisms of developmental theories, they continue to influence education. Some ideas, especially those of Steiner and Montessori, have generated systems of pedagogy that serve as alternatives to more traditional education. Often these alternative systems are more child-centered than the public schools, more experiential, and more based in arts and play, which accounts for their widespread popularity, especially amongst neohumanist educators and parents. However, a close study of the development theories behind some educational alternatives reveals some unfounded speculation as well as fundamental misconceptions. For example, Rudolph Steiner's emphasis on utilizing the "four temperaments" (sanguine, choleric, melancholic, and phlegmatic, imaginatively connected to the elements of air, fire, earth, and water) as a guide to children's development is rooted in ancient Greek philosophy but does not seem to take new research on children's personality development into account.

Sarkar's (1959) philosophy of neohumanism does not promote highly specific theories of child development and pedagogy, except to note that "it will not do to impart education through intimidation" (para. 14) and to emphasize the importance of "awakening the thirst for knowledge" in students of various ages (para. 30). He does indicate the importance of developmentally appropriate education. For example, when speaking of young children:

> Children are by nature most inclined towards play, so a thirst for knowledge will have to be awakened in children through the medium of play—children should be educated through play methods. Children are also by nature inclined to listen to fantasies and stories... Children love play and stories almost equally, so in their case the two should be equally utilized. (para. 15)

When he speaks of adolescents, he emphasizes the importance of a balance of idealism and realism:

> The dream of the future first crystallizes in the mind of the adolescent. So adolescents should be taught, without indulging in narrow-mindedness, through the medium of idealism. The minds of young adults are, however, somewhat inclined towards realism, so in their case pure idealism will not suffice. In order to educate such young adults, a harmonious blend of idealism and realism is required. (para. 16–17)

Neohumanist educators need to be acquainted with conventional and alternative development theories, but hold them lightly, and rely more strongly on their own observations and reflections, an approach which will be developed further in Chapter 6, "Contemplative Inquiry: The Art of Knowing the Child." What follows are two scenarios that suggest why intuitive observation is more important than following a rigid stage theory:

1. We know that for very young children (birth through 5 or 6 years old), a play centered environment, rich in concrete materials and characterized by music, movement, storytelling, creative drama, and a variety of visual expressions (paint, clay, etc.), offers the best opportunities for growth and later cognitive development. While some developmental pedagogies prohibit a premature emphasis on learning to read and write, neohumanist educators would be alert for an early interest in text, and support a child who clearly desires to learn to read, or who joins the school as a reader.
2. The development of logic and reason occurs at different ages and in different ways for young people. Very young children often ask "why questions"—"Why is the sky blue?"; "Why do the leaves turn brown?"; and "Why does rain fall?" Of course, good teachers know that the best way to learn more about how a child thinks is to turn the question back on them—"Why do you think the sky is blue?" If a young person persists, however, and demands more sophisticated explanations, the teacher needs to be sensitive to the developmental schema already held by the child, and make a judgment about what level of information might extend that, and provide necessary skills to explore the question further (such as helping to design an experiment and collect evidence). Lev Vygotsky (1978), the Russian psychologist, elaborated on this process with his articulation of the *zone of proximal development*, a concept that illustrates the space between what a child is capable of knowing/doing by themselves, and what can only be done with support from a teacher, or "knowledgeable other." An example of this would be a child who reads at a certain level without assistance, but needs some help sounding out more advanced words.

The two examples given above suggest a few neohumanist principles in regards to child development stage theories:

- Theory needs to be "held lightly" and not applied rigidly.
- Education decisions need to consider the differences children may exhibit, or variations from conventional development theory.

- It is important to rely on observation and intuition, informed by theory, in making pedagogical judgments.

The Focus on Norms

Most child development theories are aimed at establishing norms—what is considered usual, typical, or standard. This has been useful to the extent that it has enabled the expansion of supports for children who due to disability, injury, trauma, or some other cause, have not attained typical milestones in their development. But the weakness of this normative approach lies in a fundamental error of definition—describing difference as *deviation* rather than *variation*. This can lead to deficit thinking (focusing on what needs to be *fixed* in children).

The other weakness in the normative approach is its dependence on hierarchies of value (e.g., valuing formal logic over emotional attunement). In most conceptual frameworks, norms are constructed around what the dominant culture values (e.g., so in the capitalist West, independence/autonomy is highly valued, while caring and interconnection may occupy a lower rung). While a teacher's focus should always be on learning and growth, they need to be mindful of the human impulse to establish what is considered normal and the desire to fit all children into that mold, and to understand that established standards often represent the interests of powers-that-be, that they have often served to stigmatize people, and that they are subject to change. Unconditional acceptance that is free of judgment, and the capacity to see the divine in every child provide the most conducive conditions for learning and growth.

Universalizing Development

Early theories of child development were largely based on studies done in Western countries on White, male, middle class children. In the historical moment we live in, people everywhere are engaged in personal struggles around identity. Conventional human development theory has been challenged on the basis of gender, sexual identity, and racial identity, among other factors. Understanding these newer, more expansive frameworks is important both for people who have been marginalized and people who have benefitted from privilege. Any developmental framework that does not acknowledge the importance of these differences, especially in their relation to power and privilege, and which attempts to universalize developmental experience, will miss the mark.

The measurement of intelligence, for example, is based on Western theories of cognitive development. The tests themselves have relied on objects and processes that are often unfamiliar to non-Western or Indigenous subjects. Culturally inappropriate testing results in misdiagnoses, misunderstandings, and stigmatization. A more universal approach to viewing intelligence was put forth by Howard Gardner (1983), who defines intelligence as the capacity to solve problems or to fashion products that are valued in one or more cultural settings. It's important for neohumanist educators to hold this culturally relevant perspective in mind.

The Focus on the Individual

Historically, almost all developmental thinking has focused on the individual and their human relationships. The limitations of this way of approaching development are clear from the perspective of neohumanism's "relational ontology" (see Chapter 1) in which everything is connected to everything else. The closest Western thought has come to a relational understanding of development can be found in the ideas of Urie Bronfenbrenner (Russian-born American psychologist, 1917–2005), who developed an "ecological systems theory" of child development (1981). He proposed that a child's life is affected by an integrated process of nested living systems that included:

- The Microsystem (family, caregivers)
- The Mesosystem (interaction of the different components of the microsystem with each other—for example, relations between the parents and the child's teachers)
- The Exosystem (people, places, and events that may impact the child, even if they do not come into contact—for example, a parent's employment)
- The Macrosystem (larger, remote events and perspectives—for example, war, the economy, cultural values, etc.)

While such systems thinking is clearly an improvement over individualistic theories, his theory, while termed an ecological systems theory, is still very much human-centered in that there is no role for considering non-human nature or "more-than-human-others" (Abram, 1997; Elliott & Davis, 2018) in a child's development. What might we learn about a child if we were to take note of how they interact with plants, or carefully document their developing relationships with insects or animals (Kesson, 2003)? These ideas will be developed further in Chapter 6, "Contemplative Inquiry: The Art of Knowing the Child."

A Neohumanist Theory of Development

We need only to put the humanist ideal of the "rational, autonomous self" alongside the neohumanist ideal of an "ecological self" who is interdependent, emotionally and spiritually attuned, and empathetically related to others, to see the limitations of classic humanism and modern theories of development in terms of the desired end states of adulthood.

Our children are signaling us that something has gone entirely wrong with the environment they have been born into. In the Western world, we are witnessing epidemics of anxiety, depression, suicides, eating disorders, and substance abuse in young people, and a vast increase in such challenging conditions as autism, childhood schizophrenia, hyperactivity dysfunction, and learning disabilities. An entire developmental enterprise is now based on what are termed *adverse childhood experiences* (ACEs) such as violence, abuse, and neglect, and an educational industry has sprung up in response termed *trauma-informed pedagogy*. There are so many reasons for these developments that it is impossible to establish simple causality. Modernity in the Western world brought with it a disruption of childbirth, lactation, and childrearing practices developed over millennia. We now have hospitalized and medicated births, an alarming rate of unnecessary caesarean sections, the separation of mothers and babies following births, the substitution of chemically laced formulae for breast milk, the creation of cribs, strollers, and playpens to take the place of riding about on a parent's body, separate sleeping quarters, the increasing rapid return of parents to the workplace, and early placement in child care institutions.

The demands of our current modern society have made it imperative (in virtually all capitalist societies) that all able adults work for a wage, and many parents have little quality time to spend with their children. The nuclear, mobile family has become the primary social unit, rather than the vast and extended systems of kinship that characterized prior centuries. Plastic toys take the place of everyday items and natural objects in a child's tactile environment, and they often replace adult/child interaction. Children now spend much of their time glued to digitized screens, incorporating enormous amounts of decontextualized data into their body/minds. Few children in the WEIRD world have access to uninterrupted time in nature, time to observe the changing patterns of the clouds, to feel the morning dew on bare feet, listen for the call of birds and the rustle of wild creatures in the brush. They have not taken the time to see which flowers the bees prefer, which mushrooms grow under which trees, or which fish swim in the shallows. How can children come to love the living world if they spend little time in it?

In other parts of the world, ravaged by climate change, war, or the despoliation of their environment, adverse childhood experiences are less the result of lifestyle choices and more the result of macro-forces of capitalism, environmental catastrophe, and economic imperialism. Trauma-informed pedagogy is essential when dealing with children who are suffering from extreme poverty, injury, illness, violence, and displacement as a result of such factors.

A neohumanist theory of child development must take into consideration the desired end points as articulated in neohumanist philosophy. The end points of "spiritual awakening," "cultivating a love for all creation," "understanding the interconnectedness of all life," "awakening the intellect to multiple ways of knowing," and "living a life of service to humanity and all creation" challenge the whole edifice of development theory, which is constituted of values, beliefs about ends-in-view, milestones, accepted educational practices, prescribed ways of thinking, and so on. Just as the work of feminist researcher Carol Gilligan (1982) opened up our thinking to the gendered nature of prior developmental theories when she posited an "ethic of care" (demonstrated by many women she studied) to challenge Lawrence Kohlberg's more abstract, male oriented "ethic of justice" as the end point of moral development, so must neohumanist educators begin to articulate the challenge to conventional development theories that neohumanism presents.

To recap, while it is very important for neohumanist educators to understand the basics of conventional ideas that have shaped the field of child development, so that they might be responsive to children's interests and capacities, it is also important to question the taken-for-granted assumptions that have shaped the field concerning:

- the role of culture in human development;
- the usefulness (or not) of stage theory;
- the problem with norms;
- the idea of childhood as an inferior stage;
- the historical biases in development theory;
- human-centeredness of development theory;
- the exclusive focus on the individual; and
- the exclusion of nature in so-called ecological system theory.

In this time of crisis and transition, we need to mitigate the social conditioning that has oriented young people toward the materialism and consumerism that has created an unsustainable world. We need to help them see beyond limiting conceptions of the self and its potential. A neohumanist theory of child development is inseparable from a larger vision of the world we wish to create. Envisioning a cooperative, ecologically sustainable, regenerative and just society requires us to rethink many taken-for-granted ideas about child development and how best to create the conditions in which children can thrive and grow into contented, peaceful, productive adults.

In Chapter 1, "Neohumanism: A Philosophy of Education for Our Time" we talked about a process of human development encompassing a *chain of identity* that begins with the small self, the ego and its identification with the body and its needs and grows into awareness of the surrounding world. The individual's sense of identity expands to the family, their sense of place (geo-sentiment) and ever outwards to include one's social groups, clan, social class, race and ethnicity, religion, and so on (socio-sentiment), to humanity as a whole (human-sentiment), culminating, ideally, in love and respect for all beings, animate and inanimate, in the universe (universalism). We noted that this is the ontological task of neohumanist educators, to guide the movement of young people through this ever-expanding circle of care and connection. Our foundational theory of child development must be equal to this important mission. In order to accomplish this, we need to foreground the following elements of development:

- Recognition of the multidimensional nature of the human being, and the creation of learning environments that nurture the development of all of the layers of the body/mind.
- Understanding the nature of the individual human as deeply interconnected with everything else, and arranging for everything to be studied in this relational context.
- The cultivation of fundamental virtues, and embedding character development, ecological ethics, and the cultivation of love for all living beings across the curriculum.
- Attending to the balanced development of extroversial knowledge (learning how the world works) and introversial knowledge (learning about one's inner life).

Perhaps most important is the remembrance that, as Sarkar noted, happiness is the birthright of all human beings, and every child deserves to learn and grow in a loving and supportive environment that focuses not on their deficits but on their strengths, not on punishment but on restorative justice, and which actively works to create a family-like atmosphere characterized by affection, trust, relationship, and respect. If all of these elements are in place, we can be confident that development will proceed in ways that maximize health, harmony, and happiness.

FOR CONTINUING STUDY

> *Discussion/Reflection:* Reflecting on your own childhood, try and recall any "developmental milestones" you experienced, in terms of your physical, mental, emotional, or moral development. Tell the story of what catalyzed this growth.
>
> *Discussion/Reflection:* What are some ways we can foster the feelings of interconnectedness with all species in young children? How can we keep alive a sense of wonder and awe?
>
> *Application:* Plan to spend at least 30 minutes watching a young child of any age. Describe what they are doing (building with blocks, making a sand castle, etc.). Write down what you notice about their physical development (coordination, strength, gross and fine motor skill, etc.), their thinking (how it appears they are making sense of things), and how they are responding emotionally to their activity. If they use language, write down what they say.
>
> *Application:* Observe a parent (can be yourself) and document the different ways they seem to be responding to an infant's developmental needs (Does the adult encourage smiling; play peek-a-boo; exercise the baby's arms and legs; help them grasp objects?)

Important note: Any time you observe and document children's behaviors, be sure you have the permission of the child's caregiver(s).

References

Abram, D. (1997). *The spell of the sensuous.* Random House/Vintage Books.

Ananda Rama, A., & Brim, A. (2010). *Foundations of neohumanist education.* Ananda Marga Gurukula Publications.

Barrows, A. (1995). The ecopsychology of child development. In T. Roszak, M. E. Gomes, & A. D. Kanner (Eds.), *Ecopsychology: Restoring the earth, healing the mind* (pp. 101–110). Sierra Club Books.

Belsky, J., Caspi, A., Moffitt, T., & Poulton, R. (2020). *The origins of you: How childhood shapes later life.* Harvard University Press.

Bronfenbrenner, U. (1981). *The ecology of human development: Experiments by nature and design.* Harvard University Press.

Dewey, J. (November, 1893). Self-realization as the moral ideal. *The Philosophical Review, 2*(6), 652–664.

Elliott, S., & Davis, J. M. (2018). Challenging taken-for-granted ideas in early childhood education: A critique of Bronfenbrenner's ecological systems theory in the age of post-humanism. In A. Cutter-Mackenzie-Knowles, K. Malone, & E. Barratt Hacking (Eds.), *Research handbook on childnature* (pp. 1–36). Springer International Publishing.

Gardner, H. (1983). *Frames of mind: The theory of multiple intelligences.* Basic Books.

Gilligan, C. (1982). *In a different voice: Psychological theory and women's development.* Harvard University Press.

James, W. (1890). *The principles of psychology.* Henry Holt & Co.

Kesson, K. (Autumn, 2003). Doing good science: On the virtues of simply "messing about." *Encounter: Education for Meaning and Social Justice, 16*(3). https://kathleenkesson.com/unschooling-in-paradise/excerpt-from-chapter-4/

Kohl, H. (1994). *"I won't learn from you": and other thoughts on creative maladjustment.* The New Press.

Murris, K. (2018). Posthuman child and the diffractive teacher: Decolonizing the nature/culture binary. In A. Cutter-Mackenzie-Knowles, K. Malone, & E. Barratt Hacking (Eds.), *Research handbook on childhoodnature,* Springer International Publishing.

Sarkar, P. R. (1959). Education. In *Discourses on neohumanist education* (2nd ed.). Electronic Edition of the Works of P. R. Sarkar, version 9.0.

Sarkar, P. R. (1979). The means to save oneself from sorrow. In *Ánanda vacanámrtam,* Part 9. Electronic Edition of the Works of P. R. Sarkar, version 9.0.

Towsey, M. (2019). *Neohumanist education: A handbook for teachers.* http://prsinstitute.org/downloads/related/education/nhe/NHETeachersHandbook.pdf

Vygotsky, L. S. (1978). *Mind in society: The development of higher psychological processes.* Harvard University Press.

4

The Science of Learning

Educated are those who have learned much, remembered much and made use of their knowledge in practical life. These virtues I call "education."
— P. R. Sarkar, *Discourses on Neohumanist Education*, 1998

What Is Intelligence? What Is Learning?

It's really quite amazing if you stop and think about it: the human infant, born in a "blooming buzzing confusion" as we noted in the last chapter, and totally dependent upon caregivers, develops in just a few short years the mastery of speech, the processing of information from the environment, the development of various orders of thinking abilities and the capacity to make judgments, then goes on to invent and produce such complex products as symphonies, novels, computer programs, and airplanes. How is the acquisition of such intelligence possible?

We know that humans share with other vertebrates and many invertebrates an organ called the brain, with an attached central nervous system that receives information from the environment through sensory organs, responds to external and internal stimuli, transmits electrochemical signals

---

Becoming One With the World, pages 55–75
Copyright © 2024 by Information Age Publishing
www.infoagepub.com
All rights of reproduction in any form reserved.

55

between cells, processes and integrates information, coordinates reflexes throughout the body, and generates responses to activity in the environment. We now know that all sentient beings possess intelligence, and even very simple invertebrates such as sponges and jellyfish operate through a nervous system and nerve endings. The human brain is thought to differ from other animals' only in specifics: A larger portion devoted to vision and language processing, newer cortical structures that enable more complex processing, and more neurons in the cerebral cortex which support cognitive processes such as monitoring one's behavior, controlling actions, planning, carrying out complex tasks, and metacognition (thinking about thinking).

We now know a lot about the human brain, and research in this area has been greatly accelerated by advanced imaging technology and computer modeling. However, there is much on the horizon of discovery about everything from addiction to brain disease to musical and visual processing. Perhaps of most interest to neohumanist educators is research on the effects of Yoga and meditation on the brain, on the development of creativity, on the neurobiology of intuition, and the study of neural correlates with spiritual practices (Goleman & Davidson, 2017). On the fringes of neurological research are investigations into the mysteries of consciousness itself and the relation between the physical brain and the less tangible entity of the mind, and the even more esoteric nature of what Carl Jung called the "collective unconscious," what physicist David Bohm called the "implicate order," and what some mystics including Rudolph Steiner and Madame Blavatsky of the theosophists, referred to as the "Akashic Records." All of these areas of research are very much in their infancy, but they promise to inform theories of neohumanist education in the future.

This chapter will stick to the fundamentals of what we currently know about intelligence and learning and what are considered the best educational practices in regards to what we know about how the human body/brain/mind system works. We will look at how different learning theories have been associated with the major philosophies introduced in Chapter 1. And finally, we articulate a theory of learning that correlates with neohumanist educational values and beliefs. As with other aspects of neohumanist education, we need to keep in mind that research on learning and the brain is dynamic and rapidly changing, and it is important that neohumanist teachers study, adapt, and change along with new knowledge.

What Is Learning Theory?

Learning theory is closely related to child development, but whereas child development deals with the whole child, learning theory is more narrowly focused on cognition and the development of the intellect. How do children learn? What do we know about the human brain and how it assimilates and adapts to new information? How does intelligence grow? Building on what was learned in the last chapter on child development, we will examine different ideas about how learning occurs and what are the optimum conditions for learning.

Learning theories are drawn from foundational studies in philosophy, linguistics, psychology, neuroscience, and artificial intelligence. Interdisciplinary studies of the body/brain/mind system address issues of language, perception, memory, attention, reasoning, and emotion, with the overall aim to understand intelligence and learning. Throughout the 20th century, influential scholars including Jean Piaget, John Dewey, Howard Gardner, and Lev Vygotsky focused on how learning theory informs the education of young people. Some of the questions they asked include:

- What do we mean by intelligence?
- How do children learn to speak?
- What is the relationship between thought and language?
- How do children develop conceptual schema about the world (principles of quantity, shape, size, distance, time and space, etc.)?
- What are the social dimensions of learning?
- How can we know what a child is capable of learning?
- How can learning best be "scaffolded" (providing adequate supports to move onto the next stage)?
- Do learning styles exist?
- What teaching approaches are most compatible with how the brain works?

Despite decades of research on learning and the brain, there is no consensus on optimum teaching and learning methods, though innovative ideas are put forth about best practices all the time. There are some principles that have endured over time, however, and rather than hop on the latest bandwagon we will explore those that seem most effective and most compatible with neohumanist values. For while most learning theory is primarily concerned with the development of reason, logic, and other capacities associated with the intellect, neohumanist education is equally concerned with the development of creativity, imagination, morality, intuition, and compassion. It thus asks additional questions:

- How do we create learning experiences that awaken subtle human capacities (empathy, aesthetics, altruism, biophilia [love of nature], feelings of "oneness," etc.)?

58 ▪ *Becoming One With the World*

- What is the role of the *koshas* in learning?
- How can intellectual development be grounded in ethical thinking?
- How do people learn to love (in terms of *agape*—universal, unconditional love)?

Brain-Based Learning

In the latter part of the 20th century, a handful of education researchers attempted to extract principles of education from what we were learning from the neurosciences (see, e.g., Caine & Caine, 1991; 1997; Crowell et al., 2001; Wolfe, 2001). Though sometimes accused of oversimplification, these resources can give teachers some insights into how the brain functions and how to design learning environments and experiences that are most compatible with what we know at this point. Renate and Geoffrey Caine (1991) offer up the 12 principles that they deem most significant for contemporary learning:

1. The brain is a complex adaptive system.
   - Thoughts, emotions, sensory data, imagination, predispositions and physiology all operate concurrently as the unit mind interacts and exchanges information with the environment.
   - The brain/mind is a system that cannot be reduced to the sum of its parts.
2. The brain is a social entity.
   - The individual human brain/mind system is an integral part of larger social systems.
   - Individual development is dynamic and changes in response to interactions with its environment.
   - Learning is profoundly influenced by the nature of the relationships that people are embedded in.
3. The search for meaning is innate.
   - There is a central drive to make sense of our world.
   - The search for meaning is driven by our evolving purposes and values.
   - The quest for meaning involves basic survival, the development of relationships and a sense of personal identity, the exploration of human potential, and the quest for transcendence.
4. The search for meaning occurs through *patterning*.
   - The brain/mind system creates schema or patterns into which it fits new information.

- There is a dynamic dance between registering the familiar and seeking novelty.
- Isolated bits of information that do not connect to existing schema are rejected.
5. Emotions are critical to patterning.
    - What we learn is organized by emotions and mind-sets involving expectancy, personal biases and prejudices, self-esteem and the need for social interaction and belonging.
    - Emotions and thoughts shape each other.
    - The emotions evoked by experiences continue to reverberate through time.
6. Every brain simultaneously perceives and creates parts and wholes.
    - Popular left brain/right brain theories, though oversimplified, have some scientific foundation, but are more complex than once thought.
    - The left and right hemispheres do have distinct functions.
    - The brain perceives parts and wholes in parallel; analysis and concepts should go hand in hand for effective learning.
7. Learning involves both focused attention and peripheral perception.
    - The brain/mind absorbs what it is concentrating on (e.g., a text) but also responds to the larger sensory context (smells, sounds, feeling tones, etc.).
8. Learning always involves conscious and unconscious processes.
    - A large part of learning occurs below the level of awareness.
    - Understanding may not occur instantly, but take some time to develop.
    - The learning context should involve experiential components, plus reflection and metacognition, and the creative elaboration of skills and ideas.
9. We have at least two different ways of organizing memory.
    - Memory is a very complex function.
    - One way of organizing facts is through "taxonomies" (i.e., the periodic table of elements).
    - Spatial/autobiographical memory is how we register more complete experiences.
    - Meaningful learning is a combination of both, but memory is most effective when embedded in natural spatial memory (i.e., complex experiences).
10. Learning is developmental.
    - "Neuroplasticity" means that the brain continuously adapts and changes as the result of experiences.

- There are "windows of opportunity" (though these are not fixed) for creating foundations for later learning (e.g., second language acquisition).
- There are no limits to the growth of learning; in the absence of neurological damage, neurons remain capable of making new connections throughout life.
11. Learning is enhanced by challenge and inhibited by threat.
    - The brain requires new challenges.
    - It "downshifts" in the presence of threat (i.e., high stakes tests), becoming less flexible and reverting to primitive processes.
12. Every brain is uniquely organized.
    - We all have the same set of organic systems.
    - There are differences in genetic endowment.
    - Culture and environment play a large role in brain development.

This last principle, that of sameness and difference, is explored in Howard Gardner's Theory of Multiple Intelligences.

The Theory of Multiple Intelligences

In the 1980s, Harvard professor and cognitive psychologist Howard Gardner (1983) launched his *theory of multiple intelligences* which attempted to debunk the idea that intelligence was a singular thing that could be accurately assessed and predicted using traditional intelligence quotient (IQ) tests, and that the definition of intelligence needed to be expanded beyond the capacities to use reason and logic. Gardner first proposed seven intelligences:

- Musical
- Mathematical
- Interpersonal
- Intrapersonal
- Visual-Spatial
- Linguistic
- Kinesthetic

He later expanded his theory to include both a naturalist intelligence and an existential intelligence (see Figure 4.1). While the theory has come under fire from many quarters, including psychologists who assert that these are not intelligences, but rather innate abilities, inclinations, or

The Science of Learning • 61

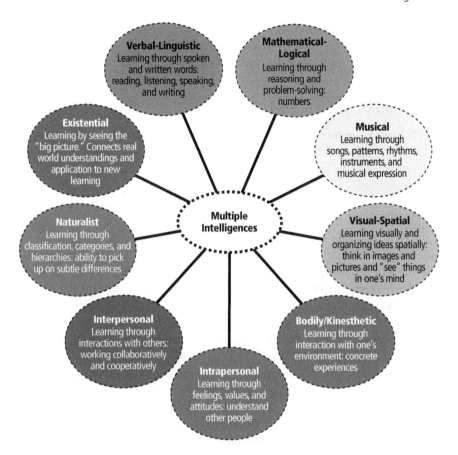

Figure 4.1 Multiple intelligences. *Source:* Retrieved from http://eflshire.blogspot.com/2013/03/week-9-reflection-1-learning-styles.html

talents, educators embraced the ideas enthusiastically, as they support an enlivened curriculum rich in experiences, social-emotional learning, and the arts, which taken together, can infuse education with joy and offer more pathways to success for young people.

Despite the contention around the theory, there are important ideas to be gained from a close study of his ideas. First is the appreciation for the vast range of intelligent capacities and their unique symbol systems; next is an understanding of how different modalities (e.g., movement, singing) can amplify learning in other domains (such as mathematics). Importantly, Gardner acknowledges the cultural specificities of learning and the great variety of valued achievements across cultures. Perhaps most meaningful for neohumanist educators is the potential of multiple intelligence theory-in-action to nourish the subtler capacities of the child— the imagination, the aesthetic sensibility, the social-emotional dimensions, the love of nature, the cultivation of intuition, and the search for transcendence/oneness.

Philosophy and Learning Theory

In Chapter 1, we introduced six major philosophies that have shaped educational thought in the Western world. Below we revisit these and see how each relates to specific learning theories.

Perennialism

Perennialists believe that knowledge is external to the learner, that it resides in classic texts that transcend time, and that it needs to be transmitted from teacher to student. The aim of learning in this paradigm is to develop the intellect by learning to think critically and use reason. Modern teaching in this paradigm consists of some percentage of time devoted to didactic instruction aimed at factual recall (lecture, reading, demonstration), some to discussion seminars aimed at concept development in which students debate ideas, and much time to academic coaching, in which teachers circulate among individuals and groups with the intent to guide and pose questions aimed at intellectual development. There is little focus on student interest or individuality, and more on a standard curriculum that promotes a shared knowledge base. Educational perennialism in the modern world is perhaps best represented by Mortimer Adler's (1982) "Paideia Proposal," which focuses on the values embedded in the "great books" of the culture.

Behaviorism

Behaviorism, as the word suggests, concerns itself with what can be observed about a young person, what they DO. Learning, in this model, must provoke some behavior change (for example, learning about sentence structure should result in the improvement of writing). Knowledge is considered to be "out there" (objective reality) and people's minds are thought to be "blank slates." Learning is predetermined by externals (what a society values) and is reinforced by stimuli, rewards, and punishments, such as grades. In this model, teaching is governed by a linear understanding of learning that generally follows four sequential principles:

1. Teacher (or textbook) defines learning objectives
2. Teacher establishes relevant learning experiences.

3. Teacher organizes these learning experiences for maximum effect.
4. Teacher evaluates the results of the learning, and revises their plans accordingly.

19th and early 20th century pioneers of behaviorism include Ivan Pavlov, known for his animal experiments on classical conditioning and B. F. Skinner for his further studies on operant conditioning (modifying behaviors through rewards and punishments). Behaviorism is rejected by many educational scholars and philosophers, but not surprisingly, given the opportunities for social control in this model, it is widely (if perhaps unconsciously) employed in many schools today.

Romanticism

The Romantics rejected this idea of the human being as a blank slate, and believed that young people are born with innate powers, or a divine spark. The word *"ēducēre"* (from the Latin, "to draw out") is often associated with this philosophy, suggesting that knowledge, in some form, already resides within the person, and needs only to be brought forth. The freedom to explore is highly valued in this model, as are activities that cultivate emotional expression, imagination, and creativity. Initially popularized by the 18th century philosopher Jean-Jacques Rousseau, who promoted the sovereignty of the "natural man," it was taken up enthusiastically by the nonconformist Romantic poets in the early 19th century, and adapted to education by some teachers and schools throughout the 20th century. These ideas reached their apotheosis alongside the countercultural movement of the 1960s with the establishment of hundreds of Free Schools and the "open classroom" movement, but mostly faded due to internal contradictions and external struggles in both the culture at large and in the educational world.

Pragmatism

While mainstream, conventional education (of the behaviorist sort) presented the fiercest opposition to the freedoms called for by the Romantics, the more compelling critique came from those who shared many of their core principles. Pragmatists, perhaps best exemplified by the philosopher John Dewey, critiqued the Romantics for their failure to engage creatively and constructively with young people when freed from conventional restraints, and for their belief that any guidance at all by adults was oppressive. Dewey's (1938) classic little book, *Experience and Education*, can be read as a rejoinder to the excesses of the Romantics.

If the perennialists and the behaviorists focus on outer experience, and the Romantics on inner experience, the pragmatists believe in a dialectical transaction between the inner world of the student and outer reality, and that people construct knowledge through having experiences and reflecting on them. It has been profoundly influential in the development of learning theories that come under the rubric of *constructivism*—the idea that learning is an active process in which people construct their own meanings out of their experiences. The pragmatists advocate inquiry-based learning, practical activities, and the cultivation of analysis, reason, and logic. Pragmatists value democracy and democratic ways of living, so teaching methods in this framework are characterized by cooperative group learning, real world problem-solving, and discussion. Unlike the more "hands-off" teaching of the Romantics, pragmatists believe that the role of the teacher is to carefully structure activities that maximize learning, and to connect young people, through their experiences and their reflection, to organized subject matter.

Social Reconstructionism/Critical Pedagogy

In the 1930s, during the Great Depression, a number of the pragmatic philosophers in the United States turned towards socialism, believing that unregulated big business was the ruination of America. In the same century, the incredible human costs of WWII highlighted the need to transform human society to create a more compassionate, just, and peaceful world. This quest to develop a better, more democratic world (through education) came to be known as social reconstructionism (Brameld, 1965/2000; Counts, 1932/1978).

In the later 20th century, influenced by the work of Brazilian educator Paulo Freire (1970), social reconstructionism morphed into critical pedagogy, a philosophy of education that takes a hard look at the social structures that construct our worlds. While it shares with Pragmatism a commitment to democracy and social freedoms, it emphasizes social justice, and insists that we acknowledge the ways that capitalist relations, racism, sexism and other forms of oppression have limited the full development of human potential, and thus the extent to which our democratic ideals have been realized.

A clear thread can be drawn from early 20th century critics of American education such as W. E. B. Du Bois (2013) and Carter G. Woodson (1933), through the mid-century work of Paulo Freire with his concept of "conscientization," into the current work of critical race theorists such as Gloria Ladson-Billings and William Tate (1995), and the many Black, Indigenous, and people of color writing eloquently today about "decolonizing education." There are many variations of critical pedagogy, but all of them support learning that is grounded in the development of critical thinking and political, economic, and social analysis in order to understand and overthrow the limitations that have been imposed on people who have been historically marginalized. It goes without saying that teachers themselves must understand the connections between colonialism, capitalism, racism, and the many ways that the structures, practices, and content of schools reproduce a social order that is profoundly unjust.

Holistic Education

The five philosophies above encapsulate various and often conflicting perspectives that have shaped the 200+year history of education in the United States and in many other places on the globe. In the late 20th century, a movement, international in scope, emerged alongside these models that drew ideas from all of them, but was unique in its proposition that human beings had the capacity for transcendence—a spiritual nature—and that any form of education that neglected that aspect failed to nurture the expansion of human potential. Holistic education, as it came to be called, draws upon the ideas of interconnection, relationship, and the evolution of human consciousness that are at the heart of neohumanism.

This minority tradition in education has historic (18th century) roots in Europe with the work of Johann Pestalozzi, who aimed to implement Rousseau's ideas in actual educational settings. Pestalozzi believed that at the heart of education must be love, and he rejected corporal punishment and rote learning in favor of emotional security and close relationships (see Miller, 1990). Friedrich Froebel (founder of the kindergarten movement) worked with Pestalozzi prior to founding his own school, and with Pestalozzi, believed that humans possessed a divine essence and that the purpose of education was to lift this essence into consciousness. Other European innovators, including Rudolph Steiner and Maria Montessori, developed their own spiritually based pedagogies in contrast with a dominant authoritarian model. The methods of these holistic educators varied, but they all shared a commitment to the unfolding of the divine in each person, to the "spontaneous and essentially creative nature of this unfolding, and cultivation of an educational environment that respects the fullness and natural stages of this unfolding" (Miller, 1990, p. 100).

Two scholars who brought these ideas into the North American academic field of education were Dwayne Huebner (1999) with his commitment to the transformation of limiting human perceptions and conditions, and James Macdonald (1995), with his "transcendental developmental ideology of education" (pp. 69–98). Huebner rejected reductionist forms of thinking about learning and the learner, and advocated instead for understanding education as attending to and caring for the journey of the self, or the soul. The transcendental developmental model, according to Macdonald, integrates many of the principles of pragmatism and critical pedagogy, but addresses their weaknesses by attending to the aesthetic and the intuitive dimensions of learning. In order to teach this way, the teacher must have more than mere knowledge of a young person; they must have a deep understanding, built on a relationship of *mutual centering*. Both of these eminent theorists agree, as we outlined in Chapter 2, "The Development of a Neohumanist Educator," that it is of central importance that the teacher be on their own soulful journey of self-knowing. A transcendental developmental approach to education, then, coupled with new research on learning and the brain, and embedded in Yoga theory, offers a solid foundation for neohumanist learning theory.

A Neohumanist Theory of Learning

Philosophy and psychology were once a unified approach to the study of mind. Western philosophers going back to the early Greeks relied on their own inward, subjective observations coupled with logic to formulate their ideas about learning. In the 19th century psychology broke from philosophy and began to call itself a science, with its claim that only phenomena that could be mutually observed, verified, and experimentally controlled could constitute valid knowledge. Thus, this new science focused almost exclusively on how young people learn about the *world out there*—the world of objects—and the resultant behaviors or interactions with that world. Sarkar calls this "extroversial knowledge" (Anandarama & Brim, 2010, p. 25). It is only now, with advances in neurotechnology such as magnetic resonance imaging that Western science is beginning to penetrate the deeper layers of subjectivity and various aspects of consciousness and higher order brain activity that Sarkar terms "introversial knowledge" (Anandarama & Brim, 2010, p. 25). There is progress, but the exploration has only begun to scratch the surface of the mysteries of consciousness.

Yoga and the Science of Mind

The intuitional "science of mind" that is the foundation of Yoga has a long history in the East; its principles and practices have evolved over thousands of years of disciplined study and observation. Yoga theory has a lot to say about the subjective world of feelings, intuitions, and the cultivation of more subtle states of consciousness. Yoga practices derive from the fundamental assumption that there are progressively more subtle layers of the human body/brain/mind system. It names the following capacities of a "self" and how that self comes to know:

- First, the *citta*, the image-making capacity of the body/brain/mind system. Images can be formed from both external objects and internal objects.
- The *aham*, corresponding with Western definitions of the ego. The sense of doership, performance of activity, whether sensing, feeling, thinking, or desiring.
- The *mahat*, or the feeling that "I exist," corresponding with an existential sense of self.
- The *atman*, a witnessing function beyond the sensory mind, beyond the ego and its wants and needs, even beyond the sense of "I exist." Its capacity is metacognitive, but defined in Yoga psychology as pure consciousness.

Paralleling these aspects of mind that constitute the sense of self are the *koshas*, which further define layers of awareness at different stages (not necessarily linear) of knowing. The *koshas* similarly progress from crude (or dense) to subtle: *annamaya kosha* (basic matter, the physical body) to the *kamamaya kosha* (senses and instincts) to the *manomaya kosha* (thinking and remembering). These capacities correspond roughly to Western psychology's conception of body, conscious mind, and subconscious mind. The body, considered to be a product of earthly evolution, comes equipped with instincts for survival, sustenance, reproduction, pleasure, and so on. The human body takes in information from the external world via the senses (in Sanskrit, called *indriyas*). The impressions from the external world (called *tanmatras*) are carried to the brain via vibrations in the central nervous system, and become "psychic objects," whereupon they take mental form according to the innate tendencies of the individual. In part, this explains why two people can have an identical experience but process it much differently, and take away different learnings from it. This is a very important idea in education, as it helps explain why even when applying the same experience, the same teaching method, and the same information, students come away with a bewilderingly different set of outcomes.

Beyond these fundamental aspects of the body/brain/mind system lies the causal mind, referred to in some esoteric traditions as the "superconscious" or "supramental" mind. Here we have the *atimanasa kosha*, said to be the seat of aesthetics, imagination, and creativity, the *vijanaamaya kosha*, where intuition, discrimination, and non-attachment are cultivated, and at last, the *hiranyama kosha*, where reside the inclinations toward universal love and spiritual longing. Though it is tempting to correlate specific kinds of learning activities to the development of specific *koshas*, there is the risk of reductionism here, of reducing the vast range of potential experiences to specific outcomes, much like the behaviorists try to do. Understanding the different capacities attributed to the *koshas*, and grasping the psychic and spiritual dimensions of the sense of "I-ness" requires us to see the human being, even the very young child, as an extraordinarily complex entity.

Human experience is also a very complex phenomenon. Let's analyze, for example, a single simple event: witnessing a sunrise. The image of the sunrise, in the context of a horizon, cloud formations, and perhaps a vast spectrum of color is assimilated via visual perception, into the human body/brain (*kamamaya kosha*). In the brain, the image meets former experiences: factual information one has learned, former experiences of sunrises. One may recall a piece of music associated with the sun, Gustav Holst's "Planets" or the popular "Here Comes the Sun" written by George Harrison and recorded by the Beatles. And we know that a chain of memory often follows upon recalling a piece of music (*manomaya kosha*). Or it might evoke wonder about the size of the sun, the angle of light emanating from it, or its relation to other planets. This might make one think about sundials and how our ancestors developed their sense of passing time. Perhaps the sunrise stimulates thinking about ancient narratives and myths—about Ra, the Egyptian sun god, or the Olympian deity Apollo, whose domain included light and the sun, or Surya, the solar deity in the Hindu tradition (*atimanasa kosha*). Perhaps we are moved to consider the fleeting quality of all experience as we observe the sun move across the sky, and ponder the nature of impermanence (*vijanaamaya kosha*). And the existential intelligence can be summoned when one thinks metaphorically about emanating light as an aspect of divinity, thus inducing deep spiritual feelings (*hiranyama kosha*).

The complexity of the human being coupled with the complexity of experience remind us that there are no simple correlates between what we hope to teach, the activities we plan, and what children actually learn. This is why teaching is an art, and not a science. We will return to this idea in upcoming chapters. Note too, all of the intelligences that could be thus activated in the simple example of a sunrise: the linguistic, the musical, the visual-spatial, the naturalist, the mathematical, the intrapersonal, the existential.

Yoga and Biopsychology

Though seemingly complex, there are very practical educational implications of understanding the human being in this multi-dimensional way. From Yoga studies, we have a sophisticated approach to the science of biopsychology, an integration of ancient wisdom and modern science that elaborates the ways that the nervous and endocrine systems work to "integrate and regulate the activity of the brain, autonomic nervous system, and endocrine glands" (Jordan, 2016, p. 28). In this system, our thoughts, whether generated through memory, sam'skára (inherited, acquired, or imposed), or fueled by new environmental stimuli, are processed in complicated neuro-chemical, nervous electrical, and hormonal impulses into physical chemistry, which then results in specific behaviors. Of course, this all happens in micro-seconds, well below the surface of consciousness. The complexity of this system is beyond the scope of this chapter, but neohumanist educators should familiarize themselves with its concepts.

The introduction of Yoga practices in developmentally appropriate ways, including quiet time, asanas, and mindful breathing, is a core principle of neohumanist education; only through attention to the harmonious integration of the complex play of energies in body, brain, mind, and spirit can we help a child find balance in a volatile world full of distractions. The concept of *pranayama* comes into play here—a word that describes the esoteric science of breath. Again, Western science is beginning to recognize the relationship between breathing and the emotions (Goleman & Davidson, 2017), but the intuitional science of Yoga has long recognized the complex interplay between breathing, perception, awareness, emotion, will, and other attributes of human consciousness. Practicing controlled breathing is said to help develop a balanced mind, and a balanced mind is fertile soil for concentration and learning.

Core Principles of a Neohumanist Learning Theory

The information overload—the sea of words, images, facts and misinformation that young people are swimming in—is an overpowering distraction and a hindrance to the concentration necessary for deep learning. Yes, information is vitally important and how wonderful that we have so much of it at our fingertips now. But there is a vast chasm between information and knowledge, and beyond that, between knowledge and understanding. Aldous Huxley (1956) framed it beautifully, in his important essay, *Knowledge and Understanding*:

> Knowledge is acquired when we succeed in fitting a new experience into the system of concepts based upon our old experiences. Understanding comes when we liberate ourselves from the old and so make possible a direct, un-

mediated contact with the new, the mystery, moment by moment, of our existence.

Understanding is an intimate and subjective act. When we *enact* our understandings with meaning and purpose, and in ways that serve the common good, understanding becomes wisdom. A balanced mind is a solid foundation for the development of wisdom. And wisdom must encompass both keen knowledge of the world "out there" and a sense of identity and purpose gained from introspection. Hence the slogan that encapsulates the essence of neohumanism: to be fully human one must embody a *subjective approach and objective adjustment.*

We are approaching the horizon of an integrative approach to learning theory that can enable a synthesis of ancient and modern ways of knowing. Research is advancing at an accelerated pace (this century has already had a "Decade of the Mind" [2007–2017]), and Western science may soon arrive at a deeper understanding of consciousness that could change the face of education. However, conventional education has always lagged far behind new discoveries in the cognitive sciences. Neohumanist educators who have integrated what we currently know of body/brain/mind research with what we know from the ancient teachings of Yoga are positioned to formulate innovative pedagogies that not only develop the keen intellect necessary to solve increasingly complex problems in the world, but that nurture the whole child, and their social, emotional, ethical, aesthetic, imaginative, and intuitive selves as well.

The following core principles drawn from Yoga teachings and contemporary educational brain research will be developed further in upcoming chapters on learning environments, teaching methods, curriculum, and assessment:

- The search for meaning should be at the heart of all educational activity. Seeking information must arise from genuine questions that young people have about the world and their place in it.
- Learning activities should be balanced between the extroversial (external knowledge) and the introversial (inner knowledge), integrating these elements in creative ways.
- A "heart-centered" approach that promotes love for all creation should permeate all subject matter.
- Learning should be holistic, engaging the many dimensions of conscious and subconscious activity—body, senses, perception, reflection, cognition, and metacognition.

- Learning should activate the subtle aspects of the personality (aesthetics, intuition, imagination, caring, empathy) as well as the intellect.
- Understanding that much learning happens below the surface of consciousness, great attention should be paid to the sensory environment, including colors, textures, scents, sounds, materials, décor. Think of the surrounding environment as a "teacher" and ask what is learned and absorbed from every detail.
- Loving kindness and safety should characterize the learning environment. Relationship is at the heart of good teaching.
- The discrete learning of facts should be contextualized in meaningful activity.
- Experience should be at the center of learning, amplified by discussion, debate, and reflection.
- There should be opportunities for students to articulate what is already known about a topic, so that new information has something to "hook" onto, and misunderstandings can be cleared up.
- Learning should be social, developing communicative skills and relationships.
- Critical thinking—the ability to reason and think logically—should be cultivated.

Novelty and challenge should both be present, tempered by support and encouragement. Teachers need to understand Vygotsky's "zone of proximal development" (the difference between where a learner is and their potential for growth) and proceed accordingly.

- There is no room in a neohumanist classroom for activities that shut down the brain (threats, negative criticism, high stakes testing, strict time limits, penalties and punitive grading).
- Engagement and joy in learning are motivators, and information thus gained results in higher levels of cognition, better long-term memory storage, connection-making, and "Aha!" moments.
- The "thirst for knowledge" should be activated; information and facts should be presented creatively, utilizing storytelling, visual artifacts, music and film whenever possible.
- Many different forms of intelligence should be valued, and students should have multiple choices about how they express their knowledge.
- A spirit of gratitude should be fostered and opportunities to engage in selfless service should be inspired.

These are simple principles, but they are based in fundamental values concerning how we should treat young people. Many students have been damaged by schooling practices that demean, belittle, and threaten them, and some leave school traumatized by their experiences. It is up to every educator to create equitable learning environments where students can find joy and pleasure, as well as challenge, in learning.

This is not a "soft" approach to education. Content is important as is the development of a well-honed intelligence. But this must be tempered by the affective environment, and learning activities that simultaneously nurture *knowing, doing and being.* Otherwise, how are we to support the development of young people for a world in which there is love for all creation, a universal sentiment of care and concern for all, and a devotion to the well-being of the planet?

Cultivating Wisdom

How do we educate for wisdom? All of the brain-based practices in the world can serve to educate for good or for ill. The aim of neohumanist learning should be the cultivation of an *awakened conscience,* what P. R. Sarkar (1982) calls "rationalistic mentality" (p. 76). This is a subtle idea that references not merely the abilities to think critically, logically, and analytically, but also the importance of bringing a discerning sense of ethics to bear on all subjects. The integration of ethical thinking into learning is a key principle in neohumanist education. *Ethos,* the Greek word at the root of ethics, means "character" or "conduct." Neohumanist education is a values-based approach to teaching and learning, and thus rightly concerned with the cultivation of an ethics in line with its philosophy. Issues of right and wrong, fair and unfair, harmless and harmful, surface in everyday life in the classroom as well as across the curriculum. The capacity for critical moral reflection is a developmental one and involves a multitude of factors, including learning to listen to one's peers, cultivating empathy, practicing mindful agreement and disagreement, observing effects and speculating about the future consequences of actions, and exploring the implications of individual and group decisions. These practices are all aimed at the cultivation of the "awakened conscience" or rationalistic mentality (Sarkar, 1982), and will be explored in more depth in future chapters.

The idea of rationality proposed by Sarkar is a nuanced one. Recall that we discussed *epistemological pluralism* in Chapter 1, a stance that acknowledges ways of cultural knowing that are distinct from Western forms of logic (including intuitional knowing, embodied knowing, ancestral knowing, etc.). Many of these alternate ways of knowing can be said to be *non-rational* in that they bypass conventional (Western) forms of logic and reasoning in favor of "felt" knowledge, or knowledge that has been passed down intergenerationally. *Non-rational* knowing is different from *irrational thinking*, which is generally grounded in faulty logic, emotional distress, or cognitive inadequacy. Our post-modern task is to identify the differences between these ways of knowing, honoring and valuing ideas that may be arrived at *non-rationally* while discarding what is clearly *irrational*, and discover new ways to integrate the rational and the non-rational in order to arrive at closer approximations of the "truth."

A Philosophy of the Future

A neohumanist learning theory, to be of real use, must be based in a strong set of values about what knowledge is important and what constitutes ethical behavior, and integrated with developed neohumanist ideas concerning the aims of education. Neohumanism is a philosophy of the future, a prophetic vision of the potential of humanity to create a world of peace, happiness, health, sustainability, and joy. Aware of the research on the frontiers of consciousness, we can peer into the future and get a glimpse of how intelligence might be thought about and developed in times to come:

- How do we learn from "more-than-human" others? (Can we learn to listen to the trees? What can the animals teach us?)
- Is there a "collective unconscious?" If so, can we learn to access information from it?
- Can we learn to access extra-cerebral (beyond time and space) memories?
- How might we communicate with other humans without using words?
- How can we invite Divine wisdom into our consciousness, aligning ourselves with the positive energy of the universe?

Back to the present, contemporary learning theory is quite narrowly focused on understanding how people take in information from the external world, how they process that information, and how it connects to other information that has been processed to become knowledge. Yoga studies offer pertinent answers to some of the perennial questions about the brain/mind connection, the mysteries of consciousness, and the relationship of mind and matter. Fusing what we know from these two poles of investigation—modern empirical science and ancient intuitive wisdom—provides us with a meaningful foundation for an integrative learning theory. Neohumanist learning theory articulates the important differences between information, knowledge, understanding, and wisdom. But learning theory alone will not answer all the questions about what a teacher should DO in order to ensure that deep learning happens and that we lay a strong foundation for the development of wisdom in our students. In future chapters we will elaborate on the teaching methods that align with neohumanist learning theory, on the design of learning environments, and on curriculum principles that can put flesh on the bones of these ideas.

FOR CONTINUING STUDY

> *Discussion/Reflection:* Out of Gardner's nine "intelligences" which ones are dominant for you? How were these nurtured in your upbringing? If they were NOT nurtured, how did you develop them?
>
> *Discussion/Reflection:* Do you feel that your own education followed any or all of the 12 "brain-based" principles in this paper? Why or why not?
>
> *Application:* Imagine that you are a teacher (maybe you are!) and consider a common unit of study that is taught at a specific grade level (e.g., Natural Selection—middle school). Keeping in mind the "core principles of a neohumanist learning theory" what are some learning activities you would design that align with these?

References

Adler, M. (1982). *The paideia proposal: An educational manifesto.* Simon & Schuster.

Anandarama, A. & Brim, A. (2010). *Foundations of neohumanist education.* Ananda Marga Gurukula Publications.

Brameld, T. (1965/2000). *Education as power.* Caddo Gap Press.

Caine, R. N., & Caine, G. (1991). *Making connections: Education and the human brain.* Association for Supervision and Curriculum Development.

Caine, R. N., & Caine, G. (1997). *Education on the edge of possibility.* Association for Supervision and Curriculum Development.

Counts, G. S. (1978). *Dare the school build a new social order?* Southern Illinois University Press. (Original work published 1932)

Crowell, S., Caine, R. N., & Caine, G. (2001). *The re-enchantment of learning.* Corwin Press.

Dewey, J. (1938). *Experience and education.* Kappa Delta Pi.

Du Bois, W. E. B. (2013). *Education and empowerment: The essential writings of W. E. B. Du Bois.* Hansen Publishing Group.

Freire, P. (1970). *Pedagogy of the oppressed.* Herder & Herder.

Gardner, H. (1983). *Frames of mind: The theory of multiple intelligences.* Basic Books.

Goleman, D., & Davidson, R. J. (2017). *Altered traits: Science reveals how meditation changes your mind, brain, and body.* Penguin Books.

Huebner, D. W. (1999). The lure of the transcendent: Collected essays by Dwayne E. Huebner. In V. Hillis (Ed.), *Collected and introduced by Pinar, W. F.* Lawrence Erlbaum.

Huxley, A. (1955/1956). Knowledge and understanding. Recorded lecture at the Vedanta Society of California, later reprinted in the May–June issue of *Vedanta and the West.* https://vedanta.org/2002/monthly-readings/knowledge-and-understanding-part-1/

Jordan, S. (2016). Biopsychology and yoga sadhana: Education for self-knowledge and social welfare. In *Proceedings: International Educational Futures Conference,* 28–33. https://prsinstitute.org/downloads/related/education/nhe/InternationalEducationalFuturesConference.pdf

Ladson-Billings, G., & Tate, W. F. (1995). Toward a critical race theory of education. *Teachers College Record, 97*(1), 47–68.

Macdonald, J. B., & Macdonald, B. J. (Ed.). (1995). *Theory as a prayerful act: The collected essays of James B. Macdonald.* Peter Lang.

Miller, R. (1990). *What are schools for? Holistic education in American culture.* Holistic Education Press.

Sarkar, P. R. (1982). *The liberation of intellect: Neo-Humanism.* A'nanda Márga Pracáraka Samgha.

Sarkar, P. R. (1998). *Discourses on Neohumanist education.* Ánanda Márga Pracáraka Samgha.

Wolfe, P. (2001). *Brain matters: Translating research into classroom practice.* Association for Supervision and Curriculum Development.

Woodson, C. G. (1933). *The mis-education of the negro.* Associated Publishers.

5

Healing the World

Decolonizing Education

> *Decolonization takes us deep inside the serpent's belly to confront the white supremacy, the savior complex, and the internalized oppression that are entrenched in ourselves, our institutions, and our society.*
> —Edgar Villaneuva, *Decolonizing Wealth: Indigenous Wisdom to Heal Divides and Restore Balance* (2018)

> *The most potent weapon in the hands of the oppressor is the mind of the oppressed.*
> — Steve Biko, *I Write What I Like*, 1978/2002

At the beginning of the 20th century, a handful of European empires ruled over a vast portion of the planet, including much of Asia, Latin America, and Africa. Colonialism was justified by asserting the moral, technological, and cultural superiority of the Western empires, and conquest proceeded hand in hand with missionary Christianity and commerce (which generally consisted of the plunder of raw materials, forced labor and the disruption of local economies).

Colonized people (mostly Brown and Black) were considered culturally inferior by colonizers (mostly White) and incapable of "civilizing" themselves. A primary aim of the colonizers was to transform the colonized into versions of themselves. The British were particularly adept at this in India, where their aims were "to produce civic, loyal citizenry and bureaucracy which will facilitate the rule of colonizer" (Sharma & Ahmad, 2019, p. 4). In one famous speech, British historian and politician Thomas Macaulay, who was responsible for the establishment of English as the language of education in India, noted that "education would produce citizens which would be Brown in colour [*sic*] but will be English in thought and action" (Sharma & Ahmad, 2019, p. 4).

In the United States, the colonialist project had many faces. United States history texts emphasize the colonial status of the European invaders, and valorize the successful revolution that brought independence from Britain. Less attention is given to the processes by which European settlers emigrated from Europe over the next few centuries and spread across the United States colonizing, dispossessing, and slaughtering the indigenous inhabitants—distinct peoples who constituted hundreds of sovereign nations. Genocide, says one historian of this period, is a term that "drills to the very core of U.S. history, to the very source of the country's existence" (Dunbar-Ortiz, 2014, p. xiii). Richard H. Pratt, founder of the Carlisle Indian School, expressed a similar sentiment to that of the British colonizers: "that all the Indian there is in the race should be dead. Kill the Indian in him, and save the man" (1973). It should be clear from these statements how important a role education played in assimilating the conquered to the values, behaviors, and beliefs of the conquering culture.

By the end of the 20th century, almost 150 former colonies had asserted their independence, often through violent revolution, and become their own nation states. Following these ruptures, capitalism became a global, homogenizing force, multinational capitalists replaced colonizers, and "economic colonialism" is now justified by asserting that people will all be better off if they are integrated into the modern, technological, global economy. Shrii Sarkar (1986) agrees that colonialism has been transmuted into new forms: "In economic life there is extreme inequality and exploitation. Although colonialism no longer exists openly in the political and economic spheres still it persists indirectly, and this should not be tolerated" (para. 11). The new forms of colonization include resource extraction, imposed models of development and austerity, and economic dependency. The winners in this game are multinational corporations; the losers most often suffer ecological and humanitarian damage to their land and cultures. As in colonialism, modernization and its handmaiden, Western education, has been accompanied by the loss of languages, the erasure of cultural identity, the eradication of traditional technologies that have evolved in response to local conditions, and the deterioration of bioregional sensibilities. Madhu Prakash and Gustavo Esteva (1998), in their book *Escaping Education: Living as Learning Within Grassroots Cultures*, write:

> Wherever education advances, homogenization establishes itself. With every advancement of education or the educated, a global monoculture spreads like an oil slick over the entire planet. (p. 7)

As we begin to understand the latest iterations of colonialism, it becomes clear that "decolonizing" is a much longer-term process that involves removing not just the material, but the intellectual and emotional shackles of the oppressor who has brought about the systematic destruction of so many of the world's languages and the great variety of cultural expressions. Decolonization is a process that recognizes the connections between what has occurred in the past, what is experienced and perceived in the present, and how we might shape a future that atones for the misdeeds of the past and heals the wounds that persist into the present day.

A Neohumanist Perspective on Decolonization

If you analyze [sic] the history of the world, you will find that whenever one group exploited another in the economic sphere, they first created psychic exploitation by infusing inferiority complexes in the minds of the exploited mass.
—Sarkar, 1982, p. 47

In hundreds of citations, we read Shrii Sarkar pointing out the problems posed by inferiority and superiority complexes. Powerful people can inject feelings of inferiority into people which then makes it possible to exploit them, socially or economically. This is clearly operative under all colonizing cultures; without the injection of internal feelings of inferiority, it would be difficult, if not impossible, to control others for one's own benefit.

Shrii Sarkar is very clear that neohumanist education must nurture a universal outlook that transcends caste, creed, color, race and gender, and that sentiments which impose limitations on human development must be rejected; this is not to be understood as universalism in the sense of uniting all people across geographic boundaries under the umbrella of Western values. Neohumanism resolves the apparent tension between universalism and cultural pluralism by emphasizing the importance of sustaining local languages, and by including learning about the histories and cultures of non-dominant groups: "Neohumanism ultimately represents a philosophy of *one* humanity existing as a multiplicity of *different* humans, while neohumanist education presents a pedagogy of diverse universalism" (Kesson & Oliveira, 2023, p. 11).

In the United States, descendants of white people from Northern Europe have constituted a majority for much of recent history—though that is changing—and they wield most of the economic and political power. People whose recent ancestors were enslaved, oppressed, or victims of genocide or dislocation can experience a range of emotions and ailments—anxiety, distrust, fear, anger, shame, grief—that both consciously and unconsciously can structure beliefs and behaviors in the present. This has been named *transgenerational trauma*. As well, there can be feelings of inferiority—internalized oppression—that can result in holding the colonizers in higher esteem than one's own Indigenous ways.

Both the oppressed and/or marginalized people in a society and the privileged (individuals and groups who benefit from the historical legacies of colonialism and occupation) have been mentally colonized by media, educational curricula, power relations, and institutional structures that create and sustain myths of inferiority and propagate racism (racism = power plus prejudice or discrimination based on an assumption that one's own race is superior) and ethnocentrism (ethnocentrism = the evaluation of other cultures according to the standards and customs of one's own). If education is to take seriously this idea of "decolonization" and be truly transformative, the stories of the past must be carefully attended to in order for healing to occur. Educators need to confront and challenge the colonizing practices that influenced education in the past and are still operative in the present. This is becoming increasingly difficult in the United States, where a politically reactionary movement is attempting to whitewash American history and remove references to the racial conflict, racism, sexism, and genocide that are part of our past in a presumed effort to eliminate information that might inflame divisions in the populace. At least 18 states (at this writing) have legislation forbidding the teaching of anything perceived to be related to "critical race theory." This is just one of the dangerous "liberal ideas" they want eliminated from the school curriculum—also off limits is comprehensive sex education, references to gender identity, and discussion of the climate crisis.

If neohumanist educators aim to achieve the radical social equality and economic and political democracy promoted by Shrii P. R. Sarkar and facilitate the epistemological pluralism that can help to mitigate the dire consequences of technocracy and the exclusive focus on the positivist science that underpins it, then the discourses on decolonizing education, emergent now from all corners of the globe, offer important concepts to our theory and practice.

A Pedagogy of Decolonization

The form of education that most modern people are familiar with is European in origin. The old German Republic of Prussia, a quasi-military state, gave the West compulsory schooling, educational technologies of surveillance and control, the idea of a prescribed national curriculum, regular testing, and state certification for professional teachers (Gatto, 2001). Complementing the influence of Prussian methods were the laboratories of Wilhelm Wundt in 19th century Saxony, where the seeds of psychological behavior modification and social control were germinated, tested, and refined. Enormously influential in western education, strong traces of these ideas remain in systems of discipline, zero tolerance policies, positive and negative reinforcement, grades, and rewards—everything from praise to pizza to degrees. Decolonizing education will require the rethinking of all of the taken-for-granted assumptions that underpin our educational theories and practices.

We should not underestimate the enormity of the task of decolonizing education. One scholar, G. T. Reyes (2019), notes that colonization has been a "global project of domination over ways of thinking, knowing, valuing, feeling, doing, being, and becoming" (p. 1). Because colonial power has been exerted historically by (mostly) White people, and the colonized have been primarily people of color, "whiteness" is a pervasive norm, and this "directly influences the ways that schools are organized and how teachers, students, and families interact" (Reyes, 2019, p. 3). These conditions often operate below the level of consciousness, and may be experienced by privileged people as natural, as "just the way things are." Hence, projects like uncovering implicit bias are prevalent in anti-racist and decolonization work.

Clearly, this is a huge undertaking and we cannot begin to do justice to its many dimensions in this brief overview. Scholars who write about the processes of decolonizing education present a number of principles that are deeply compatible with a post-colonial, neohumanist education:

- Teachers and school leaders need to study historical processes of colonization and examine their own subjectivities in relation to power, being, and knowledge.

Colonization has occurred in diverse ways in multiple places across the planet throughout known history, therefore approaches to understanding and mitigating the effects of colonization will necessarily be varied. Neohumanist schools are staffed by both local people as well as teachers and leaders from other countries. It is important for both to study if and how the land and its inhabitants have been colonized in the past, and to understand the histories of power in that locale. Subjectivities are formed by one's experience, therefore it is important for neohumanist educators to reflect on their own experienced *positionality* in relation to power and hierarchy—what social class they were born into, how they were raised, what forms of discrimination and bias they experienced in their life (either on the giving or receiving end), and how issues of *intersectionality* play out in their lives. Intersectionality is a term used to describe how a person's different aspects of identity (race, gender, ability, language, etc.) interact dynamically to form unique matrices of inequality (Crenshaw, 1989).

- School structures need to be examined for their ideological frame, and understood as ways that act to reproduce coloniality (or the dominant—white—culture).

This is an extraordinarily complex concept to unpack, as it involves nearly every aspect of a school's structure. Structures include explicit things like: how physical space is organized and set up, schedules, curriculum, instructional methods, disciplinary policies, grading systems, organizational decision-making, hierarchies of power (i.e., How are faculty evaluated? Who determines schedules? etc.). The foundation for analysis must be a deep understanding of how modernity (which includes colonialism) has shaped modern schooling in ways that no longer serve the interests of planetary well-being. From there, we can then apply social imagination to envision how things could be otherwise. What structures best serve human (and non-human) interests?

- School materials (textbooks, bulletin boards, signage, etc.) need to be analyzed for how various people and cultures are represented, and for ways that they transmit messages about power and privilege.

This follows from the former bullet point, in that the artifacts of the school need to be examined in terms of what they represent and what priorities are being highlighted. What language(s) are the public bulletins in?

What races, genders, abilities, and so on, are presented in visual images? What activities take center stage (sports trophies? children's art?)? How is the image of the school presented?

- Educators need to be aware of whose knowledge and ways of knowing are prioritized and how/when/by whom academic subject matter has been created.

This issue takes a great deal of study and requires educators to develop a critical consciousness about the knowledge that is presented to the students. Whose story is being told in the history books? Whose is left out? How diverse is the selection of authors presented to the students in literature classes? What are the interests behind curriculum materials (check to see if certain businesses have provided materials that are "friendly" to their interests)? If the school is in a post-colonial culture, are the ideas, frames of reference, and subject matter of the former colonizers still featured? Is Western science presented as the one way to truth, or is traditional knowledge recognized for its value?

- Colonizing education attempts to homogenize people; decolonizing values individual and cultural diversity.

Recall the point made earlier about the remaking of the colonized in the form of the colonizer. Attempts to homogenize a population rests in forms of standardized curriculum that require uniform thinking, school materials that are characterized by stereotyping, tests that require one right answer and do not value independent thinking, and the inculcation of Western attitudes and values. Modern education systems, under the influence of global capitalism, are oriented towards creating workers with similar content knowledge, attitudes, and behaviors who can serve multi-national corporations by being transplanted anywhere. A decolonized education must be firmly rooted in place, honor local language (while not neglecting to support a lingua franca), and be responsive to local customs, history, and culture.

- Colonizing education attempts to sift and sort students and works from a deficit model; decolonizing education works from a strengths-based model and fosters resilience.

Norms and accepted standards are most often a reflection of the dominant groups in society. For many reasons (language differences, interrupted schooling, different cultural values), students from non-dominant cultures may not match up with these. A "deficit model" of education is designed to identify weaknesses in students and "fix" them. It relies on rigid grading systems, ranking of students, and separation of students into ability groups with the highest groups having more opportunity for complex learning and critical thinking and the lower groups concentrated on remediation. A strengths-based model identifies what a young person *can* do instead of focusing on what they *can't* do and builds in supports to help them achieve the next level of understanding. It recognizes and values diversity, including neurodiversity, and designs a curriculum that opens opportunities for all young people to access knowledge. When learning groups are formed, they are deliberately structured to incorporate a diversity of learning styles and intellectual strengths, in order that all students can learn from each other.

- The narratives that constitute the curriculum must be inclusive of the many stories people tell about their lives and their relations with other species on the planet. "Counter-stories" must be unearthed and history (as just one example) must be studied from multiple perspectives, not just the narrative of the conqueror/dominator.

History, it is said, is written from the perspective of the conqueror, and this is certainly true in the history texts of the colonizers. There are many strategies for reconceptualizing the way that history (as well as other academic disciplines) are taught including the use of primary source documents (letters, texts by marginalized people, visual artifacts such as paintings and posters of the time, etc.); engaging with "sensitive subjects" such as genocide, slavery, witch-burning, colonization, and so on (in developmentally appropriate ways); showing maps that portray geographies differently; examining how certain stories have been privileged over others; and ensuring that multiple perspectives are offered on any one topic by varied texts and speakers. An excellent multi-lingual collection of resources on decolonizing education can be found at: https://euroclio.eu/2021/03/10/an-introduction-to-decolonising-the-history-curriculum/

- Classrooms must be spaces that are grounded in human values. They must also be grounded in "eco-values"—a recognition of the inherent worth of all species—if we are to survive.

Neohumanism honors the humanistic efforts to extend rights and protection from discrimination to all persons regardless of race, color, creed, gender, sexuality, ability, and all other marginalized and vulnerable groups, a global project that has yet to be fully realized. Neohumanism also recognizes that the ecological imperatives of our time require us to include the rights of non-human others as well (endangered species, rivers, air, etc.) as we work to create a sustainable future. The cultivation of values begins in the home and in the classroom as adults model ethical relationships. Ethics is at the center of neohumanist curriculum planning, with the recognition that ethical thinking and decision-making must be taught from the very beginning of schooling, as, for example, when teachers discuss issues of fairness with preschool children.

- "Decolonized education is rooted in connections to place. Place-based education empowers students and helps restore cultural knowledge" (Centre for Youth and Society, n.d.).

Place-based education emphasizes the symbiotic character of humans and nature, acknowledges our co-evolution, and has a deep respect for the carrying capacity of the local bio-system. Linking place and culture is a reminder that many pre-colonial societies lived in relative balance with their bio-systems, had a keen awareness of the relationships between people, plants, animals, weather patterns, and geography, and developed appropriately scaled technologies to make work easier. Much of this local knowledge has been lost as people and places have been colonized, conquered, polluted, deforested and destroyed in the name of progress. Some scholars argue that the decolonization project must include the repatriation and rematriation of ancestral land to people who have been forcibly displaced or removed. This is an enormously complex topic, well beyond the scope of this chapter (Tuck & Yang, 2012). It is a topic that generations to come will be called upon to engage with in the work to create a future in which all beings can survive and thrive, in which the land is held as sacred, and in which justice is realized.

- New relations between schools and communities need to be cultivated—all adults in a community need to be seen as mentors, role models, and teachers of youth.

Conventional Western schooling has been seen as a way out of poverty, away from the grip of tradition, and a way "up" in the world, generally meaning attaining improved standards of living and increased status. In order to accomplish this, schools needed to break with communities and become vehicles of mobility. In many ways, this is such a widespread idea that it has become taken-for-granted. Helena Norberg-Hodge offers a different perspective on this in her book *Ancient Futures* (1991/2016), as does the film *Schooling the World* (Black, 2016), which both look at the unanticipated negative impacts on people and communities when students are inducted into the formal education system.

Norberg-Hodge is a leading advocate for a movement termed *localization*, which has become a rallying cry for people who seek to restore the vitality to local communities, develop food security outside the global market system, decentralize manufacturing to ensure a more dependable supply chain, restore and regenerate eco-systems, and mitigate the damages ensuing from a warming climate. In order to build strong local economies and vital social networks, the schools need to open their doors to the knowledge and expertise in the community. Community schools are doing this by building partnerships, supporting community-based education, and welcoming parents and other community members in as co-teachers (Kesson, 2021).

- Decolonized education focuses on the whole person (emotions, embodiment, identity, etc.), not merely the intellect.

Conventional Western schooling has focused on the acquisition of intellectual skills, occasionally adding in ingredients to spice things up a bit: social/emotional learning, the arts, and physical education, most of which are seen as extras or add-ons. Literacy and numeracy are at the top of the pyramid, as they are essential to the creation of a technologically advanced, competitive society. A few students rise to the top of this academic food chain, others opt for secondary choices like the military or technical education, and high numbers simply drop out. With no real skills to offer society, many turn to drugs and crime. Healthy, sustainable, inclusive societies are not built on this model of education. Schooling designed to create a healthy society would value the inherent worth of every person, recognize that there are different ways of knowing, design educational experiences that meet a variety of learning styles, interests, and preferences, provide necessary supports for people to progress at their own rate, and center the idea of personal and communal well-being rather than competitive academic achievement.

- A decolonized education validates the experiences of young people, and calls forth youth voice and activism.

Young people today are facing a world of enormous challenges: climate catastrophe, the extinction of species, global conflict, domestic social unrest, pandemics, the global creep of fascism, threatened LGBTQ rights, and economic inequality and instability. In order to conquer the epidemic of despair that haunts so many youth, schooling must provide them with multiple opportunities to develop *agency* (defined here as the capacity to make choices, to act on them, to develop their potential in ways that enable them to work for a better world). Young people have a history of working for social change; the current generation has magnified their efforts with social media and new ways of organizing. Interestingly, as young people lose trust in formal political institutions and become more critical of their leaders, they "tend to increase their participation in the democratic process via alternative and more direct means" . . . including "activities such as attending demonstrations, protests, boycotts and signing petitions" (Saka, as quoted in Carnegie, 2002, para. 13). Schooling in this new era needs to prepare young people to participate in more radically democratic ways, providing the skills and training in leadership, effective organizing, communication, policy, building alliances, and working for social justice.

* * *

Every educational context is different—who the students are, the communities they come from, the values and beliefs of their families—hence, decolonizing work will look different in every setting. Common factors, however, include the necessity of looking below the surface for root causes of conditions and problematizing situations: "listening, asking questions, and drawing connections to the broader implications of systems of oppression" (Reyes, 2019, p. 7). Decolonizing education is a healing process—healing the wounds that have been inflicted by centuries of domination, exploitation, and violence perpetrated by people against their fellow human beings and the planet. Decolonizing education asks us to reconsider the fundamental purposes of education: rather than educate so that a tiny sliver of people rise to the top of the global income chain, we need to educate all people for the art of living well together on a fragile and sacred planet. A pedagogy of and towards decoloniality must be "a project of 'Re'—resisting, refusing, rehumanizing, remembering, reminding, restoring, reframing, revisioning, and reimagining" (Reyes, 2019, p. 7). Neohumanist education is dedicated to this task of providing learning environments that support the project of decolonization, and bringing about a society grounded in justice, joy, and the well-being of all.

FOR CONTINUING STUDY

Discussion/Reflection: In what ways do dominant educational practices in your locale reflect (or not) the principles of a decolonized education? What are some of the forces working for and against decolonizing?

Discussion/Reflection: Consider some of the major conflicts over educational practices. In what ways do you see these connecting to colonialism/post-colonialism?

Application: To whatever extent you are comfortable, write about your origins (birthplace, family of origin, religion, caste/class, lifestyle [family careers, etc.], schooling, relationship to geographical place). *How did your experiences shape your view of the world? What are some of the most valuable aspects of your own culture? What aspects of your culture were perhaps dogmatic or limiting?*

Application: Describe the geography of the place you live and describe the population of this place. *What do you know about the original inhabitants of the place? What do you know of the history of the place? What groups are in power now/what groups are marginalized; is there a class/caste system in place?*

References

Black, C. (2016). *Schooling the world* [Film]. http://carolblack.org/schooling-the-world

Carnegie, M. (2002, August 8). *Gen Z: How young people are changing activism.* https://www.bbc.com/worklife/article/20220803-gen-z-how-young-people-are-changing-activism

Centre for Youth and Society. (n.d.). University of Victoria. https://www.uvic.ca/research/centres/youthsociety/

Crenshaw, K. (1989). Demarginalizing the intersection of race and sex: A Black feminist critique of antidiscrimination doctrine, feminist theory and antiracist politics. *University of Chicago Legal Forum, 1989*(1), Article 8.

Dunbar-Ortiz, R. (2014). *An indigenous people's history of the United States.* Beacon Press.

Gatto, J. T. (2001). *The underground history of American education.* The Oxford Village Press.

Kesson, K. (2021). *Community schools blueprint: Transforming the school/community partnership.* The Bay and Paul Foundations. https://static1.squarespace.com/static/590cbe53ebbd1afaa38e2081/t/6137afb7ea47387a7a5a58ac/1631039450845/communityschools-blueprint_Aug31.pdf

Kesson, K., & Oliveira, M. (2023). Diversifying universalism: Neohumanism, internationalism, and interculturalism in education. *Práxis Educativa,* Ponta Grossa, v. 18, e21500. https://doi.org/10.5212/PraxEduc.v.18.21481.049

Norbert-Hodge, H. (1991/2016). *Ancient futures.* Local Futures.

Prakash, M. S., & Esteva, G. (1998). *Escaping education: Living as learning within grassroots cultures.* Peter Lang.

Pratt, R. H. (1973). The advantages of mingling Indians with Whites. In *Americanizing the American Indians: Writings by the "Friends of the Indian" 1880–1900* (pp. 260–271). Harvard University Press. https://teachrock.org/wp-content/uploads/Document-1-Excerpts-from-Richard.-.-..pdf

Reyes, G. T. (2019). Pedagogy of and towards decoloniality. In M. A. Peters (Ed.), *Encyclopedia of teacher education* (pp. 1–7). Springer Nature Singapore. https://doi.org/10.1007/978-981-13-1179-6_220-1

Sarkar P. R. (1982). *The liberation of intellect: Neohumanism.* A'nanda Márga Pracáraka Samgha.

Sarkar, P. R. (1986). Renaissance in all the strata of life. In *A few problems solved (Part 7)*. The Electronic Edition of the Works of P. R. Sarkar, version 9.0.

Sharma, N., & Ahmad, S. (2019). *Decolonizing education: Re-schooling in India.* https://sinectica.iteso.mx/index.php/SINECTICA/article/view/913

Tuck, E., & Yang, W. E. (2012). Decolonization is not a metaphor. *Decolonization: Indigeneity, education & society, 1*(1), 1–40.

Portions of this article first appeared in the newsletter *Gurukula Network* (2021, January), under the title: "Decolonizing Education" (Kesson) Issue 51).

6

Contemplative Inquiry

The Art of Knowing the Child

> *Teachers cannot be said to understand children simply because they possess a considerable amount of explicit knowledge about them. Understanding is a deeper concept. It demands a sort of indwelling in the other, a touching of the sources of the other... (it) provides for relating, for being fully there in the presence and as a presence to the other.*
> —James Macdonald, *Theory as a Prayerful Act*, 1995

Despite decades of educational research, hundreds of "models of best practices," and an industry of "research-based programs" and "data-driven instruction," genuinely effective teaching and learning remain a mystery, frustrating all efforts to identify the one best method or the most successful recipe for instruction. While much effort has gone into trying to articulate a *science* of teaching and reduce it to a list of prescribed behaviors, teaching is more an *art* than a science. It is a complex human activity with innumerable variables. Every context is different. Every child is unique. And every society holds different values about what is important and what should be taught. The neohumanist educator needs to be aware of all these differences and nuances when considering the act of teaching, and approach their work with the same creative and contemplative purposes and intentions as a painter approaches a canvas or a poet considers the rhythm and imagery of her words.

Theories of child development and how children learn can provide useful signposts in our efforts to help young people on their educational journey, but they don't get us to the deep knowing, what James Macdonald (1995) calls "indwelling," necessary to truly guide the child. In this chapter we outline an approach to inquiry that is designed to bring you closer to the *reality* of the child, so that you might better see them in all of their fullness. A quote by Patricia Carini (1979), who developed the process of child study known as the Descriptive Review, highlights the importance of *seeing clearly*, in order not to fall into a form of habitual perception, thinking, and action:

> The gift of vision ... through which observing lays claim to its fullest possibilities, requires exercise to realize its power or it relapses into a kind of blindness, in which the things in the world are perceived only as objects-of-use; that is, in terms of personal needs. (p. 11)

The approach to inquiry that we outline here is a *contemplative practice*, not in the sense of meditation that is connected to a particular religion or spirituality, but in the sense of *an active attunement to the many layers of meaning in unfolding events*. Such an attunement is essentially a practice guided by "spirit," and we use the term spirit here in a broad, secular sense, hearkening to Huebner's (1999) notion that to

> "have spirit" is to be in touch with forces or aspects of life that make possible something new and give hope and expectations. Spirit refers to the possible and the unimagined—to the possibility of new ways, new knowledge, new relationships, new awareness. (pp. 343–344)

To be open to what is not yet imagined, however, requires the deconstruction of habitual patterns of perception and action. It asks us to learn to suspend judgment, bias, conditioned responses, and hasty interpretations, allowing for more fluid and open perception. Such disciplined perception, the exercise of the "gift of vision," offers the opportunity to attend to the multidimensionality of the child. Connecting the acts of systematic observation and description to phenomenological reflection on both inner (somatic) and outer events makes this sort of clear seeing possible, providing the ground from which teachers can develop increasing insight and understanding about children and make informed moral judgments about what is in the best interest of their students. Descriptive inquiry is a meditation on the mystery of the child and their uniqueness and potential. In this chapter, we ask important questions about the act of teaching:

- How can neohumanist teachers make the child *visible*?
- How can they develop their powers of educational observation and intuition to better guide young people on their unique educational journey?
- How can teachers awaken a sense of "pedagogical love" capable of responding to the universal human needs to be cared for, to belong, and to develop their highest potential?

The Child as an Endangered Species

The child, along with the wild tigers, the sea turtles, the dolphins, and unthinkable numbers of butterflies, bees and other insect pollinators, is an endangered species. Recall in the chapter on child development the emphasis on norms. Norms are established and reified by labels that define (and some scholars would contend, *construct*) deviance. The child disappears underneath the myriad labels that attempt to classify and control: ADHD (attention deficit hyperactivity disorder), EBD (emotional/behavioral disorder), ASDs (autism spectrum disorders), ODD (oppositional defiant disorder). We locate all of these problems in the individual child. The boy with lots of energy and a strong need to move about might be described as hyperactive. The girl with little interest in a required topic might be described as having an attention deficit. Seldom do we look at the system itself, a system that often requires children to sit still and engage in prescribed tasks for long periods of time, as a cause of deviant behavior. This is not to discount the importance of supports for children who due to disability, injury, trauma, or some other cause, have not attained typical milestones in their development; rather it is a critique of the over reliance on the medical model, especially the diagnosing and prescribing of pharmaceuticals for dealing with behaviors.

In many schools the child no longer has a name, they are a number: a Level 1, 2, 3 or 4, depending on their standardized test scores. We push the academic curriculum on younger and younger children in the rush to have them read, write, and compute. We place 6-year-olds in reading recovery, an educational intervention that is necessary largely because we pressure children into reading before they are developmentally ready and then need to "remediate" them. Many schools have eliminated arts, drama, music and play time, as well as the social-emotional learning that is essential to healthy child development, in favor of extended literacy and math periods.

Test preparation (even in kindergartens) has become a staple of "low performing schools" (usually schools with large numbers of children living in poverty, children of color, or immigrants). Even pre-schools, which used to be joyful havens for free play, socializing, and exploration, now have academic standards that must be met. Pediatricians, says one expert, "are reporting worrisome levels of achievement-related stress among elementary school children" (Crain, 2003, p. 4), accompanied by headaches, difficulty sleeping, and bouts of anxiety. Parents and teachers alike are deeply worried about the future, so much so that we fail to see and value the child for who they are in the present. Descriptive inquiry aims to make the child *visible*, to articulate their strengths, and to describe them in their fullness in order to develop a deeper understanding of who they are at their core and guide their learning more effectively.

Descriptive Inquiry

Phenomenology is a philosophy of perception, and a method of objective study of subjective topics; a systematic reflection on the contents of embodied consciousness such as one's emotions, judgments, and perceptions. Phenomenological educational inquiry focuses on what is perceived, which is captured by detailed written description. It is through taking a descriptive stance that inquirers using this method engage in a form of contemplative observation, seeing "what is" rather than seeing what our experiences have conditioned us to see. Another quotation from Carini (2001):

> Describing I pause, and pausing, attend. Describing requires that I stand back and consider. Describing requires that I not rush to judgment or conclude before I have looked. Describing makes room for something to fully present. Describing is slow, particular work. I have to set aside familiar categories for classifying or generalizing. I have to stay with the subject of my attention. I have to give it time to speak, to show itself. (p. 163)

As this passage suggests, engaging mindfully in description requires several things of the investigator. One is positioning herself on the borders of her taken for granted reality, "setting aside the assumptions and concepts from her everyday lifeworld" (Bentz, 2016, p. 52) in order to become aware of preconceived notions and to work to meet what is described on its own terms. Another is resisting (or being aware of and stepping aside from) definitive judgments and instead remaining open to further experiences that generate possibilities and new understandings. A third is recognizing that moving from the particular to the general does not mean making an abstract generalization, but instead means seeing connections between different particulars that enables a deeper, more nuanced understanding. In simple language, descriptive inquiry requires the teacher to:

- slow down,
- be attentive,
- be fully present and focused,
- look and listen carefully, and
- be tuned into the child with an open-hearted caring and compassion (Miller, 2018).

These are all aspects of the *discipline* of descriptive inquiry, and should come easily to the teacher who is well established in a meditation practice of their own. Inquiry is a habit of mind, a way of learning to see more deeply into the uniqueness of each child, a way to look closely at student work in order to better understand the child and their growth patterns, and a way to examine one's own teaching practice. When a teacher engages in inquiry, they become a "knowledge maker" rather than merely someone who implements the ideas of others. Inquiry is a creative foundation for becoming a teacher, for learning to really *see* our students—their needs, interests, strengths, characters, and interactions—more clearly. This enables us to make judgments about curriculum, instruction, activities, materials, and interpersonal responses that are more thoughtful, more appropriate, more compassionate, and more effective.

The Process

Descriptive inquiry can be applied in a number of ways: the descriptive review of a child, the descriptive review of children's work, and the descriptive review of a teaching practice. This chapter will focus on the descriptive review of a child. In subsequent chapters, you will learn how to apply the inquiry process to understanding children's art works and other constructions, their writing, and their science dialogue. Though investigations are most often carried out by individual teachers, an important part of this process is the sharing of reviews amongst teachers: "Sharing descriptions with other phenomenologists provides a group of colleagues who can collectively see aspects not immediately apparent to the writer" (Bentz, 2016, p. 53). To reiterate an important aspect of this work: the process of inquiry is not designed to "fix" children so that they can better fit the mold of the school or classroom. Rather, says one experienced teacher, descriptive processes

> make a space for stepping away from a vocabulary of deficiency. Positively, they create a space for discovering a vocabulary particular to a child and a

child's work that is both apt and vivid, and so to restore to view the child as she is—a lively presence, with capacities and strengths to be counted upon. (Carini, 2011, p. 40)

All of the variations on the descriptive review involve careful observation, describing what you observe, usually in written form, and reflection on what you have seen. Teachers are constantly engaged in the act of observation, noticing what activities children are drawn to, how they make sense out of the world they encounter, how they interact socially, and how they engage with academic activity such as reading, writing, constructing, and drawing. The act of *describing* these observations in writing is a method for becoming more reflective and more systematic. When a teacher first begins this process, it seems quite time consuming, and they might wonder *what is the use* of doing this for one child? What emerges, however, is a *way of seeing*, a habit of noticing and reflecting, that results in making wiser judgments about what, when, why, where, and how to teach. It is important to keep in mind that the purpose of this mindful attention isn't to assess a child or to figure them out—and certainly not to change them into someone else. The purpose is simpler and more ordinary: to be more sensitively attuned to who they are and are becoming, so that, recognizing them as persons, we can better assist and support their learning.

Format

The double entry journal is a useful format used for recording observations. "Law-ruled" paper, which is divided into two columns, can be obtained from many office supply stores, or you can make your own. Generally teachers use handwriting, as it is less awkward than typing while in the midst of activity. It can be difficult to record observations in the moment as so much is generally happening at once in a classroom. But it is recommended that a teacher write up their observations as soon as possible after the observed event.

On the *right* hand side of the page goes your description of the student or an event. Here is where you record your perception of what you see, *uncolored by interpretation or analysis,* in as much detail as possible. These are the *facts* of the observation, *as you perceive them.* A good rule is to limit yourself to what you can see, hear, taste, smell, and touch—in other words, sensory details. It is important not to try and cover too much time in an observation. A 5-minute observation (or less) can be very rich in detail and issues.

On the *left* hand side of the paper is where you record your first impressions (both objective and subjective), thoughts about what you observe, and your analysis of the event. Here is one example of a double-entry journal (note the way that the commentary is matched up spatially with the event):

Reflection/Analysis	Description of Concrete Events
Uh oh, I thought. Here we go again. I could feel my heart race as I wondered what trouble Roberto would get into today. I find that I am relieved when he doesn't show up for school, which is often. But I feel bad about that. I really want to find ways to integrate him into the life of the classroom.	Roberto rushed into the room looking to both sides with a scowl on his face. His complexion was reddened as though he had been running. He tore off his jacket and dropped it on the floor.
I wonder how I might help him get more organized. Perhaps this is one of the reasons why he doesn't get his homework done.	He slammed his book bag down on the table he shares with Tiffany, Lorenzo, and Ophelia and the contents spilled out. The papers were loose and not in his folder.
I need to observe more carefully to see who relates positively to Roberto and perhaps change the seating arrangement.	Tiffany and Lorenzo looked at each other across the table and sighed. They turned away from Roberto and began talking to each other in low tones.

Bracketing Assumptions, Bias, and Preconceptions

The word "bracketing" in phenomenological research refers to a process of setting aside our habitual thinking about the phenomena we are witnessing. We have all been shaped since birth by the institutions of our culture: families, school, church, and media. We engage in stereotypical thinking as a result of our experiences and our conditioning. Though it is probably impossible to free ourselves of all of our habitual thinking, we can at least recognize that we have been socialized to see the world in particular ways, and admit that these preconceptions may be preventing us from seeing clearly and understanding the nature of reality. This is a good starting point.

Some of our strongest biases and assumptions are around issues of social class, gender, race, ethnicity, ability/disability, sexual orientation, and so on. These are hard to recognize, because often they are unconscious. We may act in accordance with them without consciously understanding our motivations. One example of this is the teacher who assumes that a child who dresses poorly is less intelligent, or that a quiet Asian student is a highly motivated learner. These biases interfere with our ability to reach all children and to be successful teachers.

For example, if a child is known to be a bully and we see him or her engaged in a tussle with another child, a conditioned reaction is to blame the child with the bad reputation. However, if we observe carefully, we might notice that another child is rather slyly instigating the bully. This noticing would give us a deeper understanding of the problem, and help us make more effective judgments about how to handle the situation.

In order to overcome biases, it is important to make assumptions and preconceptions *explicit.* In your double entry journal, in the reflection column, you should notice your immediate reactions to a situation and write them down. In the example above, the teacher noted her somatic response to the experience ("I could feel my heart race") and made explicit her wondering: "I wondered what trouble Roberto would get into today?" Making your reactions explicit allows you to examine them. She also confessed her thoughts of relief when he did not show up for school. The practice of noticing your somatic reactions and immediate thoughts helps you to "bracket" them, to set them aside in order to see more clearly. Next time you observe the bully, you will be looking more carefully to see what leads up to the disruptive behavior, noticing body language, glances, and the spoken words of other children.

The Use of All the Senses

When we think of perception, we usually think of vision. *Sight* is the dominant way most people take in the world. Sight gives us information about color, shape, size, movement, gesture, energy, facial expression, proxemics, and other physical actions and interactions. However, don't neglect your other senses when you record an observation. Hearing is an important sensory experience. When you listen to a group of children talking, note the sounds of their speech: What are the rhythms, cadences of the speech? What about volume? Is someone a soft speaker? Whose voice dominates? What about pitch and quality? Is a voice high? Squeaky? Throaty? Hoarse? What dialect or vernacular is spoken? Smell can be important too. What does your school smell like when you walk in the front door? Taste could play a part in an observation. And touch reveals a lot of important information about texture, temperature, strength, elasticity, and so on. Using all of your senses will give you a more complete and detailed picture and overall sense of an experience.

Using "Apt" Language

One important way to move beyond habitual thinking and begin to see events and people from differing angles and perspectives is to carefully monitor the language we use in our descriptions. Words like "mean" "lazy" "unmotivated" "pretty" "smart" or "aggressive" tend to label children and *cement* our experience of them in our minds. The idea is to be open to change, to see the child anew each time, to offer, in this way, the possibility for change to them. The language we use to a great extent shapes our thinking, so the words used in descriptive processes needs to be evocative and concrete, not jargon-y or judgmental. This is actually one of the more difficult aspects of the process to master—we are so used to evaluating, judging, and assessing based on limited data that we tend to use linguistic shortcuts in the beginning. This is an art, and it takes practice.

Seeing the Whole Child

Categories of Description

The classic descriptive review of a child encompasses five dimensions of the person: physical presence and gesture, disposition and temperament, relationships and connections, strong interests and preferences, and modes of thinking and learning, as developed by Patricia Carini and her colleagues at the Prospect School. These have been slightly revised and expanded to encompass elements important to a neohumanist educational approach.

Physical Presence and Gesture

Children are profoundly *embodied* creatures. From the moment of birth, the child is a bundle of basic physical needs: the need for comfort, for nourishment, for warmth. Their bodies are well equipped with instincts for survival, sustenance, and pleasure, and they express their needs in no uncertain terms. As they grow and develop, they gain control over more and more bodily functions and develop skills (other than crying) to communicate their needs. We can learn a great deal about a child from the careful observation of their physical presence.

A child's physical presence involves their size and build, and the way they move about in space. Are they observers of activity, noticing what others are doing before they participate? Or do they jump right in without much deliberation. Do they move quickly, with confidence? Or are they tentative in their motions? Do they like to daydream, sometimes seeming not involved in external activities? Do they have any physical limitations which may require support for them to engage fully in activities?

You will want to observe the child in different circumstances. When they are outdoors, what do they like to do? Climb trees? Ride a bicycle? Chase other children? Notice the energy, pace and gestures involved in these activities. Do they accentuate their speech with large hand movements? When in the classroom, how do they engage in active play (dress up, block building, etc.)? Do they tend to stand apart and observe? Or leap in and guide the activity? How do they engage in more quiet, solitary work, such as drawing or writing? Use all of your senses to investigate the physical presence of the child. Describe their voice: its inflection, volume, and rhythm; characteristic phrases and ways of speaking (and listening). Think about the expressiveness of the eyes, hands, and mouth; where the child's feelings can be read.

How do they approach the activity of yoga? Is it easy for them to hold still for a time, or do they find it difficult? Do they seem to take the work seriously, or tend to giggle with embarrassment when learning a new pose? The physical body is the most outward expression of the emotions, the mind and the soul, or innermost being of the child. The young child expresses their needs and wants through instincts and impulses, gradually bringing their physical expression under the control of intelligence and intention. Much of childhood is devoted to gaining mastery over the physical body: learning to work with tools, figuring out appropriate ways to interact with other children, testing the limits of speed and other capacities by running, jumping, climbing, and so on. Helping the child gain mastery over physical expression and become attuned to the inner messages of the body is an important part of early education. In neohumanist schools, a playful approach to asanas and moments of quiet time help the child become calm and reflective, and aware of their body's signals.

Meaningful data about physical presence and gesture can best be gathered when there is relative freedom of movement, not constriction. A learning environment designed for the healthy integration of body, emotions, mind, and spirit is one rich in activity: exploration, play, games, dance and creative movement, all of which will be addressed in subsequent chapters.

Disposition and Temperament
Physical characteristics can provide clues to more subtle aspects of the child's being—their inherent qualities of character and common ways of behaving and expressing themselves. Disposition and temperament focus on the emotional parts of their personality. As with everything else in descriptive work, we need to be especially cautious about labeling a child by naming them as "withdrawn" or "social" or "self-centered"—and recognize that social and emotional characteristics are *fluid, variable according to circumstances, and changeable.*

How would you describe a child's general expression? Are they usually calm, cheerful, somber? Are they easily distracted (by noises, other children, sudden changes in the environment)? Do they stay focused on a task and see it through to completion? Do they try different approaches when something doesn't work? Are they easily frustrated? Do they seem to enjoy attention? Do they tend to want what other children have? Do they share easily and readily? Are they eager to meet new people and have new experiences, or are they more cautious? Do they like predictable routines, or are they always up for "going with the flow?" Are they sensitive to the feelings of others? Do they try and soothe other children when one is upset? How do they respond to touching and being touched? The intention of identifying general moods and dispositions is to better meet the needs of the child and create a positive relationship with them.

Noticing what a child cares for deeply and what stirs deep feeling can provide insights into the inherent tendencies they bring with them to this life. Children can exhibit early inclinations towards such important human capacities as justice, fairness, affection, and loyalty, which should be nurtured by the adults around them and their educational experiences. Similarly, they may bring (through inborn tendencies or cultural conditioning) behaviors that limit their ability to engage positively with the world. Close observation and careful reflection can assist the teacher in responding positively and constructively to whatever behaviors the child presents.

Relationships and Connections with Other People and With Non-Human Others

If disposition and temperament are very personal expressions, this next category moves into looking at the child in relation to others—the social (and ecological) dimensions of personality. The child has relationships with a variety of others—caregivers, teachers, classmates, siblings. Notice the different ways a child acts when with different groups. Notice how they enter into play with a group—are they shy? Inclined to leadership? Controlling? What kinds of roles do they play in friendships? Are they comforting? Supportive? Helpful? Sharing? When describing a child it is helpful to NOT use interpretive words like these, but to describe the actions of the child. This leaves a reader or another teacher the room to make their own interpretations of behaviors.

How does the child interact with adults? Do they notice them or go right to their peers when they enter the classroom? Do they greet the teachers? Do they seek out or avoid any adults in particular? Think about possible reasons for this. Does the child ask teachers a lot of questions and seek explanations of things in the world? Do they seek comfort or affectionate touch? Do they hide behind grown-ups, as though seeking protection? Another point of reflection might be your sense of what makes the child feel safe, trusted, respected, and secure with adults (or not). If the child is hard to *see*, give some thought to what keeps the child hidden from you or others. Reflect, too, on what adult responses, interests, and ways of being hold the child's interest and which kinds of responses seem most effective.

Classic descriptive review processes focus on the relationships of children with other humans. Neohumanist education aims to cultivate the sense of self in relationship with all beings, not just other humans. This requires teachers to more deeply understand how a child develops relationships with non-human others, including plants, animals, and what we call the "inanimate" world. When walking outdoors, does the child jump in the puddles? Swing from tree branches? Clamber over rocks? Do they seem at home outdoors, or do they exhibit caution in the elements? Do they eagerly embrace changes such as rain? Do they express any fears (of thunder, of wind, etc.)?

If you have pets in the classroom, how does the child interact with them? Are they eager to hold the pet, to be in close physical contact? Do they talk with the pet? Do they express an understanding of the animal in human terms (as in "the hamster is lonely; he wants someone to play with"). Is the child gentle with the animal? How do they interact with a strange new animal (for example, a worm or a snake)? Do they recoil? Or seek contact?

When walking in the forest or the woods, where does the child gaze? At the other children? Up at the sky? Or down at the earth? Do they notice small entities—a ladybug? A caterpillar? An unusual leaf, or a new mushroom? Do they seek to investigate it further? Do they wish to hold it? To examine it? Do they have questions, or make observations? Are they curious to meet new creatures—to turn over a log, to peek in the hole in a tree? Do they eagerly pick things up—pine cones, sticks, seashells, leaves? Do they investigate textures and forms? Do they express imaginative possibilities for these materials? Do they listen—to frogs croaking, to the call of birds?

Many modern children, especially those raised in WEIRD countries, have few encounters with the outdoors. Author Richard Louv (2005) calls this a "nature-deficit disorder" and it is the task of neohumanist educators to do their best to remedy this lack in children's lives.

Strong Interests and Preferences

These are likely to offer much valuable insight in terms of the child's entries into learning and particular talents to be nurtured. Some children are persistent in their questions, and wonderings. What do they seem most curious about? What seems to stir their imagination? Do they seem obsessed with Superheroes? Or are they most interested in playing with dolls? Or blocks? Or creating environments with dinosaurs in the sand table? It's important to look for patterns, and see how these interests play out over multiple environments. Do they choose to read related books? What do they draw? Often children become immersed in a topic—dinosaurs, for example—that finds regular expression in a variety of forms.

Does the child engage in fantasy play with non-representational objects? For example, when playing with cubes or sticks or rocks, do they impart human or animal characteristics onto the objects? Does the child like to engage other children in their passionate interests? If so, how do they go about this? What role does the child tend to assume in group play? What sort of props do they use? Are they open to suggestions from children or adults about how to enhance the play? Or do they have fairly set ideas about how it should proceed? Are there rules or expectations that the child imposes on the group? What seems to make the play satisfying? What makes it "go wrong?" What generally ends the period of immersion?

Meaningful observations about strong interests and preferences can only be successfully carried out in an environment in which there are many available books, play spaces, materials, and opportunities to exercise choice over activities. Without the freedom to choose, it is difficult to discern what a child is interested in or how they prefer to spend their time.

Modes of Thinking and Learning

One of the most fascinating aspects of the careful study of children is observing how they go about making sense of their world. The young child is full of questions and ideas about everything: How high will the ball bounce? Will the toy boat float? How fast will the marble roll down the slide? What happens when I mix these colors together? Such questions can be understood as the embryonic exploration of physics, and the testing out of such ideas is essential to a child's cognitive growth. That such testing out of ideas is a trial and error affair, and often quite messy should not discourage the teacher who is dedicated to understanding how the child thinks and learns. Noticing their interests and preferences, their approach to tasks, their emotions when engaged in work, and the products they create yields important information that enables the thoughtful teacher to design experiences and environments that support children's innate meaning-making capacities.

Faced with making sense out of a puzzling situation (and to the young child, most things are puzzling) the child makes use of many strategies for figuring things out. They often ask questions. They might map or sketch or draw or construct or graph. There may be interest in taking things apart and putting them back together; or looking at things or ideas from many angles; or counting, ordering, and creating patterns. Some children learn best by watching others and remembering. Or perhaps they like to look things up in books. You can see from all these different possibilities how important it is to provide varied settings and materials with which a child can try out their ideas.

Listening carefully to children's questions and wonderings, it is sometimes possible to glimpse deeper ways of meaning-making. There may be a philosophical, reflective, and speculative faculty or the child may have a religious or spiritual predisposition, indicated by "God talk" or speculation about angels, or heaven, or even death. Some children incline toward imaginative comparisons with an eye to metaphoric likenesses between objects or events. These are the children who see dragons in the clouds or liken the rain to angels crying. Some children are drawn to the big picture and big ideas (who made the Earth?), while some are fascinated with textures, colors, and small details (why do ladybugs have spots?). Perhaps a child expresses an experimental or problem-solving slant on the world, with an eye towards understanding why things happen the way they do (why does the block tower always topple with X number of blocks?). Or perhaps they express a utilitarian initiative, using materials in imaginative ways to build and construct. It's important to keep in mind that in life children draw on all these capacities and more, and it's important not to categorize them prematurely. Human beings are complicated creatures: "Given that complexity, in my experience, creating types or categories of thinkers and learners tends not to do a child (or adult) justice or to be especially helpful in the long run to the parents and teachers responsible for that child's learning and education" (Carini, 2011, p. 17). Children are fluid, development is non-linear, and teachers need to stay open to the element of surprise, for children prove remarkably able to astonish us.

Volumes have been written on learning styles, multiple intelligences, and the many other variables in how people approach learning. Some people dive right into an experience, preferring to learn through trial and error. Some of us have to read multiple books about a topic before we try something. Some people like to watch someone else do something before they try. Some wish to be instructed by a teacher who stays with them through a process and others prefer to muddle through on their own. All of this applies to children as well as adults. Understanding different children's modes of thinking and learning may be one of the most important skills a teacher develops, for everything—curriculum design, instructional methods, even forms of discipline—all flow from these deep understandings. These descriptive processes, however, are not merely intellectual exercises designed to enhance pedagogical skill. They can open the heart to genuine pedagogical love—the capacities to embrace the child fully regardless of their characteristics, extend deep empathy, hold sincere hope for their futures, and to trust in their possibilities. For it is only through such deep caring that the child can experience and learn to express the kind of unconditional love and acceptance that reflects one of the highest aims of a neohumanist education.

Cultivating Intuition

Intuition is sometimes defined as having a "gut feeling," suggesting that the body has a kind of intelligence that precedes awareness. Indeed, humans have evolved as careful observers, using all of our senses to detect danger or threat. When we fail to pay attention to these feelings, we sometimes get hurt or end up in problematic situations (or relationships!). This is our subconscious mind, our limbic brain, keeping us alert. These instincts served us well in our evolutionary history, as our brains evolved to trust the familiar and repeat behaviors that served us well in the past.

Neuroscience has coined the term *interoception*, which means the ability to sense internal signals from your body. Interoception is related to physical well-being, as the body signals states such as thirst or threat. It is a metacognitive capacity, and has been shown to be related to perspective-taking and empathy (Heydrich et al., 2021) as well as to our emotions, accuracy of insight, and our ability to make good decisions.

Certainly, interoception plays a major role in phenomenological inquiry, as this method of study involves both perception (external input) and reflection (internal input). Though as we have seen, gut instincts can also be misleading, as we sometimes make judgments based on our own deeply embodied biases, which are a part of the information system stored by the brain. Scientists have also found that distracting emotional states such as anger, depression, and anxiety interfere with our "internal compass" or our ability to process and interpret our "subliminal sensations" accurately. This is why, in doing descriptive inquiry, we bracket our instinctive responses, in order to examine their source.

Another factor to consider is that our immediate inclinations in terms of identifying patterns or problem-solving are strongly related to expertise. An expert in a field, whether that is gemology, espionage, medicine, or education, is likely to discern the truth of a situation more readily than someone with no proficiency in the area. Of course, expertise is also vulnerable to limitations, in terms of the paradigmatic assumptions of professional fields.

In Yogic philosophy, there is another angle on intuition, the recognition that it is a property of "cosmic consciousness" or the all-encompassing mind of the creative force in the universe. Yoga is often called an "intuitional science," as it is a practice that aims to unite the individual mind with the cosmic mind. As we know from the new story emerging from many sources (quantum physics, the Gaia Hypothesis, the implicate order, and the universality of intelligence) we are but part of a greater *wholeness* and this wholeness contains all that is known. This is why in traditional spiritual paths, God is said to be "omniscient" (all-knowing). Our small minds are but reflections of the more developed consciousness available to us, and we polish this mirror by contemplative practices, by consciously cultivating stillness, so that intuition can flow to us from this source. Because meditation calms the "thinking mind" it actually increases the capacity for interoception as well. You might recall from Chapter 2, "The Development of a Neohumanist Educator," the discussion of the *koshas*, or levels of mind. In this system, the Vijinaamaya kosha is the seat of intuition, discernment, and non-attachment, a level of mind increasingly accessible through contemplative practices.

Phenomenological inquiry is thus an integrated activity involving perception, interoception, reflection, and knowledge gained from experience. Coupled with a contemplative practice, specifically a form of meditation designed to focus and still the mind and open the heart, it can yield important insights about the child that can aid the teacher in more effective guidance of the young person on their soulful journey. It can cultivate, in the teacher/student relationship, the *indwelling* spoken of in the opening quote by James Macdonald, the capacity for being fully there in the presence and as a presence to the other.

Making Inquiry Central to a School

The adoption of an inquiry approach to education is an important alternative to the enforced standardization, high stakes testing, labeling, behavior modification, and judgment that characterize conventional schools. It accomplishes this in a number of ways:

- by making the strengths and capacities of children as learners and thinkers more visible;
- by valuing the contextual knowledge of teachers;
- by learning to value the multiple ways by which children come to understand the world;
- by emphasizing the importance of having a variety of materials and experiences available for students;
- by aiding teachers to personalize learning and provide relevant individual attention to each child;
- by maximizing children's opportunities to choose what and how they learn;

- by fostering positive relationships amongst the youth and adults of a school; and
- by centering caring and pedagogical love in the culture of the school.

The skills gained in this inquiry practice can be utilized in many creative ways. Featuring student art work is a staple of most early childhood and elementary classrooms. Meaning can be added to this if a teacher transcribes what a student has to say about the work and places the text alongside. Some teachers capture dialogue that occurs in the context of observing an activity (such as sand or water play, or block building). This dialogue is then featured alongside an enlarged photograph of the event. (Of course, you want to make sure you have permission from both parents and children to display their work like this). This is a wonderful way to communicate to parents the kind of learning that is happening in the classroom. The Reggio Emelia schools have brought this sort of documentation to a level of sophistication that is central to the professional development of their teachers (Edwards et al., 1998).

A teacher is often required to write "assessments" of children to inform families of their progress. Describing a child's strengths in detail and with appreciation is an extraordinary gift for a parent (some of whom have only heard what needs to be fixed in their child). It may move parents and other caregivers to a deeper understanding of their child, and thus improve parenting practices.

In order to track student progress in school, it is important to select and collect work that illustrates different dimensions of a child's development in a portfolio. This can be a meaningful way for a child to review what they have done over time and reflect on how they see their own growth and progress. It can also be an important supplement at a parent/teacher conference. Some child-centered schools include the student in these conferences and prepare them to demonstrate what they have learned to their families or caregivers by sharing their portfolio. These portfolios travel with a child from grade to grade, providing not only useful information to a current teacher about a child's strengths and interests, but an evolving portrait of the development of the "whole child." In Chapter 11, "Visual Art and Emergence: Bringing Worlds into Being" we articulate a meaningful way to begin to understand a child's "spiritual blueprint" that the careful attention to their work can bring to light.

While descriptive inquiry is an important practice for individual teachers who wish to improve their practice, it becomes a meaningful method of school improvement when teachers engage in the work collaboratively. The method was developed by The Prospect Center for Education and Research, an independent school started in 1965 for elementary, and later, middle school children. The school closed in 1991 and the center closed in 2010. The dedicated teachers of the Prospect School kept longitudinal records of children's thinking and learning as expressed in their visual and written work. These archives have been digitized and are available through the collections at the University of Vermont. (https://cdi.uvm.edu/collection/uvmcdi-uvmcdiprospect). Protocols for the sharing of reviews (of a child, of a practice, of artwork or writing, of a space, or of a school) and many samples of reviews can be found in the online version of *Prospect's Descriptive Processes: The Child, The Art of Teaching, and The Classroom and School* (Himley, 2011).

FOR CONTINUING STUDY

> *Discussion/Reflection:* Think about and discuss some of the usual ways we "rush to judgment" based on immediate perceptions in everyday life. What are we basing these judgments on?
>
> *Discussion/Reflection:* Given the difficulties of note taking in the moment, brainstorm some ways to keep track of what you observe in the classroom.
>
> *Application:* Create a law-ruled paper based on the description in this chapter. Choose a child (with permission) to observe for a few minutes, and describe their physical presence and gesture in as much detail as you can in the right hand column. In the left hand column, write about what you thought about when viewing the child. How did you interpret their physical presence and gestures?
>
> *Application:* Try the above application with the other categories of description: disposition and temperament, relationships and connections, strong interests and preferences, and modes of thinking and learning. What are you learning about your own "habits of mind" as you carry out these observations?
>
> *Important note:* Any time you observe and document children's behaviors, be sure you have the permission of the child's caregiver(s).

References

Bentz, V. M. (2016). Knowing as being: Somatic phenomenology as contemplative practice. In V. M. Bentz & V. M. B. Giorgino (Eds.), *Contemplative social research: Caring for self, being, and lifeworld* (pp. 52–79). Fielding University Press.

Carini, P. (1979). *The art of seeing and the visibility of the person.* North Dakota Study Group on Evaluation.

Carini, P. (2001) *Starting strong: A different look at children, schools, and standards.* Teachers College Press.

Carini, P. (2011, Winter). Descriptive review of works: Guidelines for describing visual works. In M. Himley (Ed.), *Prospect's descriptive processes: The child, the art of teaching, and the classroom and school.* The Prospect Archives and Center for Education and Research. https://cdi.uvm.edu/sites/default/files/ProspectDescriptiveProcessesRevEd.pdf

Crain, W. (2003). *Reclaiming childhood: Letting children be children in our achievement-oriented society.* Henry Holt & Company (Times Books).

Edwards, C., Gandini, L., & Forman, G. (1998). *The hundred languages of children: The Reggio Emilia approach—Advanced reflections.* Ablex Publishing Corporation.

Heydrich, L., Walker, F., Blätter, L., Herbelin, B., Blanke, O., & Aspell, J. E. (2021, January 18). Interoception and empathy impact perspective taking. *Frontiers of Science,* 11. https://doi.org/10.3389/fpsyg.2020.599429

Himley, M. (Ed.). (2002; 2011). *Prospect's descriptive processes: The child, the art of teaching, and the classroom and school.* The Prospect Archives and Center for Education and Research.

Huebner, D. E. (1999). *The lure of the transcendent: Collected essays by Dwayne E. Huebner.* Lawrence Erlbaum.

Louv, R. (2005). *Last child in the woods: Saving our children from nature-deficit disorder.* Algonquin Books.

Macdonald, J. B., & Macdonald, B. J. (Ed.). (1995). *Theory as a prayerful act: The collected essays of James B. Macdonald.* Peter Lang.

Miller, J. P. (2018). *Love and compassion: Exploring their role in education.* University of Toronto Press.

SECTION II

Pedagogy and Practices of Neohumanist Education

7

Curriculum Theory and Design for a Neohumanist Future

> *I believe that education, therefore, is a process of living and not a preparation for future living. I believe that the school must represent present life—life as real and vital to the child as that which he carries on in the home, in the neighborhood, or on the playground.*
>
> —John Dewey, *My Pedagogic Creed*, 1897

The title of this chapter and the opening quote may seem to be at odds. How can we educate for a neohumanist future and also provide learning that is fully embedded in the vitality of the present life? That is the question we hope to answer in this chapter.

When most people hear the word "curriculum" the first thought that comes to mind is a list of courses or a set of lesson plans constituting a plan of study for a school or class. This commonsense definition is a given, however curriculum scholars have presented us with a much more expansive definition of the term. And with this more expansive version comes deeper and broader thinking about children, knowledge, teaching, learning, and culture.

Curriculum is not merely what is written and taught in formal lesson plans. Curriculum is *everything* that happens within the school, including extra class activities, guidance, and interpersonal relationships. Curriculum is that which is taught both *inside* and *outside* of school. Curriculum is a *series of experiences* undergone by learners in school. Curriculum is that which an individual learner *experiences as a result of schooling*. Curriculum is the *whole life experience* of the person, in and out of formal schooling (Schubert, 1986).

In this more expansive version, we must think about curriculum in terms of what students are learning from non-school social media and films, what they learn from their peers, and how they are influenced by their home culture. In some cases, the classroom can build on these experiences and integrate them into learning (e.g., appreciating the *funds of cultural knowledge,* defined here as the formal and informal knowledge and resources that families have accumulated over generations, that students bring with them); in others, the schools might need to challenge what is learned outside the classroom (for example, helping young people discern "fake news").

Who Controls the Curriculum?

For much of educational history, teachers have been in charge of designing and developing the curriculum, influenced to a large degree by a community's religious values, cultural conditions, legal strictures, and a host of other constraints. Over the past century there has been a shift as subject matter specialists in higher education, the business community, politicians, and textbook and standardized testing companies came to dominate curriculum-making. In the latter part of the 20th century in the United States, the federal government in concert with state officials, bureaucrats and large corporations had an ever greater hand in prescribing curriculum, signified by the "Common Core" (a set of standards detailing what all children K–12 should know in English and mathematics).

When coupled with a rigid system of standardized testing, common standards and prescribed learning limit the possibilities of what children learn, can represent the dominant views of society (in our current time, the corporate/capitalist perspective), and fail to present alternatives and foster critical thinking. While there is support for high standards from many sectors of society, the Common Core standards have come in for criticism on the basis of a number of issues, including but not limited to these:

- They drain initiative and autonomy from teachers.
- They ignore the vast diversity of students and promote a "one-size-fits-all" curriculum.

- There is no evidence that standards have improved educational outcomes.
- They emphasize rote learning, and de-emphasize creativity and variety in education.

The important thing to know is that underneath and behind *all* curriculum (and learning standards) are sets of values and interests. It is sometimes difficult to "unpack" these, as many curricula claim to be value-neutral. Sometimes it is obvious what the interests are—when, for example, curricula are designed and developed by timber companies and fossil fuel corporations, they present a one-sided view of environmental problems. If you look closely at textbooks, you can often find product placement in something as innocuous as math word problems; state funded math textbooks often include an array of brand name consumer products which also appear in illustrations. And now, educational videos with pop-up advertising or product placements are ubiquitous.

Less easy to recognize are the subtle but effective ways that the "language of learning" can affect the consciousness of both teachers and students. One renowned theorist of education notes the ways in which most educators fail to recognize the "metaphorically layered nature of language—and how it carries forward earlier culturally specific ways of thinking" (Bowers, 2002, p. 2). This takes a great deal of study, but one can begin by looking for signifiers of taken-for-granted aspects of modernity such as *data-driven, manipulate, achievement gap, evidence-based, delivery systems,* or analogies that liken the human brain to a computer. Teachers need to recognize how the "root metaphors of patriarchy, anthropocentrism, subjective/rational individualism, mechanism, and progress have provided the conceptual direction and moral legitimacy" (Bowers, 2002, pp. 2–3) for a narrow form of learning. Below are a couple of terms/concepts from curriculum theory that can be useful tools for analyzing curricula.

The *hidden curriculum* includes the unspoken or implicit academic, social, and cultural messages that are communicated to students while they are in school. One early example from the United States is simply the design of schools. Square classrooms connected by a hallway, with bells that ring to signify the end of one period and the start of another, was actually known as the Ford model, because it was influenced by early factory design (at a time when most students were expected to go to work in factories).

The hidden curriculum often embodies dominant culture rules and expectations about social class, race, and gender, and serves to socialize individuals to particular values and norms. An example of this would be a male principal overseeing a cadre of female teachers. Another example, identified by scholars of color, are the ways that "White supremacy culture" shows up in organizations (Jones & Okun, 2001). Such norms and values are considered "hidden" because they are not written down in official curricula or policy, but are seamlessly woven into the structures and routines of school life.

The *null curriculum* refers to what is absent from the formal curriculum—what students do NOT have the opportunity to learn in school. Examples abound in the social studies curriculum (again from the United States): Students rarely study about labor history, so they know little about the conflicts that have shaped the economic environment we have now; curricula about Black Americans often focus on slavery, but little if anything is written about African resistance to the slave trade; the teaching of Native American history may have something about the Indian Wars, but little about the Doctrine of Discovery or accurate information about the hundreds of Native cultures eradicated in the settlement of the country by European invaders. Efforts to remedy these absences, such as including more perspectives on history in the curriculum, often provoke severe backlash, as in the current efforts of conservatives in the United States to abolish treatments of Black and Indigenous history that are outside the "loyalty and patriotism" curriculum paradigm that they support. There are also efforts through state and local policy and legislation to control what young people are taught about gender or sexuality, especially targeting references to lesbian, gay, or transgender issues. The intention to limit what children learn has been taken to the extreme of banning popular books for young people by well-known authors. If these moves become dominant, then years of efforts to cultivate equity, fair representation, and inclusiveness in U.S. education will become part of the "null curriculum."

Sources of Curriculum

It is not easy to untangle *curriculum* (the *what* and the *why*) from *instruction* (the *how*). In this chapter our focus is on the former; in the next chapter, we will dig deeper into the processes of learning, how to conceptualize, organize, and deliver effective instruction. Deciding what to teach and how to organize it is a daunting prospect for new teachers. Given the practical and intellectual challenges of curriculum work, it is understandable that people want a road map, a script, curriculum guide, or at the very least, a set of expectations about student outcomes. As teachers gain experience, they are more likely to take on the creative tasks of planning, developing, and designing curriculum.

Where do ideas about what to teach come from? The answer is *everywhere!* Information is ubiquitous in the age we live in, and we are faced with innumerable choices about what to teach. A philosophy of education is a major factor in delimiting those choices, for a philosophy of education embodies a set of values and beliefs that inform what kinds of learning are most meaningful.

Neohumanism, with its holistic orientation, draws upon some of the same sources as the other philosophies of education we have discussed in earlier chapters. Like the Romantics, neohumanists believe that a divine spark exists within the incarnating person, and that this immanent energy can provide direction and interests that need to be nurtured. But the value of individual freedom, so dear to the hearts of the Romantics, is tempered in neohumanism by the cultivation of a deep sense of relationship and connection to the whole, so that the good of all might be achieved. These values can best be realized by the skillful facilitation of cooperative inquiry and inquiry-based problem-solving as reflected in the Pragmatists' approach. Unlike the human-centeredness of the Pragmatic approach, problem-solving in this model must take into consideration the inherent worth of all species, and address important issues in the environmental as well as the social worlds.

Neohumanism promotes radical social equality, so the methods of Critical Pedagogy play a major role in understanding the social world in order to become effective agents of justice and social change. In neohumanism, however, even the idea of social change is moderated by a concern for sustaining positive cultural traditions; in this model, ancestral wisdom, traditional ecological knowledge, and intergenerational knowing sit alongside modern scientific information and critical rationality. Neohumanism is a holistic paradigm; it recognizes the inadequacy of social justice movements that lack a contemplative, or spiritual dimension in the sense that they can be too easily corrupted by ego, power, or exclusionary strategies, and advocates a balance between personal development by the expansion of mind through meditation, and the fulfillment of social responsibilities by selfless service.

What is unique about a neohumanist education is the cultivation of a non-dogmatic spirituality, inner exploration, and character development with the aim of creating a sense of *oneness* or love for all creation. Lest this be misunderstood as anti-intellectualism, the cultivation of these capacities is intended to lead to an *awakened rationality*—a form of cognition in which intellectual knowledge is integrated with discernment developed by reflection and introspection.

Curriculum Design

A curriculum design has large *aims* or *purposes*, expressed in more detail as *goals* and *objectives*. There is the selection of *content* or *subject matter*. There is the *organization* of subject matter, often referred to as *scope* and *sequence*. There are the *activities* or *experiences* chosen through which to teach subject matter. And there is *assessment* or *evaluation*—the determination of the success of the learning experience. What leads to the wide variation in educational settings are the details of each of these elements: who makes decisions and at what points, how much attention is given to content vs. process, where the learning takes place, etc.

Curriculum Aims

Ask any group of twenty five people what the most important aims of education should be, and you will likely get twenty five different priorities, many of which would conflict with each other. Large aims are expressed as lofty ideals:

- Education should aim to create good citizens who uphold the values of the nation state.
- Education should aim for the healthy social and emotional development of young people.
- Education should aim for academic content mastery.
- Education should prepare people for the workforce.
- Education should aim to create a just and equitable society.
- Education should foster the self-realization of the person.

Expansive aims like these are then narrowed down to more specific *goals* and even further down to *objectives*. Take bullet one, above—the aim of cultivating good citizens. A related educational goal might then be stated as: "Students will understand how the U.S. federal government is organized." An even more discrete objective might then be stated as: "Students will be able to name the three branches of government and describe the function of each." You can see here how aims, goals, and objectives follow from each other but are expressed in progressively finer detail.

At a conscious level, aims are determined by people and are expressions of specific interests; these interests vary according to numerous factors (age, social position, professional standing, etc.). People in the business community are often most concerned with preparing young people for the workforce, parents may be focused on student readiness for college, members of oppressed or marginalized groups may be most interested in bringing about a more equitable society, and students may clamor for a curriculum that is relevant to their interests and current social problems.

At a deeper level, aims of education may be shaped by less conscious assumptions about the nature of reality and the nature of the human. We live in a complex world and a multiplicity of worldviews sit alongside each other. Government run schools are generally aligned with national interests; in most cases these are secular interests allied with the aims of the corporate state, but in some countries, there is a religious element as well.

Neohumanist education is embedded in a distinct set of aims and purposes, as have been developed throughout this text. Some of the fundamental commitments include:

- It emphasizes the essential interconnectedness of people with all of creation, expanding the heart to embrace all species.
- It aims to cultivate a deep ecological sensibility, with an emphasis on caring for land, water, plants, and animals.
- It emphasizes spiritual growth, service, and social activism in causes of universal welfare (subjective approach/objective adjustment).
- It aims to free the mind from limiting sentiments and dogma.
- It recognizes the fundamental equality of all people, and aims to repair and heal the social wounds of the past and present.
- It values epistemological pluralism, acknowledging the importance of balancing multiple ways of knowing: Western science and traditional ecological knowledge; introversial and extroversial knowing; reason and intuition.

The aims and purposes of any curriculum in a neohumanist school, along with the more detailed goals and objectives, should reflect important social concerns as well as neohumanist principles as stated above. These fundamental principles should serve as a touchstone by which to assess the value of any curriculum plan for a neohumanist school.

Curriculum Goals and Objectives

There are many different types of goals and objectives, and while not all of them may fit into a single lesson, the overall curriculum design should touch on all of them:

- *Essential question(s):* What are the larger questions that the curriculum addresses? Essential questions in a neohumanist curriculum should address issues and topics of major concern to the well-being of people and planet.

- *Content understanding(s):* What are the essential facts and information students should gain in order to address these questions?
- *Literacy understanding(s):* All subject matter can advance skills in literacy and numeracy. How does the intended learning accomplish this?
- *Learning skills:* What process skills will be developed or enhanced in the curriculum? (Examples of learning skills include inquiry strategies, analytical skills such as comparing and contrasting, problem-solving, revision, etc. For a more complete list of learning skills see Appendix A to this chapter).
- *Application:* To what uses can the learning be put? What can be done as a result of it?
- *Dispositions:* Dispositions address the personal and social development of a child (Examples include a desire to do service, learning to share, leadership development, introspection, etc.).

Note that this approach to goals and objectives encompasses the holistic domains of *knowing, doing, and being*, thus promoting the all-around development of the child.

Selecting Content, or Subject Matter

Many teachers work in schools where they have no decision-making power over what to teach. They may have a curriculum guide that specifies in exact detail what every child should learn at each grade level. These are usually very lockstep and allow for little variation or responsiveness to student interests. Some of these documents are so explicit that they require specific prompts from the teacher, and stipulate required responses from students. Often, such curriculum guides are aligned with high stakes tests that can determine what future opportunities will be open to the young person; in other cases, standardized tests are criticized because they do *not* relate to what the students have actually been taught. While some tests require a smattering of critical thinking and analysis, most are designed to reward students who can memorize large chunks of information and regurgitate these from their textbooks or test prep materials.

There are schools which consider themselves neohumanist because they do include meditation and other aspects of Ashtanga Yoga, however their curriculum may actually be quite conventional or even be aligned with a national curriculum and exam regime. While this may be unavoidable in some cases, neohumanist education should offer a meaningful alternative to the many families who do not accept that a "one-size-fits-all" curriculum fits anyone, and who desire that their children have the chance to develop their interests, their creativity, and a passion for learning. Many parents are aware that rote learning and the increasingly high pressure of the standardized tests play a large role in the epidemics of youth depression, anxiety and despair, and account for the very high level of school dropouts in many countries. They want their children to experience joy in learning, and be free from unwarranted stress.

In an ideal situation, teachers and students, acting collaboratively, have a great deal of say over the topics of study. The potential sources of subject matter in such environments are numerous: the needs and interests of the students; the needs of the community; the academic disciplines; special interests or expertise of the teachers; the study of contemporary life; hot topics and controversies. In a neohumanist school, any of these sources might be considered, with the caveat that subject matter should advance the fundamental neohumanist principles and commitments mentioned above.

Engaging Students in Content Choice

In Chapter 4, "The Science of Learning," you learned some basic ideas from the neurosciences about how to engage students in the learning process. You learned that young people have an innate drive to make sense of the world, that they seek meaning, that the brain makes meaning through patterning, that the quality of relationships influence successful learning, and that learning is enhanced by appropriate challenges but inhibited by threat.

The traditional curriculum with its disjointed and isolated facts seldom helps students connect the dots to develop a deep understanding of larger issues and concerns. It is a recipe for disengaged learning, and while some students manage to navigate this, others merely tune out what they are taught. One proven way to engage students is through immersion in a theme or topic of interest. Theme immersion is "an in-depth study of a topic, issue, or question" (Manning et al., 1994, p. 1) in which students and teachers collaboratively plan a study, pose important questions, identify resources, and design ways to express their learning.

Themes can come from current events, from experiences that students have, or from community needs. Themes are large ideas, and must be broad enough to help students connect what they are learning to the wider world. Themes do not specify content; for example, students may have become interested in the natural world around their school, and their teacher sees an opportunity to teach about the importance of biological evolution and biodiversity. The student interests in the local habitat then become the focal point for teaching embedded ideas such as the nature of a system, its components and their interactions, how changes in habitat, water distribution, climate and food sources affect the organisms living there, and what happens to species when they are no longer supported by their habitat. In the context of such a rich exploration, many forms of knowledge and learning skills can be brought in from science, language, social studies, mathematics, and the arts, thus producing an "integrated curriculum," which leads us to the topic of how subject matter is organized.

Curriculum Organization

A new teacher may know about and care for children, but have insufficient content knowledge. Conversely, an adult may have a deep knowledge of some academic subject, and yet be unable to teach what they know to children of different ages. *Pedagogical content knowledge* happens at the intersection of subject matter and teaching; it is literally the way that a teacher transforms subject matter knowledge into opportunities for student learning. This is actually a complex professional task and requires knowledge of the many aspects of child development, learning theory, the academic disciplines, local cultural knowledge and patterns, awareness of students' linguistic capabilities, familiarity with the arts, and having a deep understanding of the students, their families, and the contexts in which they live.

Determining the *scope* (the depth and breadth of subject matter) and the *sequence* (the order of information and experiences) of what will be taught is a large part of pedagogical content knowledge. This task is best begun at the level of the school rather than the individual classroom, in order to maximize learning through what has been termed the "spiral curriculum" (Bruner, 1960). The spiral curriculum encompasses the notion that a child should revisit concepts they have learned in increasingly complex ways throughout their education. In this process, teachers help them to connect new knowledge to what is already known, thus deepening and reinforcing what is learned. Teachers in a school can make scope and sequence charts by determining what "big ideas" should be focused on in the school, and then identifying the knowledge, skills, and experiences at each level of a child's development to help them attain these concepts. This is called the *vertical integration* of curriculum.

With such a school-wide framework in place, then teachers can develop the scope and sequence of their classroom curriculum units using the tool of *Understanding by Design (UBD)*, sometimes referred to as *Universal Design for Learning* ([UDL]; Wiggins & McTighe, 1998).

> The Universal Design for Learning...works to accommodate the needs and abilities of all learners and eliminates unnecessary hurdles in the learning process...developing a flexible learning environment in which...students engage in learning in a variety of ways, and students are provided options when demonstrating their learning. (Center for Teaching Innovation, n.d.)

This design process differs from earlier linear, reductive models of curriculum planning with its emphasis on a pluralistic form of design that recognizes the many differences in how young people learn, notes the importance of appealing to their interests, and provides multiple choices for how they might demonstrate what they have learned. It is also eminently adaptable to neohumanist purposes, as it begins with philosophical considerations: "What is most important to know?"; "What are the Big Ideas and Essential Questions in this topic?"; "How will we know what students have learned?"; "What will they be able to DO as a result of their learning?"

Understanding by Design

UDL is a three stage curriculum design process, which begins, as we have repeated throughout this chapter, with the big ideas and essential questions that we want students to learn (Stage 1). A student's ability to demonstrate understanding of these big ideas is the hoped-for result of a curriculum plan. Stage 2 of this process, a teacher (often with the input of students) decides how it can best be shown that a student has attained these results. What is acceptable as evidence of proficiency? This then becomes a *culminating activity* which can be either a group event or an individual event. A strong culminating activity provides a means of synthesizing the knowledge and skills acquired throughout the curriculum unit. Some examples of group culminating activities include:

- a dramatic reenactment of a story or book;
- a ritual or celebration to honor a season, a holiday, a species, and so on;
- a wall mural depicting visually the concepts learned;
- an outdoor installation such as a garden;
- a 3-D construction such as a castle with a moat.

Examples of individual culminating experiences include things like:

- a diorama depicting characters in a scene from a book;
- a scale model of an artifact from a book;
- a research paper;

- a multi-media display of an historical event (maps, timelines, illustrations, etc.);
- a content-related board game with rules, directions, and components such as cards, miniature characters, or chips.

A good culminating activity needs to be central to the purpose of the course or the unit, require students to think about important issues or questions, use important content and meet many of the specific expectations of the curriculum aims, be multifaceted (requiring a number of skills), allow for different learning styles or intelligences, assess more than one aspect of achievement, and most important, be engaging and hold the interest of students over time.

When a culminating activity is decided upon, that is when "backwards design" (Stage 3) kicks in. Teachers need to determine what will need to be taught and coached in light of the curriculum goals and objectives. How can they facilitate the successful enactment of the culminating activity? What sequence of activity best suits the desired results? This is where the careful selection of *experiences*, or learning activities happens. For a Sample Curriculum Unit Design Template using the principles of UDL, see Appendix B for this chapter. For a complete Sample Curriculum Unit Plan, see Appendix C.

Selecting Experiences

There is really no reasonable debate about the importance of "learning by doing"—the having of rich experiences as a foundation for learning. Visit any schoolroom where young children are forced to sit still at desks for hours upon hours, listen to long lectures, and engage in tasks that fail to capture their interest. Observe the body language of the children. Are they asleep? Daydreaming? Tapping their pencils? Staring out a window

Experiential learning is an active process, rather than a passive one; learning occurs as a result of the student's interaction with the world, and their reflection on the experience. Experiments are tried, and redesigned when they fail; ideas are shaped and reshaped based on these *transactions*, and knowledge becomes a living, dynamic process rather than a concept implanted in the brain that does not connect to anything in real life. Such active learning becomes a model for living, enabling students to transfer what they learn from one context to another, and to become creative problem-solvers.

In order to be educative an experience should be designed to elicit ever-more-complex thinking. A classic model of the complexity of thinking is Benjamin Bloom's *Taxonomy of Educational Objectives* (1956), which was revised in 2000 by a group of scholars and titled *A Taxonomy for Teaching, Learning, and Assessment* (Anderson et al.). Both versions show the fundamental cognitive skills of memory and recall at the base of a hierarchy of thinking, which ascends through increasingly complex cognitive processes: to understand, to apply, to analyze, to evaluate and to create (see Armstrong, 2010). Complex thinking can be built into experiential learning by ensuring that students have an opportunity to reflect on what they experienced, with generative prompts designed to draw out what was learned.

In order to be truly educative, in a neohumanist sense, an experience needs to be designed to elicit ever-more-complex *feeling* and *being*, as well as *thinking* and *doing*. There has been some movement towards developing a comparable taxonomy of the affective dimension by scholars following in Bloom's footsteps. This domain addresses the more emotional aspects of activities such as listening respectfully, responding to others, cultivating a sense of values, comparing and contrasting cultural values, and working well with others (Centre for Teaching Excellence, n.d.). This is a start, but barely scratches the surface of the principles of neohumanist education. How, for example, might we identify evidence of caring for all species? The desire to provide service? The expression of deep empathy? Or the inclination towards epistemological pluralism? How might a new theory of complex feeling/being help to shift our teaching away from the exclusive focus on rational, critical thinking towards a more inclusive, holistic expression? Complex feeling and being can be built into experiential learning by ensuring that students have opportunities for both introversial and extroversial activities.

Designing experiences is one of the most appealing aspects of teaching. Not every experience a teacher designs has the desired results. You may realize that an essential instruction was omitted. Or that you failed to anticipated the direction an activity might take. Or you don't elicit the hoped for kinds of questions from the students that you had in mind. It takes practice to successfully design the sequence of lessons necessary to accomplish a culminating activity. In order to be successful, lessons leading up to a culminating activity need to be carefully chosen to build the knowledge and skill to attain the *performance standard*, or expectations for student learning. Lessons need to be engaging and hold student interest. They need to allow for student choice, appeal to a broad range of abilities, and encompass multiple intelligences (visual, kinesthetic, musical, linguistic, etc.).

When fully understood and implemented well, UDL is beneficial to instructors because it inspires intentionality during the design process. It continually encourages the instructor to establish the *purpose* of doing something before implementing it into the curriculum. Backwards design is an effective way of designing lessons, units, and courses. Once the learning goals, or desired results, have been identified, instructors will have an easier time developing assessments that advance the students' abilities.

Assessment or Evaluation?

Neohumanism envisions a world in which all children are enabled to reach their full potential, in which each has scope to develop themselves physically, emotionally, intellectually, socially, and spirituality. A world in which they have many opportunities to discover who they are, what they love, and what they can contribute to the well-being of all. A world where all people are valued for who they are, not just what they know, or can do, or how much wealth they have accumulated. A world based on compassionate collaboration, not competitive individualism. A world that values the uniqueness of each human being, and recognizes the universal divine spark that animates us all.

Can we attain such a world when students are ranked and graded almost from the time they can walk and talk, where they are constantly judged and evaluated to see if they are measuring up? Where the adults in their lives are more concerned with their deficits than their strengths? Where they are regularly pitted against their peers in a desperate race to the top? Where compliance is more highly valued than creativity, and external motivation supersedes intrinsic motivation? Where the adults in their lives use their children's academic achievements as status symbols?

In neohumanist education, learning should be a deep pleasure, an activity that meets human needs on multiple levels, not a crass competition for achievement. It should foster curiosity, inquiry, experimentation, and personal growth. At the heart of the educational process is *relationship,* between student and student, between teacher and student, and between students and subject matter. Constant surveillance and ranked grading diminishes the possibilities of positive relationships in all of these dimensions:

- Students become rivals in a race to the top of the achievement ladder rather than cooperative and supportive peers. Social hierarchies are formed based on perceived proficiencies related to academic scores, sports abilities, and of course, wealth.
- Top–down grading by the teacher diminishes their important roles as guide, mentor, and friend, to be replaced by critic and judge. This sets up either passive compliance or active resistance, neither of which imply a healthy relationship.

- Subject matter becomes a score to be attained rather than a dynamic field of concepts and experiences to be explored, enjoyed, and integrated into their lives: "Research shows three reliable effects when students are graded: They tend to think less deeply, avoid taking risks, and lose interest in learning itself" (Kohn, 2006, para. 4).

Assessment must be aligned with our values and beliefs about the worth of all human beings. It must focus on supporting and encouraging students to do their best, not on penalizing errors. At its best, it shifts the act of determining value and quality of work to the person producing the work.

It is very challenging to shift from a graded system to an ungraded system for a number of reasons. There is a common misconception that students will perform better if they fear getting a bad grade or hope for a good one (Kohn, 1993, p. 201). Parents want to know how their child is doing, how they match up alongside their peers, and whether they will get into a good college. Teachers look at grades to determine the success of their teaching. Young people are conditioned to being graded, and they may feel untethered if they don't have these indicators attached to them. And in bureaucratic societies, entry to higher education or various professions may depend on scores or grades. Despite these obstacles, many schools have either shifted away from grades entirely, replaced them with proficiency-based systems, or been designed from the start to be ungraded. Before we look at various forms of assessment, and the alternatives available to grading, it's important to know some history.

The Origins of Testing

Testing and grading (in the Western world) can be said to have originated in the 19th and 20th centuries with the eugenics movement, a now discredited "science" which purported to improve the human race by prohibiting people of low IQ from having children. Testing was used to determine inferior and superior intelligence, and measures such as compulsory sterilization, forced abortion, and marriage restrictions ensued, primarily directed at people of color, people with disabilities, and people with hereditary diseases. The Nazis were influenced by eugenics in the United States in their WWII campaign to exterminate various groups of people including the mentally ill, people with disabilities, homosexuals, and members of racial and ethnic groups such as Jews and Roma.

Eugenics, unfortunately, is not a remnant of history. Ideas about racial and ethnic inferiority survive in educational practices and procedures.

According to one contemporary anti-eugenics group dedicated to dismantling eugenics, educational practices

> as fundamental to the system as grading echo eugenicists' preoccupation with identification, quantification and stratification. The disparate outcomes for minoritized populations are not an aberration or a failure of the system, indeed they are central to the system's intent of slotting people into their assumed societal position or role. (Eugenics Legacies Transnational Working Group, n.d.)

For an important history of the misuse of intelligence testing, see *The Mismeasure of Man* (Gould, 1996).

Another side effect of high stakes testing has been cheating (by individual students as well as schools) as well as corruption on the part of school leaders, teachers, and parents who are willing to take risks to guarantee their children's future. The limitations of standardized testing are numerous, and well beyond the scope of this chapter. For more information, you can consult the National Center for Fair and Open Testing (fairtest.org) or refer to some of the well-researched literature on the subject (Kohn, 2000; Lemann, 1999; Popham, 2001; Sacks, 1999). In high stakes test environments, many children experience *downshifting* (when the brain shifts from its "thinking centers" into lower levels, where the body processes threat). Even well prepared students can suffer test anxiety, and fail to demonstrate what they know successfully. Some test companies began including "vomit bags" and rubber gloves in their classroom kits, for teachers to clean up the students' reactions to testing.

Doing Away With Tests and Grading Does Not Mean Doing Away With Assessment

Traditional assessments in the past have been in the form of tests or pop quizzes. These generally feature items that deal with the lowest scale on Bloom's Taxonomy (memory and recall). Assessing higher order thinking, such as analysis or application is a much more complex undertaking and requires creative thinking.

The first thing to know about assessment is that individuals are always engaged in assessing their own work, especially when they have access to "benchmarks" that demonstrate high quality work. The second thing to know is that students are much more invested in teacher feedback when they have some agency in determining what kind of feedback they would appreciate. The two broad forms of assessment are formative and summative assessments.

Formative assessment is on-going and is intended to shape the instructional environment to better meet student needs. Formative assessment is designed to let teacher and students know how they are both doing in the effort to facilitate learning. Formative assessment:

- assesses progress and process;
- can be informal;
- is flexible (oral, written, individual, group, brief, in-depth, etc.);
- can be based on multiple sources: discussion, games, quizzes, drafts, exit tickets, and so on;
- helps student improve work by providing "actionable" feedback;
- helps the teacher discover misconceptions, identify struggles or learning gaps; and
- suggests what might need to be retaught.

There are many low key, creative forms of formative assessment: Individual conferencing, in which a teacher asks the student questions about their work in order to learn more about their process or their understanding; exit tickets, which are brief written exercises that seek to assess student understanding of the day's lesson; low stakes quiz-like games and polls; and importantly, self-assessment, where the student is asked to reflect on the strengths of their work and what they want to improve. Assessment such as this fosters a "growth mindset" that helps a young person overcome challenges. A growth mindset understands that mistakes and failures should be embraced as positive steps and reminds the students that it is effort that improves work, not innate abilities. Of crucial importance, formative assessment offers feedback that will help students become more adept at, and excited about, what they're doing.

Summative assessment comes at the end of a unit of study and is intended to determine the overall success of both the teaching and the learning. Summative assessments:

- generally assess final work products (projects, papers, presentations, etc.);
- are usually compared to a standard or a benchmark;
- are a more formal evaluation of what was learned;
- show how well students attain objectives; and
- sometimes use rubrics.

Summative assessments are usually high stakes and can determine things like unit grades, final course grades or even promotion. This is not necessary, however. Summative assessments *could* promote a growth mindset—if the student has multiple opportunities to retake a test or resubmit a project. If a summative assessment is intended to improve learning, then students need to have opportunities to improve. Rather than assess a student's work against a standardized benchmark, consider assessing the work in relation to work they have done before. In this way, a student is in competition with themselves, not with peers, and they are aiming to attain increasing *proficiency,* not an external standard.

Keep in mind that the tendency is generally to measure what can be easily measured (facts) while important aspects of learning such as understanding, effort, or the ability to transfer knowledge from one context to another are much more complex. If you must measure, then measure, but keep in mind the neohumanist aim of developing the full potential of the child. A summative assessment is most often of an intellectual product—we seldom assess emotional or spiritual growth (and I am NOT suggesting here that we need to do this with conventional frameworks, such as grades, only that our summative assessments provide incomplete portraits of a student). There are ways to include emotional and spiritual growth in assessments without ranking, judging, or evaluating. That is simply to move away from a point or a letter-based system to a narrative system, and then to ensure that your description of the student's outcomes are inclusive of all of the desirable attainments you (and your student) hoped for.

When teachers first start making the shift away from grading, they often turn to rubrics. A rubric is an assessment grid that clearly states the expectations for a product on the vertical Y axis and a scale of levels of quality on the horizontal X axis. Teachers use many different names for the levels of quality:

- advanced, intermediate, novice;
- exceeds expectations, meets requirements, getting there; or
- mastery, partial mastery, progressing.

Rubrics can be simple or complex, scored or not scored; what is common to them is that they demystify what the teacher is looking for in a product or performance and they provide students with clear feedback on what they need to do to improve. In many ways they are an improvement over the more subjective grades that teachers award to students.

One problem with rubrics is that often teachers transpose old grading expectations onto the rubric; a teacher provides a scale in which numerical scores translate to a grade and a student with a holistic score of 15 or 16 now knows they got an "A" or that their score of 12–14 is a mere B. Rubrics are yet another tool of standardization, and can actually inhibit creative approaches to learning, as they so clearly specify what the teacher is looking for. They also tend to measure what is most easily quantified, so the student work products become simplified rather than more complex. For example, if a writing rubric focuses mainly on mechanics, the work may be grammatically correct and uninspired. Teaching and learning then just continue to be a game of trying to figure out what the teacher wants and then giving it to him or her. And we do know, from research, that "students whose attention is relentlessly focused on *how well* they're doing often become less engaged with *what* they're doing" (Kohn, 2006, para. 14). So, much as these nice neat little boxes might be an improvement over the elusive grading system of yesteryear, teachers should revisit the values they hold most dear about teaching, and consider whether the assessments they are using are truly accomplishing the aims of a neohumanist education.

The Future of Curriculum

Integrated curriculum has become a hallmark of 21st century curriculum design. An integrated curriculum recognizes that the complex problems we are called to address in contemporary times do not fit neatly into academic boxes. Climate change, for example, requires understanding the physical sciences of ecosystem characteristics, weather, ocean temperatures and sea levels, animal migrations, and chemistry, as well as much from the social sciences: how people adapt and change, the root causes of climate change, and climate migration. In addition to the sciences, many novels and compelling poetry have been written about the climate crisis, and arts and cultural organizations are contributing to the mobilization of activism and educating the public about diverse issues such as biodiversity and pollution with innovative installations and exhibits.

An integrated curriculum recognizes that humans don't learn about life in fragmented ways that fit neatly into the boxes of the academic disciplines. The brain simply doesn't work the way that the academic disciplines are organized. A truly integrated curriculum incorporates content from multiple sources as well as skills and processes, it is of high relevance to the learner, and it must prove itself capable of solving real life problems and issues. There are a number of approaches to creating integrated curriculum designs that take us beyond the traditional single subject curriculum. These approaches constitute the *horizontal integration* of curriculum:

- *Multidisciplinary curriculum design, occasionally referred to as cross-curricular* draws on knowledge from different disciplines, but maintains boundaries. It broadens and deepens the understanding of a theme by bringing in different perspectives. An example of this might be a curriculum unit on the Revolutionary War between Britain and the American colonists taught during the social studies period, while featuring a novel about a young person at that time in the language arts period.

- *Interdisciplinary curriculum design* also draws on knowledge from different disciplines but may focus on process rather than content, using methods of study from one discipline to illuminate another. An example of this in primary school might be studying the science of weather and recording daily temperatures and rainfall for a month on a chart and then using mathematics to figure out the average temperature and rainfall for the month.
- *Transdisciplinary curriculum design* transcends the boundaries of the academic disciplines, connecting learning by a unifying theme or topic. An example of this might be the study of homelessness in your locale, which would require multiple forms of inquiry and knowledge (interviewing unhoused people, research on city planning policy, causes of poverty, history of the neighborhood, gathering statistics on housing costs, etc.).

Integrated curriculum designs really benefit from teacher collaborations and team teaching. These approaches to curriculum design are deeply compatible with neohumanist education, given the emphasis in holistic education on *wholeness*. According to one prominent education scholar, the central focus of the integrated curriculum is the search for self and social meaning (Beane, 1995). Learning that lacks coherence and a strong focus on meaning is like an enormous jigsaw puzzle without a picture: a fragmented, disconnected collection of meaningless parts. Neohumanist education, with its strong philosophy and clear focus on a new vision for society, lends itself extremely well to curriculum integration and learning that is relevant to young people. There are no hard and fast rules around this; it may be necessary occasionally to spend time on a separate subject; if students need coaching or instruction in a specific set of disciplinary skills, then teachers would be remiss to ignore this. But overall, the neohumanist curricular aim should be the integration of subject matter, organized around student interests and concerns.

21st Century Curriculum Design

With new metaphors from the new sciences come new possibilities for educational theory and practice. In earlier chapters in this book, we have looked at the powerful structuring forces of modernity/coloniality/humanism and the ways that this centuries-old paradigm has shaped every aspect of the world as we know it. Humanism paralleled the development of Newtonian physics, a reductionist science which replaced an earlier organic view of the world. Newtonian physics asserts an "atomist theory"—that the world is made up of dead inert particles moved about in space by external forces. In this model, order is defined as the predictable behavior of parts in the context of the whole within a rationally determined system of laws. Early versions of this theory presented a dualistic, supernatural framework—a "clockwork universe" set in motion by God (and then ignored). This dualistic philosophy divided the human psyche—mind from body, subject from object, knower from known. Later, atheistic sentiments replaced (incompletely) the supernatural version, but the universe was still understood as the random collision of particles, and the splits remained.

Curriculum design, for the most part, is still grounded in Newtonian theory. Direct teaching, rote learning, and exams with their desire for certainty, control, and predictability of learning belong to this outdated paradigm. In a "Newtonian model" of curriculum:

- Learning is standardized—everyone is expected to learn everything at the same pace.
- Outcomes are predictable (and measurable).
- Learning is reductionist—the examination of the parts is the priority.
- Nature is mechanistic—the guiding metaphor is the "machine."

Neohumanism is emerging in a post-Newtonian world in which these ancient assumptions about the nature of the universe are being questioned, and in many ways, discarded. We now know that the universe of waves and particles is alive, that there is intelligence in matter, that matter, mind, and spirit are interconnected, and that rather than inert parts bumping into each other the universe is a complex, fluid, intelligent, and dynamic set of relations. While predictability is possible at some level of systems (a ball rolling on a horizontal surface still slows down as it rolls), quantum mechanics brings in elements of uncertainty and unpredictability. The vocabulary of chaos theory, self-organization, and complex systems present new ideas that attempt to explain this.

Emergence is a compelling idea from this model of complexity. One scholar defines emergence as "the arising of novel and coherent structures, unexpected patterns and properties during the process of self-organization in complex systems" (Goldstein, 1999). Think about this, and what it implies for a neohumanist education that would be consistent with this new story of how the universe works. An emergent system of learning would acknowledge:

- Unseen forces are operating in every person (and in every system).
- Learning is idiosyncratic.
- The brain is a complex, self-organizing system.
- A "living system" is a more generative metaphor than a machine.

While UDL—the curriculum procedures you have learned about in this chapter—represents the state of the art in conventional curriculum design, it perhaps does not reflect the full potential of a neohumanist educational future. Good planning is an essential aspect of good teaching, and new teachers, especially, benefit from the kind of comprehensive planning outlined in this chapter. But a curriculum is not a commandment etched in stone. The best curriculum designers leave space for the free play of intuition and creativity, the interests of the moment, unexpected questions, and emergent opportunities for exploration, deeper inquiry and play. Teaching for emergence requires additional skills and dispositions.

Teaching for emergence is not a science, it is an art. There is neither a map nor a checklist. The best teaching can be likened to improvisational jazz. A teacher who is aware of the nuances of the mood and climate of the classroom, who can pick up major themes as well as minor patterns in group dynamics, who has a discerning eye for quality, who is able to think creatively about solutions to problems that present themselves, who is able to help a group of young people create something that is so much more than the sum of its parts: This teacher is an artist.

In chaos theory, "sensitivity to initial conditions" means that every point in a chaotic system lies near other points with different trajectories. Any perturbance or disturbance of one point can change the future behavior of the whole system. You may have heard the analogy of the butterfly flapping its wings which causes a tornado across the globe weeks later. Most teachers are painfully aware of how a group of young people (a complex system) is exceedingly sensitive to fluctuations (individual behaviors, the weather, interruptions from a loudspeaker). In these instances, a teacher needs to utilize careful observation and intuition to help restore equilibrium, or facilitate students' navigation into new territory.

A curriculum design process that embraces emergence and unpredictability is open-ended and fosters individuality, engagement, and relational thinking. It understands that much of what is going on in the classroom is beneath the surface. It welcomes surprises, and understands that emergent learning is contextual, collaborative, and goes beyond the norms of intended learning. Emergent learning "is about tapping into the as yet unknown and unsaid, sensing into what is wanting to be born, using collective sensemaking to manifest the 'magic in the middle'" (Chattopadhyay, 2019, para. 5).

One scholar who brought the ideas of complexity to the fore in education is William Doll (1993), who proposed that curriculum needed to reflect not the old Three R's (reading, 'riting, and 'rithmetic, but the new Four R's, and be:

- Rich (with depth of learning, layers of meaning, and multiple interpretations);
- Recursive (involving inquiry, reflection, and meaning-making);
- Relational (forming connections—between the academic disciplines, between people, and between all species); and
- Rigorous (in neohumanist terms, being both introversial and extroversial, fostering "awakened rationality").

The 21st century promises to be a volatile and uncertain period characterized by ecological devastation, political unrest, the inequalities brought about by capitalism and the globalization of the economy, conflict over scarce resources, and fragmented social structures. These multiple crises may indeed constitute a portal, an opening into a transformation of life on Earth (Kesson, 2020). If we wish to help usher in a new era of peace, economic and social justice, ecological sustainability, community resilience, creativity, and spiritual revitalization, the topics of the curriculum must advance, in a focused way, the knowledge, skills and ways of being in the world that will enable young people to survive and thrive in such a world-historic transition. The task is immense:

> To unfold the child's innate potential on all levels of being—to develop a strong and agile body, sharp senses, penetrating intellect, creative imagination, subtle intuition, and blissful Spirit. (Anandamitra, 1987, p. 199)

Neohumanist curriculum design has the potential to break though convention and offer a theoretical basis in line with new discoveries in quantum mechanics and chaos theory, with the artistry of teaching, and with all we are coming to understand about the spiritual nature of our species. In order to do this, teachers need to develop their capabilities in a multi-faceted way, designing learning environments that support students in discovering and constructing knowledge for themselves, that facilitate communities of learners that make discoveries and solve problems, and that nourish the highest ethical, intellectual, and spiritual potential in all students. In this way, we can engage students fully in the present moment, while preparing them for a just and joyful neohumanist future.

FOR CONTINUING STUDY

> *Discussion/Reflection:* Consider your own educational experience: What do you believe were the large aims and purposes of it? What evidence do you offer for this?
>
> *Discussion /Reflection:* Can you think of examples of the "hidden curriculum" from your own educational experience? What about the "null curriculum?"
>
> *Application:* Decide on a topic for a curriculum unit (one that reflects one or more principles of neohumanist education, and one that is expansive enough to include a number of lessons). Make a concept map, with the Big Idea (an aim or purpose) in the center. Brainstorm some of the main concepts that you would want young people to understand. What are some of the essential questions that you or the children might have about the topic?
>
> *Application:* Returning to the first paragraph of this chapter, write a brief opinion paper (250–300 words) on whether an education that is strongly focused on the present life of the child is a viable education for the future.
>
> *Application:* If you were to create a "taxonomy" of *feeling* and *being*, how would you structure it? What are some of the important rationales, sample learning outcomes, and sample assessments/activities?

Appendix A: Learning Skills

Analysis
Attention to Detail
Brainstorming
Cause & Effect
Challenging Assumptions
Collaborating
Composition
Concentration
Comparing/Contrasting
Creative thinking (divergent/convergent)
Critical Thinking
Debate
Defining
Describing
Digital Literacy
Editing & Revision
Evaluating
Explaining
Gathering evidence
Goal Setting
Improvising
Inquiry
Listening
Memorization
Mnemonics
Note Taking
Organizing
Planning
Presentations
Prioritizing
Public Speaking
Questioning
Reading Comprehension
Reflection
Self-Direction
Studying
Summarizing
Synthesizing
Systems Thinking
Teamwork
Time management

Appendix B:
Arts-Based Literacy Curriculum Unit Plan Template

Title of Unit: _____	Subject: _____
Topic: _____	Grade(s): _____
Designer: _____	
Duration of unit: _____	

Stage 1—Desired Results
Overarching aims:
Neohumanist curriculum principles addressed:

Goals and Objectives	
Essential Question(s):	Content Understanding(s):
Literacy Understanding(s):	Learning skills:

Stage 2—Determining Acceptable Evidence
Description of culminating activity:

Stage 3—Planning Learning Experiences and Instruction
Books and Other Resources
1)
2)
3)
4)
5)
6)

Lesson Plans—Attach detailed lesson plans				
Lesson # & Title	Subject area content	Literacy content and/or numeracy content	Arts focus	Learning skills
1)				
2)				
3)				
4)				
5)				
6)				

Assessment of culminating event:

Appendix C:
Sample Curriculum Unit Plan

Curriculum Unit Title
"Pollinators Are Our Friends"

Grade Levels
K–2

Submitted by (Designer): Kathleen Kesson

Date: May 2022

Title of Unit: **Pollinators Are Our Friends**	Subject: **Ecology**
Topic: **Pollinaton**	Grade(s): **K–2**
Designer: **Kathleen Kesson**	
Duration of unit: **6 weeks**	

Stage 1—Desired Results
Overarching aims, goals, or content standard: Students will understand the interdependence of insects, animals, plants, and humans and apply their knowledge in a practical way. **Neohumanist curriculum principles:** Respect and love for all creatures, deep ecology, contact with nature.
Goals and Objectives

Content Understanding(s):	Essential Question(s):
Pollinators are animals that transfer pollen from one flower to another, fertilizing plants and leading to seeds and reproduction. Pollinators are critical to our planet's health and survival—more than 75% of the Earth's flowering plants depend on them.	• What are some of the most important pollinators? • What plants do they like? • How does pollination work? • How are pollinators endangered? • What happens if we don't have pollinators?

Bees alone pollinate a third of the food we eat! Habitat loss, climate change, and pesticides are contributing to dramatic declines in pollinator populations.	• What can we do to protect pollinators?
Literacy Understanding(s):	**Learning skills:**
Content vocabulary (Queen Bee, honeycomb, animal names, flower names and parts, dispersal, pollen, etc.) Rhyming Sentence construction (making simple sentences about insects)	Classification Etymology Listing Attention to detail Cause and effect Describing Inquiry Planning Scale drawing Teamwork

Stage 2—Determining Acceptable Evidence

Description of culminating activity:

Students will research, plan (using scale drawings), and plant a raised bed in the backyard of the school to attract pollinators to the school garden.

Stage 3—Planning Learning Experiences and Instruction

Books and Other Resources

1) *No Monkeys, No Chocolate* by Melissa Stewart, Allen Young, and illustrated by Nicole Wong

   Young readers learn that cacao trees need the help of rain forest critters to survive: a pollen-sucking midge, an aphid-munching anole lizard, and brain-eating coffin fly maggots.

   Reading age: 5–8 years
   2018, Charlesbridge; Reprint edition

2) *Bees* by Laura Marsh

   Written for young children interested in learning more about honey bees. The book consists of two-page spreads with a full-page color photograph on the right and on the left are simple sentences with controlled vocabulary written at the first grade level. Children learn vocabulary words such as queen bee, worker bee, and comb.

   Reading age: 5–8 years
   2016, National Geographic Kids; Illustrated edition

3) *The Life and Times of a Honeybee* by Charles Micucci

   An introduction to the life cycle, social organization, and history of one of the world's most useful insects. How bees make honey, what a beekeeper does, and products that contain beeswax.

   Reading age: 4–7 years
   1997, HMH Books for Young Readers

4) *Bees, Bugs and Butterflies* by Ben Raskin

   How pollinators work, how children can help pollinators by planting the right plants and creating safe homes for them; tricks that plants play on insects. Includes engaging projects and explanations.

   Reading age: 4–8 years
   2018, Roost Books

5) *Begin With a Bee* by Liza Ketchum, Jacqueline Briggs Martin, and Phyllis Root, illustrated by Claudia McGehee

   The story of the life of a bumble bee. Young readers learn how different living things depend on each other. A picture book that will appeal to nature lovers of all ages.

   Reading age: 4–9 years
   2021, University of Minnesota Press

6) *Flowers are Calling* by Rita Gray and illustrated by Kenard Pak

   A beautifully illustrated, poetic book about the interactions between plants, animals, and insects

   Reading age: 4–7 years
   2015, HMH Books for Young Readers.

7) *If Bugs are Banished* by Ferris Kelly Robinson & Mary Ferris Kelly

   A boxed set of books that teach children about the importance of nature. Entertaining and educational, these books help the youngest stewards of our planet learn to care for the tiny little things that run our world.

   Reading age: 2–8 years
   2019, Peachtree Press

8) *Pollinator Gardens* (*Helping the Environment*) by Nick Rebman

   This book examines how pollinators affect the environment, the threats these species face, and how people can help protect them with pollinator gardens.

   Reading age: 4–8 years
   2021, North Star Editions

YouTube Videos (Ex: https://www.youtube.com/watch?v=9AuVm1jpKEA)

Activity websites (Ex: https://www.education.com/resources/science/?q=pollination)

		Lesson Plans		
Lesson # & Title	**Science content**	**Literacy/ numeracy content**	**Arts focus**	**Learning skills**
1) Why Plants Need Animals and Insects	Predators and pests Pollination	Vocabulary, naming and describing plants and pollinators		Listing Cause and effect Describing
2) Flower Friends	Smell, shape, pattern, color, parts of a flower	Rhyming	Illustration of a flower (visual art, watercolor) Create a rhyming poem about a flower (poetry)	Describing Attention to detail
3) The World of Bees	How bees help people and plants, bee habitat, life cycle	Vocabulary: nectar, pollen, hive, honeycomb, how many bees does it take to make a spoonful of honey?	Create a musical presentation of a beehive (music)	Cause and effect Inquiry

142 ▪ *Becoming One With the World*

4) How Bees Gather Pollen	Bee anatomy, pollen gathering	Onomatopoeia	Movement activity depicting pollen gathering (creative movement)	Inquiry Attention to detail
5) Why Humans Need Animals and Insects	Products related to pollinators Effects of extinction	Rhyming	Create drama featuring animals and insects speaking to humans (creative drama)	Imagining Creative thinking Analysis Synthesizing Applying
6) Creating a Pollinator Garden	Matching pollinating companion plants and insects	Flower and insect names	Design work Scale drawing (visual art)	Collaborating Brainstorming Teamwork Planning Labeling Mapping Scale drawing Measuring Carpentry Planting and fertilizing

Assessment of culminating activity:

Finishing up a **KWL** chart: Lesson #1 will have included a brainstorming about "What I *know*" about pollinators and a "What do I *want* to know?" activity. Final assessment will be a group brainstorm: "What have I *learned*?"

References

Anandamitra, A. A. (1987). *Neohumanism: A vision for a new world.* Ananda Marga Pracaraka Samgha.

Anderson, L., Krathwohl, D., Airasian, P., Cruikshank, K., Mayer, R., Pintrich, P., Raths, J., & Wittrock, M. (2000). *A taxonomy for learning, teaching, and assessing: A revision of Bloom's taxonomy of educational objectives.* Pearson.

Armstrong, P. (2010). *Bloom's taxonomy.* Vanderbilt University Center for Teaching. https://cft.vanderbilt.edu/guides-sub-pages/blooms-taxonomy/

Beane, J. (Ed.). (1995). *Toward a coherent curriculum: The 1995 ASCD yearbook.* Association for Supervision and Curriculum Development.

Bloom, B. S. (Ed.). (1956). *Taxonomy of educational objectives: The classification of educational goals.* Longman.

Bowers, C. A. (2002). *How language limits our understanding of environmental education.* http://cabowers.net/pdf/howlanguagelimits2001.pdf

Bruner, J. (1960). *The process of education.* Harvard University Press.

Centre for Teaching Excellence. University of Waterloo. https://uwaterloo.ca/centre-for-teaching-excellence/catalogs/tip-sheets/blooms-taxonomy#:~:text=The%20affective%20domain%20focuses%20on,values%20and%20acting%20upon%20them.

Center for Teaching Innovation, Cornell University. https://teaching.cornell.edu/teaching-resources/assessment-evaluation/inclusion-accessibility-accommodation/building-inclusive5#:~:text=Universal%20design%20for%20learning%20%28UDL%29%20is%20a%20teaching,process%20and%20improves%20the%20learning%20experience%20for%20all.

Chattopadhyay, C. (2019, July 3). *Six enablers of emergent learning.* https://medium.com/activate-the-future/six-enablers-of-emergent-learning-a1b9390279a6

Doll, W. (1993). *A post-modern perspective on curriculum.* Teachers College Press.

Eugenics Legacies Transnational Education Working Group. https://www.fromsmallbeginnings.org/eugenic-legacies-transnational-educ

Goldstein, J. (1999). Emergence as a construct: History and issues. *Emergence, 1*(1), 49–72.

Gould, S.J. (1981/1996). *The mismeasure of man.* W.W. Norton and Company.

Jones, K. & Okun, T. (2001). *Dismantling racism: A workbook for social change groups.* ChangeWork. https://www.whitesupremacyculture.info/uploads/4/3/5/7/43579015/okun_-_white_sup_culture_2020.pdf

Kesson, K. (2020, April 12). Three scenarios for the future of education in the Anthropocene. *Journal of Futures Studies.* https://jfsdigital.org/2020/04/12/three-scenarios-for-the-future-of-education-in-the-anthropocene/

Kohn, A. (1993). *Punished by rewards: The trouble with gold stars, incentive plans, A's, praise, and other bribes.* Houghton Mifflin Company.

Kohn, A. (2000). *The case against standardized testing: Raising the scores, ruining the schools.* Heinemann.

Kohn, A. (2006). The trouble with rubrics. *English Journal, 95*(4). https://www.alfiekohn.org/article/trouble-rubrics/

Lemann, N. (1999). *The big test: The secret history of the American meritocracy*. Farrar, Straus & Giroux.

Manning, M., Manning, G., & Long, R. (1994). *Theme immersion: Inquiry-based curriculum in elementary and middle schools*. Heinemann.

Popham, W. J. (2001). *The truth about testing: An educator's call to action*. Association for Supervision and Curriculum Development.

Sacks, P. (1999). *Standardized minds: The high price of America's testing culture and what we can do to change it*. Perseus Books.

Schubert, W. H. (1986). *Curriculum: Perspective, paradigm, and possibility*. Macmillan Publishing Company.

Wiggins, G., & McTighe, J. (1998). *Understanding by design*. Association for Supervision and Curriculum Development.

8

The Art of Teaching

> *Teachers, I believe, are the most responsible and important members of society because their professional efforts affect the fate of the earth.*
> — Helen Caldicott, *If You Love This Planet: A Plan to Save the Earth*, 1992

Shrii Sarkar held the profession of teaching in the very highest regard, noting that it is not the teacher's task merely to impart intellectual knowledge, but to be a model of good character as well. Teachers, he stated, "must possess such qualities as personal integrity, strength of character, righteousness, a feeling for social service, unselfishness, an inspiring personality, and leadership ability" (Sarkar, 1959, para. 5). Teaching is not just one profession among many, a career one chooses to earn a living or gain status in the community. It is a *vocation* (Latin, *vocare*, "to call"), denoting, as one scholar says, "a summons or bidding to be of service" (Hansen, 1995). The service is on one hand to the all-around development of the children in one's care and to the families who entrust them to you; on the other hand, the service is to society, as Dr. Caldicott suggests in the opening quotation. Teachers must hold a strong and benevolent vision of a just and

---

Becoming One With the World, pages 145–163
Copyright © 2024 by Information Age Publishing
www.infoagepub.com
All rights of reproduction in any form reserved.

peaceful society, as the shaping of people who will create the future is, at least partially, in their hands.

While much effort has gone into trying to articulate a *science* of teaching and reduce the question of instructional method to a list of prescribed behaviors, most scholars recognize that teaching is more an *art* than a science. Despite millions of dollars spent on research into the "best methods" and a plenitude of books on effective teacher behaviors, there is little agreement about what these are. Teaching is a complex human activity with innumerable variables of context and person which need to be taken into consideration when considering what method(s) of instruction to use.

An instructional method is a process employed by a teacher to facilitate student learning. Curriculum and instruction are deeply intertwined; one way to differentiate them is that curriculum is really the "what" of teaching and learning (and implicitly the "why"), instruction is the "how" (and to some extent the "when" and the "where"). The history of pedagogy is awash with instructional methods which go in and out of fashion like clothing styles. Methods include such strategies as lectures, discussions, cooperative learning, "hands-on" or active learning, Socratic Seminars, computer-mediated learning, peer teaching, project-based learning, debate, and so on.

When thinking about what method to employ, one must consider the individual learner—their cultural context, their temperament, what he or she already knows about the topic, their interest in learning, how they approach problems. The teacher also needs to consider the group of learners—their range and variety of abilities, the culture of the classroom, and their common interests. As well, a teacher needs to be self-reflective and understand their own teaching temperament, their strengths, and their level of comfort with the content. There is a vast literature on "pedagogical content knowledge" (PCK) that highlights the ways that teachers make academic content accessible to young learners using various kinds of illustrations, examples, demonstrations, procedures, and explanations specific to content areas. For example, mathematics learning often relies on providing examples of problem solving on a board or screen in front of the class; science learning often involves demonstrations of experiments. PCK also involves learning what students already know about a topic, exploring their preconceptions and misconceptions, and determining how to "scaffold" instruction (building supports into teaching new material in order for students to gain a deep understanding). This is a very short list of instructional skills; one must also be aware of larger issues such as the culture of the school, the culture of the community, parental expectations, and bureaucratic rules and regulations.

Philosophies of Teaching

Teaching methods are expressions of fundamental philosophical beliefs about the nature of the human being (ontology), the nature of knowledge and how we come to know (epistemology), the relationship between teacher and student (the philosophy of authority), and what is worth knowing (axiology). In the traditional educational paradigm of Perennialism, the teacher is the holder and dispenser of knowledge, an intellectual familiar with the great books and big ideas of the past. The role of the teacher is to impart subject matter knowledge and foster critical thinking and the ability to reason, and the primary instructional methods employed include lecture, reading, discussion, and debate.

The teacher in a Behaviorist paradigm is focused on behavioral outputs rather than the thoughts or feelings of students. Concerns with conditioning and compliance necessitate that teaching methodologies involve structures of rewards and penalties to reinforce desired outcomes. The teacher inclined towards Romanticism is a facilitator and mentor, and in order to promote personal growth and discovery, they create opportunities for students to explore their interests and values, and to take charge of their own learning.

Like the Romantics, Pragmatist teachers are also interested in personal growth, but with a social focus towards becoming engaged citizens, and so they tend to design learning experiences that are hands-on, collaborative, community-based, and involve real world problems to be solved. They spend time cultivating strong classroom communities and emphasize collaboration, empathy, fairness, justice, dialogue, open-mindedness, and a focus on the common good. Critical teachers employ a number of methods to raise consciousness about issues of social class, racism, economics and other social issues, including storytelling, dialogue, role play, and the close reading of texts, encouraging young people to become active rather than passive learners.

Teaching in the holistic paradigm draws on many of the above methods, with an additional focus on the search for meaning, the emphasis on cultivating human potential, and the attainment of self-actualization (Maslow, 1962/2011). Holistic teachers foster individual and group meaning-making by utilizing techniques such as reflection, visualization, dialogue, journaling, self-regulation, and the cultivation of understanding, in contrast to mere information acquisition.

Neohumanist Teaching

When considering which method to use it is essential to keep in mind the principles at the heart of neohumanist education, as noted in Chapter 1:

1. Expanding the circle of love to include everyone and everything.
2. Freeing the mind from dogma and limitations, cultivating a broad-minded and compassionate rationality that serves as a gateway to realizing our full individual and collective potential.
3. Awakening the desire for social and environmental justice through the practice of selfless service; translating values into action to achieve a sense of purpose and connection.

With these principles in mind, neohumanist education methodology draws from many sources, integrating and synthesizing some of the best practices devised by educational scholars and practitioners. There is no one best method in neohumanist education; central to pedagogical decision-making is the judgment of the teacher, cultivated through experience, reflective teaching, knowledge of the culture, close observation of young people, and intuition. The personal development of the teacher is at the heart of neohumanist teacher preparation, given Sarkar's emphasis on the character of the educator. Long after a student has forgotten the facts taught, they will remember the *person* who taught them, and (hopefully) will have internalized the noblest qualities of that person. A great deal of what is learned is beneath the surface of consciousness, intuitively absorbed from the *presence* of the teacher who models empathy, clarity, warmth, curiosity, engagement, strength, and an awakened consciousness. We address the concept of teacher presence in more detail at the conclusion of this chapter.

Much of the content of this book is directed towards the creation of schools. Mass schooling as much of the world now understands it is a product of modernity and coloniality, and to this day, its primary purpose is the creation of workers to sustain national or global economies, and support the forces of development, consumerism, and capitalism. As discussed in the chapter on decolonizing education, the old German Republic of Prussia, a quasi-military state, gave the West compulsory schooling, educational technologies of surveillance and control, the idea of a prescribed national curriculum, regular testing, and state certification for professional teachers. In the Western world, schools were profoundly influenced by the model of the factory, and in the 19th century (and well into the 20th), most schools (excepting the elite academies) were aimed at training workers for the emerging industrial system. In this model, young people needed to internalize behaviors of compliance, punctuality, and unquestioned submission to authority. They needed to engage in tasks that did not relate to personal interests or desires, and become accustomed to repetitious behaviors. Everyone was expected to learn the same thing at the same time in order to foster social cohesion and control. For those readers interested in the ways that modern schooling has devastated local and indigenous societies based on traditional sustainable agricultural and ecological knowledge, and ancient spiritual traditions, the documentary film *Schooling the World* (Black, 2010) is an informative source of history about the impact of Western models of schooling.

Schools the world over are remarkably similar in design, still true to their industrial origins with their rows of desks, black or whiteboards at the front of class, the teacher's desk, and perhaps a podium for lectures. They are also similar in school culture: classes are formed according to age and children are separated by grades, academic content is generally taught in separate periods punctuated by ear shattering bells, most learning is from textbooks, and children are judged and ranked according to fairly narrow definitions of intelligence.

Times *have* changed and it's commonly understood that we have transitioned from an industrial economy to an information-based economy. Goods are still produced but with the advent of robotics, AI, and other computer-assisted technologies, different kinds of intelligence and behaviors are needed to grow the economy. Schooling has responded accordingly, and now tables for groups may have replaced isolated desks, signifying the awareness that work tasks are often assigned to corporate groups; computer screens have to some extent replaced textbooks (not altogether); some schools have moved to more interdisciplinary or transdisciplinary learning, recognizing that large problems to be solved require more holistic thinking; and some systems have introduced more "personalized learning"—recognizing the importance of entrepreneurial skills. In spite of these surface changes, most modern schooling is devoted to maintaining the status quo of the system—globalized capitalism, consumerism, and modernist assumptions about progress—with little thought to the urgent need to reimagine education and reorient our systems around the health and survival of our biosystems and human societies.

Neohumanist education is a bold attempt to meet our civilizational crisis head on, and engage in the deep rethinking of all of our assumptions about schooling, including what is worth knowing, what are the most effective ways of learning, where and when does learning take place, how children should be assessed, and what is the role of the teacher. To date, this effort has mostly involved the global creation of schools, and many of these are situated in contexts of bureaucracy and government regulation. There is a small global movement, most pronounced in the United States, toward unschooling, or deschooling, with roots in the conceptual work of Ivan Illich (1926–2002) who wrote compellingly about the unhealthy intersections between modernity, capitalism, bureaucracy, and institutional schooling. Illich believed that education in the modern context could not be reformed; that it needed to be dismantled in order for something truly new to arise. He promoted the idea of establishing educational webs and networks that would link people who wanted to know something with people who could share their skills or knowledge (Illich, 1971/2000, 1973). James Moffett (1994), whom we write about in the Introduction to this book, was a well-respected scholar of English language arts whose final book, published right before his death, *The Universal Schoolhouse: Spiritual Awakening Through Education*, sketched the outline of a similar decentralized learning network that would build on what we know about how children learn best. He addresses many of the important questions we need to be asking as we move towards a truly student centered, community-based paradigm of learning: How do you provide choice in an ever-expanding universe of educational possibility, and still anchor young people securely so that they have the emotional and social support they need? What structures need to be in place to match up learners with the right resources at the right time? What kind of guidance or counseling should be available for students who have never had the opportunity to be self-directed learners? Many of his ideas are *transitional*, in the sense that if choice and freedom and personal growth and sustainability are interesting to us, we need some mechanisms to get from here to there.

Alternative Metaphors for Schooling

This chapter builds a bridge from where we are now and the practices that are currently thought of as most effective, to possible futures, with methods not yet imagined. The instructional methodologies outlined here will help the neohumanist educator design a school that is true to neohumanist principles. However, we encourage educators interested in setting up learning environments aligned with neohumanist principles to cultivate their social imaginations, and take a deep dive into alternative future possibilities, even those that involve "deschooling." There are many places to begin: home schooling or deschooling parents are often looking for creative forms of group activity to meet the socialization needs of their children; after school programs are increasingly important for working parents who want their children in safe and supportive learning environments outside of school hours; similarly, summer and weekend camps offer many possibilities for fun and learning. The implementation of creative programs is a lighter lift than the creation of a school, and can lead to the formation of more comprehensive institutions.

Metaphors are powerful ways to encode larger ideas, and metaphoric thinking is essential to creativity. We offer here some metaphors of schooling and deschooling to move us beyond the current metaphors of the *Factory* or the *Corporate Workspace* to spark thinking about possible futures: the *Atelier*, the *Journey*, the *Eco-Village*, and the *Forest School*. The link between instructional methodologies and models of schooling is a strong one; alternative environments call for innovative models of instruction.

The Atelier

The Atelier has a long history dating from Medieval times as a workshop and/or studio space for artists and apprentices. Reggio Emelia schools have incorporated the concept of the Atelier into their schools, designing spaces filled with ready tools, materials, and techniques for expressing learning in multiple visual languages—spaces for exploration, collaboration, and creativity to emerge (Edwards et al., 1998). The metaphor of the Atelier need not be confined only to arts-based learning; it is a model for centers that might incorporate many kinds of tools (agricultural, mechanical, digital, etc.) as well as interested experts available for coaching and self-directed learning.

The Journey

Wonderful things can happen when young people travel, either in educational groups or as unschooling families. Travel opens minds to new experiences and people, catalyzes interests in academic subjects such as history and geography, and cultivates self-identity and knowledge in important ways, fostering social skills, time management, executive functioning (like planning), and communication. A new term—*worldschooling*—has emerged to describe this form of experiential learning.

The Village

Schools have long been separated from their communities, literally and figuratively cut off from local knowledge and skills available. The *community school movement* aims to remedy that, by bringing young people into the community and the community into the school in meaningful ways that support local culture building (Kesson, 2021). Localization, in terms of the models highlighted by the work of Helena Norberg-Hodge (https://www.

localfutures.org) or the Schumacher Center (https://centerforneweconomics.org) provide guidance for ways to make learning more community-based, whether in traditional self-sufficient villages or modern eco-villages. Education in such sites offers students opportunities to build skills of sustainable living: agro-forestry, organic farming, small scale invention, building and manufacturing, domestic arts and crafts, foraging, and democratic community building.

Forest Schooling

Outdoor education is becoming increasingly popular as adults come to realize the physical, social, and psychological benefits of exploring nature and learning in the woods or forest. Richard Louv, with the publication of his book *Last Child in the Woods* (2005) brought to popular attention the need to save our children from "nature-deficit disorder." Outdoor education can involve adventure, team-building, survival skills, and conservation activities, as well as incorporating more conventional academic skills. First popularized in Scandinavian countries, where there are even pre-schools that spend most of every day, no matter the weather, outdoors in the wilderness exploring, playing, and learning about the world around them, the forest school is capturing the attention of families who have come to appreciate the many lasting benefits of a childhood spent in nature.

These are just a handful of alternative models that can help shift education from the conventional industrial, corporate model to a more holistic model that can better achieve the aims of a neohumanist education: to develop connection and compassion towards other people and the more-than-human others with whom we share the planet, to develop one's own authentic identity, to learn how to live in balance with the rest of nature, to engage in meaningful work and learning that is self-directed, and to cultivate the skills to create a better world. In these models, teaching generally shifts from the metaphor of the *sage on the stage* to the *guide on the side*, suggesting a realignment of the power differential between teacher and student and an opening to new possibilities of relationship.

Overview of Instructional Methods

Even if the intent is to start a school, complete with walls and classrooms, aspects of alternative models can be built into the structure and culture of the schools. And whether a traditional school or a forest school, it is still true that adults are very important in the lives of young people. Whether the adult is a state certified teacher, a parent, or a community member with an interest to share, all adults can benefit from learning more about how children learn, and what methods are most likely to accomplish this. Instructional methods vary greatly according to the age level of the young people, but they do fall into some general categories: design of the environment (spatial), rhythm of the day (temporal), participation structures, social/emotional climate and community building, discipline and behavior management.

Design of the Environment

The typical early childhood classroom is designed to foster learning in centers for dramatic play, music-making, science and math, visual arts, a reading corner, library, large motor movement (balls and balance beams), and other activities. The neohumanist school utilizes color and natural materials to create a calming, uplifting, and imaginative atmosphere, and includes living plants, perhaps insects and animals (keeping the ethics of captivity in mind), as much natural light as possible supplemented by soft lighting, comfortable cushions and pillows, magical spaces (hidey-holes, climbing structures, indoor forts, fairy lights, draped natural fabrics) and the liberal use of basketry and other natural containers to hold supplies. Children's work should be displayed tastefully, and in such a way that invites further reflection and learning. The environment should evoke in adults and children alike a sense of wonder, awe, fantasy, and imagination. The environment in a neohumanist classroom carefully reflects the philosophy and inherent values of neohumanism. For example, there may be a mural depicting animals, plants and humans living harmoniously, or an arrangement of costumes and props may be available for children to act out a favorite story.

Too soon, children often graduate into a typical primary school, with its rows of desks or perhaps tables, and often cluttered and busy environments filled with book covers, word walls, vocabulary lists, graphs and charts, number charts, lists of rules and regulations, and a huge array of other clutter. An overabundance of visual stimuli creates competition for children's attention, and can overpower their ability to concentrate. The neohumanist primary school should adhere to the same aesthetic principles as the early childhood center if we hope to sustain the qualities of wonder, awe and enchantment alongside the development of the intellect.

In a neohumanist school, depending on the space available, the outdoor environment should be much more than just a playground. Outside is every bit as important as inside, and a year around outdoor curriculum should be in place, with such activities as paper-making, planting, cooking, dyeing, composting, seed saving, and building. According to neohumanist early childhood professor Ruai Gregory with inspiration from the Nature

Explore Classrooms of Arbor Day Farm (natureexplore.org), the outdoor environment should include the following elements:

- an entry feature (a totem, arbor, or magical door);
- an open area for large motor activities (climbing, running, circle movement and games, etc.);
- a building area, with tools and materials, and many sizes and shapes of handmade wooden blocks;
- a nature art area;
- a music area (with instruments made of natural materials: maracas, drums, stringed instruments, claves, whistles, rainsticks, wrist and ankle shakers, clappers);
- a sand area;
- greenhouse, permaculture garden, and composting site;
- nature trails; and
- shaded nooks and crannies.

Neohumanist education shares with the Reggio Emelia approach an understanding of the environment (indoor and outdoor) as a teacher. Learning environments should be warm, welcoming, safe, invite exploration, be flexible and responsive to children's needs and interests, stimulate the imagination, and nurture the children's growth and development in multiple ways.

The Rhythm of the Day

There is no one right rhythm to the school day; each teacher and each school must plan together for the most effective use of the time allotted. Children, especially very young children, do need some level of predictability in terms of the rhythm of the day, a certain amount of repetition, and reoccurring rituals. This is not to discount the importance of occasional novelty or surprise to alleviate boredom or complacency! An important aspect of rhythm is transitions—when children shift from one activity or environment to another (arriving at school is a transition, coming together in a morning circle is a transition, getting ready to leave is a transition, etc.). Children handle transitions differently and a mindful teacher accommodates the variety of needs in creative ways.

In setting up a rhythm for the day, the neohumanist teacher utilizes careful observation of the individuals and the group, and intuitive interpretation to figure out the appropriate balance and sequence of quiet time, group projects, individual choice time, structured learning, outdoor exploration, and of course, significant time devoted to exercise, cooperative games, and sports for young people of all ages. The one thing that should be invariable at both the start of the day and the end of the day are circle times. These can include a variety of activities—songs, stories, check-ins, chanting, discussions, games, meditation, seasonal rituals—but are essential for individual development and group cohesion. The activities change as the children get older but some form of morning and closing circle is an important aspect of neohumanist schools.

Participation Structures

A participation structure is a way of organizing the communication between students and teachers and students and peers. Different structures have strengths and weaknesses, and need to be carefully calibrated to the aims of the lesson.

Lecture

Perhaps the most familiar structure of teaching and learning, the lecture is a one-way transmission of information from a teacher (usually at the front of the class, and standing) to the students, arranged in rows and seated. Teacher talks, students listen. Teacher is active, students are passive (though in some instances where a teacher is an engaging speaker, neurons may be firing!) Lectures are felt to be efficient ways of transmitting information; they are less effective at cultivating understanding. While it may sometimes be necessary to impart information in a lecture format, it is essential to keep in mind the attention span and engagement of the students, and use active learning strategies to keep things lively (mini-lectures, breaks for questions, pair-sharing, short writing assignments, problem-solving, etc.).

Augmented Lecture

In a nod to the need for some students to see, some to hear, teachers may hand out written notes to follow, or utilize a technology such as PowerPoint. Worst case scenario, teacher simply reads what is on the screen; somewhat better is the use of visual images that supplement the understanding of the material presented.

Self-Paced Learning

Heralded by many (especially software developers) as the modern antidote to the "one-size-fits-all" model of education, self-paced learning is promoted as the magic button that personalizes learning, allows students to complete learning tasks at their own level of competence, skip topics they have already mastered, repeat things as needed for comprehension; it even steers students towards resources tailored to their interests. It is highly individualized, offering little opportunity for building relationships.

Software is a seductive fix, especially programs that promise to liberate teachers from the routine tasks that take up much of their day, to customize learning to each individual student's needs, to offer content unavailable in small, isolated schools, and to replicate the fast-paced, hyper stimulating media environments that young people have grown accustomed to. This instructional model sits uncomfortably close to the digitized business model that tailors services and products to accommodate specific individuals, discernible in the Internet recommender systems that analyze our preferences through data mining and steer us towards books, films, and products that we may enjoy based on past purchases. In this sense, self-paced learning supported by personalization software might be understood as merely the latest weapon in the arsenal of late capitalism, branding our young people's interests and mining their data in order to squeeze maximum profits out of future consumers.

Modeling

When a teacher models an academic behavior, they are performing a task in the way they hope students will perform it. Instances where modeling is often used include step by step solving of math word problems or algebraic equations, or demonstrating the revision process for a piece of writing. In an early childhood classroom, it may be showing how to measure an ingredient in a recipe and stirring it into a bowl. Modeling at its best is not merely showing students how to do something, it should engage them in describing what they see, analyzing, thinking, estimating outcomes, conjecturing explanations, and proposing solutions, with the aim that students will be enabled to take the reins and perform the task independently or in groups.

Discussion

There are a multitude of ways to structure conversation in a classroom, ranging from the *pair-share* in which you have two students turn to each other and discuss a prompt; a *brainstorm*, in which a group of students generate creative ideas about a problem; a *debate,* a formal structure in which students explore the pros and cons of an idea; a *fishbowl* in which students sit in two concentric circles, with the circles alternating discussing, listening and providing feedback; or a *Socratic Seminar*, a formal discussion based on a text, facilitated by a discussion leader generating open-ended questions that foster collaborative inquiry.

Cooperative Learning

Cooperative learning, sometimes called collaborative learning, is based on the idea that young people have a lot to learn from each other, that knowledge is best constructed through socio-linguistic interaction, and that working together is good preparation for the kinds of problem-solving that adults engage in. Well planned cooperative learning allows students opportunities for language use and for practicing the interpersonal and social skills necessary for solving problems (learning to listen, examine different perspectives, experiment with solutions, give feedback, be accountable to others), whether they be practical problems, artistic problems, or political problems.

Cooperative learning can be used to work out the answer to a complex math word problem, build an architectural model of a bridge, analyze a text, or write a short play. There are many varieties of the basic model, such as the *jigsaw* method, a way of cultivating expertise in aspects of a topic and sharing it in rotating groups.

Gallery Walks

Different groups of students are assigned different aspects of a topic or problem to work on cooperatively, resulting in posters that can be displayed on the wall. Usually a student stays with the poster as other students circulate around the room studying the posters and asking questions, sometimes adding sticky notes to the posters with additional comments or questions.

Project-Based Learning

Project-based learning (PBL) involves the identification of a problem-to-be-solved (meeting a community need, painting a mural, creating a garden and composting system, putting on a play, or lobbying the local government on an issue of importance). Projects are organized around central driving questions that are complex, authentic, and of relevance to the learner(s), and they involve multiple and extended activities over time. They involve planning, design, inquiry, activity, feedback, and reflection, draw upon diverse academic subject matter, require the on-going acquisition of knowledge and skills, and often result in a publicly presented, culminating event or a product (Kesson, 2019).

Role Play

Role play is a fun and engaging form of active learning that can serve many purposes—warm-ups for other theater games, exploring literary elements such as characterization and dialogue, practicing decision-making and/or conflict resolution, or raising consciousness about social issues.

Role play and other theater games are featured extensively in Chapter 14, on creative drama.

Active Learning Games

Games can be used to teach a huge variety of topics, everything from letter sounds, to number sense, to vocabulary, to anatomy, to music theory. Games can involve large motor movement (you can learn more about this in Chapter 13 on creative movement) or quiet activity such as playing and/or designing board games. Well-designed games can improve cognition, increase the retention of ideas, provide motivation, energize children, and activate perception. Games are effective because play is the natural way that children learn, and the truth is, we never outgrow our need to play. The resourceful teacher is always thinking about how a topic can be presented or worked on in a way that involves kinesthetic movement and/or other creative, playful activity.

These are just a few of the innumerable pedagogical approaches that can be used. Varying the participation structures in a classroom provides the novelty necessary to keep students engaged and alleviate boredom. Important questions to be asked of any participation technique include these: Is everyone included in a meaningful way? Does the structure allow for different ways of learning? Different types of contributions? Does the method increase opportunities for deep understanding? Does it support human development writ large (social, emotional, physical, cognitive)?

Nurturing Community—Social and Emotional Learning

In 1995, *Emotional Intelligence* became an international best-selling book. The author, Daniel Goleman, spent time in India under the tutelage of Neem Karoli Baba, who was also the guru of Baba Ram Dass, of *Be Here Now* (1971) fame. Goleman and his colleague Richard Davidson (2017) have become premier neuroscience researchers of Yoga, meditation, and the brain. Davidson established the Center for Healthy Minds at the University of Wisconsin–Madison, dedicated to the research and practice of emotional well-being and meditation practices in education and the workplace. Just as Howard Gardner, the theorist behind the multiple intelligences theory, linked the intrapersonal and the interpersonal intelligences, these scholars have brought to popular attention the close relationship between self-knowledge and emotional awareness, personal transformation, and a healthy society.

Neohumanism is not merely a philosophy of individual spiritual development; it is equally devoted to the common good, the improvement of society towards greater equality, justice, and sustainability. For the neohumanist educator then, the cultivation of a spirit of community is essential to their practice. At this point in humanity's development, and despite the ways that big money and vested interests have eroded faith in democratic ideals in capitalist societies, democratic participation remains the most promising way to ensure the greater good. Since schools are the primary social institutions that have sustained contact with children throughout their formative years, it is important to instill the habits of mind, skills and dispositions necessary to enabling all students to find their voice and become empowered to participate in public life. And this happens not just through a few isolated lessons in civics, but through a comprehensive approach that includes attention to curriculum, instructional practices, governance, school culture and structures, relationships, and opportunities to practice civic learning in real life situations. There are a number of democratic dispositions to be cultivated in the context of class meetings and collaborative learning, which include both social and emotional learning. These include:

- sense of connectedness and understanding of the importance of relationships and sociability;
- sense of fairness and justice;
- recognition of the fundamental equality of all people;
- care and concern for both friends and strangers;
- acceptance of difference;
- willingness to take the perspective of another;
- open-mindedness—the willingness to incorporate new information into prior conceptual schema; and
- capability to modify beliefs in light of new experience and information.

Along with these habits of mind, neohumanist teachers help students develop skill sets that will help them become engaged social beings, including:

- ability to write and speak coherently and persuasively;
- ability to think critically and utilize the tools of logic (recognizing hasty generalizations and faulty arguments, weighing evidence and evaluating truth claims);
- ability to question the motivations and interests underlying points of view, and detect bias;
- ability to listen actively and respond empathetically to the varied perspectives and opinions of others;
- ability to deliberate, negotiate, and dialogue across differences;

- ability to think imaginatively and come up with creative solutions; and
- ability to work together collaboratively and appreciate the varied skills and talents that others bring to a situation (see Kesson et al., 2002).

These dispositions and capacities are developmental. While they can all be fostered from the earliest ages, they are designed to come to fruition as students approach adulthood. However, they must be consciously nurtured and supported throughout a student's entire education.

Discipline and Behavior Management

Beginning teachers invariably run into issues of how to control the behaviors in a classroom in order for learning to take place. Classroom management is the term often used for strategies to organize and control student behavior, movement, and interaction during lessons. Faced with unruly actions such as making noise, fighting, cursing, cheating, bullying, sleeping, talking out of turn, or just being unprepared for class, teachers often resort to rigid classroom management strategies such as rewards and punishments, isolating students with problematic behaviors, sending misbehaving students to a higher authority such as the principal, or in extreme cases, expulsion or suspension. Corporal punishment (inflicting pain, usually with a paddle, to control behavior) is still allowed in nineteen states in the United States (as of 2018) and is prevalent in many countries. Neohumanist teachers recognize that most problematic behaviors are signs of trauma, abuse, neglect, or are misguided communications about *need*, and understand that short term responses such as the above do little to remediate the deeper causes of anti-social behavior.

The best classroom management begins with cultivating, maintaining, and restoring *relationships* with young people, and establishing environments of understanding, trust, and connection. As well, the thoughtful educator establishes structures, such as democratic class meetings, in which students learn to communicate with each other, solve interpersonal problems, and cultivate positive relationships. Students need to be involved in creating the rules by which they will live, in determining what is and what isn't appropriate behavior, and in considering the consequences for inappropriate action. They need to discuss how to show respect for each other, and explore what creates a safe and trusting learning environment. This kind of proactive involvement in the creation of the classroom culture creates conditions in which problems are less likely to surface, and when they do, provides some of the skills to solve them.

One particularly effective classroom strategy includes what are called *restorative practices*, a social intervention that began in the judicial system as *restorative justice* but is now implemented in many schools. Restorative practices include community-based processes by which wrong-doers have opportunities to heal and mend harm that has been done. It is a relationship centered approach that requires the kind of prior culture building discussed in this chapter (Amstutz & Mullet, 2015). Learning to live together in peaceful, inclusive, democratic, and caring communities is a key aim of a neohumanist education. Therefore it is essential that this way of life is taught and practiced in neohumanist schools.

Cultivating *Presence*

In this chapter, we have focused extensively on methods. But methods are mere techniques, and no technique, no matter how skillfully executed, can substitute for what has elusively been called *teaching presence*. What is this teaching presence?

> I believe that teachers cannot really develop the "teaching presence" without being willing and able to love. Knowing the limitations to perspective, skill or self-mastery in the young, a loving teacher feels deep respect for the essential humanity—the depth of feeling and capacity for wisdom—in even the smallest child. (Kessler, 2007)

A neohumanist definition of presence goes beyond competence, or even the charisma or creativity of an educator. It is, as noted in other places in this book, a capacity for *indwelling*, the deep empathy that is required to lead a young person on their soul's journey, a capacity "to touch and be touched by another in terms of something fundamental to our shared existence" (Macdonald, 1995, p. 95). A teacher with presence is attuned to individuals and the pulse of the group, receptive to the implicit and explicit messages that are being sent, empathetic and connected to the feelings circling about, and ready to respond in the moment with intelligence and compassion to what is needed to facilitate the best next step in the learning process. They must be alert to what we refer to in the chapter on curriculum design as *emergence*, a term difficult to define but suggesting an attunement to the underlying order in a self-organizing system, a subconscious understanding of the "patterns that connect" (Bateson, 1978).

Emergence, literally the process of coming into being, suggests a condition seeking to be born, a spontaneous movement in time and space that must be *felt* in order to be perceived. A stunning example of self-organization among a collective of beings can be seen in the murmuration of starlings in flight, "a breath-stealing wonder, a pulsating, swooping, living, harmonized whole" (Donovan, 2021, para. 2). Perhaps we can replace the term classroom management, with its implications of control and social engineering, with *classroom murmuration*, implying the ability of teachers to choreograph relational, connected forms of learning and socialization in which the parts function together to create a harmonious, purposeful whole.

FOR CONTINUING STUDY

> *Discussion/Reflection:* Recall a teacher that had a strong and positive presence in the classroom. Describe the behaviors exhibited by this teacher. How did this affect you?
>
> *Discussion/Reflection:* What kind of group activities do you recall from your own schooling that helped to build community in the classroom? What ideas might you add to the ones presented in this chapter?
>
> *Application:* Create your ideal classroom, for whatever level learner you choose. Design a floor plan, and describe in great detail what the environment looks like. Explain the choices you made and how you believe they align with neohumanist principles.
>
> *Application:* If you are a teacher, try one of the participation structures that is new to you. Reflect in writing what the results were, and what you might do differently next time.

References

Amstutz, L. S., & Mullet, J. H. (2015). *The little book of restorative discipline for schools: Teaching responsibility: Creating caring climates.* Good Books.

Bateson, G. (1978). The pattern which connects. *The CoEvolution Quarterly* (Summer), 5–15.

Black, C. (2010). *Schooling the world.* https://www.filmsforaction.org/watch/schooling-the world-2010/

Donovan, J. (2021). *The secrets and science behind starling murmurations.* https://animals.howstuffworks.com/birds/starling-murmurations.htm

Edwards, C., Gandini, L., & Forman, G. (1998). *The hundred languages of children.* Ablex Publishing Corporation.

Goleman, D. (2005). *Emotional intelligence: Why it can matter more than IQ.* Random House Publishing.

Goleman, D., & Davidson, R. J. (2017). *Altered traits: Science reveals how meditation changes your mind, brain, and body.* Avery Books.

Hansen, D. T. (1995). *The call to teach.* Teachers College Press.

Illich, I. (1973). *Tools for conviviality.* Marion Boyars Publishers.

Illich, I. (1971/2000). *Deschooling society.* Marion Boyars Publishers.

Kessler, R. (2007, March 26). *The teaching presence*. https://www.creducation.net/resources/The_Teaching_Presence.pdf

Kesson, K. (2019). Project-based learning: Whole class thematic investigations. *VTLFF Occasional Paper Series, 2019*(1). https://static1.squarespace.com/static/590cbe53ebbd1afaa38e2081/t/5d69370f9b5867000190937d/1567176516174/Occasional+Paper+%231-sept2019.pdf

Kesson, K. (2021). *Community schools blueprint: Transforming the school/community partnership*. The Bay and Paul Foundations. https://www.vtlff.org/community-schools

Kesson, K., Koliba, C., & Paxton, K. (2002). Democratic education and the creation of a loving and just community. In J. S. Thousand, R. A. Villa, & A. I. Nevin (Eds.), *Creativity and collaborative learning: A practical guide to empowering students and teachers.* Paul H. Brookes.

Louv, R. (2005). *Last child in the woods: Saving our children from nature-deficit disorder.* Algonquin Books.

Macdonald, J. B., & Macdonald, B. J. (Ed.). (1995). *Theory as a prayerful act: The collected essays of James B. Macdonald.* Peter Lang.

Maslow, A. H. (1962/2011). *Toward a psychology of being* Martino Fine Books.

Moffett, J. (1994). *The universal schoolhouse: Awakening spirituality through education.* Jossey-Bass.

Sarkar, P. R. (1959). Education. In *Human Society Part 1*. Electronic edition of the works of P. R. Sarkar, Version 9.0.

9

Arts-Based Learning at the Center

> *The practice of art... is a spiritual discipline that offers a powerful antidote to an age of suffering from its loss of center... In this coming age we will see a big shift in human consciousness, away from the mental, egoistic, toward more spiritual ways of being and knowing.*
> — Kenneth Beittel, *Zen and the Art of Pottery*, 1989

Painting, drawing, carving, sculpting, singing, dancing, poetics, music-making, jewelry, costume and decoration, story-telling, dramatic enactments. These behaviors have been around since the dawn of human evolution. Why? What is art for? Why has it remained such a central aspect of human development? Long before the invention of the museum, the gallery, and the stage, art was an integral part of human life.

What Is Art For?

Aesthetic theorists who debate this question have come up with many explanations. Evolutionary biologists, faced with overwhelming evidence of the universality of the arts in human culture, posit that the arts have survival value; they contribute to evolutionary fitness (Dissanayake, 1988). Art processes and products are so interwoven into the fabric of the world's cultures that many languages do not even have a word for "art." Throughout history, the arts, coupled with ritual, festival, and ceremony, have served multiple functions that create stability, connection, and continuity in human culture:

- The arts can point beyond the surface of things to a deeper reality, connecting people to a more timeless experience (as in traditional mandala art).
- Symbolism, for example in masks, totems, or stained glass windows, remind a people of their shared mythic history, thus supporting cultural continuity.
- Coloration in art (e.g., on flags or shields) can remind people of essential cultural ideals (fertility, honor, courage, victory, peace).
- The arts can encode and transmit moral messages that enable survival (e.g., the importance of preserving water, caring for plants, honoring the power of the elements).
- They can facilitate individual and communal healing (Some, 1995).
- They mark important passages in collective life (the changing of the seasons) as well as in individual life (rites of passage to adulthood).
- The arts can establish essential interconnections with the worlds of non-human others (Macy & Brown, 2014).
- The arts can reinforce moral values of reciprocity and the gift economy (Vaughan, 2007).
- They contribute to joyful celebrations of survival and well-being (harvest festivals).
- They can highlight social unity and shared values (parades and processions).
- They can focus a people's collective supplications of divine intervention (rain-making, good harvests) thus cultivating a sense of shared purpose and intention.
- They can forge strong links between past, present, and future (as in honoring ancestors).
- They can introduce novelty, uncertainty and surprise into culture (as in masquerades).

As we can see from the list above, the many art forms have evolved to make certain events that are important for survival or social cohesion more salient, pleasurable, and memorable. They accomplish this by the making of specific objects, behaviors, and events (a major food crop such as corn, a wedding, the solstice) *special,* embellishing the moment with song, decoration, dance, poetry, or dramatic enactments. These experiences are *participatory,* rather than *spectator events.*

It is the participatory nature of these experiences that accomplishes what Dissanayake proposes is perhaps the most compelling explanation for the evolutionary necessity of the arts: they nourish the capacity *to experience transformative or transcendent emotional states and extraordinary states of consciousness.* It is in this that the important links between arts experiences and the cultivation of spirituality are forged. The capacity of (especially) the temporal arts (music, song, drama, dance) to heighten emotional responses, foster a sense of timelessness, unity, grace, communalism, ecstasy, or mystical understanding is recognized by the academic world (Gablik, 1991; Laski, 1961), by followers of ecstatic religions, and by anyone familiar with the contemporary dance music culture of Europe and the United States, a participatory scene in which the music and lighting (and often, chemical augmentation) are finely tuned to produce altered states of consciousness. Interestingly, this "rave culture" has inspired a postmodern, drug free, "cosmic mass" with deep roots in both Eastern and Western spiritual traditions, developed by the well-known theologian Matthew Fox (1997). Just as the various arts can provoke transcendent states of consciousness, so too can meditation or other forms of contemplation inspire the making of or appreciation for art.

Pseudo-Culture and the Arts

While inspiriting and inspiring aesthetic rituals still take place, art in the modern world has taken on different functions: as commodity, as entertainment, and spectacle. Much of what we call art today falls into the category of *pseudo-culture,* a term that Shrii Sarkar introduced that characterizes cultural products imposed by forces of colonialism and capitalism, leading to the denigration of local and folk cultures. In contemporary capitalist culture the arts are commodified—art is a product bought and sold in the marketplace with ascribed value based on notions of uniqueness and scarcity. Profit is a primary objective and the artist is not expected to be overly concerned with the welfare of society. Art practices have become the province of a talented few, rather than rooted in the everyday experience of ordinary people, and while some artists achieve enormous success and accumulate great wealth, most practicing artists struggle to make ends meet, and the creatively inclined among us have little time to engage in the practices of "making special."

168 ▪ *Becoming One With the World*

French philosopher Guy Debord (1967/2021) spoke of the way that modern capitalism exercises social control through the use of the "spectacle"—mass communication (print, television, news, propaganda, advertising, etc.) and mass entertainments (musical extravaganzas, video games, interludes in major sports events, popular movies, and the lavish spectacles of U.S. megachurches)—to distance us from genuine experience and supplant experience with representation, creating a *pseudo-world* that can only be viewed, not experienced. He speaks of the way that so much of modern culture has us drugged, hypnotized, alienated: "The spectacle is the bad dream of a modern society in chains and ultimately expresses nothing more than its wish for sleep. The spectacle is the guardian of that sleep" (p. 21).

The philosophy of neohumanism, at its core, is about *awakening*—awakening our intellects and our spirits from the chains and delusions and limiting sentiments that block individuals from experiences of enlightenment, connection, and bliss, and which perpetuate social ills such as war, inequality, oppression, environmental degradation, and other crimes that humans wreak upon each other and the non-human others with whom we share the planet. Neohumanist education is about awakening and nourishing the sense of wonder, awe, and joy that is the birthright of all. This is why the arts have long been at the center of neohumanist education—their capacity to enliven the educational experience and human expression with the beauty, mystery, heightened awareness, imagination, creative ability, and sublime feelings that can be aroused when we make the ordinary *extraordinary*—when we *make special* the everyday events of our lives.

Neohumanist Education and the Arts

Making choices about the inclusion of the arts in the context of neohumanist education requires reflection on the philosophical aims of education. We note here some of the key principles of neohumanist education outlined in Chapter 1, "Neohumanism: A Philosophy of Education for our Time":

- A neohumanist education (NHE) is equally concerned with "extroversial knowledge" (understanding the external world) and "introversial knowledge" (awareness of the subtle inner dimensions of the self).
- NHE emphasizes the essential interconnectedness of people with all of creation, expanding the heart to embrace all species.
- NHE explicitly cultivates a deep ecological sensibility, with a commitment to care for land, water, plants and animals.

- NHE recognizes the fundamental equality of all people, and aims to heal the social, political, and economic wounds of the past and present.
- NHE emphasizes service and activism for the common good.
- NHE values the specifics of culture and place, and cultivates a universal sentiment as well (a "diversified universalism").

There is more, but these key ideas are important to keep in mind as we analyze the intentions and the outcomes of arts processes and practices in neohumanist education.

Art is, essentially, the creation of culture. One's personal identity is strongly influenced by one's cultural heritage—the transmission of language, story and dance forms, rituals, visual images, and mythologies. And yet today, due to migrations, dislocations, digital communications, and the ease of transport in a global society, we live in a time of *syncretism*, the encounters, conflicts, and fusions of multiple forms of culture. There are very few pure cultures left in the world. Neohumanist educators value the language and cultural expressions of particular places and groups; they are also aware of the way that cultural forms are evolving through syncretism.

Adding complexity to arts integration in this multicultural environment is the risk of cultural appropriation—the use of cultural elements without permission. For example, many traditional cultures, societies that lived in close relationship with their environment, enacted rituals and ceremonies enriched by the arts to express this harmonious balance. It can be illuminating to view films or photographs of these practices and gain inspiration from them, however, it would be considered cultural appropriation to imitate a ritual or ceremony for educational purposes, or to copy sacred cultural artifacts. People living in modern industrialized societies cannot adopt Indigenous spirituality, as the practices are specific to tribe or clan or community and often deeply connected to specific places and histories. Aboriginal artists in Australia, for example, who have been recognized for introducing one of the most exciting contemporary art forms of the 20th century, inherit the rights to express certain stories in their art through family lineages (https://www.aboriginal-art-australia.com/aboriginal-art-library/the-story-of-aboriginal-art/). Modern people must find their own ways out of the thicket of materialism and consumerism in which so many have been imprisoned. The arts offer profound opportunities for revitalizing old and cultivating new rituals, ceremonies, and festivals that can serve the creative cultivation of our "ancient futures" (Norberg-Hodge, 1991/2009).

Different Approaches to Arts Education

There are varied perspectives on and approaches to arts education. These are often thought of as distinct practices, but it is possible to draw what is strong and relevant from each in the development of a neohumanist curriculum.

- *Separate subjects.* Maintaining the disciplines of the arts as distinct curricular areas, taught in studio formats that build specialized skills in forms like drawing, painting, sculpture, or musical instrumentation.
- *Discipline-based arts education.* A highly academic approach which includes elements of art production (studio art) as well as art history, art criticism, and philosophical aesthetics.
- *Curriculum enhancement.* Utilizing various arts as strategies to support other curricular areas (e.g., singing the ABC song without learning anything about melody or rhythm).
- *Multi-arts integration.* Creative engagement with two or more disciplines in order to deepen learning in both (all) modes. For example, in a study of the abolition of slavery in the United States (social studies), students learn not just to sing freedom songs but gain knowledge of melody, lyrics, and style, as well as historical information about the creators and the contexts of the songs.

Neohumanist education emphasizes multi-arts integration for a number of research-based reasons:

- There is growing scientific evidence that activity in the arts has measurable effects on the brain and its structure, creating new synapses and enlarging the cerebral cortex; researchers believe that this increases the capacity to learn other skills, for example, in math and science (see Ross & Magsamen, 2023).
- The arts increase the brain's plasticity—its ability to adapt in response to new experiences (Ross & Magsamen, 2023).
- Arts experiences support the diversity of learners in a classroom and allow for multiple entry points into knowing.
- They enhance sensory development in multiple modalities.
- They offer "catalyst" experiences that can foster later focused interests and skill development.
- The arts are uniquely capable of connecting personal interests with subject matter.

- Arts activity lends itself to problem solving by strengthening spatial reasoning (the capacity for organizing and sequencing ideas) and developing conditional reasoning (theorizing about outcomes and consequences).
- Arts foster creative and divergent thinking (openness, brainstorming, originality, elaboration, flexibility).
- Involvement in the arts nurtures the capacities of active engagement, disciplined and sustained attention, persistence, and risk-taking.
- Learning in one modality (i.e., music) can enhance development in other areas (i.e., math); another example: dramatic experiences have been shown to improve writing skills. Research is new in these areas, but promising.
- Engaging in the arts improves mental health, relieving stress and anxiety and releasing "feel-good" hormones.
- Perhaps most important, integrating the arts creates a learning environment of "serious play," creativity, and joy!

As children grow and learn, and begin to develop strong interests, it is important to provide opportunities to develop specialized skills in the visual or performing arts or music. Too often, higher level arts training is only available outside of school, and generally not affordable for all families. The neohumanist educator seeks to provide equitable opportunities for all young people to develop their skills and talents through creative community partnerships with local arts practitioners, artist residencies, and by continuous development of their own creative processes.

Art as Experience—Going With the "Flow"

American pragmatist philosopher John Dewey (1934) wrote extensively about aesthetic experience, proposing that a "work of art" is not necessarily a static object but rather *a special kind of dynamic experience*, differing from everyday undertakings by virtue of its special refinement or intensification. In the course of daily life, we are *experiencing* continuously—sensory inputs (images, sounds, conversations), feelings (responses to the environment), tasks (eating, drinking, walking, playing, working). Most of our experiencing is habitual—programmed behaviors dictated by cultural norms, rules, customs, schedules, expectations. Our perception and our thinking, too, become habitual, closing the doors on new insights, *Aha!* moments, or new ways of approaching life. Ordinary, habitual experience, in Dewey's view, differs from "an experience"; *an experience* has structure, with a beginning and end, and is characterized by:

- awakening us from the dream-like state of daily repetition;
- forcing us to confront life consciously and non-automatically;
- engaging the forces of cognitive disequilibrium and equilibrium; and
- bringing a sense of wholeness, organic unity upon consummation/completion.

The Hungarian psychologist Mihaly Robert Csikszentmihalyi (1990) introduced us to the concept of *flow*—an optimal psychological state characterized by total immersion, engagement with activity, intrinsic motivation, focus, intense concentration, and a release of the ego into a state of mindfulness. Both Dewey's idea of aesthetic experience and Csikszentmihalyi's notion of a flow state are essential components of happiness and well-being, and indicative of long term learning, achievement, and the fulfillment of personal goals. Both perspectives capture the essence of *making special*.

What is the relationship between the free flow of creative expression and skill development in the arts? Let us take an example from arts education. When learning a musical instrument, there are endless exercises and repetitions to go through to begin to get decent sounds from an instrument, to master durations and pauses, to understand rhythm patterns, to learn the mathematics of tempo. Numerous variables enter into the equation of learning to make music: kinesthetic skill (holding a bow correctly), hearing the sounds you produce (audio sensing), matching your sound to external stimuli (as in the Suzuki mode of teaching) or integrating symbols on a page with activity of the brain and body—an enormously complicated set of tasks.

A new level of experience is attained when one first mingles their sounds successfully with those of others, resulting in an orchestral piece. Research abounds on the ways in which musicians often experience a deep flow state. There is a sense of accomplishment, a sense of completion, a collective experience that results in a great sense of satisfaction. One can be said to have had a true *experience* then, and the listeners as well experience this sense of wholeness, or completion. For Dewey, the arts are not just about what the artist creates, the artistic *experience* lies in the dynamic interaction of the creator and the listener or the viewer, who bring their own prior experiences and perceptions to the act of observing or hearing the created object, thus creating new expressive meanings.

It is a long road, however, between the first squeaks by a novice violin student and Elgar's "Serenade for Strings." The educator has a major role to play in establishing the conditions that support optimal learning and continuous engagement and development in the arts. As we have explored in past chapters, it is essential that the teacher be attuned to the capabilities, the interests, and the purposes of the children in order to provide materials and strategies that support such experiences. Beyond this, what steps can an arts-based educator take to ensure that student interest in making music (for example) doesn't give way to frustration and feelings of inadequacy? That the developing visual artist does not compare their sunflower unfavorably with those of Vincent van Gogh? A few reminders:

- Support student choice and self-direction in the use of materials and forms of creative expression.
- Provide structured and in-depth instruction in the use and care of materials.
- Create opportunities for a flow state *at every skill level* by setting challenging tasks that are attainable.
- Ensure that a child's work is not interrupted when they are immersed in creative activity.
- Withhold both positive and negative judgments about creative work; rather learn to *describe* what you see or hear, and ask pertinent questions (other than "what is that?").
- Ensure that all children can participate in arts-based group experiences at their own comfort and ability level, even if that means dinging the triangle at the end of a song.
- Share multiple varieties of art from various cultures and traditions, ancient and modern, so that students have a large and varied ensemble of models, making sure to avoid stereotypical representations, trite and/or cliché symbolisms, or the marginalization of non-Western art forms.
- Balance skill development with improvisation and free expression.
- Create many opportunities for young people to share their work and talk about it with peers.

Cultivating Creative Thinking

Good education requires encounters with what is unknown, the introduction of novelty, uninhibited explorations, and new experiences, all of which can result in behavioral changes, insights, and new ways of thinking and acting. It is the task of neohumanist education to reclaim the arts as central to human experience, as uniquely able to engage young people in dynamic making and doing, and in the important cognitive and affective processes inherent in the creative process. In Chapter 4, "The Science of Learning" you were introduced to Howard Gardner's theory of multiple intelligences. You may recall that he first proposed seven intelligences:

- Musical
- Mathematical
- Interpersonal
- Intrapersonal
- Visual-Spatial
- Linguistic
- Kinesthetic

which he later expanded to include both a naturalist intelligence and an existential intelligence. Many of the intelligences he identified are clearly related to the arts, especially the visual-spatial (drawing, painting, sculpture), musical and mathematical (instrumentation and singing), kinesthetic (dance), linguistic (poetry), and so on. Though he presents the intelligences as distinct, in reality they interact with, enhance, and in fact, amplify the effects of each other.

A key idea in his theory is that every intelligence has its own unique symbol system. In the linguistic realm, the symbol system incorporates sounds, letters, words, sentences, and so on. In mathematics, children encounter numbers, quantity, patterns, ratio, units of measurement, and so on. In music, the symbol system indicates pitch, tones, volume, melody, rhythm, tempo, and so on. The human acquisition of symbolic learning is developmental; it is a long road from the infant's first burbling sounds to the recitations of the professional poet. Education is the bridge that connects the young person's symbolic development across the span of early life.

We associate thinking with intelligence; with Gardner's theory, we understand that thinking can take many different forms. It is important to note that Gardner sees the concept of intelligence as culturally specific; in other words, traits that are highly valued in one culture (such as logical thinking) may be less valued in a culture that values skill or social competence or even empathy more highly. He notes too that specific intelligences may manifest differently depending on the cultural context. For example, one culture may identify the kinesthetic intelligence most ardently with dance, another with competitive physical sport, and yet another with skill in weaponry. Intelligence is thus differentiated, not only within cultures, but across cultures as well. His ideas help us shift from a narrow definition of cognition that values logic, memorization, and linear thinking as the apex of intelligence to a more robust view that values multiple modes of intelligence; this supports the neohumanist principle of "epistemological pluralism" as outlined in Chapter 1.

Conventional ideas about education posit the importance of "teaching as telling" (what Paulo Freire calls the "banking model of education"), memorization, and the regurgitation of these "intellectual deposits" on tests. Students who score highly on tests are thought to have superior intelligence. We are beginning to understand that this narrow definition of intelligence is not necessarily an indicator of success in life—that other ways of thinking and more authentic modes of assessment are more likely to produce meaningful educational outcomes such as the ability to solve problems, to invent and discover, and to apply knowledge in novel ways. The ways of thinking and problem solving that we find in the arts have applications in other disciplines such as science and math. Some of these thinking processes relevant to the arts as well as to the other academic disciplines include:

- the generation of ideas (identifying key problems; divergent thinking; brainstorming);
- awareness of process (discovering intrinsic motivation, tapping into personal experience, self-assessing, making choices and noting consequences;
- experimenting (testing hypotheses, questioning, risk taking, combining and mixing ideas, synthesizing; and
- engaging multiple perspectives (considering different points of view, perceiving relationships and patterns, attending to both details and the big picture).

Creative thinking is essential, now more than ever as we confront the enormous problems resulting from the choices humans have made in the past. As we of necessity move in the direction of an ecologically sustainable society, a post-capitalist commitment to degrowth, and towards the decommodification of the many aspects of life that have been violently inducted into the market system, we must help young people to understand and enjoy lifeways that do not depend on consumerism and commercialism. While there are many examples of decommodified activity (service, care, play, sport, etc.) the arts will play a central role in moving us away from the conversion of all of nature, including human beings, into objects that can be monetized, and towards ways of being in the world that honor life by making ordinary experience extraordinary.

Spiritual Development and the Arts

The research-based benefits of the arts in education are manifold (see ArtsEdSearch, a main site for research in the arts). Music, visual arts, dance, theater, and the many offsprings and subsets of these enliven the curriculum, nurture social-emotional learning, inspire cultural knowledge, boost learning and achievement across the curriculum, motivate young people to stay in school, offer more pathways to success for young people, and infuse education with joy.

If that weren't enough, the arts have a special purpose in neohumanist education, the aims of which go beyond social adjustment and finding a worthy career, important as these are. For people raised in modern industrialized cultures, neohumanism is an emerging paradigm, a worldview that understands all of creation as deeply interconnected, supremely alive, and intelligent. It understands the person as a *multi-dimensional being* with attributes, potentials, and capacities aligned with the cultivation of relational ways of being in the world. Education, for the neohumanist, is not merely about training the intellect or equipping people with social and emotional skills. It is about laying a foundation for consciousness to develop in evolutionarily important ways, about cultivating the subtle human faculties such as aesthetics, ethics, gratitude, peace, introspection, intuition, discernment, and spiritual discovery. Real education, according to Shrii Sarkar (1981), should awaken a sense of universalism in the child; it should "lead(s) to a pervasive sense of love and compassion for all creation" (para. 6). It is this pervasive sense of love and compassion, the universal feeling of love for all creation, that is to be cultivated, and to that purpose, neohumanist educators ask the following questions of their practice:

- How can the arts cultivate individual spiritual expansion and development?
- How can they help us imagine new narratives for a livable, sustainable, peaceful, just, and joyous future?
- How can the arts make everyday experiences—sharing meals, welcoming guests, greeting teachers and classmates, celebrating birthdays—*special* with simple etiquette and rituals?
- How can the arts enliven the curriculum and bring joy to the classroom experience?
- What can make each day special and introduce novelty and humor into the life of the school (*Hint:* Did you know that in the United States, January 16th is "Appreciate a Dragon Day" or that February 26th is "Tell a Fairy Tale Day")?

- How can the arts foster ecological awareness and cultivate "biophilia" (the love of nature)?
- How do we create learning experiences that awaken subtle human capacities (empathy, aesthetics, altruism, feelings of "oneness")?
- How are the higher *koshas* activated?
- How can the arts bring a sacred (not religious) element into education and culture?

In the chapters that follow, we explore how the disciplines of visual arts, music, creative movement and creative drama address these questions in particular ways. We redirect attention from art as individual talent and achievement to the many ways that the arts can inspire concern for the welfare and uplift of society. We pay special attention to the ways that communal aesthetic participation, as in the making of music or song, offers us the opportunity to enter a state that transcends individuality "in which we are not (as is usual) separate and sequential but seem to partake of a timeless unity" (Dissanayake, 1992, p. 71). We explore how songs, stories shared, sand paintings, contemporary urban murals, rhythmic processions and sacred circle dances construct vital bridges between separate lives and community solidarity. We look at how neohumanist educators create *cultures of enactment*, involving young people in participatory experiences in which they create and recreate the fundamental stories of our existence—our human bonds, our relationships with plants, animals, sea and sky, and the mythic stories that carry forth and transmit the blueprints of a moral universe. In these, and other ways, we hope to make the case that the creative arts are essential to education, to human development across the lifespan, to ecological consciousness, and to the advent of a more enchanted, luminescent, spiritually awakened world.

FOR CONTINUING STUDY

Discussion/Reflection: Recall a time when you participated in a group arts experience: a school play, an orchestra, or a mural painting. What was the experience like for you? What did you learn from it (think about skills, dispositions, habits, etc.)?

Discussion/Reflection: Choose any of the bulleted questions at the end of this chapter, and discuss it in depth, adding examples whenever possible.

Application: As an individual or as a group, recall the idea of a "culminating experience" as introduced in Chapter 7 on curriculum design. Think about an arts-based experience that might culminate a specific unit of study, and brainstorm all of the skills needed to carry it off, and the experiences necessary to build these skills.

References

ArtsEdSearch. https://www.aep-arts.org/

Csikszentmihalyi, M. (1990). *Flow: The psychology of optimal experience.* Harper & Row.

Debord, G. (2021). *The society of the spectacle.* Critical Editions. (Original work published 1967)

Dewey, J. (1934). *Art as experience.* Penguin Group.

Dissanayake, E. (1992). *Homo aestheticus: Where art comes from and why.* The Free Press.

Dissanayake, E. (1988). *What is art for?* University of Washington Press.

Fox, M. (1997). *Confessions: The making of a post-denominational priest.* Harper Books.

Gablik, S. (1991). *The reenchantment of art.* Thames and Hudson.

Laski, M. (1961). *Ecstasy: A study of some secular and religious experiences.* Cresset.

Macy, J., & Brown, M. Y. (2014). *Coming back to life: The updated guide to the work that reconnects.* New Society Publishers.

Norberg-Hodge, H. (2009). *Ancient futures: Lessons from Ladakh for a globalizing world.* Sierra Club Books. (Original work published 1991)

Ross, I., & Magsamen, S. (2023). *Your brain on art: How the arts transform us.* Random House.

Sarkar, P. R. (1981). Talks on education, Excerpt F. In *Prout in a nutshell,* Volume 4, Part 18 [Electronic edition of the works of P. R. Sarkar, version 9.0].

Some, M. (1995). *Of water and the spirit: Ritual, magic and initiation in the life of an African shaman.* TarcherPerigee Publishing.

Vaughan, G. (2007). *Women and the gift economy: A radically different worldview is possible.* Inanna Publications.

10

Multiple Literacies

The Role of Language and Story in Neohumanist Education

> *The way people can express their thoughts and ideas in their own mother tongue cannot be done in any other language. People feel uneasy when they speak in a language other than their mother tongue. If they constantly feel such uneasiness... their vital force will be weakened.*
> —P. R. Sarkar, A Few Problems Solved, 1981

Shrii Sarkar wrote extensively about language, linguistics, and literacy, contributing thousands of pages of analysis on a range of topics from philology to grammar, with a deep focus on root languages such as Sanskrit and Latin. Language is a universal capacity, he said, noting that all living beings have their own inherent tendency to express and symbolize; he included other-than-human species in this observation. He further emphasized the importance of one's home language (called variously one's primary language or one's native language) as deeply connected to their most inner essence, or "Práńa Dharma." Shrii Sarkar (1998, p. 112) is firm in his insistence on the preservation of local languages, for a number of reasons:

- the empowerment people feel when they express their thoughts and ideas in their mother tongue;
- the psychological crises and debilitating effects of not being able to express in one's mother tongue; and
- the imposition of inferiority complexes in people whose languages are suppressed, leading to their socio-economic exploitation or even annihilation.

Language policy is highly contested, especially in post-colonial countries, multicultural societies, or areas experiencing high levels of immigration. Language is power, determining (or influencing) one's access to employment, political position, and social status. In this respect, Shrii Sarkar's guidance is highly useful, providing as it does a nuanced understanding of oppression and empowerment as it relates to language and literacy.

What Does It Mean To Be "Literate?"

Literacy is the essential aim of education in the modern world. Mass literacy is considered fundamental to socio-economic development; having well educated, skilled workers is a requirement for the improvement of health, sanitation, agriculture and other basic needs, not to mention scientific and technological development. Literacy is now considered a human right, and like many other rights, women proportionally have less access to it. Literacy rates continue to increase, and the gender gap continues to decrease, but as of 2019, we were still about 13 percentage points away from global literacy, with the rates of literacy varying widely across countries (and in some cases, within countries).

In contemporary thought, literacy means the ability to decode written text, to comprehend the meanings embedded in it, and to analyze, interpret, and evaluate what is read. In addition to reading, literacy implies the ability to write down one's own thoughts in order to communicate them to others. Reading and writing constitute the basic ingredients of education. Literacy, however, is a complex phenomenon, for education is much more than the learning of alphabetical symbols and how to make sense of them.

Education is never a neutral process, rather it serves one of two purposes: it either facilitates the integration of people into the logic of the existing system or it becomes, as the well-known Brazilian literacy educator Paulo Freire (1970) noted, the practice of freedom. Expanding Freire's revolutionary literacy praxis of educating for freedom from oppression, neohumanist educators are also tasked with the cultivation of educated people who have a deep love for and sense of relationship with all created beings, who value multiple ways of coming to know the world, and who reflect an integrated personality (body, mind, emotions, spirit in harmony).

Anyone serious about the teaching of language and literacy should consult some of Sarkar's original texts on the topic. This chapter extracts what we believe are the salient points about language learning that are necessary for teachers to understand. In it, we propose incorporating a *pedagogical multiplicity* of literacies, a neohumanist approach to communicative competence that straddles the border between what is required for survival and success in modern culture, and the requirements of a postmodern, posthuman society, in which human beings live sustainably in deep relationship with all species. As with all principles and practices of neohumanist education put forth in these chapters, differences in time, place and circumstances must dictate the choices that are made about subject matter and instructional methodology.

Pre-Text Societies

Educated people often divide humans into binary categories: literate/illiterate; modern/primitive; smart/dumb. These categories embed some deep cultural assumptions: that history is a linear narrative of material progress; that humans are getting smarter; and that our lives are improving immensely with rapid developments in science and technology that make us safer and more comfortable. In these assumptions, we often fail to understand that progress in the material sphere of life is double-edged: we have antibacterial drugs that save lives (to which harmful bacteria simply adapt and become more powerful); we increase the yields of common crops through applications of chemical fertilizers and pesticides (which pollute the groundwater and destroy the long term fertility of the soil); we fly around the planet in airplanes (and contribute to global warming and climate change), and so on. Almost all indicators of material progress have their largely unexamined shadow side.

Cultural groups that have not developed a written text are considered to be inferior, less intelligent than modern, text-based cultures. However, pre-text societies did manage to survive and thrive for many thousands of years prior to the invention of such modern artifacts as paper and written alphabets, printing presses, cameras, and now, the binary coding of the digits 0 and 1 to represent words and images, along with the storage of enormous amounts of information on tiny digital devices. With the advent of these technologies, some cognitive capacities have atrophied, including orality and memory, capacities that pre-text societies developed to a high degree.

What has also diminished with the advent of text is our inclination to engage sensorily with the animate and inanimate worlds, the capacities that once made it possible for the kinds of deep relationships and connections that created the sense of universal love for all beings. As we struggle now to reweave some threads in the animistic fabric of the world, we need to examine some of the assumptions about the role of text in our individual and social development.

Language and Place

In many Indigenous societies, some of which have lived in relative balance with their biosystems for thousands of years, language, memory, and information are deeply connected to *place*. The landscape itself is often linked to vital intelligence, which might be further encoded in song, dance, myth, story, or ceremony. It is difficult for modern rootless people to understand the tragedy of land loss, such as what happened to many Native American people when they were forcibly relocated away from their homelands onto reservations. The loss of ancestral burial locations and sacred ceremonial sites contributed to a loss of cultural memory and identity, which is taking generations to begin to recapture.

Some pretext cultural groups used the skyscape as a memory device; you may have heard of the navigational feats of island people who used information from the stars, wind patterns, bird migrations and a strong oral tradition to guide their long ocean voyages for thousands of years. Research verifies the prodigious memory skills of many Indigenous people; one study, for example, shows that Navajo elders memorize and classify more than 700 insects, including their identifying features, habitats, and behaviors (Kelly, 2017). And that is just one aspect of their place-based knowledge.

Why is this important for neohumanist educators? Just as so many thousands of insect, bird, plant and animal species are becoming extinct due to the incursions of our industrialized, capitalist society (Kolbert, 2015), so are the languages of thousands of people disappearing as land-based, Indigenous cultures are forcibly assimilated into existing modern societies. Of the more than 7,000 known languages of the world, almost half of them are endangered. While there are moral imperatives for preserving Native language and culture, there are very pragmatic ones as well, which might prove more compelling to self-interested modern people. Along with the diminishing bank of cultural knowledge, ways of knowing, and different ways of perceiving the world (worldviews) the loss of language has tragic consequences that are only beginning to be understood. One example: all contemporary mass market medications are derived from medicinal plants—everything from aspirin to morphine. A recent study that investigated thousands of plant species and their relationships to endangered languages revealed that 75% of the uses for medicinal plants *are known only in one language* (see Cámara-Leret & Bascompte, 2021). When the language is lost, so is the potential for important medical advances.

Language, for modern people, is *decontextualized.* It has been torn from its home in the rocks, in the stars, and in the waters. Many modern people do not experience a deep sense of connection to place. Easily transportable languages such as English are unequal to the task of helping people to establish relationships with the natural world that lead to long term regeneration and sustainability. With the click of a finger on a keyboard, people in Vermont, Kenya, and Singapore can "communicate" at a basic level. But as theorist Chet Bowers (2014) highlighted so well, the transmission of words and facts via computer is not a neutral technology, but rather has culturally transforming effects. Most prominent among these are the reinforcement of individually centered relations, decontextualized ways of knowing, and the loss of local and intergenerational knowledge. Certain human capacities are amplified; others are diminished. As just one example, the acquisition of information through "sound bites" and hyper-linked ideas may threaten the kinds of deep understanding that one might obtain from reading a sophisticated text, let alone the extended sensory observation of a phenomenon.

Importantly, language shapes the way we see the world. In some languages, nouns change based on their context, qualities, or relation to other objects. Researchers have documented over 47 different Inuit words for snow, based on things like "snow on the ground" or "snow in the air." The Inuit people's attunement to the environment is greatly enhanced by these numerous nuances. Native American author and scientist Robin Wall Kimmerer (2013) writes eloquently about "learning the grammar of animacy" in her book *Braiding Sweetgrass.* As just one example, she notes that when we call a plant or an animal an "it" we create an *object*, "we put a barrier between us, absolving ourselves of moral responsibility and opening the door to exploitation" (p. 57). "It is all in the pronouns," she says, and perhaps a grammar of animacy

> could lead us to whole new ways of living in the world, other species a sovereign people, a world with a democracy of species, not a tyranny of one—with moral responsibility to water and wolves, and with a legal system that recognizes the standing of other species. (pp. 57–58)

Neohumanist educators faced with the teaching of language and literacy have an important mission: to cultivate not only the basic capabilities of decoding written text, but to infuse language with meaning and life, and foster (through language) ways of coming to know the world that bring about a deep sense of connection with, and love for, all species, as well as a passionate commitment to live sustainably and in harmony with our biosystem. To begin our pedagogical discussion, we turn to one of humanity's oldest forms of sharing knowledge and passing on cultural values: storytelling.

Storytelling

Since the dawn of human evolution, our ancestors have told stories around campfires and hearths. Stories contained the hard won wisdom of the past, whether about the uses of edible or medicinal plants or advice about hunting or of the interpersonal ethics required to keep peace and harmony in the tribe. Stories told of origins, of how the universe was created, where a people came from, what was known of their ancestors. Stories contain archetypes and metaphors that help to shape human behavior, and stories create a context for the development of our personal identity. Why is it that stories have such an enduring legacy?

Some neuroscience researchers believe that our brains are actually "hard-wired" to the storytelling, or narrative, format. But what is that format? Stories include a plot—things *happen* in stories. Other story elements include characters, settings, catalysts (events that set a story in motion), conflicts, climaxes, and resolutions. Good stories use these story elements to make meaning, to convey an idea of importance. Stories generally engage us at an emotional level, and they stimulate a number of cognitive capacities: imagination, speculation, inference, intuition, and memory. Stories can activate multiple sensory channels in the brain: olfactory, auditory, kinesthetic, visual, tactile. Researchers refer to *neural coupling* or *mirroring* to describe the communicative process when brains are aligned in the process of sharing stories. The complexity and variation of effects provide some hints as to why learning is more effective when it is embedded in a narrative structure.

Facts are information that has been extracted from stories and presented as data, isolated ideas, theories, and/or formulae. Facts are often communicated in dry, abstract language, rather than in compelling visual symbols or with captivating adjectives. A dry lecture simply does not light up many parts of the brain, as any undergraduate who has nodded off in a huge lecture hall can testify. Facts alone, as found in many textbooks and PowerPoint lectures, don't often generate emotional responses, and so it is difficult for the brain to create patterns or meanings, and in the absence of patterns, memory is not stimulated. A common complaint from disaffected and disengaged students is the fragmented nature of the content they are learning. When one learns facts in this isolated, decontextualized way, no coherent story of the world and one's place in it can emerge. Students need a greater narrative in order to construct a meaningful personal identity. Humans in general need to feel a sense of purpose, of how one fits into the larger narrative.

For these and many other reasons, neohumanist educators are encouraged to study the use of narrative and make it a central part of their pedagogy. Early childhood educators know and value the uses of storytelling and picture books in engaging pre-readers. Hearing stories builds bridges to literacy development by enabling concept development, character study, and enhanced awareness of narrative structure, temporal sequencing, grammar, and vocabulary.

There are many tried and true methods of amplifying the storytelling process in early education that create a fertile soil for later literacy. Teachers should familiarize themselves with musical storytelling (singing and song making), fingerplays (hand and finger movements coordinated with a song, rhyme, or short story), finger-puppets, flannel story boards, or using small figures to enact a story. Such props activate multiple sensory channels and aid in stimulating memory functions, which are often exercised by having children retell stories. Retelling stories supports oral language development, grammatical knowledge, narrative structure, sequencing, supporting details and other elements central to later reading and writing abilities.

As Kieran Egan (1986) of Australia has pointed out, storytelling is not just for pre-readers, but should become a central part of curriculum planning and design across the curriculum, at all grade levels. What, after all, are the academic disciplines, if not stories? Science is a story of exploration and discovery, and of the solving of problems and the improvement of life through the application of knowledge. The origins of the universe in the Big Bang is a story. Human evolution is a story. In Yoga philosophy, Brahmacakra, the cosmic cycle of creation, is a story that elucidates ultimate human purpose. History is perhaps the most obvious narrative discipline, constructed as it is of the stories that have come to us from the past. Teachers can engage students in making sense of the world by presenting subject matter in ways that make use of what we know about how stories light up the brain.

Conventional Thinking About Literacy Pedagogy

In the modern rush to fill the heads of children with information in order to better fit them for an advanced, technological, consumer society, we have neglected the important role of fantasy and imagination in the development of thinking. Many conventional preschool and kindergarten classrooms are (mis)guided by the notion that the sooner the child is presented with a realistic version of the world, and the earlier they are taught to decode symbols on a page, the smarter and better adjusted the child will be. Each day begins with a calendar activity, laying the groundwork for number sequencing and the concept of time. They record the weather, and children sometimes have a moment to share an object or an experience with their class.

Classroom learning is often structured by themes. One popular preschool or kindergarten theme is community helpers, offered on the assumption that what the child is most interested in are firefighters, doctors, police and mail carriers. Teaching materials are often generic, cartoonish, and devoid of real meaning. Children spend large blocks of time on various literacy activities, practicing sight words or phonics, and if they are lucky, they have some free time to look at picture books. In some classrooms, children are taught test-taking skills, practicing at a tender age to fill in appropriate answer bubbles while a timer ticks away. These are all considered "best practices" in education, not universally, but in many modern settings.

A guiding idea here is that children learn best by starting with the concrete, the world that is around them, and moving outward from that towards greater abstraction. Related to this is the idea that we must start with the part and only gradually move to the whole. Start with the nurse, the doctor, the firefighter as objects of interest. Start with phonemes, digraphs, and diphthongs—the building blocks of language—and build up to words, then sentences, then eventually books. The practices are consistent with the philosophy of mind as a "blank slate" upon which can be written any cultural story. Consider, however, what we learned in earlier chapters on neohumanist child development about alternative ways of thinking about the potential of the child:

- the animistic state of the young child's mind, in which everything is alive, enchanted and endowed with meaning;
- the multidimensional nature of the human being, and the many "layers" of the body/mind;
- the nature of the individual human as deeply interconnected with everything else, and the importance of cultivating "relational thinking"; and
- the need for balanced development of extroversial knowledge (learning how the world works) and introversial knowledge (learning about one's inner life).

If we apply these principles to literacy development, then we can begin to understand the limitations of the "blank slate and social realism" theory of learning. What if we turned conventional wisdom on its head, and moved instead from the whole to the part, recognizing that children live in a world permeated by feeling, that everything they encounter from the sweet smelling rose to the complicated grasshopper is endowed with meaning and purpose, that they are intensely interested in big ideas (good and evil, life and death, abandonment, monsters, rewards and punishments, justice, magic, mystery and love) and that their minds are not blank slates, but rather repositories of ancient archetypes and ancestral memory?

Fantasy and Fairy Tale

> *The wonder is that the characteristic efficacy to touch and inspire deep creative centers dwells in the smallest nursery tale—as the flavor of the ocean is contained in a droplet or the whole mystery of life within the egg of a flea.*
> —Joseph Campbell, *The Hero With a Thousand Faces*, 1949

Recent research on fairy tales suggests that the narratives we usually think of as arising in 1500s Europe may actually date back thousands of years to our prehistorical past. Researchers using strategies developed by evolutionary biologists have traced the roots of 275 fairy tales through complex trees of language, population, and culture (Blakemore, 2016). Is it any wonder that children are immediately captivated when we gather them into a circle, and whisper "Once upon a time, in a faraway land..."?

According to philosopher Douglas Sloan (1983),

> Because fairy tales are based on a time tested primeval human wisdom, there is in them a depth and substance, layers of meaning upon meanings, which cannot be exhausted by neat explanations, and which can continue to light up in the understanding even into adulthood and old age. (p. 228)

Sloan goes on to say that much of the contemporary reading fare in classrooms, designed to bring children with all due haste into the grown-up (disenchanted) world, and "often itself presented as a scrubbed, smiling, and utterly monotonous world" (p. 229) seems trivial.

Bruno Bettleheim (1903–1990), a controversial thinker whose work focused on emotionally disturbed children, claimed that traditional folk and fairy tales, with their intense themes of abandonment, curses, evil witches, trolls, giants, and miraculous transformations allow children to grapple with their very real fears in symbolic ways, aiding their emotional growth and health (Bettleheim, 1975/2010). Often tales contain tests, trials, and tribulations that mirror the human experience, helping children to internalize ideas of morality, justice, faith and loyalty long before such abstractions could be grasped. Fairy tales have perhaps rightly been criticized for their excessive cruelty, violence, and stereotypical gender representations. But in virtually all such tales, good wins over evil in the end, and benign powers triumph over cruelty, bloodlust, cunning, and flattery. Fairy tales reduce the structures of the human psyche to their rawest form. Other forms of tales, like fables, myths, and legends, also deal with universal themes, usually in the context of a particular culture, but fairy tales, in their elementals, appeal most strongly to the young child. Shrii Sarkar (1957) appreciates the timeless value of fairy tales: "The thirst for the distant, and the earnest zeal to know the unknown that abides in the child's mind must be fulfilled by drawing pictures of magical lands and relating colourful [*sic*] fairy tales" (para. 108). Neohumanist educators need to become cultural archaeologists, digging deep to uncover the tales that embody the ancient wisdom of the culture in which they teach, studying the archetypal forms that mythic characters have assumed, and learning to narrate the cultural story. In these ways, we can connect young children with their ancestral heritage and provide them with rich opportunities to engage with the inner fears and conflicts of childhood. We can strengthen their powers of visualization and conceptualization, and generate a rich bank of symbols and metaphors for them to draw upon in their creative work.

Stories and Enactment

In our current world, governed by modernist customs and a capitalist economy, the arts are set apart from life, and primarily act as commodified vehicles for individual expression and celebrity-making, and as a means for status expression. But the arts serve much older imperatives than this. As art theorist Ellen Dissanayake (1992) notes, "homo-aestheticus" is a far more ancient species than "homo-economicus." In her important cross cultural, historical study of the role of art in human experience, she notes that the arts—encompassing a broad range of visual art, sculpture and modeling, decoration, singing, poetry, music making, drama, puppetry, and more—have stayed with humans for millennia because they serve the important purpose of making the ordinary *extra-ordinary*—what she calls making special. The arts appeal to multiple cognitive necessities: the needs for pattern making, for order, for clarity, balance, proportion, and continuity. Even more important, she claims, is that the arts *feel good*—they are pleasurable, appealing to our senses and our emotions. She concludes that human beings have a universal, biologically based need for art (1992; 1988). From this evolutionary perspective, art is something humans do *because it helps them to survive.*

Consider the early connections between art, story, ritual, and ceremony in many societies, as well as contemporary artistic expressions in cultures such as those of the Southwestern Hopi Indian or traditional Balinese, which have not yet lost their time-honored bonds to the biotic community. The role of participatory aesthetic ritual in such cultures is multi-faceted: Stories embedded in rituals affirm life processes and re-inscribe positive social values; confirm the human interdependence with the surrounding natural world; unify the social order; facilitate individual and communal healing; and mark transitions (rites of passage). Perhaps most important for understanding the evolutionary purposes of art, aesthetic rituals nourish the capacity *to experience transformative or transcendent emotional states and extraordinary states of consciousness* (Dissanayake, 1988).

This last point, the awakening of the spirit and higher levels of mind, should make it clear why the arts play such an important role in neohumanist pedagogy. The arts embody "multiple literacies"—visual—musical—social—emotional—linguistic—kinesthetic—literacies. Separate but distinct, these pedagogical multiplicities, applied in integrated ways, can amplify and enhance learning in any modality. Neohumanist educators need to expand their repertoire of "intelligences" and seek out the numerous creative opportunities that present themselves in the classroom.

Enactment is how we create and recreate the fundamental *stories* of our human existence. Enactment can involve drama, song, expressive movement, or ceremony—constructed actions that arise from more fundamental human activities. The Japanese Tea Ceremony is an example of a highly ritualized enactment that elaborates on a fundamental human activity. The Sacred Corn Dance of southwestern Pueblo Indians celebrates the seasonal renewal of life, fertility and the magic of birth and growth. In Thailand, many people honor the Water Goddess and the Buddha in a festival called Loy Kratong by floating lighted baskets and lanterns on the water; in this enactment they give thanks for their use of water and apologize for polluting the waters. Many Waldorf schools hold seasonal enactments that celebrate traditional religious holidays or natural events, such as the arrival of summer on May Day. Enactment, in this sense, is not a spectator sport. It is a participatory event, requiring embodied involvement in a shared, communal expression.

Enactment, in all of its various forms, is both the base and the core of literacy instruction in neohumanist schools. Central to neohumanist educational philosophy is the idea of cultivating a deep love for all living beings. This relational dimension is unlikely to flourish in an educational environment in which language is divorced from its meaning-making capacities. It is important to recognize the profound rupture that occurs when the spontaneous participation of children in their "synaesthetic encounter with animals, plants, and streams" (Abram, 1996, p. 131) is refocused to symbols on a flat page. When inert letters on a page begin to speak to us, says Abram (1996), "the stones fall silent... the trees become mute, the other animals dumb" (p. 131). Text-based reading and writing are indeed vital ways of learning about the world, but in the early years, and continuing on up through the grades, language needs to be given expression in multiple creative ways, thus becoming a *living thing*, rather than mere marks on a page. As language becomes a living thing, so the world is animated. The Earth begins to breathe, and if we listen carefully, attune to the more subtle energies of the living world, we might begin to comprehend the speech of the more-than-human-others: the call of the crow and perhaps even the electric waves of vibration amongst the chattering mycelium, the songs that connect the trees of the forest at their most elemental level. As David Abram says so eloquently: "Only if words are felt, bodily presences, like echoes or waterfalls, can we understand the power of spoken language to influence, alter, or transform the perceptual world" (p. 88).

Our literacy challenge, then, is that we need to slough off the logo-centered biases of our modern worldview, and then reconstruct and reintegrate the positive aspects of this tradition with the folk cultures and wisdom traditions of the world that have sustained a reciprocal relationship with the many other-than-human species with whom we share the planet. We need to cultivate ways of knowing and being that respect the texture and immediacy of reality as well as the power and elegance of abstract thought. We need to create meaningful stories and rituals of enactment for (modern) people who have lost their deep sensory engagement with the natural world, and who see decontextualized bits of information as the central road to truth and wisdom (Kesson & Oliver, 2002). There are many ways to engage young people creatively in enacting the stories of their lives, and in the process making language come alive in ways that invigorate personality development, foster emotional and social intelligence, and develop creative and original thinking. These will be explored further in upcoming chapters on creative movement and creative drama.

Thoughts on Literacy and Pseudo-Culture

Shrii Sarkar (1982, p. 55) cautioned against the imposition of "pseudo-culture"—roughly translated this implies false culture. This is related (but not identical) to Freire's concept of *false consciousness*, in which oppressed people come to feel they have no opinions of value and little self-worth (O'Conner, 2015). Neohumanist educator Arun Jacobson (2012) identifies three related reasons why many modern aesthetic expressions fall into this category:

- The priority of corporate culture is to make money; the long term effects on a child's psychology is not a determining factor in what (movies, books, songs) gets chosen for sale and distribution.
- The tendency towards instant gratification and simple instinct are powerful dynamics; psychic movement towards subtle ideas and states of consciousness requires more purposefulness.
- Artists of great subtlety of ideation and expression have trouble surviving economically in late capitalist, corporate culture. Therefore culture building is too much in the hands of people who lack insight and vision.

Determining what is and what is not pseudo-culture is very tricky. There are elements of taste involved, elements of social class, and tendencies towards unwarranted bias and racism. One is likely to see one's own favored cultural expressions as "true" and others as "false." Sometimes pseudo-culture is glaringly obvious. Once I visited a school in India in a small rural village. There was a nicely constructed educational compound built in a circle. Around the school on every wall was a mural based on Disney fantasies, populated with pale skinned, blonde Snow Whites and Sleeping Beauties. This seemed to me one of the most egregious impacts of pseudo-culture—the imposition of inappropriate (and foreign) standards of beauty and femininity likely to create feelings of inferiority in the young girls of the school. Given that India has an extraordinarily rich cultural bank of mythic images and folklore to choose from, the imposition of Disney ideals in the aesthetic of the school was clearly a lingering effect of colonialism.

Tang Taminga (2013), a neohumanist educator in Taiwan, decries the "Disney-ized" fairy tales that have overtaken the shaping of Chinese children's imaginations, and advocates for the primacy of stories from the local culture in the education of children: "Only these tales offer the child the imagery that can help them not only learn the psychology and values of the culture of the land, but also the spiritual wisdom" (para. 1). Chinese tales, he says, "teach children their place in the cosmos and how all life forms are interconnected" (para. 3) and help them to discover deeper dimensions of the self.

Pseudo-culture is deeply connected to issues of colonization and economic imperialism; all culture has political dimensions. As noted in Chapter 7, politicians, unduly influenced by fundamentalist religious groups in the United States are attempting to ban hundreds of books written for children and young adults. Many of these include issues relevant to LGBTQ (lesbian, gay, bi-sexual, transgender, questioning) youth and many of them are written by people of color and deal with issues of racism and equity. The groups sponsoring the bans claim that the books are subversive, immoral, and threaten the "American way of life." But there is clearly a political agenda here, one group of people deciding what is true culture and what is false based on their own prejudices.

Given the complexity of the issue, how should neohumanist educators approach the role of deciding what is and what is not true or false culture? Are there objective standards that can be applied? In his article, Jacobson asserts that banning media or technology, or yearning nostalgically for some presumed "true" cultural past are both counterproductive. Rather, he says, neohumanist schools should hire the most thoughtful and talented literature and arts teachers and charge them with the task of sifting the wheat from the chaff in local, regional, national and global expressions of culture, and working collaboratively with other teachers to replace pseudo-culture (which most children will have had vast exposure to) with meaningful aesthetic activity that aims to foster cultural integrity and empowerment, self-realization and universal love. This is a very large task, one that will require in-depth discussions among faculty and families.

Throughout these chapters, we have iterated the core principles of neohumanist education, which can here be rephrased as questions: Does this literacy/aesthetic experience express the essential interconnectedness of people with all of creation, expanding the heart to embrace all species? Does it cultivate a deep ecological sensibility, with an emphasis on caring for land, water, plants, and animals? Does it value the specifics of culture and place? And perhaps of most importance, does it connect genuinely with the needs and interests of the children?

Literacy Pedagogy in the Early Years

All of this is well and good, you say. Now I understand the importance of immersing young people in rich language environments. I perceive how pseudo-culture operates. I appreciate the importance of putting local language and culture at the center of learning. And I see the value of infusing language with vitality. But what about the ABC's? How should neohumanist educators address the nuts and bolts of reading and writing?

The Reading Wars

Whole language? Phonics? Phonemic awareness? Word recognition? Vocabulary lists? Spelling tests? Context clues? Direct instruction? Informal acquisition of skills? Fluency? Comprehension? Drop everything and read? Throughout much of the past century and on into this one, battles have raged over the best method to teach reading. Should the child be immersed in a fertile language environment alive with stories, play, and drama? Or should they have a structured, workbook-based program that leads them step by step into the process of reading?

In much of the Western world, the structured approach was dominant until the 1980s when a teacher-led movement called *whole language* began to move the field toward more meaning-centered pedagogy. The phrase whole language became common currency in educational conversations. Whole language approaches do not disregard the teaching of discrete literacy skills such as phonics, spelling, or capitalization; the difference is that skills are embedded in much larger contexts of meaning. It is only recently (in the 2000s) with additional research on the increasing numbers of children who come to school not knowing English, or who struggle with dyslexia or other inhibiting conditions, that the argument has begun to refocus on structured approaches.

Conventional education has pushed the expectations for reading readiness lower and lower. Kindergarten used to be a haven for children to learn social skills, explore the world through play-based activities, and get acquainted with printed language in pleasurable ways. That is no longer the case, and now children are expected to leave kindergarten as readers. If they fail at this, there is "reading recovery" in the first grade. Teachers feel a great deal of pressure to teach and test academic skills, to prepare children for the next stage, rather than honoring their developmental needs. Research from the neurosciences confirms that while children's brains are plastic and capable of rapid growth and development, there is wide variation in brain development related to reading readiness. Several studies document the negative effects of forcing reading instruction prematurely on children who are not yet developmentally equipped to handle the academic pressure of such early expectations (Shepard & Smith, 1988).

Alternative, holistic schools often have a more relaxed approach to academic instruction. Waldorf schools, for example, do not even allow the teaching of reading until the "change of teeth" (at around the age of seven). There is much to be learned from studying the methods of Waldorf and other holistic educators in literacy pedagogy; more important, however, than any "rule" about when to commence formal reading instruction, is the cultivation of an *inquiry stance* in neohumanist educators, so that teachers might make informed judgments about their teaching based on careful observation of individual children (see Chapter 6 in this volume: "Contemplative Inquiry: The Art of Knowing the Child").

The transition from immersion in the sensory world to the world of abstract signs is a major event in the life of a child (earlier in this chapter, we call it a "rupture"), and should be approached with the reverence it deserves. The origins of alphabets lie in pre-history, with pictorial representations of plants, animals, serpents, and events in the lives of people. David Abram (1996) reminds us that "the glyphs which constitute the bulk of these ancient scripts continually remind the reading body of its inherence in a more-than-human field of meanings...they continually refer to our senses beyond the strictly human sphere" (p. 97). A child's first relationship with symbolic meaning making is pictorial. Just as "babbling" is a precursor to speech, young children will begin to scribble on paper with crayons, experimenting with lines and creating increasingly recognizable shapes. They may begin to name their scribbles (Mommy, Sun, Dog), thus demonstrating an emergent understanding of the relationship between symbols on a page and the world of objects. Children will often engage in storymaking while they draw, an important stage in the development of written literacy. The more opportunities a young child has for making art (and for talking), the easier it will be to acquire reading and writing proficiency.

Volumes have been written about the fascinating development of children's art, and we have more to say about this in Chapter 11 ("Visual Art and Emergence: Bringing Worlds Into Being"); suffice it to say, for our purposes, that these early scribbles are a child's first attempt to use symbols to communicate an idea. Of such scribbles are composed the basic alphabetical forms. Many parents and teachers believe that learning the alphabet is the most important aspect of reading readiness. People are overjoyed when a child comes home singing the alphabet song. But learning the names of the letters is not the most important literacy skill. Deep acquaintance with the many and various sounds the letters make is even more important. However, the ways in which letter names and sounds are introduced to the child largely determines if reading will be a dull affair or if it will awaken the personality, stimulate the layers of the mind (the koshas), and deepen the sensorial engagement with the external world.

Waldorf educators have developed specific pedagogical strategies for maintaining a strong connection between the world of objects, the world of speech, the world of pictures, and the world of alphabetical symbols. The alphabet is introduced in an imaginative pictorial way in a context of storymaking. Children might be introduced to the letter M, for example, when a character in a story has to climb a *mountain*, or to the letter K depicting a *king* with a raised sword. For the neohumanist educator, this pictorial approach is ripe with creative potential.

Just one example is the making of a story wall, a long sheet of newsprint the size of a classroom mural. Each day, when the class takes their walk, teachers can collect a list of natural objects the children observe and can name (bee, rock, ant, etc.). Back in the classroom, the teacher can depict an image of a chosen noun, with its beginning sound written next to it, and/or the name of the object. To develop the understanding of interconnection, objects should be depicted in relationship with other objects. Perhaps the children notice ants crawling into a hole into the ground—the drawing should then represent the tunnels made by the ants underground. A bee should be depicted nosing its way into a colorful flower. These kinds of illustrations can stimulate ongoing conversations about how objects in the world interact with each other, and stimulate interest in books about the creatures.

The children can also duplicate each letter and its relationships in their own notebooks, thus creating their own alphabet textbooks. The story wall can become an increasingly complex text, inviting new objects and characters, and encouraging the children to make up stories about the images. Compare this to the usual factory made alphabet strip, with the predictable "A is for apple" in a linear strip around the room above the blackboard. The story wall is made by the children and the teacher and grows out of real life experiences, it is embedded in the surrounding environment, it contains an ever growing scene of storymaking possibilities, and it keeps alive the connections between experience, objects, pictures, and the alphabet. When letters and words are taught pictorially, the child develops the capacity to visualize, a skill that is essential to achieving later reading comprehension. The ability to create moving pictures in the mind as one reads enhances involvement with text and encourages meaning-making.

In Chapter 13, "Neohumanist Education and the Lively Arts: Integrating Creative Movement Across the Curriculum," we note the importance of linking the awareness of sound and form with kinesthetic movement and actual speech. Too many literacy lessons see children hunched over their desks, pencils gripped, facial muscles tense, as they are obliged to write, erase, rewrite, and edit their emergent stories. A skilled creative movement teacher understands that language must be enacted in vibrant and imaginative ways in order to be integrated with the will and creative power of the child. Letter sounds stimulate certain kinds of movement: the Ah of a short "a" sound is an opening upwards; the hard sound of a "d" might result in stamping. Movement is linked to verbs in the kinesthetic classroom: jumping, twirling, tiptoeing, reaching. Vocabulary is built and internalized as movements are made to new words: whisk, seethe, bubble, collapse. Prepositions are taught as children build bridges and go over, under, and around structures. Obstacles are encountered and strategies developed for getting through a narrow tunnel, crawling over a fallen oak tree. Emotions are linked to words through movement, as outlets are provided to express joy, anger, fear, strength. Muscle and mind develop in sync with each other.

Art forms such as creative dramatics and creative movement will be elaborated upon in future sections of this topic of the arts-based curriculum. Once a teacher's creative impulses are awakened, many opportunities for games and dramatic activities that enliven literacy instruction will present themselves.

So who has won the reading wars? It seems almost magical the way many children absorb the complexities of syntax, tense, and semantics merely by participation in a robust linguistic atmosphere. Children who have the benefit of a rich language environment such as what we have described, who have been told stories and read to, who have drawn and painted and danced their way into language, often learn to read seemingly effortlessly, on their own timetable. This is especially true of children who come from language rich homes, where many in-depth conversations happen over the dinner table, where they enjoy regular story time before bed, and where they are surrounded by books. All this can be considered the "cultural capital" of readers.

Not all children come from such environments, and for various reasons (lack of fluency in the primary language of the school, neurological damage, trauma, or what is now referred to as "neurodiversity") do not make the transition to reading easily. These children may need a more structured and systematic approach, such as the Wilson Language Training or the Orton-Gillingham approach, which is especially designed for children struggling with dyslexia. The best of these approaches do insist on being combined with a literature-based language arts program for best effects. What is most important is that the teacher not rely rigidly on one particular method, but have at their disposal numerous tools to meet the many and varied needs that children present.

Literacy Assessment and Evaluation

The last few decades in the Western world have brought an obsession with standardized testing in literacy. The results have often been counterproductive to the implementation of excellent literacy programs, as preparing for and taking standardized tests uses up an enormous amount of time that could otherwise be devoted to quality learning. Standardized language exams often focus on discrete skills (like phonemic awareness) that do not occur in a meaningful context. Instructions to children are often confusing. They do not allow for personal (or cultural) interpretations of questions, and thus generate "wrong" answers. They do not account for language differences among socio-cultural groups, nor do they consider the wide differences in social capital among children. Many tests are timed, and thus exert undue pressure on young people, many of whom suffer from test anxiety. Applying a single number, or measure, to a child has resulted in lowered self-esteem for thousands of children who begin to think they are simply not competent readers.

All this, and multiple studies fail to show improvement in literacy since the advent of the tests. Test results that might actually help teachers revise their instruction are generally not available at the individual or classroom level. The "achievement gap" between rich and poor children has not decreased. Scores on international tests have not risen. The only beneficiaries of the standardized testing movement have been the testing corporations, who rake in billions of dollars from their tests and their test preparation materials (Kohn, 2000).

Evaluation and assessment are one of the most difficult areas of teaching. We know that appropriate feedback on our work is the best way to improve. *Authentic assessment* is an educational movement that provides a counterpoint to standardized testing. Authentic assessment is a daily, ongoing process that asks the teacher to collect, record, interpret and analyze multiple sources of data: data from observations, anecdotal records, interviews, conferences, learning logs, and running records. Unlike in standardized exams, where the test items often have nothing to do with what the children have learned, authentic assessment is embedded in the content and activity of the literacy classroom. In order to use these informal processes well, teachers need a thorough knowledge of child development and language acquisition, they need to be clear about their beliefs and values about children's learning, and they need to be flexible and experimental in their approach.

Students should have multiple and self-directed ways to express what they know and can do: exhibitions, conversations, performances, and portfolios. Self-assessment and learning to edit and revise one's own work are key elements in becoming proficient readers and writers, so these process skills need to be built into the curriculum. A major aim of instruction should be the development of students who can talk about their own learning processes, reflect on strategies that they have tried, note their own progress, and set new goals.

Neohumanist educators need to become skilled observers of student growth and progress and cultivate the art of constructive criticism, always mindful that kindness and compassion and a genuine concern for the welfare and progress of the student should be at the heart of any feedback. The issues of assessment and evaluation are complex, and involve a major commitment when moving from an exam-based educational culture to one of authentic learning and assessment. It is important to consult the excellent literature that is available to guide this process (see, e.g., Hart, 1994; Perrone, 1991; Routman, 1994).

Literacy and the Cultivation of Critical Thinking

As children master the primary tasks of cracking the letter-sound code of written symbols and putting together sounds to make words, and then recognize more and more words instantly, reading fluency and understanding what they read becomes of prime importance. Recall the introduction to this chapter, and the statement that education is never a neutral process, rather it serves one of two purposes: it either facilitates the integration of people into the logic of the existing system or it becomes, as the well-known literacy educator Paulo Freire (1970) noted, the practice of freedom. As children advance through the grades and become accomplished readers, neohumanist educators must assist them in not merely reading the *word*, but in reading the *world*.

This has become an increasingly difficult task, given the prevalence of social media. Young people today swim in a sea of contradictory messages and media noise, engulfed in a hundred shades of truth and misinformation in online spaces with little or no curation. Critical media literacy is an educational response that expands the notion of literacy to include different forms of mass communication, popular culture, and new technologies. It is designed to teach young people to think critically about texts (writ broadly) and analyze the connections between media, information, power, and audiences. Critical media literacy can help them develop the skills that are necessary to untangle the miasma of conflicting and misleading information and learn to participate in an informed way in a democracy. It can foster the practice of freedom.

Critical literacy extends, to a greater and greater degree, into all subject matter. In math classes, young people can be taught how the manipulation of math facts can lead to faulty inferences. In health classes, students can be taught to look objectively at the information about timely issues like vaccines, and determine who is propagating what information and to what ends. In science, they can be aided in understanding the economic and political interests behind climate denial "research." In social studies classes, they can study media representations of gender, social class, sexuality and race in order to better understand how biases are formed. And in English language arts, the study of argument, persuasion and propaganda could again assume a primary role (as it once had in the United States), in terms of developing a democratically inclined citizenry. Critical media literacy combined with support for an idealistic vision of how to create a better world can help young people develop the skills to do their part to bring about a more just and sustainable society. In these ways, neohumanist educators can foster what Sarkar (1998, p. 123) terms the "awakened conscience," or "rationalistic mentality" that will enable them to reject all limiting sentiments on the road to the liberation of intellect. We summarize below some principles that can guide neohumanist teachers in their efforts to foster this liberatory intellect.

Principles of a Neohumanist Approach to Literacy

- Neohumanist educators need to recognize that children enter school with much knowledge about literacy, just from hearing people talk and learning to speak in a cultural environment. Literacy acquisition should be seen as a natural extension of this learning.
- The child has many "funds of knowledge" gained from their interactions in home and village. These ways of knowing need to be honored in literacy instruction.
- Instruction should occur in the children's native language; when appropriate a lingua franca should be taught.
- Neohumanist educators need to be familiar with the literature on bi-literacy, multi-literacy, second language teaching, and trans-languaging (learning to move fluidly between languages).

- Reading and writing should be taught only when informed observations indicate a child's readiness and interest.
- Literacy development should draw its inspiration, motifs, and themes from the lifeworlds of the students.
- Neohumanist educators need to have a great variety of literacy instructional tools in their toolkit, to be applied when their professional judgment indicates the needs of a group or individual.
- Literacy instruction should be enlivened through the liberal use of the arts: poetry, storytelling, puppetry, sculpting, creative movement and drama, visual art.
- Academic literacy skills should be practiced through games, rhymes, and other pleasurable activities.
- Oral literacy is an essential aspect of language development. A classroom should provide many opportunities for children to talk (sharing experiences, making observations, speculating, making inferences) in front of a large group, in pairs, and in small groups.
- Students should never be shamed or humiliated, as so often happens when struggling children are forced to read aloud.
- Neohumanist teachers should maintain a playful approach towards language, demonstrating for example, the humor in rhymes, or the delight in playing a character from a story.
- There should be multiple informal opportunities for writing in the classroom: letters, lists, journal writing, note-taking, brainstorming, and so on.
- Authentic assessment should highlight strengths the students exhibit, not merely weaknesses or deficiencies. Criticism should always be offered in a spirit of kindness and consideration for the welfare of the child's sense of self as well as their academic proficiency.
- Literacy should be considered a vital aspect of all subject areas.
- Children's creativity should be fostered from the earliest stages of literacy, for example in the making and "publishing" of their own books.
- In a neohumanist classroom, cooperative groups should not be formed on the basis of ability, though ad hoc groups can be pulled together for specific instructional purposes.

We close this chapter with a quote by P. R. Sarkar that illuminates both the importance and the limitations of literacy, and reminds us of the ultimate neohumanist educational aims of human development, the social aim of democratic culture building, and self-realization:

> Education does not only mean literacy or alphabetical knowledge... real education means proper, adequate knowledge and the power of understanding. In other words, education should impart an understanding of *who I am and what I ought to do*. Full knowledge of these things is what education means. (2018, p. 244)

This quote takes us back to earlier chapters, and highlights a fundamental aim of neohumanist education: to aid the young person in the construction of their identity, and provide many opportunities for them to find meaning and purpose in life and learning. It is a reminder that the liberation of intellect is, in very practical terms, the practice of freedom.

FOR CONTINUING STUDY

Discussion/Reflection: What do you remember about learning to read? Do you know what "method" was used to teach you? Describe what made it easy or hard for you.

Discussion/Reflection: Brainstorm as many imaginative ways as you can to link ecological learning with literacy learning.

Application: Review a popular children's picture book. How does the author make the story come alive? Do you detect any literary tools (repetition, similes, metaphors, alliteration, rhyme, personification)? What devices does the author use to keep the reader turning the page? What traits do the characters have? Is there a problem that gets resolved? Is there a "moral" to the story?

Application: Time to let *your* creative juices flow! Write a short children's story for a specified age range. Think carefully about character, plot, setting, and what neohumanist principle you hope to convey, as well as some of the literary points above.

References

Abram, D. (1996). *The spell of the sensuous*. Vintage Books.

Bettleheim, B. (2010). *The uses of enchantment: The meaning and importance of fairy tales*. Vintage Books. (Original work published 1975)

Blakemore, E. (2016). *Fairy takes could be older than you ever imagined*. https://www.smithsonianmag.com/smithsonianmag/fairy-tales-could-be-older-ever-imagined-180957882/

Bowers, C. A. (2014). *The digital revolution and the unrecognized problem of linguistic colonization*. https://cabowers.net/pdf/The_Digital_Revolution_and_the_Unrecognized_Problem.pdf

Cámara-Leret, R., & Bascompte, J. (2021). *Language extinction triggers the loss of unique medicinal knowledge*. Proceedings of the National Academy of Sciences. https://www.pnas.org/content/118/24/e2103683118

Dissanayake, E. (1988). *What is art for?* University of Washington Press.
Dissanayake, E. (1992). *Homoaestheticus: Where art comes from and why*. The Free Press.
Egan, K. (1986). *Teaching as storytelling: An alternative approach to teaching and curriculum in the elementary school*. The University of Chicago Press.
Freire, P. (1970). *Pedagogy of the oppressed*. Continuum.
Hart, D. (1994). *Authentic assessment: A handbook for educators*. Addison-Wesley Publishing.
Jacobson, A. (2012, November). Pseudo-culture vs. true human culture. *Gurukula Network*, 35. https://gurukul.edu/newsletter/issue-35/gems-of-neohumanism/
Kelly, L. (2017). *The memory code: Unlocking the secrets of the lives of the ancients and the power of the human mind*. Atlantic Books.
Kesson, K., & Oliver, D. (2002). On the need for a conceptualized theory of experience. In W. Doll & N. Gough (Eds.), *Curriculum visions* (pp. 185–197). Peter Lang.
Kimmerer, R. W. (2013). *Braiding sweetgrass: Indigenous wisdom, scientific knowledge, and the teachings of plants*. Milkweed Editions.
Kohn, A. (2000). *The case against standardized testing: Raising the scores, ruining the schools*. Heinemann.
Kolbert, E. (2015). *The sixth extinction: An unnatural history*. Picador.
O'Conner, C. (2015, October 26). *The continued relevance of Freire's pedagogy of the oppressed*. British Educational Research Association. https://www.bera.ac.uk/blog/the-continued-relevance-of-freires-pedagogy-of-the-oppressed
Perrone, V. (Ed.). (1991). *Expanding student assessment*. The Association for Supervision and Curriculum Development.
Routman, R. (1994). *Invitations: Changing as teachers and learners K–12*. Heinemann.
Sarkar, P. R. (1957). The practice of art and literature. In *Discourses on Neohumanist Education* (2nd ed.). Electronic edition of the works of P. R. Sarkar, version 9.0.
Sarkar, P. R. (1982). *The liberation of intellect: Neo-humanism*. Ananda Marga Pracaraka Samgha.
Sarkar, P. R. (1998). *Discourses on neohumanist education*. Ananda Marga Pracaraka Samgha.
Sarkar, P. R. (2018). *An outline of Prout*. Ananda Marga Pracaraka Samgha.
Shepard, L. A., & Smith, M. L. (1988, November). Escalating academic demand in kindergarten: Counterproductive policies. *The Elementary School Journal*, *89*(2). https://doi.org/10.1086/461568
Sloan, D. (1983). *Insight-imagination: The emancipation of thought and the modern world*. Greenwood Press.
Taminga, T. (2013, November). Local story traditions in schools. *Gurukula Network*, 37.

11

Visual Art and Emergence

Bringing Worlds Into Being

with Alieta Belle and Leeza Stratford

> *The artistic process ... is the chance to encounter dimensions of our inner being and to discover deep, rewarding patterns of meaning.*
> —Peter London, *No More Secondhand Art*, 1987

The River School near Maleny, Queensland (AUS) began its life in the 1980s as part of a community housing cooperative on 52 acres in a beautiful rainforest. The school now serves over 200 children and their families, and is recognized globally as an exemplary neohumanist school. With a core focus on educating the whole child, River School offers an inquiry approach to learning, daily Yoga and meditation, and a curriculum strongly oriented around arts and the environment, often as wholly integrated subject matter. This chapter will tell a bit of the story of the River School in order to create a dynamic picture of the role of the visual arts in neohumanist education.

As well as infusing art across core subjects in order to create enjoyable ways to learn, students at the River School each have a weekly art lesson in a dedicated arts space called the Art Shed. This space is an *open studio*—welcoming, filled with light and abounding with aesthetic possibility. Shelves filled with donated art materials, natural fibers from the local environment, and recycled materials line the walls, and student artworks fill the spare spaces. Alieta Belle has been the art teacher at the River School for the past 10 years. She is a passionate advocate for the arts, and a gifted mentor to the students who enter her Art Shed. We share here a bit of her personal story about how she approaches the teaching of visual art.

* * *

I start each art session with the students and I sitting around a circle mat, allowing us all to become fully present in time and space, let go of any worries or stresses, and connect with each other. I introduce the basic artmaking focus and materials, often with a simple demonstration. I ensure there is always choice with artmaking activities and materials. A strong emphasis is placed on students being exposed to and experimenting with different art processes and techniques and exploring different materials, and for students to find resonance and expression with these.

I see myself as a facilitator of the arts space. I believe in the power of art to balance and support students deeply, and I believe in the inherent and unique creativity (life force) in all students. And so, I see my role to connect students with arts experiences and to connect students with the well of creativity and expression that dwells within themselves, by simply providing the space and provocation for creativity to happen. My skill as an arts teacher is to hold space for the magic to happen, to trust in the process of artmaking and the knowing hands of the artmaker, suggest materials to students, be curious about what students are making, and provide space for students to communicate nonverbally through the language of arts, in order for what they are processing or experiencing to find form and become visible through art-making.

I have observed over 10 years in the Art Shed working with children the transformative power of gifting children space to make art that is initiated by them. Preserving/reserving space in childhood to make art without being directed is a powerful thing. We are teaching students that creativity is within them, and they have access to it as a resource and a support for life. Artmaking brings feelings of joy, wellness, and connection, and can help children bring self-awareness and to transform difficult emotions.

From the place of showing students that they have permission to create and are safe to express themselves, students engage in the process of artmaking in an open studio environment. There are a range of materials on shelves students can choose from. Students can act on an idea they have and see it come into physical form, they can engage art in a sensory way, processing known and unknown feelings, they can work collaboratively with others. What is gained is far greater than a pretty end product (which can also be an outcome). What is developed is student access to self-expression, self-reflection, emotional regulation, curiosity, agency, self-awareness, joy, creative thinking, problem solving, development of symbolic language, flexibility, confidence, wellness...the list goes on. Fortunately, this is no longer only an opinion of arts advocates. The new science of neuroaesthetics, sometimes called NeuroArts, which has brought together research from "neuroscience, cognitive science, the arts, neurology, public health, psychology, and many other disciplines to create a highly interdisciplinary field" (Magsamen & Ross, 2023a) is bringing scientific evidence to us of the remarkable physical, emotional, and mental transformations towards well-being that happen when we participate in the arts—and how this knowledge can improve our health, enable us to flourish, and build stronger communities. Neuroscience research in the arts is confirming that artmaking is an essential need of humans (Magsamen & Ross, 2013b; Zaidel, 2010).

The children's art does not have to look good to the adult. Yes, we can teach students specific skills with different art mediums, and this can be inspiring for students as starting points, but tapping into the power of ART is bigger than skills development. While students love to experiment with new art techniques, it is important to de-emphasize the skill, or technique, as a vital component of artmaking. There is no right or wrong with artmaking, nor should adult judgment inhibit creativity. All children can make art and they innovate all of the time. This needs to be remembered by the educator. The neohumanist educator needs to keep in focus the bigger outcomes of artmaking—one of these being connection to the inner self and feelings of well-being when artmaking. It is essential that students are given space to freely create, and this is balanced with introducing new materials and techniques in a scaffolded way. Art is a language.

* * *

To pick up on Alieta's point, art, like verbal and written linguistic expression, is a language, with symbols and meanings, and its making of visual two-or-three-dimensional signs to communicate. If meanings are perhaps more ambiguous in art, or lend themselves to wider interpretation, the main idea is that it is the elements of art and the principles of design that work together to form communicative meaning, just as it is phonemes and words and sentences that construct meaning in oral and written language. In this chapter, we explore some of these basic elements of art and the related vocabulary, in order to broaden the pedagogical possibilities for teachers, and to introduce more supportive ways of talking about art with young people. We look at art and development, and explore what we can learn about young people from observing them at work making art. We then explore the relationship between spirituality and art, a topic that has not received the attention it deserves. And finally, we return to a narrative about the River School, and their insightful approach to helping children to develop the love for all creation that is essential to neohumanism.

Visual art is an umbrella term for drawing, painting, sculpture, ceramics, design, photography, video and film—constructs that generally involve *seeing* as a primary perceptual activity. Elliot Eisner (2002), a leading theorist of arts and education, notes that the "arts help us learn to notice the world... art provides the conditions for awakening to the world around us" (p. 10). To truly *see*, says Frederick Franck (1993), "is that specifically human capacity that opens one up to empathy, to compassion with all that lives and dies" (p. 39). Besides bringing the "outside" into consciousness, the arts also bring the "inside" out, allowing the imagination to generate images from the psyche, "the bringing of thought to life, permeating concepts and abstractions with life-giving images and inner energies though which thinking can penetrate and participate in the fullness of reality" (Sloan, 1983, p. 192).

Much of our thinking and feeling is based upon the visual images that we take in from the world outside ourselves or from images constructed from information given (e.g., "The color orange is somewhere between red and yellow"). Mental images become bridges between external objects and events and internal symbolic representations (such as language) and imagination. Vision is our primary tool (for those people who have sight) for making sense of the world and the processing center in the human brain for vision is the largest and most complex of all the senses.

Image-making is a sensory experience; in its *receptive* stage, light rays emanating from objects enter the cornea of the eye, are directed towards the pupil and the iris, to the lens, and are transformed by the retina at the back of the eye into electrical signals which are then transmitted to the primary visual cortex via the optic nerve. The brain decodes these electrical impulses, forming visual maps. This mental perception interacts with a neural network that connects information from various other parts of the brain: earlier images, information from other senses, language, and feelings connected to past experiences. *Transformation* occurs; we are able to imagine new images, see things from different perspectives, or think of new ideas. And in its *productive* stage, the artist, or maker, then converts the contents of consciousness into form, using materials (stone, clay, paper, paint). What was a privately held image in the individual brain becomes a public image, thus becoming an act of communication. In such ways, imagination serves to create possible futures, to share images of what might be, realities that could be created. In this way, the making of visual art can serve the cosmic purposes of *emergence*—of bringing imagined worlds into being.

Elements of Drawing and Painting

In this section, we focus on the primary components of art-making: color, line and shape, composition, and dimensions, with the aim of developing an arts vocabulary. Every academic discipline has its own specific vocabulary. Just as literature has its own terminology (metaphor, meter, irony, character, allusion) so too does the discipline of visual art (symmetry, background, foreground, harmony). Learning to talk about art opens up new possibilities for both the student, who is provided with concrete ways to continue to experiment and expand their perceptual horizons, and for the teacher, who has more tools for developing creative arts exercises and expressions, and for giving more helpful feedback to students.

Color

Psychologists and spiritual thinkers have ascribed different meanings as well as magical powers to different colors. These can be compelling, but it must be noted that all such symbolic meaning is filtered through a person's own experience, even souls such as Johann Wolfgang von Goethe, who was one of the first to develop a theory of color in the West. All symbolism is influenced by culture, and so while one cultural group may see red as signifying passion or sexual energy, others may see it as a symbol of war, others as a symbol of faith, happiness, honor, or good luck. What we can draw from this kaleidoscope of meanings is that color has a profound impact on the human psyche; it evokes emotions, can affect our mood, and has expressive power, in terms of communicating ideas.

Understanding the science of color does not diminish its magic and mystery; if anything, its existence becomes even more enchanting. To evoke wonder and curiosity, one only needs to hang a prism in a classroom, ideally one that transmits rainbows throughout the day. For color is basically white light, broken up into different wavelengths. These waves interact with objects and with the human eye, and are transformed by the light sensitive cells in the cones of the retina into the spectrum of colors that we see.

The exploration of color is an important topic in neohumanist education, from the perspective of physics as well as art. Immersing oneself in the study of color opens up vast new sensory possibilities, ways of seeing a world more luminous and resplendent than the everyday world we take for granted. In developmentally appropriate ways, students learn the language and the processes of creative color work: how primary colors cannot be mixed or formed by any combination of colors; how secondary colors are formed by mixing primary colors; how tertiary colors are formed by mixing a primary and a secondary color; what analogous colors are; what complementary colors are; what color value is; how hues can be desaturated (weakened) by adding white, black or gray to tint, shade, or tone a color. Learning this vocabulary of color and having regular access to exploring and experimenting with color through different processes can expand children's capacity for seeing the nuance, complexity, and beauty of the external world.

In Waldorf schools, children are introduced to color in teacher-guided activities that use wet watercolor paper and paints. In these exercises children begin to see what happens when colors blend, what colors seem to come forward, or exude warmth, and what colors recede (the cool colors). These colorful abstract paintings are thought to foster children's relationships to each color, to allow the "personalities" of the colors to emerge so that eventually

> when they have learnt [*sic*] to allow the forms to arise out of the gestures of the colours [*sic*], it will be quite natural for them, when illustrating a fairy tale or legend to choose scenes in which people and things can grow out of the harmony of colours [*sic*]. (Carlgren, 1976, p. 47)

This is what gives Waldorf students' paintings such a unique ethereal appearance; we might say that this artistic practice is a technique by which form can arise out of color and color can represent consciously a felt sense.

Form

Where does the world of forms come from? How can we explain the physical objects we see such as chairs, giraffes, the human body, the rose? Thinkers as distant in time from each other as Plato, with his transcendent world of Ideal (non-physical) Forms, Carl Jung, with his Archetypes (universal patterns of thought or images present in the collective unconscious of human beings), and Rupert Sheldrake, with his morphic fields (non-material fields of energy that encode patterns of growth and behavior) all proposed a transcendental level of forms that bring the physical, substantial world into being.

Many esoteric systems include sacred geometric forms that are thought to influence consciousness in certain ways. Circles can represent oneness, squares often represent stability and strength, and triangles can symbolize balance and harmony. While shapes (squares, circles, rectangles, triangles, hexagons, pentagrams, stars) are consistent across cultures, people make different meanings of shapes, just as in color theory.

Lines are the essential components of form. Lines can be curved, straight, angular, jagged, thick, thin, zigzag, horizontal, diagonal, vertical, curly, or spiral. When repeated they can create pattern and texture (as in the technique of *hatching*); with variant pressure, they can create illusions of depth and intensity. When lines are joined, they enclose, creating shapes—both geometric shapes and organic shapes (irregular forms that are found in nature). In specific configurations, they can create recognizable symbols across cultures and languages (bowls, houses, alphabets). Lines can create boundaries that separate shapes, as in map-making.

Lines compose children's most elemental attempts to communicate with marks on a surface. In the beginning, their lines are random squiggles or jagged marks as they experiment with the tools provided. Art theorist Rhoda Kellogg identified twenty basic scribbles including definitions like "roving open line," "multiple diagonal line," "single loop line," and so on (Orbach, 2020, p. 55). Children's scribbling is now considered an essential aspect of emergent literacy, suggesting as it does the beginnings of writing, "with the shapes of the letters only a matter of learning where to start and stop" (Kantner, 1990, p. 94). As the scribbles progress, lines are joined and shapes appear, and at some point, it becomes clear that the children are using their new skill to represent objects in the world. Along the way, teachers may lead the children in simple drawing exercises (such as drawing parallel lines or concentric circles) designed to gain control over tool use, learn new vocabulary, and develop techniques.

Imaginative teachers find ways to enhance the teaching of forms through creative movement activities, drawing in other materials such as dirt or sand, providing beautiful manipulatives such as colorful wooden rods or blocks (such as Tangrams), introducing with demonstrations more intricate forms such as spirals, bringing attention to patterns in nature, or providing creative lessons in ideas such as symmetry. It is important that children have a range of choices in terms of materials, as Alieta mentioned; much can be learned from their decisions about the use of tools such as pencils, paint, chalk, or crayons, the size and shape of paper, and the colors they work with. Older children often enjoy drawing tools such as rulers, protractors, and compasses to experiment with geometric and precision drawing; such implements expand the possibilities of integrating art and mathematics.

Composition

As we have seen so far, the visual arts experience of the young child is composed of colors, textures, lines, and shapes, and eventually recognizable forms. When these basics have been mastered, the child will begin to arrange the objects they wish to represent in relation to each other, expressing size, scale, and proportion in a complex whole. They may add features such as a horizon, or even a meandering road, giving their pictures some perspective. Details come into play—eyes, nose, and mouth in the circle of a head. Fingers radiating at the end of stick arms. Clothing. Leaves on the trees. They might experiment with overlapping shapes, or playing with the borders of the paper.

Learning to compose the objects one sees or imagines is all about the relationships between those objects. This is where the elements of composition come into play—ratio, proportion, balance, perspective, contrast, emphasis, pattern, unity, space, movement, and rhythm. Subjective elements play an active role here—when a child depicts a family, how does relative size come into the drawing? What aspects of the figures are dominant? It is possible that for the young child, much of this is happening below the surface of consciousness; for Elliot Eisner (2002), "the conscious realization that form can be managed to express feeling comes late in childhood" (p. 82), which does not negate the notion that prior to this *conscious realization*, the child *is* expressing feelings through form. It is one role of the arts educator to create opportunities to express one's feelings through artistic means, to bring form to the chaos of emotions that swirl in every child, providing the opportunities for self-reflection and understanding that can happen when some distance is created between an internalized feeling and an externalized expression.

Art and Development

In Chapter 3 you read about the many different aspects of child development that are studied to better understand how children grow and learn: physical, emotional, social, cognitive, and moral development. Scholars also study artistic development, a vast field that encompasses animal behaviors (such as bird song), cultural evolution, creativity, art production, art reception, and the psychology of art, as well as child development.

A popular quote is attributed (rightly or wrongly) to the painter Pablo Picasso: "Every child is an artist. The problem is how to remain an artist once we grow up." The quote speaks to the natural tendencies of most children to scribble marks on paper, to shape wet sand into castles and to mold clay into shapes, to the nature of art-making as playful, experimental, and inherently satisfying, and to the (sadly) atrophy of aesthetic inclinations as the child becomes increasingly bound by rules, norms, restrictions, logic, linear thinking, and a focus on the hard skills of reading and mathematics, as well as the insistence on proper technique in the arts.

In artistic development, there are three main human systems at play: perceiving, feeling, and making. These systems interact, feed each other, modify each other, and find expression in increasingly complex integrated forms. Numerous cognitive skills are acquired and sharpened along the developmental spectrum in art-making: perception, memory, language, fine motor control, spatial reasoning, and imagination (Pelowski et al., 2017) as well as technical skills such as "perspective, use of color, (and) accuracy of representation" (Gardner, 1973/1994, p. 220).

In the current fields of arts and well-being, there are useful frameworks that closely overlay conventional child development frameworks. The *Expressive Therapies Continuum* (Hinz, 2020) is one of those that may support educators when working with the arts. The Expressive Therapies Continuum closely overlays Piaget's cognitive development theory, explaining the development hierarchy in terms of the Kinesthetic/Sensory Level (0–7yrs), Perceptual/Affective Level (7–teens), and the Cognitive/Symbolic Level (teens–adult).

Referring to Lisa Hinz's (2020) work, the Kinesthetic/Sensory Level posits that information or learning is processed through sensation and movement: "Feedback loops support learning through senses and through repetitive movement" (p. 8). At this stage, when artmaking with toddlers the educator would look to use materials such as clay and paper. Drawing tools would be used primarily to facilitate sensory-motor development. For example, we might see the child use the crayon to bang the paper rather than draw, and to take pleasure in feeling the clay on the skin rather than make a functional object. Further development through the Kinesthetic/Sensory Level might find the 4–year old discovering form amongst repetitive scribbles and we might find "pre-school aged students begin to draw concentric scribbles" (p. 8). As Kellogg (1970) and Lowenfeld and Brittain

(1987) note, as form develops, round forms become differentiated from one another and are named.

The second level of the Expressive Therapies Continuum (7–16 years) is the Perceptual/Affective Level, where children are learning about their world and the forms around them. This level covers most of the primary school aged children. Artwork is infused with emotion and personal meaning, a sense of trial and error, and possible solutions; the child is learning about their own world. As Hinz (2020) notes, "Perceptions of reality are neurologically based, culturally influenced and different from other children's perceptions" (p. 8).

Group art making at this level may bring into awareness social or emotional challenges that can be explored with a safe degree of separation from a specific child or children or from the "real world" of emotions. As the educator, holding a sense of curiosity is important to provide space for alternative stories to emerge within the artmaking: "In order to have fulfilling relationships, it is helpful for people to understand the concept of representational diversity and be open to new perceptual experiences" (Hinz, 2020, p. 8). A safe way for children to play this out can be through art experiences; trying things out that they can't try out on the playground.

An example of this is children exploring their friendships, which are charged with emotion, as they work together on an animation project. At the River School, a group of three nine-year-old students spent the entire art lesson making detailed plasticine figurines and negotiating where to place these on their animation table to create a collaboratively imagined scene. They each had different ideas and it appeared as though they were squabbling. When asked, the children said they were fine, and were fully engaged in their process. The teacher observed that an important process was unfolding. The function of the students making this artwork together served to assist them to see different perspectives, negotiate, and practice new ways to relate to each other in a healthy way. Through this lesson, the students found solutions and worked through something "bigger" that was driving their relationship. The animation scene was a visual reminder of a transformative relational process.

The next level of the Expressive Therapies Continuum is the Cognitive/Symbolic Level (adolescent–adults). This is where the young person starts to process information outside of their own lived experiences. Adolescents are starting to be able to delay impulses, making space for problem solving and critical thinking. Art images and processes become more complex and the use of symbols for feelings, thoughts, sensations, and events is evident, as in, for example, graffiti, collage, or mask making.

The Creative Level of the Expressive Therapies Continuum may exist at any or all levels and suggests a sense of integration. Immersion in the creative process supports the uniqueness/gift/purpose/growth of the art-maker, expressing a core-sense of self where the artist feels a sense of flow, deep satisfaction and moments of joy. This sense of self is articulated well in Maslow's theory of a hierarchy of needs, which was first proposed in 1943, but made popular in his 1962 book *Toward a Psychology of Being*, in which he proposed the close relationship between self-actualization, creativity, transcendence, and purpose. Creativity is what holds the Expressive Therapies Continuum framework together in its supposition that the creative process itself can instill a sense of openness and connection to all.

Facilitating Creative Process

The astute educator can learn much from the way a child approaches art-making: The pressure they exert on a medium, levels of frustration, problem-solving ability, patience, risk taking, curiosity, and their range of feelings, which are reflected in their spontaneous drawings. Children will "devote more attention to subjects they care about, and will highlight those features in drawings about which they have strong positive or negative feelings" (Gardner, 1973/1994, p. 219). Art is such a window into the feeling life of young people that a field of study—art therapy—has evolved that utilizes art-making to help children express their perceptions and emotions, and to make sense of their lived experiences. Educators who are untrained in the therapeutic dimension of art, however, should refrain from making psychological judgments based on children's art. Though it is true that careful observation and description of children's art can yield important insights into their perceptions, their interests, their interpretation of experience, their view of the world, their assimilation of academic content, and their skill level, it's best not to over-psychologize their work.

It is important to understand that even when it *seems* that a child has just mindlessly scribbled some lines on a paper, there is apt to be a lot more going on in the mind of the child than the adult imagines. For example, a strong line drawn quickly across the page may look like just that to an adult—a line across the page—but to the young child it may be a truck zooming across the highway, a sight that impacted them greatly due to the size, noise, and intensity of the experience. Paying close attention to a child when they draw, and asking open-ended questions can yield some amazing findings. Children's scribbles often represent complex narrative structures. The attentive teacher might record these conversations, and with the child's permission, post the transcript by the drawing. Parents are often amazed to discover the depth and complexity of events transpiring in the consciousness of the child, and are impressed with their determination to communicate these thoughts in art, leading to a greater appreciation for the developing intelligence of their child.

If a child draws a rainbow and teacher or parent says, "Oh that is so pretty," chances are they will continue to draw rainbows rather than chance drawing something that might not be met with praise. Merely praising a child's art work is not useful in terms of skill development, creativity, or motivation. Better to just say, "Tell me about your artwork," and allow for the sometimes surprising things you might learn about the child's intentions. Being told, "That's a great picture," does not really communicate to the child that you are paying close attention to the work; asking process questions like, "How did you get that color of blue?" or noting the "bubbling purple and black look of the sky" notices elements that the child likely put a great deal of thought into, and can encourage further experimentation. Asking them to talk about the work inspires them to share what is inside of them, and possibly to edit, refine, or try some new things next time.

Many children abandon the free and expressive drawing of their young years at about nine or ten years of age, which some theorists attribute to their increasingly critical eye and the realization that their drawings are just not representing reality very well. Interestingly, Alieta has not experienced this in the Art Shed. She attributes this to the fact that she does not align representational drawing with good art, but rather exposes her students by the ages of 9–10 to many different ways of drawing/painting. Her aim is to preserve students' expressive nature and their confidence in this, rather than imposing ideas of what "good art" is. For many students, realistic representation is important to them and skill in this can be supported; as you will see in a later section of this chapter, it can be linked in an integrated way to scientific or botanical drawing, for example. For children who aim to improve their representational abilities, a skilled teacher can help to bring the images in the mind's eye into sharper focus and suggest techniques to assist in manifesting their vision.

Modeling and Sculpture

The natural interest of children in constructing three-dimensional models is apparent in a general inclination towards playing with blocks, cubes, Legos, and other building toys. Neohumanist educators need to think carefully about which of these artifacts further the principles of neohumanist education, and which do not. Model kits of tanks and fighter jets are obvious examples of what not to include in a classroom, and it's best to avoid artifacts and models based on popular animated shows, as the children are likely to have those at home. Less commercially oriented building toys include models of animals, birds, and insects and architecture or machines. While commercial models can be fun to assemble, creating original three-dimensional forms from wood, clay, or other modeling materials calls upon more imagination and skill.

Creating simple artifacts of everyday life such as bowls and cups from clay, baskets from natural grasses, carved wooden spoons, or woven fabrics draws us back into ancestral time. It is very important for children who have lived their lives in industrial cultures to understand how the necessities of life have been made for much of human history from the simple ingredients offered up by nature. This leads to the understanding of the abundance of the natural world, and the joys of creating useful items with this bounty. Modeling with dough, clay, beeswax, soap, cardboard, or paper, or creating sculptural pieces with items found in nature such as wood, stones, vines, leaves, nuts, or seeds leads the child into a 3-dimensional creative world.

Different media require different tools and processes. To model clay, one uses hands and tools such as a rolling pin to press, roll and create basic shapes. Local nuts and leaves can be used to imprint beautiful patterns in the clay. Simple tools such as popsicle sticks and toothpicks can be supplemented with inexpensive sculpting tools. To do soap sculpture, one chips and chisels away the material to reveal the form. Assembling constructions, as children might do when building a city from cardboard, requires scissors and glue. Creating a hanging sculpture or mobile can utilize all sorts of materials hung with thread, wire, or ribbon. Wood carving, whittling, and building simple items or scrap wood sculptures require some skill with sharp tools, and supervision. Fortunate is the school with a wood working area and an interested teacher or parent to facilitate.

In our current trajectory towards the future, 3D printing looms on the horizon, a technology that promises to "democratize" the creation of objects of use. Community Maker's Spaces and some schools have already incorporated this technology, which fosters computer skills, geometric knowledge, creative thinking and model-making. Neohumanist teachers need to think carefully about the pros and cons of immersing young children in technology and at what ages this is appropriate. While the world of 3D printing offers software for children as young as four, it is more important to instill the love and appreciation for the natural world in the early life of the child than a fascination with the world of machines. This topic is discussed at length in the chapter on teaching science, math and technology.

Model making can lend itself to an integrated curriculum in wonderful ways. Three-dimensional dioramas, for example, capture the world in miniature, and can be on-going constructions that extend a study for many weeks. When learning about the ecology of the local forest children can replicate the flora and fauna with clay or beeswax, and situate everything in a rich setting of moss, wood, and stone. Or they can create a fantasy world with felted fairies and elves, constructing tiny houses for them to reside in. The class might decide to create a 3D world of a story that they particularly like, and act it out with the figures. Anyone who has spent any time at all with young children knows the fascination with small worlds that draw them into imaginary play. They role play, manipulate the figures, and try out actions and words, all the while building a sense of self.

Viewing and Responding to Art

Thus far, we have focused on art-making. In Chapter 9 on arts-based learning, we spoke of John Dewey (1934), the American philosopher of pragmatism who expounded at length on aesthetic experience. Dewey reminds us that art is a communicative act that takes place both in the maker and in the viewer. Learning to look at and talk about art has many benefits, and is easy to implement in a classroom. It's best to have a vivid print of an art work to do this, but it can be displayed on a screen if the image is of sufficient size and clarity. The words noted earlier in this chapter that describe aspects of color, line, form, and composition are words that can be used when describing a visual image, along with responses to questions such as:

"How does this artwork make you feel?"

The first thing to remind ourselves of is that there is a lot more going on in children's heads than they have words for. Learning the language of visual art enhances the range of vocabulary children can bring to noticing and talking about the world, and to their emergent writing as well. This includes the metaphors and visual language that children can generate from a drawing, that can then enrich their descriptive writing. The exercises involved in viewing and discussing are especially useful for working with children who are learning a new language; the multi-sensory act of connecting language and image gives children more tools to make connections and to learn and remember concepts.

Examining composition, technique, or inferring meaning from a painting is similar to analyzing a text. When facilitating an activity like this, you may notice that adults and children alike almost always jump to *interpreting* both abstract and realistic images (What is the artist representing? What does it mean? That big blob looks like a dinosaur! It makes me think of war), and skip over the important stage of describing. It takes practice and skillful facilitation to assist viewers to start with and stick to description, using the vocabulary of visual art to say what they *see* rather than *what they make of what they see*. You'll soon discover that this process builds on itself, starting with simple observations and introducing more complex language: colors can be bright, vivid, garish, dull, flat; compositions can be formal, flowing, symmetrical, off center; brush strokes can be bold, precise, irregular. Only after intensive description should you move to response to the work; the sustained exploration of the elements of art will result in more meaningful interpretations. Keeping in mind that every person's interpretation of an artwork is unique, open ended questions can spark meaningful exchanges:

- What is happening in this work of art?
- What do you see that makes you think that?
- What more do you see?
- What does that make you think about/feel?
- What do you think the artist means to say?

Description entails shared perceptions (people can agree that a line is curved, that the color blue is situated next to the yellow); when you get to interpretation, personal impressions and subjective experiences enter in and students learn that each other's experiences of a work of art may differ. One viewer may feel a work of art is gloomy or sad; another may experience this same picture as calm or restful. This is a profound lesson—to learn that everyone responds in their own way to phenomena, and that the intersubjective world is composed of multiple perspectives.

Looking at and talking about each other's art is an important aspect of arts education. By learning the language of visual art and to describe what they see (rather than merely say "I like it") young people learn what it means to give and receive constructive feedback and engage in what Elliot Eisner (2002) terms "connoisseurship," or the art of appreciation. The point of peer reflection and critique is not to judge, not to evaluate, but to point out what is noticed and what that evokes (pp. 187–188), with the aim that everyone benefits in the development of narrative imagination and technical competence. In the Art Shed, Alieta invites her students to take turns holding up their artwork and talking about it. Other students are encouraged to make a positive comment about the artwork, or share what they see in the work. If the work is incomplete, Alieta may ask the maker what are their next steps/ideas? She has explored many creative alternatives to this process of peer reflection and feedback; on one occasion where the children made extraordinary nature spirit masks, students wrote and then shared one word that came up for them when viewing the mask. These words then became an "offering" to the maker.

The strategy of viewing and discussing art is not limited to formal paintings or to art produced in the classroom. Analyzing a photograph can help develop critical thinking and aesthetic judgment, and young people can develop "historical empathy" from viewing art and photographs from different time periods. Historical empathy refers to the intellectual and emotional engagement with historical figures, and an understanding of the context in which they lived, and how this influenced their actions and decisions. Here too, prioritizing description, rather than interpretation, is important.

Media literacy, an important contemporary pedagogy, relies to a great extent on the ability to look at, describe, decode, and analyze images in order to better understand the messages they are sending. Developing visual literacy is considered of prime importance in neohumanist education, living as we do in an image-saturated environment in which children's identity, self-esteem, values, and how they understand the world are becoming shaped by a continuous barrage of visual information. Understanding how an image was created, by whom, and with what intentions and then exploring its impacts ("How does this image make you feel?"; "What does it make you want?") is a key element of critical thinking, developing informed opinions, and making sound judgments.

The Spiritual Dimension of Art-Making

There is a sacred aspect to art, not in the sense of propagating a particular religion (though it has certainly been used to that end through history) but in the sense of awakening subtle human capacities such as empathy, aesthetics, altruism, and feelings of "oneness"—aspects of what we might call the *big me* rather than the *little me*, or as Franck (1993) defines it, "The ego liberated from its isolation and infinitely, cosmically extended" (p. 27). It can be difficult to judge whether art comes from a place of self-absorbed ego or a place of transcendence. Philosophers attempt to distinguish these qualities by defining the former as art that does not come from an authentic space, or is merely created as a commodity, whereas the latter comes from a more genuine level of feeling, resonates with something more universal in the human experience, and has the capacity to touch those elevated dimensions of the human mind wherein reside experiences of beauty, bliss, harmony, and divinity.

One can leave the argument to the art theorists, and say here that art-making does have the unique ability to draw out the deepest aspects of the self, and that the neohumanist educator has a responsibility to teach more than technique or the assignment of replicating the "great masters." An essential principle of neohumanist education is cultivating the capacity to access the inner world, and the layers of mind/soul/spirit where we can touch metaphor, archetypes, deep empathy, compassion, values, purpose, imagination and vivid fantasies, and where we can attune to the "metaphysical background" of the world.

Stephen Buhner (2014) describes the metaphysical background of the world as the reality that lies beyond the normal range of perception and below the surface of everyday consciousness. It is the deep knowing that all matter is energy, that what appears solid is mostly empty space, that everything comes into being from a common creative source, that everything in the universe is alive and intelligent, that there are underlying patterns that connect all of creation, and that human perception is capable of "seeing the hidden links between the ghosts of things" (Robert Bly, as quoted in Buhner, 2014, p. 337). Cultivating the awareness of the metaphysical background of the world is an essential element of neohumanist ontology, which understands everything in the universe as deeply connected, profoundly interrelated, and interpenetrating. But such perception requires attention, discipline, practice, a conducive environment, and guidance.

Nona Orbach (2020), art therapist and art teacher, claims that the availability of an open studio, with well curated and aesthetically arranged materials (like the Art Shed), calls a person to engage, express, and learn more about those dimensions of self that lie beneath the surface of consciousness, and perhaps beyond the range of everyday perception. The skilled art therapist or teacher facilitates "creative processes and emotional and spiritual dialogues within the client" (p. 118). Orbach introduces us to the idea of a *spiritual blueprint*: "the particular expression of each individual, in their marks left on materials, which is both unique and at the same time overlaps with the archetypical map of symbolism characteristic of humanity as a whole" (p. 19). She believes that these patterns of development, "weaving between the universal archetypes and the personal ones in endless variations," are present as seeds in early childhood and "mark us as a distinct human being and creator" (p. 35). This observation is critical to the "art of knowing a child" that we elaborated in Chapter 6 on Contemplative Inquiry and leads to a central expectation of a neohumanist education—that teachers keep detailed and well-organized collections of children's work. Orbach is worth quoting extensively here:

> The wonder of an individual's specific phenomenology can be revealed and identified by displaying and examining a chronological collection of that person's artwork. These phenomenological observations yield manifestations of patterns: repeated choices of color, line, shapes, texture, signs, composition, rhythm, ornamentation, perspective, and so on. And those patterns are one's spiritual blueprint. (pp. 36–37)

Keep in mind that the pedagogical purpose here is not to analyze or diagnose, but to develop a deeper and more empathetic relationship with the child, so as to better assist them in their spiritual and academic journey. We refer you again to the Prospect School Archives at the University of Vermont, specifically their extensive chronological collections, for exemplary examples of detailed, informative, and insightful descriptions of children's artwork (https://cdi.uvm.edu/collection/uvmcdi-uvmcdiprospect). This is perhaps one of the finest collections in the world demonstrating the importance of the close examination and careful documentation of young people's work in order to learn more about their unique spiritual blueprint.

Orbach (2020) reminds us that while looking for patterns and describing the processes of children's artwork we need to remember "the astonishing phenomenon that our personal growth is laid upon ancient archetypes and patterns, inherited from our ancestors and culture" (p. 51). As neohumanist educators, we can speculate that these marks and patterns that children use to communicate their inner worlds may also have roots in *samskaras* (in Yogic philosophy these are defined as the reactive momenta of our thoughts, intentions, and actions that contribute to our character traits and behavior patterns across lifetimes). This is a vital area of inquiry to be conducted by teachers in neohumanist learning environments—the practice of careful observation to discern patterns of learning and behavior that might enable us to truly *see* the child, to offer unconditional love and acceptance, and to help them transform patterns that are blocking them from achieving their potential.

The Art of Mandalas

The word *mandala* comes to us from the Sanskrit, meaning *circle*. Mandalas are designs characterized by repeating, symmetrical, geometric shapes and other forms, and are present in a great variety of cultural and religious traditions, from Eastern forms of Yoga, Hinduism, and Buddhism, early forms of esoteric Christianity, ancient Mayan and Aztec civilizations, and contemporary Native American art and ritual. The mandala is a sacred form with various purposes: cultivating concentration, withdrawing from the sensory world, gaining knowledge of one's inner world, focusing on a deity, and/or for bringing order to the contents of consciousness. According to one transdisciplinary artist/philosopher, mandalas have regenerative and curative powers; they can make the invisible visible, reveal the unity between human experience and the cosmos, and give expressive form to intuitive insights into spiritual truth (Cornell, 1994, p. 2). Materials vary—some are painted on silk or paper, some are constructed with colored sand on a floor or table, and some contemporary mandala makers use materials from nature: flowers, stones, seeds and twigs.

The psychologist C. G. Jung is largely credited with bringing an interest in, and understanding of mandalas to modern Western culture. Jung himself painted numerous mandalas during his "introspective period"—a fruitful number of years in which he formulated his theory of the collective unconscious (Jung, 2009). During that time, he noted the emergence of universal symbols, shapes and forms from his dreams and other psychic experiences that were also found across cultures and through time. It was this observation that led to his theory of archetypes—instinctive, innate energy patterns (akin to psychic DNA) residing in the collective unconscious that affect human thought and behavior. While these patterns represent archetypal figures their characteristics differ across cultures (a trickster, or jester archetype, e.g., may appear as a raven, or a coyote, or a clown). While Jung's ideas continue to be debated in scientific psychology, the impact of his ideas on the practice of "making art from within" is significant.

One profound body of research comes to us from the work of Marguerite Smithwhite, a disciple of the great Indian Yogi and philosopher Sri Aurobindo (who is credited with the creation of Integral Yoga). Smithwhite, influenced by the work of Carl Jung as well as her study of Eastern philosophy, carried out research for 3.5 years on teaching children meditation and observing their drawings immediately following. Her work began in the London Borough of Southwark at the Crampton Primary School but extended around the world in many cultures. She called her method "a new education with a soul," with the stated aim of leading children to the awareness "that everything is alive, that the Divine is everywhere, that there is consciousness even in stones" (Le Touze, 2006, p. 12), a quotation with a profound connection to neohumanism. Smithwhite began her research with a series of inquiry questions:

- Could children be taught to meditate?
- What would happen if they were asked to do colored drawings immediately after meditation?
- Would there be an increase in creativity?

- Would they display unusual knowledge different from the usual children's drawings?

She was guided by a profound belief that every human being possessed a gift that, freely shared, might benefit the evolution of humanity. She therefore structured her guided meditations with children on the theme of peace, in order to help them realize that "when one receives something very precious, like peace, love, joy,—the greatest joy is to radiate that lovely gift out to other people and indeed to the whole world" (Smithwhite, 1988, p. 6). We can see here the genuine connections between this particular practice of art-making, the expansion of love to all beings, and fostering the desire to be of service.

Smithwhite's oral visualizations as well as an extensive collection of the children's drawings, sometimes accompanied by the stories the children told about them, are contained in the beautiful book *Children's Art Through Meditation* (Smithwhite, 1988), which is unfortunately very difficult to obtain. We offer here some details about the work, with the hope that neohumanist educators might allow their imaginations to soar and draw from Smithwhite's research their own processes for integrating contemplative practices and art-making.

The procedures Smithwhite (1988) outlined are actually quite simple. Children are provided with felt tipped pens and paper, and she always included gold, as she felt that its effect on children was often "quite startling" (p. 7). They may have a discussion beforehand about the theme of the work (for her it was "peace") followed by a guided meditation that can include visual images such as raindrops or flowers, instructions to experience the *feeling* of peace in the body, and/or guidance to send these feelings out to the world. She sometimes accompanied the meditations with peaceful music. When eyes are opened and the music and meditation cease, the children then draw (or paint) freely, expressing whatever has emerged for them in the process.

The research findings, gleaned from the close observation and description of the hundreds of detailed and expressive drawings were quite remarkable:

- Archetypes were very prevalent in the children's drawings—eyes, caves, mountains, stairs, rainbows, snakes.
- The idea of a mandala, or a drawing emanating from a center point, was not introduced until a few years into the research, but many of the drawings reflected the mandala from early on.

- Symbols appeared in children's drawings that they could have had no prior contact with.
- Some drawings reflected a shaded "energy field" outside of a structured form.
- Some drawings represented the seven chakras, represented by children who had no influence from the families or culture of the existence of these.

The researcher also recorded children's verbal descriptions of what transpired for them in meditation, noting the frequency of expressions involving light, tunnels with lights at the end, or stairs or ladders climbing to the stars. She also recorded many children's creative stories that expanded on the drawings that they did. The stories suggest, according to Smithwhite (1988), that the child is not a blank slate, awaiting knowledge to be poured into their brain, but that "ALL knowledge, ALL perception, ALL comprehension, are actually there, captive in more senses than one, awaiting release and fulfillment" (p. 45).

Just as we emphasized in Chapter 6 on Contemplative Inquiry, Smithwhite (1988) cautions the inquirer not to "make a cut-and-dried diagnosis of the whole, for it is now my long experience that different people, looking at the same piece of work, will have very different intuitions about it" (p. 9). What is important, she says, is not diagnosis or interpretation, but

> the infallible indication that something extraordinary, illuminating, and with a different kind of wisdom or knowledge, has taken place, thus proving the existence in the unexplored depths of a person of something mysterious, superconscious, an indication of some of the qualities of transformed man [sic]. (p. 9)

Smithwhite hoped that more and more people might recognize the necessity for the education of the inner psychic and spiritual person, so that young people might be enabled to share these gifts of the spirit with the world, and bring about an era of peace.

Becoming One With The World Through Art

Artist Peter London (2003) sees the rejoining of ourselves and the rest of the natural world as "the great requirement of our civilization at this pivotal moment in time" (p. 1). As we draw closer to nature, says London, "the entire world takes on new degree of poignancy, luminosity, preciousness, subtlety, mystery, and intimacy...we increasingly experience ourselves in just the same way: as poignant, luminous, precious, subtle, mysterious, and intimate" and in this arts-based process, "we draw closer to our Selves" (p. 2).

To become one with the world, to develop the love for all creation that is at the heart of neohumanism, young people need immersive experiences with soil, air, water, rocks, plants, insects, animals, birds, sea, and sky. For as Peter London suggests in the previous quote, humans *are* nature, we are of the same shared substance as the world we call nature. The creative integration of art and science in the education of children is an important facilitator of these awakenings.

If we are to move in the direction of an ecologically sustainable society, degrowth, and decommodification, we must help young people to understand and enjoy lifeways that do not depend on consumerism and commercialism. While there are many examples of "decommodified activity" (service, care, play, sport, etc.) art-making plays a central role in making the ordinary extraordinary. The practice of handcraft, for example—the making of baskets, garments, home décor, jewelry, pottery—offers an alternative to rampant consumerism and fast, trendy fashion, cultivating meaningful activity grounded in sustainability, self-reliance, and skill sharing. Students can begin by learning about the materials and basic structures of craft such as weaving, carving, or sewing, and work their way into creatively breaking the rules, experimenting with form and structure, and thus blurring the boundaries between art and craft.

In the early years of Western scientific discovery and continuing well into the 19th and early 20th century, people were fascinated with natural phenomena—shells, rocks, fish, trees, flowers—and drawing the natural world was a widespread passion. Just as modern people likely have numbers of Facebook friends who share their nature photography, ordinary people observed, described, and depicted the flora and fauna of the world, inspiring a great enthusiasm for the new discipline of science. In schools, art and science were true companions, as the natural world often formed the subject matter for the teaching of art, and art was often used to better connect with and understand phenomena. Anyone who has ever taken a botanical drawing class is keenly aware of the way that the careful observation and replication of a leaf or a flower, for example, draws us deeper and deeper into the intricacies and special details of every item found in the natural world.

Beyond mere observation and replication, today's educational nature journal can also serve as a repository for concepts better understood visually (the water cycle, erosion, pollination, stratification, metamorphosis, etc.). There are many benefits to the creative use of student nature journals, defined here as the process of integrating drawing and writing in response to observations and other learning about the natural world:

- It requires the observer to slow down, and pay attention to detail.
- It improves the recognition of species and the understanding of eco-systems.
- It has a positive effect on the abilities to draw and write.
- It helps to clarify complex concepts and retain information.
- Subjectivity is enhanced as the journal includes inner thoughts as well as outer observations.

To close this chapter, we return to the River School for an illustration of the multifaceted way that art can lead and enrich education and make learning enjoyable in a school setting. We feature the voice of Alieta again, who co-created an interdisciplinary multi-modal arts project "Connection to Country" with Leeza Stratford, an expressive arts therapist and parent at the school.

* * *

Connection to Country

"Connection to Country" was an arts-based inquiry that integrated science, English, humanities, and local First Nations knowledge. It was transdisciplinary, as the children did not always know which 'subject' they were learning. It was the engagement with creative processes that fused the learning together. The setting was the "surround" of the school, the ecologically rich hinterland of the Sunshine Coast near Maleny, Australia. Home to rivers, waterfalls and a sub-tropical rainforest, as well as farms, the area offers a multitude of possibilities for immersion in the natural world and developing relationships with more-than-human-others. The visual arts inquiry engaged the students in multi-sensory, multimodal experiencing, supporting personal meaning-making and emotional connections to the natural world around them. From this place the children were then able to further explore relevant topics and try out opportunities for different ways of being with their surroundings.

"Country" is the term often used by First Nations Australian peoples to describe the lands and waters to which they are connected. In Australia, there are hundreds of "countries" within a country. The term country encompasses many things: the ecology, customs, relations with ancestors, spiritual practices, identity, and much more.

Neohumanist education emphasizes epistemological pluralism, highly valuing the traditional ecological and Indigenous knowledges of local people and places. The River School is fortunate to have relations with a number of Jinibara and Kabi Kabi custodians and experts in ecology and culture. Some of the questions generated by the children and addressed by the First Nations custodians in the study included:

> ~ How can we learn to "read" Country? ~ What are the connections between different species (that we are studying), seasons and the environment? ~ What are the needs and roles of the animals we are studying within the broader ecosystem? ~ What can we learn through study of the chosen iconic species that is important to our area and community? ~ How does the indigenous concept of a totemic species contribute to how we could investigate, celebrate, and communicate the importance of these species within our community? ~ How was this place cared for by First Nations people before colonization? ~ Can we become better place-makers, caring for and protecting the places in which we live, by integrating indigenous perspectives? ~ How can we protect our threatened animals and plants? ~ Can we connect with any local conservation groups to help protect the threatened species in our area?

The inquiry into local endangered animals became a centerpiece of the unit of study. Students made excursions to their local creek and other habitats equipped with magnifying glasses, nets, and notebooks to seek out the Cascade Tree Frog, the Giant Barred Frog, the Marbled Frogmouth, the Maleny Spiny Crayfish, the Spotted Quoll, the Mary River Turtle, the Mary River Cod, and the Lungfish. First Nations Custodians taught the students the original words for these animals. Throughout their fieldwork, students were reminded to notice what they see, what they hear, and what they feel in their bodies.

Children each selected an animal with whom they resonated, and filled their nature journals with drawings and information about this animal, exploring what the animal looks like, where it lives, what it eats, how it behaves. They made individual clay rings with three dimensional depictions of the creatures, their habitats, and other visual information about them, and discussed the stories that the clay rings represented. These rings were fired and eventually stacked on a pole, creating a collaborative artifact, a totem of endangered species that was installed at the wooded entrance to the rainforest school creek, showcasing the endangered animals of the local area to the school community. The clay models sparked creative storytelling, with the student artists giving voice to their animal (engaging their empathy and becoming custodians themselves). Students responded to questions on behalf of their animal, "If your animal could speak our language, what would it say to us?" (Can you help me with my habitat loss? Help us! Try and stop the people destroying our habitat? Look out for me! Try not to pollute the waterways!)

The adopted endangered animals found new expression in new materials. The drawings were rendered into prints, and then onto silk screened t-shirts, so that the children could actually "embody" their animal. Studying the animals so closely and sharing their knowledge in collaborative mural-making led to an interest in investigating the creek, and the many connected streams and tributaries leading to a larger river. More excursions included using the school bus to follow the water and stopping along the way to explore their animals' habitats, and taking to the water in kayaks to get closer to the aquatic habitats. The children discovered areas where people were replanting trees in order to replenish habitat that had been lost to logging. And so, loaded with new knowledge, compassion for the animals and love for the local environment, the students ventured to their school creek to make some changes. Their mentor, Matt, cleared a planting site and provided them with native plants to revegetate the riparian zone. Over 200 hundred trees were planted by the children for the welfare of the local animals.

The students confidently presented their new knowledge to members of the Sunshine Coast Community at the "Kids in Action" Environmental Conference, with the theme *Connecting to Country: Celebrating Nature's Icons*. Their process and findings were shared through artmaking workshops, video, display, and movement. The children invited peers from other schools to represent their own iconic animal or plant using clay. The class invited their new friends to select a resonant environment on the floor mural landscape to place their clay sculpture. After two workshops, the clay representations of over 40 students filled the mural. Teaching other students how to creatively explore what they know represented a cyclical ending to a wonderfully rich process. The video link showcasing the marvelous project can be accessed at: https://vimeo.com/386084057

* * *

This rich example of a student-driven, multi-layered, integrated curriculum is a demonstration of neohumanist education at its best. The "emergent" study was largely directed by student questions as they explored their own local place. Teachers offered occasional prompts for discussion, supplied the children with new materials for creating artifacts, and provided support and scaffolding for exploration. The extended study accomplished many things; while art was the central vehicle for expression, students were engaged in studying the science of ecology, the local knowledge of First Nations Custodians and their histories, learning new languages, studying the geology and geography of their local place, the waterways and aquatic culture, and more, depending on where their interests led them. They were encouraged to develop an emotional connection with an endangered animal and learn as much as they could about their animal; out of this came the passion to care for the creatures and preserve their habitat, and concrete actions to accomplish this. This perhaps is how we help young people cultivate the "love for all creation"—one Spiny Crayfish at a time!

FOR CONTINUING STUDY

> *Discussion/Reflection:* What do you remember from your visual arts education? What captured your interest? Turned you off, or on?
>
> *Discussion/Reflection:* Group activity: Choose a cartoon, print, or poster from an historical time. Go around the group, each person adding one descriptive detail about what is seen, until the group runs out of details. Use the vocabulary learned in this chapter. When you finish describing the artifact, engage in meaning making, asking interpretative questions. What was learned about the historical period?
>
> *Application:* Spend at least a half hour with a leaf, flower, tree, and so on. Using a simple paper and pencil, or graphite drawing pencils, draw your artifact with as much accuracy and detail as you can.
>
> *Application:* Spend at least 15 minutes in meditation. Use music, or not. Have a piece of drawing paper and some felt tip pens (including gold!) or crayons handy. Following your meditation, draw whatever image(s) flows from your experience. Be expansive, allow images to emerge.
>
> *Application:* Sit with a young child while they engage in a painting activity. Record what they say as they paint. Feel free to comment, but don't guide the process or press them for information. Transcribe the recording later and study it. What did you learn about this child and/or the artmaking process?

References

Buhner, S. H. (2014). *Plant intelligence and the imaginal realm: Into the dreaming of earth*. Bear and Company.
Carlgren, F. (1976). *Education towards freedom*. Lanthorn Press.
Cornell, J. (1994). *Mandala: Luminous symbols for healing*. Quest Books.
Dewey, J. (1934). *Art as experience*. Perigree.
Eisner, E. W. (2002). *The arts and the creation of mind*. Yale University Press.

Franck, F. (1993). *Zen seeing, Zen drawing: Meditation in action.* Bantam Books.

Gardner, H. (1994). *The arts and human development.* Basic Books. (Original work published 1973)

Hinz, L. D. (2020). *Expressive therapies continuum* (2nd ed.). Routledge.

Jung, C.J. (2009). *The red book.* S. Shamdasani (Ed.). W. W. Norton & Co.

Kantner, L. (1990). Visual arts integration and multiple intelligences: Before implementation. In W. J. Moody (Ed.), *Artistic intelligences: Implications for education.* Teachers College Press.

Kellogg, R. (1970). *Analyzing children's art.* Mayfield Publishing Company.

Le Touze, C. (2006). Meditation and painting: A research project. *RITAM, 3*(2). http://wiki.auroville.org.in/w/images/7/7c/Ritam_3-2_February_2006.pdf

London, P. (1987). *No more secondhand art: Awakening the artist within.* Shambala.

London, P. (2003). *Drawing closer to nature: Making art in dialogue with the natural world.* Shambala.

Lowenfeld, V., & Brittain, W. L. (1987). *Creative and mental growth.* Prentice Hall.

Magsamen, S., & Ross, I. (2023a, May 25). How arts can save your life: Exploring power of art on our health and wellbeing. *IAI News.* https://iai.tv/articles/how-the-arts-save-us-auid-2486

Magsamen, S., & Ross, I. (2023b). *Your brain on art: How the arts transform us.* Random House.

Orbach, N. (2020). *The good enough studio: Art therapy through the prism of space, matter, and action.* Independently published.

Pelowski, M., Leder, H., & Tinio, P. P. L. (2017). Creativity in the visual arts. In J. C. Kaufman, V. P. Glăveanu, & J. Baer (Eds.), *The Cambridge handbook of creativity across domains* (pp. 80–109). Cambridge University Press.

Sloan, D. (1983). *Insight-imagination: The emancipation of thought and the modern world.* Greenwood Press.

Smithwhite, M. (1988). *Children's art through meditation: A book of peace.* Ch. Falk-Verlag, Planegg.

Zaidel, D. W. (2010). Art and brain: Insights from neuropsychology, biology and evolution. *Journal of Anatomy, 216*(2), 177–183. https://doi.org/10.1111/j.1469-7580.2009.01099.x

12

The Superpower of Music

> *Life is a symphony, and the action of every person in this life is the playing of his particular part in the music.*
> — Hazrat Inayat Khan, *The Mysticism of Sound and Music*, 1996

Music does really hold enormous and varied powers! It is hard to overstate the importance of music in human life. It has existed across the millennia in virtually every culture known to us. The spiritually uplifting notes of the Indian Raga, the passions evoked by music of the classical masters, the heartbeat of the Earth conjured by Native American drumming, the transport to intense memories called up by popular music, soothing lullabies sung to newborns, joyful games and songs sung in early childhood centers, the energy and longing for social change sparked by contemporary music, or the hypnotic states induced by trance music—all of this attests to the huge and varied selection of music available to us today. Music has the power to heal, to help us relax, to bring joy, to bring tears, lower our blood pressure and reduce anxiety, increase motivation and provide stamina, help us sleep, wake us up, and perhaps most important, to create connections between and amongst people and even, between humans and the non-human others with whom we share the planet. As we will see in this chapter, it has the power to elevate our minds above the mundane concerns of everyday life, to foster transcendent emotional states, and to experience subtle awareness of the beauty, harmony, and bliss available to all.

Michael Spitzer (2021), author of *The Musical Human* (a book with the somewhat hubristic subtitle, *A History of Life on Earth*), suggests that music was born when our species first became upright and began to walk on two feet 4.4 million years ago. The rhythmic, kinesthetic patterns of walking created for us a sense of time, and forged in our brains a link between sound, motor activity, and the brain. It also implanted in us the metaphor of music as movement, and Spitzer notes that all pieces of music are a journey from one place to another, an imaginary journey, a kind of time travel. Jeremy Montagu (2017), historian of music, notes that "there are four evident purposes for music: dance, ritual, entertainment personal, and communal, and above all social cohesion..." (para. 1), according to the historical record. All of these purposes find their place in the education of young children. We add to these historical purposes self-transcendence, or as art theorist Ellen Dissanayake (1988) claims, *ecstasy*, a sense of unity or timelessness.

Music and the Human Brain

Neuroaesthetics—the cognitive neuroscience of aesthetics—is a relatively young sub field of neuroscience that studies the various forms of art and their effects on the brain. Music is probably the most researched of the arts in this emergent science. Music, unlike sculpture, painting, drama or dance, has no physical form, but exists in the air around us. A string is plucked, a skin is pounded, or a breath is blown through a pipe. With these movements, particles are displaced from a state of equilibrium and they move back and forth, creating *vibrations*. A *wave* is a disturbance or a vibration that travels and carries energy from one place to another. *Sound* is an acoustic wave that is perceived by the human brain.

How does sound register in our consciousness? Hearing is a complex phenomenon, oversimplified here for our purposes. Sound waves from the air enter the ear canal and travel to the eardrum, a membrane which then vibrates and in turn activates three tiny bones (the malleus, incus, and stapes) which amplify the vibrations and send them on to a fluid-filled organ, the cochlea. This structure recognizes different pitches, which allows us to determine whether a sound is low or high. The vibrations are amplified and turned into electrical signals which travel along the auditory nerve to diverse areas in the brain, which turns these into sounds that we recognize:

the rushing of ocean waves upon the shore, the cry of an infant, the mew of a kitten, the bass drum of a rock band.

As we know now from scientists such as Albert Einstein, everything that exists consists of invisible vibrations and waves. Things that appear solid are actually energy in motion. Things that don't appear solid such as SOUNDS are also vibratory. Frequency is the term given to the rate or speed at which things vibrate. New research in the fields of neuroaesthetics tells us that our brains react chemically to sound frequencies, vibrations, and tones, and that "these chemical triggers can dramatically alter mood, perception, and even address neurological and emotional ailments" (Magsamen & Ross, 2023, Loc 44). These chemical triggers account for the emotions evoked by music; certain collections of sound waves can flood the brain with neurotransmitters such as dopamine. Music is so closely connected to emotion that a therapeutic field has emerged in the last few decades that links music, therapy, and physical and mental health.

Many different parts of the brain are activated when we perceive a piece of music, depending on the type of music heard, and whether it is being listened to, played, or composed. Consider orchestral composition. There are many different approaches to composition, but all start with some inspiration—a memory, an image or a melodic fragment. The composer brings various aspects of knowledge together—harmony, melody, chord progressions, rhythm. They must be able to imagine what every instrument in the orchestra sounds like, hear this in their own brains, and somehow weave it all together in a form that can be notated and then reproduced by over 100 players making sounds on instruments by plucking, strumming, or bowing strings, blowing through tubes and pressing valves down, or striking, shaking, or rattling various percussion instruments. When we listen to this finished composition, different regions of our brains are responsible for discerning pitch, rhythm, tone, time, and memories, and these areas must coordinate to integrate the multi-layers of sound in order for us to "hear" the musical composition. A complex set of cognitive tasks indeed!

While playing a musical instrument is an important way to experience the benefits of music, nothing more than the human voice is needed to make music. Research on the positive physical and mental effects of singing, especially singing in groups, is extensive; the decrease of anxiety and depression, higher satisfaction with life, and stress reduction. One important area of research has been the use of song to improve brain function for people with neurological issues. Research on singing is also pointing to important connections between singing and language development. Because singing combines music and words, it "strengthens the brain networks involved in word production and articulation, in addition to the right hemisphere circuits involved in fine control of pitch and melody" (Menehan, 2015, para. 23).

Elements of Music

Just as we explored a vocabulary for the visual arts, we look here at the common words used to talk about music. *Pitch* is the basis for many of the elements in music: scales, harmony, chords, and melodies. But what is pitch? Earlier we looked at sound waves and the process by which our brain actually hears music. Pitch refers to the frequency of the sound wave, which is how fast the cycle of the wave is. The higher the frequency, the higher the pitch, and vice versa. To get a bit into the weeds on this, pitch is measured as the number of times a sound wave can repeat in one second, a number that is displayed in Hertz (abbreviates as Hz). In music, a *note* refers to a specific pitch, and Western music is made from 12 notes, the *chromatic scale*. *Timbre* is the quality of the sound emanating from an instrument or a voice, with such descriptors as warm, pure, buzzy, harsh, smooth, sweet, and so on. Think about how the same note from a flute and from a tuba registers differently—that is timbre.

The most fundamental life processes are rhythmic: breathing in/breathing out, heart beating, pulse racing, sun rising/sun setting, walking, running, night/day, body clocks, ocean waves. Musical *rhythm* is shaped by *beats* (regular or irregular combinations of notes and *rests*) and *tempo* (the speed at which a piece of music is played). *Meter* is a rhythmic pattern produced by the grouping of strong and weak beats (e.g., BOOM-boom-boom-boom or ta-DA ta-DA ta-DA).

A *melody* is a sequence of notes, or a series of pitches, usually organized in a pattern that is a recognizable unit of sounds. An *interval* is the distance in pitch between any two notes. *Volume* is how loud or soft a note is played. *Harmony* is what you hear when two or more notes are combined; harmony is said to give music its *texture*. When all of these elements come together—rhythmic impulses, variations in pitch, melodies, harmonies—we have MUSIC! And this is about how far into music theory we need to go.

Benefits of Music in Education

Given all of the physical and psychological benefits to music that are being discovered, it is strange indeed that music is not considered as basic to learning as is reading or math. The emphasis on high stakes testing in many countries over the past few decades has led to the disappearance of music and art in many public schools. But we are beginning to understand the many reasons why these arts, aside from the benefits they offer on their own, are important adjuncts to other academic disciplines.

Music and Math

By understanding beat, rhythm and scales, children are learning how to count, divide, create fractions, discover ratios, and recognize patterns. Really, all music is about division—a musical composition is divided into measures, measures are divided into beats and beats are divided into notes. Thus, a measure is a fraction of a musical piece, a beat is a fraction of a measure, and a whole note beat may be divided into regular parts: half notes, quarter notes, eighth notes, sixteenths. All music happens in time—melody and rhythm work together in time to create what we call music. The ability to count and keep a steady beat is fundamental to all music and may have larger effects on such basics as walking, running, playing sports and of course dancing.

Basic rhythmic learning teaches patterns. When learning a simple repeating rhythm that combines knee slapping and clapping (slap slap clap rest) a child is introduced to the idea of patterns, which are essential elements of mathematics. Old time clapping, slapping and chanting games are very popular with children and they can make endless variations. Learning to recognize patterns brings order to the world, and helps the child make sense out of the complexity of life. Recognizing patterns is an essential foundation for mathematics learning—number patterns (evens and odds), sequencing, arithmetic patterns, geometric patterns.

What are ratios? Simply put—the relationship between one thing and another. If you fill up glasses of the same shape with water in varied proportions (¼ full, ½ full, ¾ full, etc.) and tap each gently with a wooden mallet or metal spoon or fill plastic bottles in the same way and blow across the top, you'll notice that sounds of different pitches are made. The frequency or pitch of the sounds is proportional to the amount of water, because sound waves have to travel through the water and more water results in a lower pitch. Many exciting experiences can come from this simple experiment—try having children create a familiar tune by filling glasses with different amounts of water!

Music and Language

In the "old days" (early 1970s), when brain research was in its infancy, speech and music functions were thought to be located in the left and right hemispheres of the brain, respectively. Newer research is suggesting that things are much more complicated than this, that these functions have much in common, overlap in many ways, and in fact may benefit from each other (Jäncke, 2012). Both speech and music, according to one study, "are auditory signals that are sequential in nature (in contrast to visual information) and that unfold in time, according to the rules of syntax and harmony" (Besson et al., 2011, p. 2). In listening to music and in reading, the brain employs *prediction* (anticipating what note or chord or word comes next). The brain responds differently to familiarity and to novelty, experiencing some discomfort and prediction difficulties when encountering new forms of music or language. New studies suggest that musical training may enhance prediction abilities in language processing (Patel & Morgan, 2017).

Emergent research also suggests that reading and writing skills are closely related to pitch awareness and musical expertise. There is even evidence pointing to the positive effects on reading fluency by learning to keep a steady beat. Research aside, common sense tells us that memory is enhanced when embedded in music—think about some of the jingles you may have heard on television decades ago, and how they stick in your brain. Most children in English speaking countries learn the *alphabet song* and it's probably a challenge to find an adult who cannot sing it on command years later!

Music and Social/Emotional Learning

In terms of the education of children and their ability to create and sustain a healthy society in the future, perhaps the areas of most importance are in the social/emotional realm. There are so many ways that music listening and music making can enhance a young person's sense of self and emotional life: It can help a person get in touch with their own feelings, help them relate to what their peers are feeling, release bottled up emotion, stimulate mental imaging, express both joyful and sad states, help them to relax, and tune them into new worlds of experience. Aside from solo performance, music is most often a group event, leading to the development of social skills including leadership, discipline, working as a team member, relating to a diversity of others, and adjusting to, adapting to, cooperating and coordinating one's actions with others. One macro-study confirms the social-emotional benefits of music listening and music-making in these diverse areas as well as lowering incidents of bullying (Blasco-Magraner et al., 2021). Coordinating with others or synchronizing music making or moving stimulates positive emotions, and "(s)haring rhythmic behaviors such as singing, dancing, chanting, or talking together can increase social bonding" (Heshmat, 2022, para. 7).

Studies are proliferating on the effects of music on memory, mood, language development, well-being, learning, cognitive function, and even happiness. The coming years are likely to yield more information than we ever thought possible on all these connections. The findings, at least at this point in time, are complex, but boil down to a simple conclusion: "Music can activate almost all brain regions and networks, it can help to keep a myriad of brain pathways and networks strong, including those networks that are involved in well-being, learning, cognitive function, quality of life, and happiness" (Budson, 2020, para. 7).

Lest we think that research on the effects of music is limited to humans, it should be noted that there is a field of study looking at therapeutic uses of music, specifically on "captive animals"—domestic pets, farm animals, and non-human residents of zoos. Results are tentative in this emerging field, but we are beginning to understand that music has a wide range of effects on animals depending on their unique sensory and communication systems, and musical preferences vary widely both across species and within species. We do know that certain species of monkey prefer Mozart to heavy metal, but in those same studies we also discovered that they preferred silence to Mozart (Snowden, 2021)!

The jury is still out on whether or not plants grow larger, faster, or better when music is played for them, but apparently they do not appreciate rock and roll! Interestingly, most of the research on music and non-human-others is carried out by playing human-created music for them and documenting their response. The exception is birdsong, which humans have incorporated into their music for centuries, either by imitating birdsong, or more recently incorporating recordings into compositions, or in some cases, playing duets! There are experiments going on at the fringes of research, using computers to track sounds of creatures such as crustaceans, and then composing musical pieces to accompany them, indicating an interest on the part of some humans to attune to the actual language and sounds of the non-human others and collaborate creatively with them!

Music and Culture

Music is most often a reflection of the culture and era it was composed in. Exposing a child to multiple types of musical genres (e.g., classical, contemporary, rock, jazz, blues, raga, folk, or medieval) will allow them to have a glimpse into the past. Music is a sort of time travel and understanding the origins of music can give children a deeper understanding of what they are playing and perhaps increase their affinity for it.

As noted in the beginning of this chapter, music has been an essential part of virtually every culture known to us through time. Children gained cultural knowledge as well as traditional dance and music skills through active participation in regular rituals, ceremonies, and celebrations. In many pre-colonial traditional cultures, children absorbed their cultural identities through music related to social rites such as celebrations of births and marriages, through games, songs and storytelling, and through multi-layered entertainments that included song, music, dance, gestures and stories that carried messages about how to live and what was valued. They experienced the community commitment to the well-being of the whole, when the tribe or clan came together to help the sick through ceremonies, dances, drumming, prayer and chanting.

Neohumanism commits humans to developing deeper relationships with non-human nature than we are, to date, familiar with in the modern Western industrialized world. Dissanayake (1992) writes about the Kaluli people of Papua New Guinea, for example, who are extraordinarily aware of and attuned to their aural rainforest environment—the birds, the rustling leaves, dripping water—to which they fit their own talking, work, storytelling, movement, and music-making. To Dissanayake, such attunement *densifies texture*: "In other words, the music of nature becomes for the Kaluli the nature of music" (p. 118). She goes on to say, "We whose lives are compartmentalized and often out-of-sync with our surroundings can only admire and envy a society in which the cultural and the natural, art and life, can seem so seamlessly one" (p. 119).

Music is considered by some scholars to be essential to reestablishing indigenous knowledge and values in post-colonial cultures. Colonialism, with its introduction of Western formal education and the imposition of Christian liturgical processes, disregarded the pre-existing indigenous materials and forms or actively sought to suppress them, so this vital way of transmitting cultural values and literacies was largely lost. One Ghanian scholar, Benjamin Adjepong (2019), notes how "the rapid socio-economic transformation taking place in Africa and for that matter Ghana, is denying children the opportunity to acquire indigenous performing arts experiences in the traditional society" (p. 102). He highlights the importance of exposing students to the music and dance cultures of their ancestral history:

> Teaching students how to play rhythms on a traditional drum, sing an indigenous song, recite a traditional poetry, and perform an indigenous dance or drama provides opportunities for them to acquire skills and knowledge

which enable them to participate and engage actively in the societies in which they belong. (p. 103)

With the on-going colonial and post-colonial dislocations and ruptures in societies, it falls to the school to include these native arts in the current school curriculum, as a means of reinforcing traditional cultural values and skills. Adjepong notes a problem (which is present in neohumanist schools as well)—the lack of competence and training on the part of most school teachers to prepare children in the performing arts. It is costly to bring in professional personnel to prepare students for the annual cultural festivals which have become an important part of Ghanian education, and also expensive to provide the professional drums and other materials for performing arts programs. This requires partnerships with community arts organizations and collaboration with professional artists to provide workshops, in-service, and other professional development to regular classroom teachers so that they can gain the confidence and skills to perform these tasks. Fortunate is the neohumanist school that can afford a qualified music teacher; absent this benefit, neohumanist teachers need to call upon their own creative resources and community connections to teach the basics of music.

Bringing Music Into the Classroom

Leah Landau, who teaches music in the neohumanist teacher preparation program, emphasizes beginning with simple activities that don't require talent or even a degree in music. She emphasizes that the early years, up to age five, should be experiential, not goal or performance focused. It is important to instill a love of music making and the joy that comes from learning simple rhythms and melodies. There are many types of music activities that can be varied in the early childhood and primary classroom: singing, listening to music, making up lyrics to familiar tunes, acting out lyrics or song stories, dancing to music.

Basic rhythm activities involve the whole body—clapping, stamping, walking, jumping. Nursery tunes are familiar to everyone, and they can be the basis of an early childhood music lesson. A complex rhythmic activity can be taught by picking out the "macro-rhythm" (the whole of a measure) and then perhaps swaying back and forth to it, and then inserting the micro-rhythms (the notes in the measure), by clapping the hands. Combined with a simple tune and lyrics, this sort of activity embeds the notion of measures, beats, notes, and rests.

The love of hearing words in melodic ways begins, for most children, in the lullabies that parents or other caretakers might sing to them. There are lullabies in virtually every culture—melodic songs that calm and relax babies, help adults and babies to bond, and can even help to heal from traumatic events. Lullabies, says Shrii Sarkar (1957), "have enormous value in the formation of children's character" (para. 119). Lullabies can embody elements of the natural world, teach about cultural customs, convey messages of love and safety, transmit a heritage, and carry traces of our ancestors. Researchers have found that the language of the lullaby makes little difference in its ability to relax the child; it is "something in the kind of DNA of lullaby that helps to calm infants" (Mehr, as quoted in Simmons-Duffin, 2023).

> Lullabies are part of the fabric from which caregivers create safe spaces that are necessary for dreams to unfold... (they) remind us that we are not alone, and in the dark of night, they seem to hold a promise that on the other side waits the light of morning. (Morales, 2020, para. 46)

Just as the newborn is not concerned with whether the person rocking them to sleep can carry a tune, so too is this not an issue for young children. Teachers who are worried that their abilities might be judged have many options: Just jump in and sing without worrying, enlist the children to help you sing, play a recording to teach the song, or bring in a parent, grandparent, or community member to lead the singing. There is no need, in the early years, to "teach" a song—just start singing and invite the children in. Make up songs to accompany classroom processes ("It's time to eat our lunches, our lunches, our lunches, it's time to eat our lunches, yum, yum, yum, yum, yum."). Try this simple tune in 3/4 time doing the rhythmic macro and micro beats!

Children enjoy making up new words to familiar tunes. There are many versions of this musical game—they can substitute one word in the song ("Old Macdonald had a *zoo*"), or they can make up a whole set of lyrics to a tune. Singing becomes a form of early literacy, a means to facilitate the absorption of rhyming, alliteration, syllables, word recognition, all of the components of reading and writing. But most of all, it should be fun, and create a feeling of community.

With just a few recycled resources, one can create simple musical instruments: Fill small, empty plastic bottles with rice, dried beans, seeds or stones to make shakers with different sounds; make a drum set out of different sized pots or cans with lids; make a xylophone out of PVC pipes; make rhythm sticks from short pieces of dowelling, chopsticks or rulers. Once children have played with the instruments, you can start making music together. Play a simple beat, and ask them to repeat it with their instrument or hands. Don't forget to switch jobs so that the children can lead as well. Once children get the basic rhythm patterns down, you can mix them up to create even more complex rhythm symphonies.

As children get older, their music development stabilizes somewhat. They can continue to grow musically after this, but by nine years of age, important patterns have been laid down.

> The songs and sounds they've absorbed are...now part of the musical *lingua franca* or the music that is "normal" for them. They're familiar with the musical genres, timbres, modes, and instruments, rhythmic and melodic patterns, and have learned the culturally acceptable cadences, harmonies, texture, and so forth. (Sarrazin, n.d.)

The range of notes they are capable of reaching with their voices has expanded, and they also probably have a fairly substantial repertoire of songs, if they have been in an early education setting that focuses on singing. They are ready for more complex songs, more sophisticated subject matter, and multiple vocal parts such as simple harmonies or rounds. They are ready to engage in instrumental music in which two or more parts are played by different instruments. Any of these activities stimulate the brain to concentrate deeply on one's own part, while simultaneously keeping the whole in mind.

At this level, teachers really do need to have some musical training, in order to help children find a comfortable pitch, and facilitate the more complex singing and orchestral pieces. As children get older and approach the middle grades, they develop a strong interest in competence, and more formal music instruction can be introduced. Every child should have the opportunity to study a simple instrument such as the recorder in the primary years, so that they can learn the basics of music notation, the symbol system that communicates the language of music.

Music and Spirituality

> *Music is one of our most powerful gateways to connect to our spiritual nature—our divine source—the unseen, as well as to the universe around us and those other divine beings that inhabit it with us.*
> —Frank Fitzpatrick, *Why Music?*, 2013

Music is an art form that can delight us, amuse us, entertain us, teach us. To spiritual teachers of all faiths, it also has transcendent purpose. Indian Sufi Master Hazrat Inayat Khan (1996) explains it this way:

> The soul who is seeking for truth is in search of the formless God. Art, no doubt, is elevating, but it contains form; poetry has words, names suggestive of forms; it is music only which has beauty, power, charm, and at the same time can raise the soul beyond form. (p. 4)

There is a reason, says Khan, why many of the great prophets of religious traditions were musicians. Krishna is often depicted with his flute, and Shiva is considered the inventor of the veena (an Indian stringed instrument). The Christian Bible has references to music and prophecy: "But now bring me a minstrel. And it came to pass, when the minstrel played, that the hand of the Lord came upon him" (2 Kings 3:15).

Shrii Sarkar explains the spiritual power of music in terms of Yogic philosophy. In this narrative, all life, animate and inanimate, emanates from a single cosmic source (the psycho-spiritual equivalent of the big bang). Behind all of the waves created, there is sound (Krishna's flute is a metaphor for the music that pervades all creation). Humans experience the arts through their five senses and in our evolutionary history these have evolved to appreciate ever more refined expressions (consider the first humans who perhaps made rhythm with rocks or sticks, then consider the contemporary symphony orchestra); this movement from crude to increasingly subtle is what accounts for what Sarkar terms *aesthetic science.*

As a person develops increasingly subtle sensibilities, they come to understand that their feelings of beauty, harmony, and bliss emanate from an infinite space, one attainable only through the heart. They develop feelings of devotion, and the various choral, musical, and kinesthetic forms that people have devised to express their devotion, or attraction to the Cosmic source (the formless God), are termed, in this framework, *supra-aesthetic science.* Thus, in virtually all religious and spiritual traditions, music and song are a key element, whether it is the Samgiita and kirtan of the Yogis, the mysticism behind the musicality of the Javanese gamelan, the Gregorian chants of the Medieval Catholic Church, or the call and response gospel singing said to have originated in ancestral African music. Devotional music facilitates the disassociation from the "small self" (the individual ego) and connection with the essence of all beings, the feeling of "oneness" with all creation. Recognizing the urgent need for a cultural renaissance that might facilitate the all-around progress of the human species, Shrii Sarkar himself has contributed a huge corpus of work (5018 musical compositions) to the devotional repertoire of Yogic songs (Sarkar, n.d.). These are currently being translated into numerous languages and spread across the globe to nourish the spiritual sentiments—the "longing for the Great"—emerging everywhere.

The word Yoga, in Sanskrit, comes from the root *yug*, meaning to yoke, or to unite. The various Yoga practices are designed to unite body, mind and spirit, or to unite the personal consciousness with the cosmic consciousness. This harmonious integration is the developmental aim of Yoga practice. Infusing music and song into the lives of young people can foster delight, and inspire the increasing subtlety of perception that can lead to a devotional state of mind, a love for all beings and a deep connection to all of creation. It is therefore essential that a neohumanist education find ways to include music across the entire curriculum, whether in the form of "good morning songs," in songs that celebrate and *make special* the events of daily life, songs that reinforce empathy, friendship, and service, in music that awakens ancestral connections, in music-making that encourages the expression of feelings, in music that generates mental images of peace and well-being, or in singing that brings laughter and joy and togetherness. Young people in neohumanist schools will have access to many different kinds of music in the home and the wider community; it is the job of the neohumanist educator to carefully choose music and songs that uplift the spirit and embody the principles of neohumanism, as elaborated throughout this book: principles of oneness, of care, of connection, and of service.

In this chapter, we have focused on the neuroscience of music. The research on the effects of musicality on the brain have contributed much to the field of music therapy, which utilizes listening, singing, song writing and improvisational music-making among other musical processes to help address neurological and psychological problems. In recognition that a robust engagement with music can actually *prevent* some of these conditions, there is a slight shift in the music therapy world away from a medical model "into the bio-psycho-social-spiritual model, giving credence to all aspects of a person's needs and systems" (Roskam & Reuer, 1999, p. 140), and a turn towards studying the effects of music making on healthy active older adults. Findings have included "significant increases in the human growth hormone, which is an important factor in maintaining immunity from disease... (and) a significant decrease in anxiety, depression, and loneliness" (p. 140).

Conventional schooling emphasizes competitive academic achievement and workforce preparation; education designed to prepare young people for a "survival of the fittest" world of capitalist production, endless growth, consumerism, rapacious use of the planet's finite resources, conflict and competition between nation states, and a tacit acceptance of the realities of inequality. In most educational settings, the interests of young people themselves do not feature prominently: school attendance is compulsory, adults decide what needs to be learned, schedules must be rigidly adhered to, and textbooks present material to be memorized in ways that do not inspire enthusiasm or meaning-making. We see the results of this approach to education with the high drop out and failure statistics, with the epidemic of anxiety and depression in the young, and with the extensive substance abuse disorders so prevalent, at least in Western societies.

Neohumanism "changes the story" of our planetary existence to a narrative of living within ecological limits, technological advancement that benefits all humanity, ensuring that the basic needs of all people are met, guaranteeing that no culture or race is considered superior to another, and caring for the Earth and its non-human inhabitants. With this narrative, it follows that a neohumanist education centers the aims of well-being, health, creativity, happiness, and student agency—the ability and opportunities to make a positive contribution to one's world. Academic achievement is not devalued in this model; it is merely placed alongside other equally important outcomes, and all subject matter is taught from a critical ethical standpoint, with the aim of establishing a world in which all people and non-human others can thrive.

Music, along with the other art forms of dance, painting, sculpture, and drama, has a key role to play in bringing about such a healthy and thriving society. To facilitate the shift away from materialism and the longing for more and more *stuff*, pleasurable experience must take its place, the kind of joy that comes from creative pursuits. We will not enact the profound economic and cultural transformations that are necessary if we are to survive as a species and sustain the conditions for non-human species to survive as well, unless the alternatives to consumption, capitalism, destructive resource extraction, and militarism are more attractive than the status quo.

One of the most important emotions in our human repertoire is *awe*, a sense of the power and vastness of the world, an overwhelming feeling of reverence and wonder. In a new book, *Awe: The New Science of Everyday Wonder and How It Can Transform Your Life*, psychologist Dacher Keltner (2023) concludes that music is perhaps our most important human gateway to the sacred, because it

> breaks down the boundaries between self and other and can unite us in feelings of awe... When we listen to music with others, the great rhythms of our bodies... merge into a synchronized pattern... a pattern of energy, an idea of the times, or what we might call the sacred. (p. 153)

Music is a source of joy, of pleasure, of learning, of community, and of transcendence. In a future neohumanist society, the music will ring out from every direction—songs of gratitude, sonatas of appreciation, interspecies symphonies, Deep Earth drumming, and the music of the spheres. We will hear the twinkle of the stars, rejoice in the singing of the wood thrush, listen for the song of the humpback whale and learn what they are teaching us, revel in the rustle of the quaking aspen leaves, dance to the pattern of the flying geese, strum to the tempo of the gurgling brook; we might even learn, as the Kaluli seem to know, how to fit into the totality of the ecosystem to which we belong, to find ourselves truly "at home" on Planet Earth.

FOR CONTINUING STUDY

> *Discussion/Reflection:* In a group, discuss the various ways that music has played a formative role in your identity. Consider your relationship to music and how it has evolved through the years of your life.
>
> *Discussion/Reflection:* Think about the ways that you could bring in music that is very popular with youth, and use it to explore important social issues.
>
> *Application:* If you are a musical "novice" try the simple exercise in this chapter. Choose a simple nursery tune, such as "Mary Had a Little Lamb" and print out a copy of the musical notation from the Internet. It's a simple tune, with quarter notes, half notes, and a whole note at the end. Pick out the "macro-rhythm" (the whole of a measure) by swaying back and forth to it, and then insert the micro-rhythms (the notes in the measure), by clapping your hands. Think about how you might introduce the musical notes to a group of youngsters.
>
> *Application:* Imagine that you (parent, teacher, student, or community member) are an advocate for retaining or funding a music program in your school. Write a brief but impassioned speech for your local school board on the importance of music to the education of the children in your local school.

To watch a complex singing activity by students in a Waldorf School in Saratoga Springs, NY, click the link below: https://www.youtube.com/watch?v=dUNDemrHt0U

References

Adjepong, B. (2019). Performing arts in the basic schools cultural festivals: Educating the Ghanaian student. *European Journal of Education Studies, 4*(1). https://oapub.org/soc/index.php/EJSSS/article/view/513/1092

Besson, M., Choobert, J., & Marie, C. (2011, May 12). Transfer of training between music and speech: Common processing, attention, and memory. *Frontiers in Psychology, 2*(94). https://doi.org/10.3389/fpsyg.2011.00094

Blasco-Magraner, J. S., Bernabe-Valero, G., Marín-Liébana, P., & Moret-Tatay, C. (2021). Effects of the educational use of music on 3- to 12-year-old children's emotional development: A systematic review. *International Journal of Environmental Research and Public Health, 18*(17), 3668. https://doi.org/10.3390/ijerph18073668

Budson, A. E. (2020, October 7). Why is music good for the brain? *Harvard Health Blog*. https://www.health.harvard.edu/blog/why-is-music-good-for-the-brain-2020100721062

Dissanayake, E. (1988). *What is art for?* University of Washington Press.

Fitzpatrick, F. (2013, May 3). *Why music, part 9: Music and spirituality*. https://www.huffpost.com/entry/music-spirituality_b_3203309

Heshmat, S. (2022, June 30). The importance of rhythm in everyday life. *Psychology Today*. https://www.psychologytoday.com/us/blog/science-choice/202206/the-importance-rhythm-in-everyday-life

Jäncke, L. (2012, April 27). The relationship between music and language. *Frontiers in Psychology, 3*(123). https://doi.org/10.3389/fpsyg.2012.00123

Keltner, D. (2023). *Awe: The new science of everyday wonder and how it can transform your life*. Penguin Press.

Khan, H. I. (1996). *The mysticism of sound and music*. Shambala Publications.

Magsamen, S., & Ross, I. (2023). *Your brain on art: How the arts transform us*. Random House. [Kindle edition]

Menehan, K. (2015, December 4). *Singing and the brain*. https://chorusamerica.org/advocacy-research/singing-and-brain

Montagu, J. (2017). How music and instruments began: A brief overview of the origin and entire development of music, from its earliest stages. *Frontiers of Sociology, 2*. https://doi.org/10.3389/fsoc.2017.00008

Morales, H. R. (2023, January 20). *What the lullabies we sing to our children reveal about us*. https://education.nationalgeographic.org/resource/what-lullabies-we-sing-our-children-reveal-about-us/

Patel, A. D., & Morgan, E. (2017). Exploring cognitive relations between prediction in language and music. *Cognitive Science, 41*(Suppl. 2), 303–320. https://doi.org/10.1111/cogs.12411

Roskam, K., & Reuer, B. (1999). A music therapy wellness model for illness prevention. In C. Dildeo (Ed.), *Music therapy and medicine: Theoretical and clinical applications* (139–147). The American Music Therapy Association.

Sarkar, P. R. (n.d.). *Saṁgiita: Song, dance, and instrumental music*. Electronic edition of the works of P. R. Sarkar, version 9.0.

Sarkar, P. R. (1957). The practice of art and literature. In P. E. Sakar (Ed.), *Discourses on Neohumanist Education* (2nd ed.). Electronic edition of the works of P. R. Sarkar, version 9.0.

Sarrazin, N. (n.d.). Music and the older child. *In Music and the Child.* https://courses.lumenlearning.com/suny-music-and-the-child/chapter/chapter-9-music-and-the-older-child-3/

Simmons-Duffin, S. (2023, June 2). *A lullaby really can work magic: Science tells us why and how.* https://www.npr.org/sections/goatsandsoda/2023/06/02/1179434534/a-lullaby-really-can-work-magic-science-tells-us-why-and-how

Snowden, C. (2021, September 11). Animal signals, music and emotional well-being. *Animals, 11*(9), 2670. https://doi.org/10.3390/ani11092670

Spitzer, M. (2021). *The musical human: A history of life on earth.* Bloomsbury Publishing.

13

Neohumanist Education and the "Lively Arts"

Integrating Creative Movement Across the Curriculum

Dance as an art has to do not only with the body but also with the spirit, another dimension of the self.

—Sue Stinson, *Dance for Children: Finding the Magic in Movement*, 1988

The body—the Annamaya kosha—that incredibly complex system of muscle, bone, blood, nerve, glands, skin, water, and empty space (yes, the largest constituent of your body is empty space!) is not merely a simple machine, but "the vessel of the individual's sense of self, his most personal feelings and aspirations, as well as that entity to which others respond in a special way because of their uniquely human qualities" (Gardner, 1983, pp. 235–236). The body is the human being's fundamental means of communication and creative expression.

Long thought in dualistic Western philosophy to be a separate and inferior partner to consciousness (where all knowledge was thought to originate), current thinking emphasizes the active and significant role played

---

Becoming One With the World, pages 249–268
Copyright © 2024 by Information Age Publishing
www.infoagepub.com
All rights of reproduction in any form reserved.

by the body in the development of mind. Theories of embodiment and embodied learning are consistent with a relational ontology, as described in Chapter 1, as the body is an integral part of interlocked systems—the biological, psychological, and cultural milieux in which it exists. Without the body and its organs and limbs operating in space, we would not have perception, imagery, memory, or reasoning powers. Yoga philosophy does posit a "causal" or formless mind that can affect bodily impulses and sensations, but this relationship is non-dualistic, as it acknowledges the reciprocity between what we call body and what we call mind, spirit and/or soul. The metaphysics of the mind/body/spirit/soul connection are well beyond the scope of this chapter; suffice it to say that in neohumanism, these aspects of being constitute a holistic, integrated system.

Movement—the body in motion—should be an essential part of the education of all children, not just in early childhood but throughout their development. Modern children living in technologically advanced societies move less and less and their time is largely spent at desks or in front of screens, even in their "free" time. This has brought about an epidemic of obesity and falling levels of physical fitness. In neohumanist schools, children should be engaged in everyday motor tasks—peeling vegetables, sweeping the floor, washing windows, putting away materials. Every day should involve a LONG walk outdoors (school children in Norway spend at least an hour of each day on walking excursions, and they have one of the healthiest populations on the planet). Students should be learning subject matter like math through active learning, using manipulatives and tools to solve problems. A robust physical education program should be in place, with games, sports and of course, Yoga. And *creative movement* should be an essential part of learning across the curriculum. In this chapter, we develop the justification for and theoretical foundation of a creative movement program, and outline the main components of such a program.

What Is "Creative Movement?"

Creative movement is a kinesthetic discipline that builds upon ordinary, everyday movements in ways that foster communication, somatic and emotional awareness, social skill development, self-esteem, and creativity. It not only fosters physical fitness; it can play a significant role in an integrated pedagogy to augment learning across the academic disciplines and enhance other "intelligences." A strong creative movement program should hold a special place in the education of young children, as the cultivation of kinesthetic intelligence is important to a number of adult outcomes. The skilled surgeon possesses deep medical knowledge gleaned through linguistic and mathematical sources, but without highly developed eye-hand coordination and manual dexterity, her knowledge could not be exercised. The violinist with a highly developed musical intelligence could not perform without bodily-kinesthetic expertise. And sculptors and painters would be hard pressed to express their creative visual intelligence without the refined skills of the body to wield brush and clay. Yet, we too often take the body for granted, until some injury or disability reminds us of its centrality to our lived experience.

All of the arts provide ways in which people can bring shape, order, and meaning to our world. Creative movement provides a primary medium for expression involving the total body, not just one part, like the voice, or in the case of painting, the eye, the arm, and the hand. As with other art forms, it incorporates elements of thinking, feeling, and sensing that find unique expression in movement. Closely related to dance, there are some significant differences. It is not bound by stylistic concerns (as in ballet, flamenco, or jazz). Creative movement is not primarily in service of a product or a performance, but is more concerned with process. The development of technique is not of concern; rather the focus is on exploration, improvisation, active imagination, and expression. It can evoke a symbolic representation of the child's ideas, feelings, and sensory impressions. A child's identity, self-concept, and self-direction are improved in relation to such use of the body's movement, and the innermost selves of children can be *made visible* through skillful teaching.

In the next section, we offer practical guidelines for a beginning creative movement program that can be incorporated into any learning environment, given a bit of space, a block of time, and a teacher willing to explore and experiment along with her charges. We start with an explanation of the appropriate context for a program, outline the main components of a movement program, and then provide some curricular suggestions.

The Creative Movement Program

There are many possible designs for a creative movement program. We offer here a simple system, planned so that any teacher with an interest, even if they are not trained in dance or physical education, could conduct movement classes, or integrate creative movement into the teaching of other subjects. We start with the basic organization of a creative movement program, and outline the fundamental pedagogical elements that will be covered. We then introduce a simple process that includes the investigation of themes using guided exploration followed by discovery. We show you how to start with the most fundamental aspect—movement words—which can then be built into movement sentences, and then into longer and more complex movement narratives, or stories. You will begin to see how closely connected movement activity is to the development of vocabulary, the creation of mental images, and such cognitive skills as sequencing and patterning. We close with some curriculum suggestions—how to integrate creative movement into virtually any subject area. While this chapter provides a survey of the components of a movement program, you can find many more ideas and strategies in a full text on the topic such as one of those listed in the references.

Environmental Space

Yes, children need space in which to move. The ideal situation is an empty room with wood floors (wood is the kindest building material to young feet and bodies). If you lack an empty room, the next best thing is to be able to rearrange desks or other furniture to create a large central space. If you have pushed back furniture to create space, you might want to mark its boundaries with masking tape, so that children aren't tempted to hide under desks or climb up on chairs! The size of your space will determine the number of children that can be accommodated. They must be able to all be in motion occasionally without bumping into each other. Creative movement *can* happen out of doors, if there is a smooth grassy spot where children can safely move in bare feet. Certain limiting factors such as acoustics may present themselves.

If you lack a space where the more vigorous movement activities can take place, don't give up. In Chapter 14, on creative drama, we will discuss the process of "storymaking" with young children, in which a teacher makes good use of a very small space to do some movement activities. There are even activities that can be done while children are sitting at or standing beside their desks—movement breaks that involve exercises, wiggles, jumps, or stretches, or academic tasks like making the shape of a letter with their bodies. Even small amounts of movement can break the tedium of too much seat time.

Materials

Children should dress in comfortable clothing that allows for maximum movement—shorts, leggings or tights, and t-shirts. Bare feet are the ideal—socks can be slippery and cause accidents, and athletic shoes don't allow for the freedom of foot movement.

Neohumanist Education and the "Lively Arts" ▪ 253

It is not necessary to have available recorded music, though you may choose to use a piece at some point. What can add interest to the activities are sound making instruments that include:

- rhythmic instruments (hand drums, claves [hardwood sticks], blocks, castanets)
- rattling instruments (maracas, tambourines, sleigh bells, rain sticks)
- ringing instruments (gongs, cymbals, triangles, chime bars)

It is important that a teacher have a variety of instruments at hand. If you have the resources, it can be useful to also have instruments for the children to use. This chapter will not include instructions on making instruments, but that is certainly an option if you want the children to have access to sound-making accessories. Though not necessary, you may choose to occasionally provide age-appropriate props for the children to explore. These can include scarves, stretchy bands, hoops, foam balls, ribbon streamers, or parachutes!

Rules

As in any democratically run classroom, rules and norms are best established collaboratively, with the children taking the lead. Teachers may wish to establish certain behavioral boundaries, as in requiring that all motion !STOP! when she or he says the word !FREEZE! This simple rule can help to mitigate the chaos that can ensue when young people start to feel the freedom and joy of exuberant movement. If you post the rules where all can see them, children may choose to add more as they engage in movement experiences. These might include: respecting personal space, no touching unless invited, no pushing, etc.

Elements of Creative Movement

Space, time, and energy are the broad categories which children can explore through creative movement activities and together constitute a strong foundation for helping children explore their somatic potential. The elements of these categories provide the variables that are applied to movements to add interest and create different effects (Boorman, 1969).

Space is literally the physical surround in which all objects exist and move (whether we are talking about the solar system or your living room). Space is the container in which the child can explore their movements. Moving in space implies *direction, pathways, levels, expansion, contraction,* and *shapes*. One may travel forward, backwards, or sideways; they may move in a straight line, or a zigzag pattern, or in a curving or circular pathway; movements may occupy all the height a child can reach, or they may shrivel down to the ground, or operate midway between these levels. Movements may expand outward and upward, opening and stretching, or they may constrict, drawing in to occupy the smallest possible amount of space. Basic space words include forward, backward, near, over, under, around, sideways, up, down, and so on.

Time is an extraordinarily complicated construct in regards to child development. In the 1940s, inspired by Albert Einstein, Jean Piaget launched upon his study of how children develop temporal concepts. Since then, decades of research have been devoted to understanding how children come to grasp intervals, duration, sequences, and linear time. Much of the primary curriculum is devoted to teaching the mechanics of passing time: reading analog and digital clocks, learning the days of the week, the months of the year, the structure of the calendar. Creative movement helps a child to internalize a sense of time within their bodies, and to apply this sense to their creative movement expression. If they are instructed to "walk slowly across the floor," and then to "walk quickly across the floor" they learn, somatically, that the time it takes to cross a distance is relative to both the distance and the speed of movement. Time in creative movement deals with the relationship of one movement to another. With repeated experiences, children develop a sense of timing within their bodies. They become aware of rhythm, pulse, speed, pause, and phrasing; with this, comes the ability to understand music and to harmonize their movements with a soundscape.

Energy is the force that drives movement and gives it its intensity. Children need to explore tension/relaxation, bound/free, heavy/light, and ebb/flow to understand the ways that different intensities contrast with each other. Just as the painter adds white to a color to create a lighter hue, or black to give a color shade, dancers apply tension or relaxation, lightness or heaviness to movements to add interest and expand the range of expression. Each of these elements provides an opportunity for the child to open up their imagination and explore. How does one walk when feeling heavy? How does one move when feeling free? What does it feel like to tighten one muscle at a time, until the whole body is "clenched?" Then how does it feel to release the tension, to relax more deeply with each breath?

Starting Points for Movement

In order to symbolize expression through movement, the child must build a movement vocabulary, just as we have shown in visual arts and in music.

Creative movement teachers generally categorize these words as action words and stillness words. Action words can "travel from place to place" (crawl, walk, run, roll, or skip) or "happen in place" (jump, shake, stretch, or twist). Stillness words imply an end to movement (freeze, grip, collapse, shrink). Here is where movement pedagogy begins—with the simplest of instructions to warm up the body/mind by expressing these basic movements:

- Using action words to travel across the room.
- Staying in place to explore other action words.
- Bringing movement to an end by using stillness words.

As children grow comfortable with expressing these everyday movements, the vocabulary can be expanded: leaping, twirling, pouncing, creeping, prancing, collapsing, swooping. The possibilities are endless. Body parts can be isolated and explored both standing and sitting on the floor—heads can rotate in circles or look from side to side or touch ear to shoulder, elbows can reach, an arm can swing, a leg can extend. When children have developed a substantial movement vocabulary, it is time to combine action and stillness words. Combinations can be made: Hands can shake and then grip; whole bodies can expand, then wiggle as the body contracts. Again, endless varieties of movement combinations are possible. Longer sentences can be built—one can run, then leap, then twirl, and then fall. One can gallop and then freeze, spin, and then collapse. Percussion instruments add another dimension to these tasks; children learn to listen, process, and respond both to a voice and to a sound.

Just as the beginning artist gives form to her ideas by applying pencil or crayon to paper to create lines and shapes, and the beginning musician combines notes on the piano to create simple tunes, so the movement artist begins to create form and structure out of fundamental movements; thus are the beginnings of dance.

Expanding Movement Stories Using Space, Time, and Energy

Now we have a vocabulary of simple movements—how can they be made more expressive? In this section we consider the variables of space, levels, direction, energy, and time, and how these relate to the processes of Guided Exploration (teacher providing instructions) followed by Discovery (students explore and improvise, alone or in groups).

Space/Levels (high/mid/low)
Guided exploration:

- Imagine that you are painting your room a new color. Think about what color you would like this to be, and picture that color of paint in a bucket. You dip your brush in the bucket and then wipe the excess paint off of it. You are going to paint the low overhead ceiling first, so reach high and paint with broad brush strokes.
- When the ceiling is finished, you are going to paint a wall, covering it with paint until you get to your mid-section.
- Finally, you need to paint the lower half of the wall, being careful not to get any paint on the floor.

Discovery:

- Create an action sentence using two action words and one stillness word. Enact this sentence at a high level.
- Create an action sentence using two action words and a stillness word. Enact this sentence at the mid-level.
- Create an action sentence using two action words and a stillness word. Enact this sentence on or close to the floor.

Space/Direction
Guided exploration (horizontal and vertical space):

1. Imagine that you are standing on an "X." This is your "place."
   - Jump in place, using as little space as you can with your body.
   - Jump in place, using as much space as you can with your body.
   - One person at a time: Jump from place to place, using as little space as you can.
   - Jump from place to place, using as much space as you can.
2. Imagine there is a large tunnel (or a bridge, etc.) in the middle of the room. One child at a time, follow the teacher's commands! (Teacher calls out instructions using prepositions: "Ramona, run around the tunnel"; "Joshua, creep through the tunnel"; "Mira, tiptoe over the bridge"; etc.).

Discovery:

- Create an action sentence using three action words and two stillness words. Do this action moving first forward and then backward.

- Create an action sentence using three action words and two stillness words. Do this action while covering the floor in different patterns (zig zag, curved, etc.).

Time

Guided exploration:

- Walk across the room as slowly as you can.
- Walk across the room as quickly as you can without running.
- Skip across the room as slowly as you can.
- Imagine that you weigh 300 pounds and skip across the room as slowly as you can.

Discovery:

- Invent a movement sentence using four action words and a stillness word. First, do this action as slowly as you can. Then do the action as quickly as you can.

Intensity/Force/Energy (lethargic, strong/confident, weak/timid, aggressive)

Guided exploration:

- Imagine you are a feather falling from the sky. Feel yourself drifting slowly down to the ground.
- Imagine you are a bolt of lightning. What shape do you make? How do you strike?

Discovery:

- As a group, decide on an action word. In a circle, move towards each other using weak movements. Make sure the circle keeps its shape and do not touch anyone.
- Using the same action word, and keeping the circle shape, move away from each other using strong movements, while not touching anyone.

The above strategies are only examples drawn from innumerable possibilities—You should use your own creativity to design activities suitable for your group of children. As they become comfortable with the process, you can increase the complexity. For example, have them create movement sentences and then vary them using at least two of the variables (time and intensity, level and space, etc.). Experiment with changing the variables.

It is important to build in time for reflection after an extended movement activity. Because movement is a holistic, integrated form of activity, feelings and emotions can surface during activities. Teachers can model debriefing ("It made me feel powerful when I leaped across the room" or "When I curled up in a little ball, it reminded me of what was like to feel afraid") to let children know that there are no right or wrong responses, and it's okay to express vulnerability. Sharing strong feelings is not always easy, so children should be invited, not forced to share.

Investigating Concepts Using Guided Exploration and Discovery

So far, we have focused our attention on the close ties between movement and language development. When children have a substantial movement vocabulary and are familiar with the many ways that movements can be varied and made more interesting, you can begin to up the game to teach concepts in other academic areas as well. You may find that new ideas can take root in deeper and more lasting ways if they are "embodied." Geometry is a common academic subject that deals with lines, points, shapes, and surfaces; it becomes increasingly complex as students move through the grades. Here, we demonstrate how very young children can be introduced to some fundamentals of geometry.

Concept: Angles

Guided exploration:

- Discuss angles—what are they?
- Sitting on the floor, explore all the different ways your body parts can make angles.
- Point out the different types of angles using developmentally appropriate terminology (narrow, open for young children; acute, obtuse, right, straight, etc. for older children).

Discovery:

- In pairs, create a statue of interconnected angles. Have class watch one pair at a time, and ask for volunteers to point out the angles they see.
- In groups of three, create tableaux of interconnected angles. Have the rest of the group assess the different kinds of angles.
- Start with calling on one child to make an angle with a body part, call on another child to hook on to that child, making a new

angle, until all children are part of the tableaux. You might want to play a sharp rhythm with sticks when each angle is formed. Then have everyone reach up to the sky (or walk around for a few seconds) and then make a new angle with another person next to them. You might use a rain stick to accompany the interim movements, having them make the new tableaux when the sound ends.

Concept: Curves
Guided exploration:

- Discuss curves—What are they? Explore all the ways your body can make curves while standing still. Be sure to name what you see: "Candace is making circles with her fingers"; "Robert is making a circle with his arms over his head"; "Janet is bending her whole body to one side."

Discovery:

Repeat the activities from Concept 1 (angles).

- In pairs, create a statue of interconnected curves.
- In groups of three, create tableaux of interconnected curves.
- Start with one child making a curved shape, have another child hook on to that child, making a new curve, until all children are part of the tableaux. Then have everyone reach up to the sky and make a new curve with another person next to them.

Advanced Group Practice

- Variation 1: For the count of ten, move around the room in curved directions, not touching, and end in a curved tableaux on the count of ten.
- Variation 2: Secretly whisper a "level" into each child's ear—tell the group that their final tableaux should reflect these levels.

In Sync

Learning to synchronize one's movement with others take skill and practice. There are many forms of synchronization in human activity: marching, dancing, crew rowing, clapping. Non-human-others also demonstrate synchronicity, as in the swarming of bees, the murmuration of birds, or the harmonizing of light flashes by male fireflies! Scientists have begun to study the ways that synchronization of movements "build even stronger social ties and create a greater sense of well-being... increases generosity, trust and tolerance toward others, often beyond effects seen in more disorderly doings" (Zaraska, 2020, para. 2). This phenomenon is just beginning to be understood, but so far we know that synchronous movements do activate the brain's reward system, and that synchronized movements result in synchronized brain waves. Researchers have speculated that such activity led to greater bonding amongst humans, and that from an evolutionary standpoint, this has survival value. It is safe to assume that it can be one factor in the creation of a healthy classroom community, one in which all children can feel a sense of belonging. We start here with mirroring, a simple pair activity that lends itself to many variations (see, for example, https://www.childdrama.com/mirror.html#basic).

Concept: Mirroring
Guided exploration:

- In pairs, have the children stand about three feet apart. One starts as the "leader" the other as the "follower" with the goal of replicating exactly what the other is doing. Have them move simply and slowly, only from the waist up, while looking into each other's eyes. The goal is not to "trick" the follower, but to move in perfect unison. At a signal they can exchange roles.

Discovery:

- In the same pairs, the children experiment with changing roles without an external signal.
- As children get adept at mirroring, they can advance to using the whole body, or even moving slowly.

Concept: Synchronization
Guided explorations:

- Standing in a circle, instruct the children to begin applause, as though they have just witnessed a fantastic performance. Tell them that their aim is to all shift into clapping together. Once they all start clapping in sync, let it go on for a moment or two.
- Have children simply walk about randomly, not touching each other. Give them a signal like a bell or gong to start walking "in tune" with their closest neighbor, matching their pace (Make sure that everyone gets hooked up with a partner; if necessary, teacher joins in). After some time, have each pair hook up with another pair, and this larger group synchronizes their movements. Continue until you have the whole group moving togeth-

er, as one organism. Be sure to debrief these activities. Did they find it easy or hard to align their movements with another? What did it feel like when everyone was moving as one whole entity?

Discovery:

- Have children in small groups—leader creates a short body percussion series (some combination of clapping, stamping, slapping a body part, etc.) with a particular number of beats. They should do it until they can sustain a synchronized pattern for a while; then a new leader can take over, and try one with more beats and perhaps some rests.

Concept: Leading, Following, and Responding
Guided exploration:

- Start this exploration by moving two at a time across the floor. Teacher calls out an action word—when children are halfway across, change the action word.
- Variation: Start with half the group on each side of the room. When two children reach the other side, they tag two children who haven't had a turn.

Guided exploration—variables:

- Four at a time, in a line, one child leads the group around the room using an action word. When the bell rings, they go to the end of the line and the next person leads with another action word, until everyone has had a turn leading.
- Four at a time, in a line, one child leads the group around the room using an action word while moving in a floor pattern (straight line, curves, zigzag, etc.). When the bell rings, they go to the end of the line and the next person leads with another action word in the same pattern, until everyone has had a turn leading.
- Further variations: Movements can be changed according to level, intensity, direction, or speed.

Concept: Coming Together and Moving Apart
Guided exploration:

- In pairs, have children stand at least five feet apart. First, have them walk slowly towards each other until they are almost touch-

ing. Then have them walk backwards until they reach their starting point. Then vary the instructions.
- Taking very small steps and leading with your elbow, move together and then apart.
- Using an action word (leap) and a stillness word (crouch) move together and then apart.

Discovery:
- In pairs, make a movement sentence using any combination of action words and stillness words in which you explore coming together and moving apart. Synchronize your movements.

Curricular Applications

Creative movement offers young people unique opportunities for working collaboratively. Solving a movement problem as a group involves practicing active listening, brainstorming, weighing and assessing ideas, negotiating differences, adapting one's own ideas, and building consensus. Actually moving together requires acute awareness of others: aligning rhythms, assessing proxemics, holding a spatial pattern. Group choreography can become increasingly complex as children learn the skills of planning and implementing group movement activities.

As children get comfortable with the basics of creative movement, it is possible to shift from a very literal form of representation to more symbolic representations. Many children are familiar with pantomime. In pre-school, they may have been instructed to "wiggle their ears like a bunny" using their hands, or asked to "hop like a frog." Though they share similarities, there are important differences between pantomime and creative movement. Pantomime is a specialized form of communication in which an actor literally depicts a story or idea (e.g., being trapped inside a box, or juggling). Creative movement is less literal, more symbolic. It is an attempt to capture the *essence* of an emotion or event. Here's an example that clarifies the difference: a common pantomime exercise might be "pouring." A child is instructed to visualize a glass in one hand, and a carton in the other, and literally pour the milk into the glass as though the items actually exist. It is a bit like the game of Charades; people should be able to guess what action someone is depicting. To illustrate "pouring" with creative movement might involve starting from a standing position and then sinking to the floor using wavy movements—a symbolic representation of the pouring motion. The mover captures the *phenomenon* of pouring without literally depicting it.

Exploring curricular concepts through creative movement is rigorous in the sense that a movement expression needs to embody accurate re/presentation of this essence. When searching for ideas, think about: What do the stimuli offer for varied bodily activity? How can the idea be made animate with changes in time, space, movement and force?

The initial discussion component is important—children collaboratively examine what they know about a topic, what they need to learn in order to be able to create a movement piece about it, and they engage in creative problem solving. These activities have a number of purposes: from a curricular point of view, the activity can reinforce concepts. From a creative point of view, the curricular ideas provide stimuli for the production of creative movements. All creative activity should be followed by description and reflective evaluation ("What did we do?"; How did we do?"; "Did we accomplish what we hoped?")

Suggested Steps in Curricular Applications

- Brainstorm with the children a curricular idea that might be expressed through movement.
- Choose one that will be enhanced by students having to think it through in terms of its components.
- Brainstorm all the facts known about this topic.
- Research what is unknown, or gaps in understanding.
- Discuss (and demonstrate) the different kinds of movements that might express the content. In this "idea generating" stage of the process, all ideas should be considered. This formative stage is where young people can learn to listen to other's ideas, engage in divergent thinking, and imagine outcomes.
- Experiment with the different movements generated. Keep in mind the action words, the stillness words, and the variables. Here students can learn to plan, to assess, and revise, managing the ambiguity that comes with creative processes.
- Work together as a group to plan the sequence. Here is the opportunity to practice cooperation, engaging multiple perspectives, careful listening, taking risks, combining and mixing ideas, synthesizing.
- Try to create movement statements that are at least three minutes long. Think about beginning, middle, and end.
- After a group performs, using the skill of descriptive inquiry, have the "audience" say what they saw (using the movement vo-

cabulary they have learned). Example: "The whole group moved with a lot of intensity, and then the movement got weaker and weaker until you were all lying on the floor."
- Have students say how the piece affected them: "It made me feel sad when everyone curled up on the floor" or "I felt happy when everyone was jumping up and down."
- Discuss how the movement piece accomplished its purpose. What might be changed if it were revised?

The Machine

One popular activity to introduce group work is the creation of a "machine." First comes a whole class brainstorm of what a machine is, what are its essential parts, and what kinds of sounds it makes. Each individual child then chooses a part that moves a certain way (gear, pulley, belt, chain, brake, drill, saw, etc.), and comes up with a noise that expresses it (whirring, humming, clanking, grinding, creaking, etc.). The teacher should encourage the use of different body parts and different levels as well as different sounds (with the voice, the breath, or with other body parts such as stamping or clapping). One by one, each child hooks onto another machine part enacting their own movement and sound until the machine tableaux is created.

Extension activities:

- Practice "freezing" then starting up again.
- Experiment with volume and speed.
- Try to move the whole machine as an integrated unit across the floor.

Activities such as "the machine" are helpful in developing awareness of the whole group, and how the parts come together to create something larger. Once these ideas and processes have been mastered, young people are ready to create more sophisticated movement scenarios to represent what they have learned about a topic. The example below is an outline of a culminating activity such as was described in Chapter 7 ("Curriculum Theory and Design for a Neohumanist Future"), which takes place after an extensive period of study that included plant morphology, photosynthesis, transpiration, and other related concepts.

Curricular Example: Leaves (Boorman, 1969)

Potential Concepts	Movement Content
Leaves are attached to a tree or bush and as they grow, they take on different shapes.	Body parts. Body shape. Extension into space. Different levels in space.
Leaves are affected by outside forces (temperature, rainfall, drought), so they continue to change shape and eventually drop to the ground.	Changing body shape. Changes of time and energy. Traveling through space using different levels.
Leaves on the ground are blown by the wind and many come together and move apart again.	Traveling using different body actions. Meeting and parting.
Leaves gradually break down, join with other elements and become part of the soil.	Levels, intensity.

Other curricular content that might be explored and expressed through movement: the water cycle, mathematical sets, ocean currents, the solar system, oppression and liberation, punctuation, etc. Always remember that the planning time is as much a learning opportunity as the "performance."

Academic Learning and Creative Movement

Literacy

It should be apparent the many ways that movement activities can enhance literacy. In terms of vocabulary development, connecting verbs and their bodily expression can help to internalize the meanings and nuances of words. Learning to put action and stillness words into sentences helps with sequencing and pattern making. When students plan movements, they visualize a series of actions, using any one of a number of multi-sensory strategies: They may imagine an olfactory sensation or a sound, or see a mental picture, or think about an emotion connected to something. Visualization (the ability to form and see mental images) is a core reading strategy that contributes to reading comprehension. Students practice "retelling" a story in different ways—in words and in movements. And by linking emotions, words and bodily sensations, they can expand their understanding of character development in narratives.   Teachers can indirectly introduce linguistic concepts and increase phonemic awareness in movement activities long before a child is ready for formal instruction:

- Onomatopoeia (acting out words that sound like what they mean: hiss, buzz, boom, splat, bang, pow!)
- Rhyming (repeating patterns of sounds and patterns of movements)
- Rhythm and meter in poetry and movement
- Metaphor and simile (walk as if you are walking through peanut butter; drizzle your fingers like a light rain)

Other Academic Subjects

Students can explore cause and effect and learn the basic physics of movement, which they might not encounter formally until later in their education (linear movement, rotary movement, periodic movement). The possibilities of demonstrating arithmetic and mathematical concepts through movement games are endless. To explore life cycles in nature, students can portray metamorphosis. They can use movement to represent the relationships between air masses, wind, and weather events. And while some students may be adept at memorizing *facts*, they are often perplexed when called upon to *enact* the concept (e.g., planetary motion, blood flow, the Big Bang theory, the states of matter, the movement of electrons). Figuring out to represent concepts with the body often requires deeper and more complex inquiry and thinking about a topic. Many children are kinesthetic learners who need movement, to be actively engaged with their whole beings, in order to learn, understand, and remember.

Conclusion

How might creative movement cultivate the philosophical movement—the movement towards love for all creation, the sense of oneness with the universe—that is at the core of neohumanist education?

Movement is more than gross and fine motor development and it is more than basic body awareness. It is fundamental to the learning of the child. The basic elements of creative movement pedagogy are awareness, connection-making, exploration, invention, improvisation, experimentation, rearrangement and integration. These are the elements of all creative processes from art-making to scientific discovery. Creative movement develops a child's faculties for creative thinking and imagining and also critical thinking abilities such as problem-solving, critical judgment, decision making and a multitude of other mental processes.

There is much in modern society and in conventional pedagogy that has resulted in a mind/body split, as well as creating a hierarchy of value;

for example, the valuing of academic knowledge over practical knowledge. Students who are on the "college track" are considered superior to students on the "vocational track." Mathematical and linguistic expertise is considered more important than the visual or kinesthetic intelligences. There is the denigration of embodied activities (cooking, cleaning, childcare, gardening) in favor of more conceptual, academic labor, and the historical gender discrimination against those who perform the former. The body (flesh) has long been considered inferior to mind and spirit.

With the dismantling of such hierarchies of value, a new paradigm of body/mind/spirit integration becomes possible. Creative movement is holistic in that it seeks the positive and balanced integration of all of these levels of experience. Like few other disciplines, the creative expression of movement engages the whole child, and holds great potential to develop the child's self-image, self-awareness and self-direction—important phases of growth in the child's cosmic journey towards enlightenment and self-realization. The very act of creating has a profound influence on the formation and discovery of the self and its relation to the world. The exploration of movement and the feelings evoked—standing upright, reaching towards the heavens, expanding the body through breath, then allowing gravity to pull one to the floor, down to the earth—the push and pull of above and below—all reflect fundamental experiences of what it means to be embodied. Crawling on all fours, slithering like a snake, creeping and pouncing towards prey, the fearful scurrying of a small animal, the soaring feelings of an eagle in flight, can transport us into imaginary embodied experiences of other species.

Relaxing, allowing visual imagery to present itself, and cultivating meta-cognition or mindfulness are gateways to deeper contemplative experiences. And learning to express the insights one feels in an authentic way is fundamental to one's development as a human. As artists in every discipline can tell us, when one is just beginning to explore a creative process, the mind is busy—thinking, planning, assessing. But at a later stage of the process, the dancer becomes the dance, the potter becomes one with the clay, and the busy mind gives way to a state of pure being, the integration of all the levels of the mind in the creative act, the joining of the small self with the larger flow of the universe.

FOR CONTINUING STUDY

Discussion/Reflection

- Do you believe that creative movement should be a part of neohumanist education at the early childhood and primary levels? Why, or why not?

- How comfortable are you with leading movement activities?
- What more do you need to know about integrating creative movement into the curriculum?

Application: Referring to the Lesson Planning Template (Appendix D in Chapter 7) choose a topic and grade level for a creative movement lesson that is part of a larger curriculum unit. Fill out the template. If you are part of a class or group, you can do this in pairs.

Application: Create a list of curriculum topics, specified by age or grade level, that could be enhanced by incorporating creative movement.

References

Boorman, J. (1969). *Creative dance in the first three grades.* David McKay Co.

Gardner, H. (1983). *Frames of mind: The theory of multiple intelligences.* Basic Books.

Zaraska, M. (2020). Moving in sync creates surprising social bonds among people. *Scientific American, 323*(4), 64. https://www.scientificamerican.com/article/moving-in-sync-creates-surprising-social-bonds-among-people/

Additional Resources

Barlin, A. L. (1971). *The art of learning through movement: A teachers' manual movement for students of all ages.* Ward Ritchie Press.

Barlin, A. L. (1979). *Teaching your wings to fly: The nonspecialist's guide to movement activities for young children.* Scott Foresman & Co.

Hawkins, A. M. (1991). *Moving from within: A new method for dance making.* A Cappella Books.

Stinson, S. (1988). *Dance for children: Finding the magic in movement.* AAHPERD.

Sullivan, M. (1982). *Feeling strong, feeling free: Movement exploration for young children.* National Association for the Education of Young Children.

After reading this chapter, you might wish to view a creative movement learning experience in action. Here are links to YouTube videos that illustrate the basic concepts:

https://www.youtube.com/watch?v=yaN7TXB35IQ
https://www.youtube.com/watch?v=OQKEWtTBJbI

14

Neohumanist Education and the "Lively Arts"

Integrating Creative Drama Across the Curriculum

> *In every human being there exists the impulse to mime and to play. From sacred play came ritual: poetry, music, and dance were a part of play. Philosophy and wisdom found expression in words.*
> — Nellie McCaslin, *Creative Drama in the Classroom*, 1980

Drama—the creative enactment of a story or idea involving pantomime, action, and/or dialogue, usually featuring emotions, conflicts, and themes. We are mostly familiar with drama as a theatrical performance, a form of narrative communication presented by professional actors to an audience. Theater in its various forms has been with humanity since the beginnings of recorded time. According to Hindu holy books, gods and demons engaged in war prior to the creation of Earth, and Brahma asked the gods to reenact this drama for their own entertainment. Thus was born Indian theater, as far back as the eighth century BCE. In Africa, Yoruba theater sits alongside other regional theater histories, with its roots in ritual and the pantheon of gods in Yoruba religion. Ancient Greek theater was both performative

---

Becoming One With the World, pages 269–285
Copyright © 2024 by Information Age Publishing
www.infoagepub.com
All rights of reproduction in any form reserved.

and participatory, and closely associated with religious ritual, healing, and festivals. Throughout the Roman empire, theater developed and expanded across Europe, and important works of literature that were performed in Greek and Roman culture survive to this day.

Creative drama, variously termed educational drama, drama for learning, or dramatic pedagogy, is concerned with the communicative event *between participants*, rather than between performer and audience, and with the shaping of an educational experience. Often incorporating improvisation, theater games, pantomime, and movement, creative drama begins in the world of natural children's play and develops it further, using theater techniques, to create learning opportunities for young people.

Creative drama is a natural extension of creative movement, explored in Chapter 13, but spoken language plays a significant role. In this chapter, we will progress more or less sequentially, beginning with the early dramatic processes of fantasy play and *storymaking*. We then highlight the important role of warm-up games and exercises that help young people get acquainted, break the ice, warm up the body, get the creative juices flowing, and build community. We take a look at pantomime, the art of telling a story or conveying ideas without words. We share some ideas about how to facilitate improvisation, and the ways that role-playing can foster social and emotional intelligence. And finally, we explore the synthesis of creative movement, pantomime, improvisation, and role playing, in the fine art of acting out familiar stories and in the creation of new ones.

Fantasy Play and Storymaking: The Early Roots of Creative Drama

Most communication from young children who have learned to string words together in sentences consists of *stories* about events or personal experiences:

> I saw a bluebird on the way to school.
>
> Harry knocked my block house over.

Children's narratives may begin with a collection of unrelated events:

> The boy ate dinner. The snake crawled in the grass.

Simple isolated phrases progress to having connected elements:

> The baby lives with mommy and daddy. At night, a lion came into her bedroom. Mommy turned on the light and scared the lion away.

Eventually more details are added, or stories may begin to demonstrate cause and effect:

> The boy knocked over his milk. Mommy yelled at him. Then he had to clean it up.

Stories can evolve to contain plot elements, sequences of events, conflicts, and resolutions.

During early fantasy play, children often come up with story lines. They assign characters, and the characters "act out" stories. Such fantasy play activates creative thinking as the children solve problems. It offers opportunities to explore cause and effect and experience consequences for actions. It can help to work out emotional issues such as fears. Other benefits of fantasy play are vocabulary building, the development of representational thinking (turning a blue blanket into the sea), practicing planning, self-regulation, and negotiation, and of course, the development of imagination.

Too often, teachers abandon children to their fantasy play while they sip tea or prepare lessons. But storytelling and "pretend play" are the universal learning medium of young children. The wise teacher brings an inquiry focus to this important work of children, in order to better understand how they are making sense of the world, what they are struggling to understand, and how they are beginning to narrate their lives.

Author and master teacher Vivian Paley (1929–2019) is considered a pioneer of the use of storymaking. Her detailed descriptions of life in the classroom, lovingly narrated in thirteen books, demonstrate clearly the ways that children use storymaking to make sense of the world (Paley, 1990, 1993, 2005). Her method of collaborative storymaking involves the teacher first listening carefully to the stories children tell, then taking them down word for word in dictation, either in the group setting or privately. The stories are then "made special" in ritualized ways. A stage is laid out with masking tape. The teacher and children gather around the stage in a circle and the teacher begins to read the dictated story, encouraging certain children to take on roles and act out the events inside the stage space using movement, sound, and gesture.

When children enact their own stories, many important things can happen: they can try on new roles and see how they fit, get in touch with their feelings, share new ideas, or practice new ways of expressing themselves. The shy child who roars like a lion may discover a new energy of assertiveness. The rambunctious boy who cradles a make-believe baby kitten may experience a new feeling of protectiveness. The girl who slays the dragon may discover a new level of courage. There are endless ways to engage young people creatively in enacting the stories of their lives, and in the process making language come alive in ways that invigorate personality development, foster emotional and social intelligence, and develop creative and original thinking. Dramatic play and enactments of this sort should be at the heart of early childhood literacy learning in a neohumanist school.

As the children advance through the grades, early creative story making finds expression in more advanced work in pantomime, improvisation, role-playing, reader's theater, choral reading, creating plays from simple stories, and writing and performing original stories and plays.

Preparing the Way: The Importance of Warm-Ups

Many people feel a natural reluctance to "act," either from shyness or fear of saying something silly, or the misconception that acting is something that only professionals with exceptional talent can do. To lessen such concerns, it's important to ease into creative drama activities with various warm ups, and one can find hundreds of these theater games online or in books. Warm ups tend to fall into a few distinct categories:

Movement Warm-Ups

Stretching, wiggling, and rotating body parts loosens up tense muscles and shakes off inhibitions. Exercises can be individual ("Everyone close their eyes and make a silent scream!") or collective, as in group juggling, where a ball is tossed from one to another, establishing a pattern, and then another ball is added, and then another. Many movement warm-ups include activities that guide students to imagine a situation (i.e., walking through pudding, walking through clouds, etc.) and conform their movement to the imaginary situation. Follow the leader games fit in this category, as in following and mimicking a leader who is walking while leading with their elbow, then switching leaders and following one who is leading with their toe, and so on, until everyone has had a chance to lead.

Students can practice making tableaux in small groups; with little time to prepare, they must quickly use their bodies to plan and depict a scene (the beach, a playground, the library, a factory) that others need to guess. Movement warm-ups should bypass "thinking" in favor of spontaneous participation, and warm ups should be FUN and stress free.

Vocal Warm-Ups

These can include breathing exercises, such as breathing deeply, expanding the stomach with hands on the belly, and exhaling slowly while saying "ha ha ha ha" as the belly contracts. This will help teach proper diaphragmatic breathing. Exercises can include tongue twisters (Peter Piper picked a peck of pickled peppers). Humming exercises are fun as a group, varying the volume and intensity of the hum.

Pantomime to Enhance Physical Communication

Pantomime is the art of using one's body to depict the use of an object or a relationship to space, with no props or speech. Depicting simple tasks such as sweeping a floor, pouring milk, or wrapping a present requires sustained concentration and focus, visualization skills, and attention to physical, spatial, and temporal details. Such exercises can be carried out individually or in groups (e.g., a pitcher and a batter miming a time at bat). Movements, gestures, and facial expressions are exaggerated in order to convey emotions and thoughts, and to further depict the imaginary movement of objects (e.g., the batted ball soaring high overhead).

Pantomime stimulates the imagination. One game has the teacher giving an ordinary object to a small group of students (say, a black or whiteboard eraser). She instructs them that the object is something else entirely—a knife, a baby rabbit, a diamond necklace. They must handle it, look at it and react to it, investing in it all of the qualities of the suggested object. Activating the senses, if only in the imagination, pushes the children into a deeper engagement with the world. Pretending to touch velvet, hold ice, smell a skunk, or see a sunrise cultivates the sensory imagination.

Pantomime helps with developing characterization skills. Students practice the basics of depicting character types (dreamy, evil, scheming, clumsy) with their bodies and facial expressions, then can move on to mirroring activities in pairs, and group activities (e.g., students stand in a circle and one passes a facial expression to the person next to them, who much first replicate it, and then change to another expression to pass to the next person).

Dialogue Exercises to Increase Verbal Communication Skills

Dialogue exercises are the basis of improvisation, a way to ease gently into more complex improv activities. Improvisation fosters a number of capacities: divergent thinking, the tolerance for uncertainty and ambiguity, affective well-being, and confidence. It is an excellent way to strengthen students' listening skills and practice creating meaningful narrative threads and dialogic continuity. Improvisational dialogue compels spontaneity and is unpredictable; there is no way to tell where a conversation might lead.

It thus develops the capacity to "think on one's feet" and to bypass the usual internal editor/censor. The teacher can start things off with a written prompt spoken by one of the characters. Some examples:

- Finish what you are doing. We need to talk.
- I saw you coming out of that house. What were you doing there?
- I won't do this unless you go first.
- I can't believe you just said that!

You can use the same dialogue prompts, but assign different characters: a grandfather and grandson; an employer and an employee, romantic partners, teacher and student, and so on. See how the conversation changes with different characters. In this way, students can explore a range of relationship issues across differences of age, gender, social role, and so on.

Moving Beyond the Warm-ups: Creative Drama Enactments

Various techniques are employed in creative drama pedagogy, all of which have a basis in the warm-ups and theater games that you can start with, but which can grow into ever more complex enactments.

Role Play

Viola Spolin (1906–1994) is often credited with the creation of theater games and forms of role playing devised to teach acting skills and the formal rules of the theater (Spolin, 1986). She is considered a founder of 20th century improvisational theater. Role play and theater games, however, date back in the Western world to the Commedia dell'arte tradition of 16th century Italy. Role play seems almost "programmed" into the human species—children's fantasy play often involves assuming roles and playing out situations between characters.

Role play is basically adopting a persona other than one's own, and then depicting their motivations, gestures, behaviors, ways of speech, and probable actions in a way that is true to their character in a fictional setting. It usually involves two or more people, who respond to and build on what other characters say and do and create a collaborative narrative. The outcomes of role plays are inherently unpredictable, and players must give up any efforts at certainty and "go with the flow."

Role play can serve many purposes. It can simply be in the repertoire of warm-up games, designed to loosen inhibitions. It can be employed in the service of developing more formal stories, a way of experimenting with dialogue and characterization. Teachers often use role play in classrooms as a way of exploring decision-making or conflict resolution. Brazilian theater director Augusto Boal (1992), influenced by the political pedagogy of Paulo Freire, developed a comprehensive system of role playing techniques to raise the consciousness of how power and oppression operate in social systems. Role play is even used in psychology—drama therapy or psychodrama—using techniques such as role reversal, mirroring, and dream re-enactment to explore complex psychological issues. Playback theater is a psycho-social form of improvisational work in which people tell stories from their lives which are then enacted in a ritualized process that utilizes mime, music, and spoken scenes. It is considered to facilitate the healthy integration of the personality, this sharing of personal narratives and the empathy of those players who "bear witness" to the story.

Puppetry

Puppetry is an ancient form of theater first recorded in Greece in the 5th century BC, but which is thought to be much older than that. Many different kinds of puppetry exist across cultures; what they have in common is that they all use various forms of inanimate objects—human figures, animal figures, and props—to tell a story. From basic finger puppets and sock puppets to more elaborate hand puppets, to the very complex rod puppets and marionettes with their amazing movement possibilities, puppets have always been enjoyed by young and old.

Puppets are used to entertain. They can be characters in political theater, often speaking truth to power, or participating in protest, as in the 14th century European marches against feudalism or the contemporary political enactments by Vermont's Bread and Puppet Circus (https://breadandpuppet.org). Some cultures use puppets in religious rituals and funerary rites. Shadow puppetry, originating in Southeast Asia, is a compelling visual experience that features flat characters made of leather or paper on a rod against a screen with a light source behind them. In modern times, television, film, and the digital manipulation of images have enabled the development of new forms of puppetry and it has become a high art.

Puppets have an important role to play in the education of children. Teachers sometimes use puppets to communicate to young children, especially about sensitive or complicated topics (stranger danger, bullying, etc.). They often utilize them in classroom management—to give verbal cues to children to clean up, or move between activities, or to remember to respect each other. Puppets can model appropriate behaviors and polite language. Therapists use them to help children talk about their feelings or their problems. They are a skillful way to teach values and ethics, with a teacher acting out a scene between two puppets or between a child and a puppet.

Most importantly, children can be engaged in the entire process of puppetry—designing and making puppets, developing skits, performing for their peers and parents. A puppet theater should be an indispensable part of a neohumanist classroom—anything from a simple cardboard frame to a more beautifully crafted wooden stage. Puppets can inspire language development, cooperation, teamwork, imagination, and creativity. Puppets are magical creatures that ask the watcher to suspend disbelief and enter into the imaginative world of the animated/inanimate creatures. Puppets are uniquely qualified to enact situations that human actors cannot: They can fly, they can climb to a rooftop, they can get hit over the head and bounce right back up, they can sit on a cloud.

Creating Dramas From Simple Stories

Creative drama can deepen and enrich young people's interaction with literature by bringing the characters to life, enabling a child to place themselves in a text, form impressions of the work, examine it critically, and make deeper meaning of the words and ideas. All fairy tales and folktales have a moral center, some lesson that is thought important for children to internalize. With these tales, the neohumanist teacher will find many opportunities to highlight aspects of Yoga ethics, such as those in the Yama/Niyama code. There are many tales from different cultures that deal with common themes. It's useful to start with a familiar story from the culture of the children in your class, one that holds meaning at different levels for different ages.

One common theme that is related to multiple aspects of Yama/Niyama (asteya [non -stealing], aparigraha [overcoming greed], santosha [contentment, appreciating what we have]) addresses the human tendency to daydream about great wealth, and the sometimes negative consequences of greed and dissatisfaction (i.e., *The Milkmaid and Her Pail*, attributed to Aesop; *The Daydreamer*, from India, and many others). In these tales, a person walks along, having come into possession of some resources (a basket of eggs, a pail of oil, etc.) and daydreams about what they will do with the proceeds, fantasizing about ever greater accumulations of wealth. Something happens to them when they get carried away with their fantasies, resulting in the breakage or loss of their original resources. The moral of this story is not to dream of future riches and neglect the care of one's current resources!

To start with, a teacher might read (or tell) a culturally relevant version of the story, and have the children retell the story, so that everyone knows the basic plot and characters. When the children are thoroughly familiar with the story, some theater games can help build to a larger enactment. We will use this story theme to illustrate some creative ways to structure activities.

Solo Pantomimes

Start with some simple solo pantomimes (enactments of one character). These can be done singly, in pairs, or as a whole group depending on the comfort level of the students. Have children pretend they are a character in the story.

- How do they look? How do they walk? Do they skip? Meander?
- How do they depict what they are carrying?
- What do they say to themselves as they begin to daydream?
- How do they act when they get distracted? Do their facial expressions change?

Mirror Images

Similar tales of greed and imagining riches and power contain more than one character and can lend themselves to group activities. *The Fisherman and His Wife* (The Grimm Brothers), for example, tells of a poor couple who live in a dirty and decrepit hut by the sea, where the fisherman goes out each day to fish. One day he catches a flounder who tells him he is not really a fish but an enchanted prince. The kindly fisherman throws him back into the sea, and returns home to his wife, who berates him for not asking the flounder to grant him a wish. Against his better wishes, the man returns to the sea, and asks the fish for a better house, and the wish is granted. This happens over and over, with the wife always dissatisfied, the reluctant husband returning to the flounder, and the fish granting increasingly excessive and extravagant wishes, until the wife is finally Queen of a castle. She continues to complain, and at last she is returned to her filthy shack.

In pairs, students take turns making a frozen facial expression of either the fisherman or his wife as they argue. The other partner must mirror it. Take turns. Add one body part at a time until you have full body statues to mirror.

Narrative Pantomimes

In this activity, the teacher tells a section of the story and in pairs, students take different parts (man and fish, man and wife). They act out the story part only using gestures and facial expressions. They repeat it, using the whole body, and moving around. Then they exchange parts. New pairs of students do the activity, and what happens is they often build on something the prior pair did, or change something up.

Frozen Pictures

In small groups, organize "frozen pictures" (tableaux) depicting major scenes, perhaps of the successive wishes granted (the two of them in the palace, being served fine food by servants, the wife with her slipper being kissed by kings and emperors).

Pantomime Skits

When children have been introduced to pantomime through simple theater games, solo pantomimes, narrative pantomimes, and frozen pictures, they are ready to enact longer story sequences without dialogue. Working on extended pantomime skits, with or without a narrator, gives young people an opportunity to explore character without dialogue, through movement, facial expression, and gesture. In this story sequence, players can enact the drama without words, with one scene following another. First, the couple arguing in their dirty hut, then the fisherman catching the flounder and then tossing him back in, then returning to see the greatly improved house, and so on.

Improvisation

Improvisation, like role play, is a method of unscripted dialogue, where no one knows what each other will do or say next. It can be a fun way to play with a story; often "improvs" can become scripted dialogue that children then memorize and enact. In this story, characters can try our various improvisations (in one version, perhaps the wife starts out being old and wizened, and grows progressively more glamorous, in another version, the fisherman might display more and more symptoms of illness or distress as he is forced back to seek even greater riches from the fish). Teachers may need to provide prompts.

Choral Reading

Choral reading—reading in unison—is an ancient dramatic technique that pre-dated Greek theater, and was incorporated into later Greek drama. It has its origins in religious ceremonies and festivals of all people. Choral reading is a terrific way to invite all children, even shy ones, to participate. In one version of *The Fisherman and His Wife*, for example, there is a recurring poem that the fisherman recites when he visits the fish:

> Mandje! Mandje! Timpe Te!
> Flounder, flounder in the sea!
> My wife, my wife, Ilsebill,
> Wants not, wants not, what I will

Children will feel the emotion build each time they collectively recite this, as the story grows to a climax.

Choral reading is not prevalent in schools today, though it is worth consideration for including in the neohumanist language arts curriculum for a variety of reasons:

- It develops a sense of the group, in contrast to the singular individual, and can foster social cooperation.
- It can be done without any additional resources.
- It honors the tradition of oral cultures.
- Clear diction can be taught without embarrassing the individual.
- It can incorporate students of a range of abilities—everyone can be included.

Keep in mind that many young children value repetition. There are many versions of different tales and children enjoy hearing new, but familiar stories with different characters. Each version may have different bits of dialogue and some rhyming, though there are common elements.

Once children are accustomed to the various creative drama processes, they can apply them in new situations. Theater games with stories are an effective way to instill ethical ideas and pro-social behaviors.

Reader's Theater

Another seldom used, but very beneficial drama technique is *reader's theater*, which integrates literacy instruction and drama and fosters improved reading, listening and speaking. It can also integrate writing, if children are creating their own scripts. Reader's theater does not use props or movement, it just focuses on reading either a story or a script. It's an important way to become familiar with the lines in a story or play, and helps to develop vocal expression as well as reading fluency. The whole group can read a story (in whole or in part) in unison. Or there can be a narrator and assigned parts for a dramatic script. With reader's theater, roles should be exchanged so children can practice saying the lines in different ways. The important thing is for everyone to get comfortable with the dialogue. At this point, different groups of children can plan their own version of the story to act for each other, either using the standard lines or making up their own versions. Meaningful enactments can be created around reader's theater by incorporating lighting, sound effects, and/or music.

Extension Activities

Dramatic storytelling does not have to end with mini-performances. There are a number of ways to keep the creative juices flowing. You can add characters (give the fisherman and his wife some children; add servants, or even ladies-in-waiting as the wishes progress). You can alter a character's "arc"—maybe the fisherman decides he really does like high living after all! You can experiment with alternate endings (the wife goes mad after losing everything, or conversely, they have a heart to heart talk in which they realize that happiness is not dependent upon riches). Maybe you can have the fisherman return to catch the fish, and ask how he might help him return to his enchanted condition. What might it be like if the prince then visited them in their dirty old hut? You can try setting the story in the modern world. There are no limits to what can be done with story and educational drama when the imagination and creative opportunities are set free.

Debriefing

Just as in creative movement work, an important component of creative drama is the debriefing that follows any activity, signifying the educational idea that experience alone does not constitute learning, but must be amplified and clarified by reflection on the experience. One procedure utilized by many teachers of creative drama is the "playing, discussing, replaying" method. Students perform an enactment. The group then engages in constructive feedback:

- Did the story come across?
- Were the characters strong?

- Was anything left out?
- Did we understand the ending?
- When we replay it, what might we add or leave out?

Depending on the interests of the children and the time available, a scene can be played and replayed multiple times. The purpose of this? To increase young people's ability to communicate clearly. To develop more detail and stronger characterizations. To gain comfort in improvisation, and ease with "mistakes." To overcome self-consciousness. With experience, groups of children may begin to initiate dramatic activities themselves and organize small plays on their own.

The Many Uses of Creative Drama

We have provided ideas for initiating creative drama with young children in this chapter. As children grow older, the same techniques can be used to explore many topics. Social- emotional intelligence is fostered when young people engage in role plays and enactments depicting the contemporary issues they face every day as they explore relationships and behaviors. Augusto Boal's (1993) *Theater of the Oppressed* is a powerful way of exploring social justice issues. Subjects like literature and history can be brought to life with well facilitated dramatic activity (see, e.g., Heathcote & Bolton, 1995; O'Neill & Lambert, 1982). Some teachers, when teaching a novel, parallel each chapter with work on a scene. With drama, students can explore the motivations of a character more deeply. They can experiment with seeing events from different characters' points of view. Enacting a book can illuminate the author's intentions, and generate more significant meaning-making than ordinary reading and discussion. It can be especially helpful when trying to teach literature from another period of time, such as the Shakespearian rite-of-passage every Western high school student goes through.

There are many resources available in books and online to enrich your drama pedagogy. It is well worth the effort to start small, and bring in drama exercises to the classroom, even if a school does not have a formal drama program. Educational drama fosters opportunities for all of the intelligences to be at play, and it promotes inquiry, critical thinking, and problem-solving. Young people experience growth in understanding one's self, human behavior and relationships, and in grasping the large and complex issues in the world. They learn and practice empathy for people different from themselves. They can experiment with solutions, solving social problems in a safe space where consequences can be explored and discussed. There is no better way to explore issues of ethics and morality than in acting out the multiple consequences of complex scenarios. Imagine for example, a class enacting a town meeting about how to make use of some forested land the town has been bequeathed. Characters can include children, teachers, loggers, conservationists, bird-watchers, and so on, trying to come to consensus about how to solve a local problem in a way that requires knowledge, study, and ethical decision-making.

Engaging in creative drama is a key element of creating one's identity. Young people gain confidence in expressing their ideas when safe and fun spaces have been provided to practice this. They can begin to see their contributions accepted by the group but also learn that their contributions might be modified by others. As they begin to understand the power of the dialogic process, they can become more comfortable with changes in their thinking and their beliefs. They can begin to understand how they have been socialized in thinking and being certain ways, and to cultivate the agency to question and reconstruct those habits and beliefs that are not serving them well.

In unique ways, educational drama allows young people to play with identity, trying on different moods, beliefs, values and ways of being in the world to see what "fits." In this way, it is a meaningful adjunct to neohumanist education's emphasis on self-knowing, the ability to look within and imagine who you might become and what your purpose in life might be.

Cultivating Neohumanism Through Drama

In this chapter we have focused on a mostly human-centered approach to creating educational drama. Though many of the techniques offered lend themselves to neohumanist themes, there is a new approach to drama emerging with an even more explicit mission to address ecological issues and empower young people to take action in service to the "more-than-human" world. Artists and playwrights have often addressed environmental themes in their work (see, e.g., Kesson & Oyler, 1999, for an example of how Henrik Ibsen's play *An Enemy of the People* is integrated into a school curriculum).

Eco-theater takes this further: It not only incorporates themes like pollution and global warming, it also insists on ecological design (re-usable, found materials and even edible sets; energy efficient lighting, non-toxic paints, dyes, and make-up; digital ticketing). What makes this approach so promising for the educational setting is the integration of science and drama, bringing in experts on environmental issues to present current scientific information and then working with playwrights to compose dramas that feature these themes.

Neohumanist Education and the "Lively Arts" ▪ **283**

The innovative drama or classroom teacher in a neohumanist school figures out imaginative ways to foster the sentiment of love and appreciation for all beings.

- How might we make a tree the central character in an enactment?
- How can we make the animals talk in a non-anthropocentric way?
- How can we make non-humans the teachers in a drama?
- What are some innovative ways to depict human and non-human interaction?
- How can drama foster ethical thinking towards others who are radically different from ourselves?
- How can we shift drama locations from indoors to outdoors?
- How can nature become our setting for enactments?

Imagine, for example, if the town meeting to discuss forested land included as characters children, teachers, loggers, *birds, moles,* conservationists, bird-watchers, and *trees,* and so on, all trying to come to consensus about how to solve a local problem in a way that requires knowledge, study, and ethical decision-making. The interests expressed and debated would be even more expansive, and force the inclusion of neohumanist perspectives.

Again, the sky's the limit to what we can do with educational drama. Then again, maybe the sky is not the limit! Perhaps we can extend our dramatic thinking out to the cosmos, depicting the big bang, or Brahmacakra (the cosmic cycle) with talking stardust, dancing helium, poetic hydrogen, and singing microvita, those sub-microscopic entities thought to organize energy to create forms and structures (Rudolph, 2017). In such ways, we can, as Maxine Greene (1995) urges us, release the imagination in order "to awaken, to disclose the ordinarily unseen, unheard, and unexpected" (p. 28), in order that we might better make the ordinary, *extraordinary.*

FOR CONTINUING STUDY

Discussion/Reflection: If you have never incorporated drama before in your teaching, brainstorm some simple ways to get started. Consider the various academic disciplines: literature, history, science.

Discussion/Reflection: In a diverse classroom, with many nationalities and multiple first languages, what are some considerations when introducing drama pedagogy?

Discussion/Reflection: In a creative drama environment, the unexpected can always happen—strong emotions can surface, stereotyping or bias events can occur, physical play can get out of hand. Brainstorm some things you might anticipate, and discuss strategies for preventing or dealing with them.

Application: Referring to Appendix B in Chapter 7, the Arts-Based Literacy Curriculum Unit Plan, choose a children's book (picture book for pre-K–1, or trade book for older primary children) as the primary resource for the unit. Fill out the template, creating at least six creative drama lessons that lead up to a culminating experience. If you are part of a class or group, you can do this in pairs.

After reading this chapter, you might wish to view a creative drama learning experience in action. Here are links to YouTube videos that illustrate some basic concepts:

Magic Rock game with pre-schoolers
https://www.youtube.com/watch?v=9TF84pZuuEo

Creative drama games for grades 4-6
https://www.youtube.com/watch?v=u8VEuS-32JM

Drama warm-ups with teenagers
https://www.youtube.com/watch?v=x4J487QtUIM
https://www.youtube.com/watch?v=PYbXdJEZhbA

References

Boal, A. (1992). *Games for actors and non-actors*. Routledge.
Boal, A. (1993). *Theater of the oppressed* (C. A. McBride, Trans.). Theater Communications Group.
What Is Eco-Theater. (n.d.). Super Hero Clubhouse. http://www.superheroclubhouse.org/what-is-ecotheater/
Greene, M. (1995). *Releasing the imagination: Essays on education, the arts, and social change.* Jossey Bass Publishers.
Heathcote, D., & Bolton, G. (1995). *Drama for learning.* Heinemann Books.
Ibsen, H. (1999). *An enemy of the people.* Dover Publications.
Kesson, K., & Oyler, C. (1999). Integrated curriculum and service learning: Linking school based knowledge and social action. *English Education, 31*, 135–149.
O'Neill, C., & Lambert, A. (1982). *Drama structures: A practical handbook for teachers.* Heinemann Books.
Paley, V. G. (1990). *The boy who would be a helicopter.* Harvard University Press.
Paley, V. G. (1993). *You can't say you can't play.* Harvard University Press.
Paley, V. G. (2005). *A child's work: The importance of fantasy play.* University of Chicago Press.

Rudolph, H. J. (2017). *Microvita: Exploring a new science of reality.* AuthorHouse.
Spolin, V. (1986). *Theater games for the classroom: A teacher's handbook.* Northwestern University Press.

15

Teaching Ashtanga Yoga to Children

with MahaJyoti Glassman

We spend many years training the brains of young people to do sums, to think critically and logically, to comprehend the written word, to write coherently, and all sorts of other academic skills. Daniel Goleman, co-founder of the movement for SEL (social/emotional learning), and his research partner and co-author, Richard Davidson, a leading figure in the field of contemplative neuroscience, pose the question:

> Kindness, caring, and compassion all follow a line of development that our educational system largely ignores—along with attention, self-regulation, empathy, and a capacity for human connection. While we do a good enough job with the traditional academic skills like reading and math, why not expand what children learn to include such crucial skills for living a fulfilled life? (Goleman & Davidson, 2017, p. 280)

Education has concerned itself largely with the study of the external world, ignoring the reality that we have inner lives wherein lie capacities for empathy, emotion, compassion, discernment, aesthetic judgment, kindness, and expanded awareness of the subtleties of the sensory world. Neohumanist education is dedicated to righting this imbalance, providing tools that enable young people to catch a glimpse of their highest potential and anchor them in the best version of themselves.

In our current volatile and unpredictable times, in which young people are inundated with a barrage of things to be frightened of (pandemics, gun violence, climate crisis, economic insecurity—and this is just the short list) young children and youth are suffering a range of mental health issues ranging from social anxiety to addiction, depression, eating disorders, and behavioral problems. Untreated mental health in childhood can lead to difficulties navigating life's complexities, developing positive adult relations, poor academic outcomes, and even a higher engagement in crime. If we hope for all children to attain their highest emotional, social, and academic potential, then a foundation for positive development needs to be laid in childhood.

There are numerous contemplative paths, both in countries with ancient traditions as found in Southeast Asia, and in the West, including older Christian contemplative traditions as well as modern practices that have been secularized to promote health and well-being. Everyone, note Goleman and Davidson (2017), "has different preferences, needs, and the like" though contemplative paths share some common characteristics, in that they are

> a doorway beyond ordinary experience. At a practical level all forms of meditation share a common core of mind training—e.g., learning to let go of the myriad distractions that flow through the mind and to focus on one object of attention or stance of awareness. (p. 263)

The basic principles of Ashtanga Yoga in the *Yoga Sutras*, often attributed to Patanjali and written sometime in the early years of the Common Era, lay out an "Eightfold Path" sometimes referred to as the "Eight Limbs of Yoga," a comprehensive set of practices that include ethical guidelines, Yoga postures, breath control, and contemplative processes including concentration, inward focus, and meditation.

Neohumanist education has its origins in the ancient practices of Ashtanga Yoga, but acknowledges and honors the many approaches to developing a holistic, spiritually based (but not religious) learning system for children, one that nurtures the multiple dimensions of the student—body, intellect, heart, creativity, intuition—as well as fostering ecological awareness and a spirit of universal care and compassion.

While serious practitioners of Yoga may spend a lifetime investigating the depth and complexities of the inner world, the practices have also been adapted for ordinary people in contemporary societies seeking greater harmony of mind and body, mindfulness, composure, calm, and enhanced well-being. The essence of Yoga and other contemplative practices is *liberation from suffering*, achieved by training the mind to transcend the innumerable distractions, impulses, negative emotions, desires, and other unproductive mental busyness, and attaining a state of *witnessing*, a calm awareness that allows us to "observe what is happening in the mind itself rather than simply being carried away by it" (Goleman & Davidson, 2017, p. 286):

> A mind free from disturbance has value in lessening human suffering, a goal shared by science and meditative paths alike. But apart from lofty heights of being, here's a more practical potential within reach of every one of us: a life best described as flourishing. (p. 53)

Human flourishing may be said to be the aim of neohumanist education. But human flourishing does not occur in an individual vacuum; it is the result of a healthy interdependence in an ecosystem that includes all life, animate and inanimate. The air we breathe, the mineral kingdom, the dirt, the plants and trees, the insects, the beings of the air, all beings who walk or slither or hop on the earth, and all who swim and thrive in the seas—human beings share spiritual kinship with all of creation. Neohumanist education balances the introspective practices of Yoga with a pedagogy that incorporates service, in recognition that the brain's circuitry for happiness is energized when one acts on the loving concern for others (including more-than-human-others).

The science of meditation or "contemplative science" is a young field, but the hundreds of neuroscientific studies on meditation and brain function are leading to some remarkable conclusions. Even beginning meditators experience less reactivity to stress, better focus, less mind-wandering, improved memory, and increased capacity for empathy. For longer term meditators, the benefits are even greater, including a "greater neural attunement with those who are suffering, and enhanced likelihood of doing something to help" (Goleman & Davidson, 2017, p. 273). It is here that we begin to glimpse the transformative possibilities of contemplative practices. People who have attained a level of contentment with their lives, in whom the transcendent *states* achieved in moments of contemplation have become enduring *traits* are able to extend kindness, care, and generosity outward, in ever expanding circles, and "these positive altered traits have the potential for transforming our world in ways that will enhance not only our individual thriving but also the odds for our species survival" (Goleman

& Davidson, 2017, p. 291). We can see here the necessity for engaging in disciplined contemplation in order to realize the neohumanist aim of extending the feelings of love to all creation. In Shrii Sarkar's (1981) words, "The sense of universalism should also be awakened in the child. Etiquette and refined behaviour [*sic*] are not enough. Real education leads to a pervasive sense of love and compassion for all creation" (para. 6).

The contemplative sciences are brimming with studies on adult practitioners of meditation, but little systematic research has been carried out on the effects of this with children. In neohumanist schools, introspective practices are often integrated with other learning, for example using visualization when working on a math problem, or practicing controlled breathing or deep relaxation in the context of a movement class. But Yoga is also taught as its own subject in developmentally appropriate ways. Neohumanist educators have honed and refined the teaching of Yoga to children over the past 30 or so years, ensuring that the practices are play-based, fun, positive experiences that lay a solid foundation for a healthy lifestyle and the cultivation of enduring traits such as composure, patience, empathy, kindness, ethical conduct, and goodness of character. MahaJyoti Glassman is an experienced neohumanist educator who has written about teaching Yoga to children. Like many neohumanist practitioners who have been doing this for years, her understandings of the benefits to children and the learning environment of Yoga practices are based on observation and experience as well as on the studies that do exist. We offer in this chapter some of her advice on the teaching of Yoga to young children, and hope that holistic educators find practices of value in her play-based, integrated approach.

* * *

A Yoga Origin Story

Once upon a time long, long ago, people wanted to know how to be together in sweetness and live cooperatively with the animals on Mother Earth. The creatures flew in the sky, walked or slithered on the earth, and swam in the waters. The early families wanted to live in peace with all of nature as well as the plants and trees.

The people began to carefully study every creature. They watched the birds and the sky. They watched the whales and the sea. They watched the deer and the land.

The people wondered, "If I act just like a lion, will I become as powerful and courageous as a lion?" "If I pretend that I am a mountain, will I become as strong and magnificent as the mountain?"

The people practiced copying the lion and the mountain. They noticed that they did feel different. They did feel more powerful like the lion. They did feel stronger and magnificent like the mountain. So, the people decided to keep imitating these natural beings of the Earth. Then, their leader, whose name was Shiva, came and showed them how to sit quietly, listen to the Inner Shining One who lies deep within the heart, and speaks to all. Today, we call this meditation or inner listening. Shiva showed the people how to live with tenderness and caring for themselves and for every member of their Earth family.

Yoga is when we can flow together. Yoga is when we are holding hands. Living Yoga is to be friends, no matter what! Yoga is looking at every ant and elephant as part of our family. Even those who aren't liked very well, every snake, every bird, every scorpion, every rock, every tree—they are all members of our family.

The Eight Limbs of Yoga

Eight-limbed Ashtanga Yoga encompasses thousands of years of practicing Yoga living. To understand the basic elements of life in the most centered and connected manner, a blueprint is needed that will keep everyone on the road of positivity, balance, confidence, and peacefulness with others and with ourselves. Life requires tools that enable children to catch a glimpse of their highest potential and anchor them in the best version of themselves.

Ashtanga Yoga practices promise greater harmony of mind, body, and heart. These Ashtanga Yoga activities for young children differ from Patanjali's Eight Limbs as they have been interpreted for young children, though effort has been made to retain the essence of each practice. The philosophy and practice includes Yoga Ethics: (a) *Yama* ~ Living in Harmony With Others and the World; (b) *Niyama* ~ Living in Harmony With Oneself; (c) *Asana* ~Yoga Postures; (d) *Pranayama* ~ Breath Awareness; (e) *Pratyahara* ~ Deep Relaxation/Sense Withdrawal; (f) *Dharana* ~ Focused Concentration; (g) *Dhyana* ~ Meditation; and (h) *Samadhi* ~ Self-Actualization/Enlightenment.

Within Ashtanga Yoga, children are encouraged to consider themselves as being more than a physical body, more than a bundle of emotions, more than little thinking humans, but as spiritual beings who guard and nurture the inner radiance in themselves and in others. All are encouraged to move from the feeling of "mine" towards the feeling of "ours," transforming the needs of me or "I" and moving towards "us."

The loving approach of caring, connection, and respect is extended to all beings. This expression is shared with insects and other entities that some children may fear. These wondrous relationships are explored and the love of the diversity of beings and versatile environments of this amazing planet is fostered. What is the value of our fellow Earth clan members, their needs, and the gifts that they share? How can we help support them? How can we move together in harmony? This is the cornerstone of neohumanism.

In a neohumanist school, all cultures, ethnicities, nationalities, and genders are welcome. The school becomes a microcosm of what a compassionate world community can look like. Every child is embraced and celebrated for their uniqueness as teachers strive to help them realize their fullest potential. Coordinated cooperation and teamwork are widely encouraged. Morality is the foundation of the curriculum with artistic creative expression integrated into each area of study.

Kids Yoga Asana time is quite different from adult Yoga where everyone is standing obediently on their individual mats and interactions may be limited. Kids Yoga is an interactive, cooperative, and collaborative exchange that invites mutual respect of all classmates and nature friends. Asana poses and activities inspire relationship building with each other, the teacher, the world, and with all. Through Asana, Yoga games, Yoga breath, meditation, art, deep relaxation, and benevolent social interactions, let the fun begin!

Yoga Ethics

Yoga ethics are the first two branches of Eight-limbed Yoga. Within Yoga ethics, there exist 10 steps in the stairway of ideal human behavior of Yoga living. They are called Living in Harmony With Others and the World or *Yama* (in Sanskrit) and Living in Harmony With Oneself or *Niyama*.

Living by this moral roadmap, children advance mentally and spiritually, living more harmoniously with others and self. The 10 steps are introduced through conversations, teacher modeling, songs, stories, artistic expression, games, and dramatic play. Since the very young child resides comfortably in the creative brain, the best practices for reaching out to them with age appropriate and brain appropriate techniques is through laughter, working together, and creative expression. By providing a clear moral foundation for interactions, children's stress, frustration, and confusion levels are reduced. Empathy for all is encouraged. Yoga ethics enhances a sense of safety and comfort, and establishes a greater harmony when consistently modeled and encouraged.

Each step of Yoga ethics begins with a descriptive summary of the principle, followed by *role playing and short drama* opportunities which are a series of activities in which students gather to discuss how they manage social situations and feelings with their classmates. Children may brainstorm these elements and eventually develop (with teacher input) their own personalized strategies for approaching difficult situations. Ideally, every student should have their own formula that fits them, not a one-size-fits-all strategy, but alternative choices. Expanding the behavioral choices for children establishes more of a buy in, more of a personal investment, when faced with challenges. When children are provided opportunities to discuss and practice social-emotional skills, they feel more confident. Their socio-emotional intelligence can grow in leaps and bounds, especially if the strategy is one that they have chosen and practiced.

Living in Harmony With Others and the World
Yamas

The first five steps of Yoga Ethics initiates activities for developing sweet relationships with friends and the world. These concepts bring peace to all.

Kindness ~ Ahimsa   I am friendly. I wear my "sunny heart" every day. I am sweet to others.

Cooperative living and a compassionate lifestyle are prerequisites for living in harmony with others. Kindness is expressed in how we think, what we do, and how we speak. Ahimsa invites tenderness in our behavior. In neohumanist Yoga, educators encourage "having good relationships," which embraces vast possibilities, including others (your human peers), and the other-than-human world (the squirrels, the bugs, the plants, the rocks). The more students experience this, the more successful their journey will be as they navigate the choppy waters of life.

Very young children are dominated by thoughts of "mine and meness" which is absolutely age appropriate for 2–3-year-olds. Teachers strive to eventually stretch students beyond this developmental phase into more interactions conducive to relationship building. Frequently, young children see the entire creation as theirs, perhaps because they are still connected to all beings on some deeper level.

Young ones still want to develop the skills of helping and maintaining friendships. To do this requires stepping outside of the "ego room" and moving towards sensitivity to other's feelings, extending connections with the school family and the world. Staff need to lead the way and hold their hands. Concepts that seem to be common sense to adults may need to be explained very simply and concretely to students with frequency. Concrete examples are offered to young children as their life experiences are few, explaining what kindness is and what kindness looks like.

Teachers stage opportunities to support children to: (a) be kind to themselves, (b) be kind to others, and (c) be kind to things (including furniture, rocks, and the air). One of the keys to understanding kindness is feeling gentleness. Opportunities to experience what being gentle is like are offered by caring for plants and animals.

Mutual Respect ~ Satya   I speak and act truthfully.
I speak sweetly to all.

Sweet verbal communication is the key to expressing benevolence. The differences between kind words and hurtful words are clearly identified. Teachers explain how students can make better choices and why these are desirable. Teachers compile a list of hurtful and kind words from everyday interactions to be analyzed by the class.

Students are encouraged to listen to the whispers of their "inner sunny voice." When a student's sweet words slip away, they may be asked: "Were you listening to your sunny voice or your monster voice?" Children are not punished for saying falsehoods, but are guided gently towards preferred sweet speech. Lying happens when someone is afraid. How can teachers create the safest emotional environment so that students will not have a desire to lie? Staff are sure to praise a child for remaining honest and truthful in a difficult situation. Everyone strives to be sweet in words and actions.

A significant part of any conflict resolution process is observing the face and feelings of the injured child. Student conflicts are resolved by discussions, sitting down and talking things out. Acts of biting, hitting, and kicking are discouraged and active strategies present alternative considerations for children when the urge to become violent grows strong. Students are asked: "How does that feel? How are you feeling? Look at Mario's face. How is he feeling?" When a child is observing the face and listening to the sounds of someone in pain, they are listening with their heart.

Unconditional love is shown by staff regardless of the unfortunate behavioral choices children make. There are no bad or wrong behaviors, just behaviors that reflect a lack of skill and understanding. For teachers to forgive children who have not yet developed these skills is showing the greatest patient love. Teachers make a commitment to guide students towards kinder expressions and in hopes that expressing kindness will someday be more personally fulfilling than wielding a dominating power over others.

Students can learn to utilize "I messages" to express their feelings, needs, and concerns. These communications usually begin with "I." Examples for children are: "I don't like that"; "I'll play with you later"; "I feel like playing alone"; "I feel mad when _____ hurts my heart (feelings)."

Teachers model respect by using polite words *very frequently*, that is, please, thank you, you're welcome, excuse me. Students learn best when teachers are constantly saying these words and modeling this ideal behavior. Children practice situations in which these "helping words" are used: "How do you ask for something sweetly?"; "How do you get something you want?"; "What do you say when you hurt someone by mistake?" Students learn this is another way to show others that you care. These words are used to sweeten a relationship, make people happy, and make them smile.

Just like watering a plant to keep it happy, friendships require a certain amount of watering. Magic words are one way of watering our relationships. Where polite words are shared, mutual respect is established. Satya is about having the kind words to express social justice for others, getting your needs met, maintaining relationships, and overriding your emotions to communicate or connect with someone.

**Responsibility ~ Asteya   I take responsibility for my actions.
I do not grab things.**

It is the responsibility of teachers to unconditionally attune to each child and express love and respect to them, even if teachers do not like the child for some reason. Young children are pure intuitive beings who pick up on signals right away if someone does not like them.

For many very young children, *Everything belongs to me!* Children are reminded to not take possessions that belong to others or take something when a child's turn is not over. Teachers remember that young children come from homes where many things may be theirs. Other students in the class can openly share their feelings about others grabbing their toy when they are playing with them. Students may respond more effectively to missteps in their behavior when other students vocalize their displeasure rather than when teachers intervene. The most effective teacher is the child's peers.

Young children who are new to the school experience may not have any concept of cooperation, of working together, of being generous, or of sharing. These are all skills required for cooperative classroom living. They may or may not be required to use these skills at home.

Misbehaviors often reflect a need to practice new skills, such as turn taking, sharing, problem solving, and anger management. Students practice raising their hand in class when they have something to say. If the environment is supportive and children have many opportunities to practice turn-taking, sharing, generosity, and patience, they realize that most of their needs are met in time. On a personal level, self-restraint leads to self-control which in turn leads to mental peace of mind.

As teachers, it is our responsibility to help students on the path to emotional intelligence and greater understanding. This does not mean denying their feelings: "Don't cry"; "Don't be sad." A significant part of developing emotional awareness is to help young ones to visually recognize and interpret facial expressions. Teachers may say: "I can see that you are sad. Tell me all about what happened." Teachers acknowledge children's feelings and may say: "It's ok to be sad" or "It's ok to cry. Sometimes I am sad." When teachers share their personal experiences, it has a profound impact on children.

As their mentors, teachers may verbally reflect back to children what they perceive the students are feeling to increase their emotional awareness. "You don't like it when Giuliano takes your shovel. I can see that you are very sad. Remember to use your words." This is learning empathy, identifying feelings. Many reminders and opportunities to practice these skills in class before situations happen empower children to stop themselves before hurting others.

An important aspect of socio-emotional intelligence is learning to read body language. A game that young children enjoy is "Putting on a Face." Have one student "put on a face" (happy, sad, angry, hurt) and everyone must guess what feeling goes with that face. Everyone copies the face. How do students respond when they see this face? What does it mean? Practice this every day for a week or so.

Teachers communicate to over-emotional children with a calm voice and calm body language. When communicating with students, 30% of the communication is in your tone of voice, 55% is in body language, 7% is verbal or what you say. Teachers are consistent in their loving communications.

Responsibility for advancing socio-emotional intelligence falls on the shoulders of students and teachers. Both need plans for maintaining personal balance and peace. Both are constantly sharpening and refining their compassionate verbal skills concerning pro-social skill development.

Love of All ~ Brahmacarya   We are different. I love you.
All children are members of the Earth family. Students all hold the same inner light in their hearts. This light is not only inside, it surrounds us. The cosmic presence resides in every entity, animate or inanimate. This principle re-defines and spiritualizes every being on the planet. Every atom, rock, air particle, sand, even furniture is vibrated by cosmic energy.

There are countless diverse life forms on this Earth, and there are many levels of existence and consciousness. Some entities are very aware of themselves. Some entities are more static and may not have developed a sense of self-awareness. Every being, regardless of its state of existence, is respected and honored, be it a rock, a frog, an elephant, a blade of grass, a bird, the sky, a volcano, a coatimundi, a scorpion.

> We believe that the spirit pervades all creation and that every creature possesses a soul in some degree, though not necessarily a soul conscious of itself. The tree, the waterfall, the grizzly bear, each is an embodied Force, and as such an object of reverence. (Ohiyes, in Eastman, 2001)

Cultivating a love for all species means unconditionally accepting and showing respect to every entity (even scary, poisonous creatures who we may not wish to be friends with!), embracing every rock, every sunbeam, the dirt, the trees, the rivers, with deep feeling, and ultimately recognizing all as reflections of the Infinite.

Naturally, children find it difficult to love creatures whom they fear. When irrational fears surface, staff develop a multi-faceted approach for trying to help the child overcome it. Yoga educators may perform a Yoga asana with a story about that creature and its positive gifts to the planet. Students may read books about it. Art projects are developed. Teachers may create sayings such as, "When I am nice to the bee, the bee won't sting me." These are rhymes that a child can repeat like a mantra when the fear begins to surface again. When they contain rhyme, rhythm, and repetition they can be more effective.

Creative Activities that can help build connections include:

- Partner Dancing ~ Play some lively music and encourage all students to dance, holding the hand of a friend. When the lights flicker, each child will release their hands and turn to a new friend. Holding the new friend's hands, the dance continues.
- Web Building: Have children (less than 10) sit in a circle. Give one child a ball of yarn in one hand and the end of the yarn in

the child's other hand. The child rolls the yarn ball to another child while holding the string end in the other. The second child holds a piece of string and rolls the ball to another child. Everyone needs to hold on to string pieces or the web falls apart. Everyone must do their part, or it doesn't work well.

Helping young people to see the Divine in All and overcome fears, doubts, and negative emotions is the work of the teacher. We are all connected to the same Inner Light.

**Simple Living ~ Aparigraha   Just one or two will do.
I have what I need.**

Sometimes children are tempted to take as much as they can. This can be regulated by saying, "2 hands. 2 items, please." The benefits of self-restraint, delays in personal gratification, and patience are explained and perhaps dramatized. Emphasis is placed on how needs are met in time. Recycling products, such as paper and other items, saving energy (light, etc.), reusing water bottles, and so on are practiced when applicable.

The cultivation of non-attachment is a key part of simple living. How to teach non-attachment to children? Simple seasonal activities are important—understanding that, for example, when leaves die and fall from the trees, they are making way for the new. Imagining what it feels like to be the tree, and to let go of the leaves. *What are we ready to let go of?*

Learning to live simply and cooperatively can be reinforced in many ways in the early years. Here's an example of a creative activity that can affirm the importance of simple and cooperative living, and which demonstrates the truth that when everyone shares, there is plenty to go around:

- Friendship Salad ~ Each child brings some fruit, nuts (depending on allergies!). With students, the fruit is cut and mixed with coconut or fruit juice and served. This can also be done with vegetables and cooked into a Friendship Soup.

If everyone in the world has just what they need, as opposed to what they want, there will be enough material goods, there will be enough nature, there will be enough peace for all.

Living in Harmony With Oneself – Niyama

The next five steps are for each student's own personal growth and balance. These bring peace to self.

Cleanliness–Shaoca   I put away what I use. I clean my thoughts.
Physical, mental, and environmental hygiene are a service to the world, humanity, and self. In addition to basic personal hygiene, children maintain neatness and orderliness in the school. Experiences are provided for them to assist with routine cleaning. Students are an integral part of caring for the environment. They also have an active role in making the environment aesthetically pleasing. Student art is displayed everywhere. Plants and animals (if possible) are in the school as well as gardening opportunities to encourage the caring for nature. What makes our minds "muddy"? An unhealthy, un-nutritional diet can contribute to this. Too much junk food can cause agitation in the body and the mind. A review of what foods are healthiest can give young children a clearer understanding of how foods affect the mind and body. Healthy foods may be grown in the garden.

Spiritual practices improve our clarity and keep the "inner mirror" of the mind from collecting excessive dust. Teachers strive to help students keep their inner mental mirror polished with unconditional love and caring, and maintain a mental balance with their thoughts. Knowing which thoughts to listen to and which thoughts to discard and throw away. Sunny feelings are positive emotions such as being happy, feeling brave, calm, or confident. Cloudy feelings are when we feel sad, angry, afraid, frustrated, or stressed. When students are experiencing cloudy feelings (mental distortions), we don't want them to hang out there all day. Teachers assist kids in moving from mental cloudiness to heartfelt sunniness by offering activities that the student absolutely loves. Much of the Shaoca practice has to do with weeding the negative thoughts out of our gardens. Enriching, amending the soil, and watering the greenery are also involved in the greening of our minds and thoughts.

Contentment–Santosha   I am happy. I am at peace.
Anger clouds the mind. Once anger overtakes the mind, the child is adrift. There are many strategies for defusing angry feelings. Some responses to angry feelings can be:

- Take a walk in nature or outside (re-directs mind and is calming)
- Sit down and do some breathing exercises (settles nervous system)
- Get a drink (re-directs mind and is calming)
- Walk away (4-year-olds and up)
- Tell a teacher how you feel
- Go to a safe, cozy corner (reading corner)
- Deliver an I message (I feel like I don't want to play with you when you hurt me.)

- Play in dirt, water, or sand (naturally relaxes nervous system)
- Draw an "angry" picture (re-directs mind and is meditative)

Re-directing our feelings is one of the most vital aspects of finding peace.

Emotional equilibrium is nurtured by identifying feelings, conversing, art, nature activities, negotiation, and redirection. Any of these techniques can support children in switching emotional gears and moving on. A diversity of sensory nature experiences—walking in nature, seeing nature, hearing nature, smelling nature, and touching nature are essential to finding personal contentment, tending to naturally iron out the wrinkles in the mind and heart. There have been a number of scientific studies on "Forest Bathing" (originating in Japan in the 1980s as *shinrin yoku*), which demonstrate nature's power to enhance well-being, bring joy, and foster peace and contentment.

To sustain contentment, mental equipoise and a strong self-image are reinforced. Support for mental equanimity is nurtured so that the mind neither gravitates towards superiority or inferiority. Humility is always nurtured. This concept of finding peace can be one of the most elusive characteristics of Niyama. However, unlike happiness, peace is a permanent resident of the heart. Clarity is provided for young children concerning what are acceptable behaviors and what are not. Peace comes from moving through certain emotions and finding solace in those things that send your heart and mind to the sunny side of life.

Helping Others ~ Tapah I like to take care of my friends. What can I do?

At the earliest age, children are habituated towards feeling compassion and empathy, with an emphasis towards giving and helping. Empathy exists in varying degrees from individual to individual. To assure the continued development of empathy, caregivers vigilantly watch for and create activities to engage children in helping others so that this joy of serving others flourishes. Young students are encouraged to stretch beyond selfishness and to think of others' well-being.

Supportive activities, discussions, and dramas about how to help others (be they peers, plants, insects, animals, or the environment) can easily be orchestrated in the classroom or outside. These activities expand the mind and heart, eliciting a sense of joy and happiness that is self-sustaining. Children enjoy the appreciation from those who are helped and receive validation as worthy members of the community. These events grow their self-esteem while lightening the troubles of others. Ultimately as students get older (elementary) an emphasis is placed on serving others without the expectation of anything in return. Helping others becomes a selfless habit.

How can students be helpful? Children can be helpful when someone is having difficulty taking off their boots, getting dressed, going outside, if something has been dropped or needs to be passed out to students, if someone has fallen or gets hurt on the playground. Instead of teachers doing all the helping, utilize student helpers whenever there are things to get done. It may make the day a little longer, but it also makes the day a little happier and fulfilling.

Concrete examples may be re-enacted with classmates of what it looks like when someone is having trouble. Students discuss why it is important for children to help someone (not always the teacher). What happens if we don't help them? How do you feel when you help? Children find joy and meaning when they can place a light in someone's hand on a dark day.

Understanding ~ Svadyaya I enjoy getting to know myself.
On this journey where children learn about the mysteries of life, they need assistance in understanding the many internal voices. How do they align themselves with the Inner Sunny Teacher when there is so much noise in their heads and hearts? Yoga activities and art sharpen the intuitive faculty of inner listening. 'Understanding' for students includes participating in a variety of experiences to learn how and why some behavioral choices of caring are preferred. Children journey forward to understand their feelings and urges, and how to better respond to social situations.

"I was listening to the Monster Voice when I did that." Children reenact dramas and role playing games to practice what they have learned so they can access that information when they come into stressful situations. Students can also practice chanting positive affirmations loudly in class together in Yoga asana classes, as part of meditation, seated together in any class, or when practicing new social skills.

"Understanding" for students encompasses physical and emotional responses that bring happiness and contentment to all. This takes time and practice to integrate these possibilities into the child's heart during a time when the world is just full of experiences. It involves many heart-to-heart conversations, questions, and observations (individual and collective). Love is the key. Understanding is the cure.

Iishvara Pranidhana ~ Taking Shelter in Goodness. I am One with everything.
Very young children are innately connected to all things spiritual. Their umbilical cord to the inner Divine remains unaltered. They look for

the external signs to confirm their inner understanding, feelings, and natural benevolence. Like magnets, they are drawn to spiritual practices, uplifting music, and the wonders of nature. They long for the spiritual nurturing from within and without.

How can teachers nourish students with the omnipresence of their Inner Friend? It is important to engage in Ashtanga Yoga spiritual activities (asana, yogic breathing, chanting, meditation, deep relaxation) every day to encourage the experience of inner awareness and joy. At times like this educators remember that education is not the information that teachers give students, it is a natural unfolding that occurs within each student, from the inside out.

Frequently, the teacher gives unconditional loving shelter to the child as a compassionate caregiver. While the parent is the first caregiver, the next love giver is the teacher. The staff need to be spiritually and emotionally grounded to accomplish this. Through thought-provoking questions, intuiting what the child is feeling and intuitional problem solving, teachers introduce other considerations to the students about life.

The teacher reminds each child of the Inner Voice that they carry. This Inner Friend is always with the child. Sometimes the Sunny voice is a faint whisper. Sometimes the ego or Monster Voice IS LOUD! Teachers remind students of this dance. The teacher reminds children of their innate Oneness with the World.

Yoga Ethics embodied in the aspects of Yama and Niyama, conceptualized in age appropriate ways, generate a sense of mutual respect, promote compassionate consideration, and reinforce our natural loving nature. These go a long way towards nurturing friendships in each child's life and in the long term, creating a sense of connection with all the world.

May all beings dwell peacefully on Mother Earth. May all beings be free from suffering. May all beings see the bright side of everything. May all beings be healed.

Yoga Postures—Asana

Asanas are the physical postures or poses of Yoga that have many demonstrated benefits: increasing flexibility and strength, stress management, improved circulation, managing pain, and many other aspects of well-being. Kids Yoga is age-appropriate and can be quite a bit different from the adult practice. Children's asana classes are based on how they learn best during the early years of their lives. Students are not necessarily on mats, or in rows and columns, with minimal social interaction. While the teachers may have mats for older students, kids are moving around, hearing, making sounds, looking around, problem solving, using all their sensory organs. Their classes demand creativity and social interaction.

Children's Yoga can assist in strengthening muscle tone, improving self-regulation, harmonizing behavior, and learning more about relationship building with others and oneself. Yoga Asana is about greeting all life with benevolence.

Opportunities abound for greater focus and concentration. Connections with the world, all beings, each other, and the Inner Teacher are strengthened through the Yoga experiences. Art projects and non-competitive games are part of the Yoga curriculum.

In the elementary ages, references are still made to caring and connection with self and the world as well as the Inner Light that resides within the heart. Yoga class tools are presented for developing self-awareness and thoughtfulness. How can the Yoga teacher provide insights to enhance social, intellectual, and emotional well-being? Yoga experiences, activities, and discussions can support students in developing respect for others, building self-confidence, coping with body image issues, moodiness, and/or negative emotions, and with developing a positive attitude towards life. These are all considered foundational goals for Yoga Asana. Yoga activities are presented for the whole mind, whole body, and interweaving them with the whole heart.

A Yoga Asana is a position comfortably held (not like the Olympics or football) with proper deep breathing and mental composure. Breath awareness and positive reinforcement are effective in establishing an atmosphere of harmony and joyfulness. Neohumanist Yoga Asana is a means by which we connect students to the diverse entities residing on Planet Earth, how they are living and what is our relationship with them.

Yoga is stretching. Yoga is feeling your breath. Yoga is finding your balance. Yoga is listening inside. Yoga is relaxing. Yoga feels good! Yoga is love! There are many potential benefits to Asana practice for children. These include:

- Stress relief

Young children have countless challenges in their lives. Emotional issues for young children can include chronic illness, death of a loved one, betrayal of a friend, sleep deprivation, academic challenges, verbal or physical violence, or fears related to bullying. Stress can arise from not only the thoughts but from various influences in the environments at home, school, and neighborhood. Divorce is second only to death as a significant source of stress in children's lives. The emotional costs can be far reaching.

External and/or internal stimuli can cause physiological and/or psychological responses that can knock children off balance, causing the stimulation of the fight or flight response. The sympathetic nervous system can activate the release of stress hormones and neurotransmitters that send cues to the heart, circulation, lungs, metabolism, immune system, and skin to resolve a perceived threat which may result in hyper- or hypo-activity of the child.

Asana practice can support the process of releasing emotions. Yoga techniques such as deep relaxation, simple breath awareness, and Yoga ethics can minimize the physiological and psychological effects of stress. These Yoga toolkit supports can be carried by the individual throughout life to safeguard one's well-being on the life journey.

- Sensory integration and special needs

There are many aspects of Yoga and Asana practice that can minimize learning challenges for some students. Many children face physical, psychological, and intellectual challenges. In the case of the physically challenged, gymnastics and physical exercise may not be something that they can engage in effectively. The stretching and toning of muscles may be an Asana activity they can practice and enjoy multiple benefits. The teacher may even help move their limbs into the desired positions with input from a physical therapist or doctor, with attention to the breath when practical. Yoga movements even with teacher assistance can create flexibility in the skeletal and muscular system, especially if there is muscle rigidity.

Yoga practices can support peace of mind, help children remain calm, and lower their levels of aggression, social withdrawal, and anxiety. Specialized Yoga practices can increase attention, build self-esteem, release energy, enhance digestion or elimination issues, minimize asthma, reduce anxiety, and boost some aspects of memory retrieval. The key concept here is *improving* physical and mental health through engaging positive supportive experiences and minimizing negative experience. Yoga in and of itself may be not a cure, but it is a complementary therapeutic helping practice. Every situation brings variable results, depending on the root cause.

- Physical development

Many school districts around the globe are recommending that school curricula include very specific physical exercise movements. These activities can easily be woven into a class lesson plan. Some enjoyable movement activities are somersaulting, rocking in a seated position (side to side and forward/backwards), floor rolling lengthwise like a pencil, twirling, kicking, stomping, bouncing, jumping, galloping, walking legs up the wall, shaking, wiggling, crawling, climbing, spinning, pressing into the wall with the hands, back, hips, shoulder, feet, shaking those sillies out! Animal walking can include being a crab, bear, or dinosaur. Yoga can be easily integrated into a creative movement class, and vice versa!

Teaching Methodology

Yoga games and exercises can be seamlessly integrated throughout the day. Many neohumanist schools do reserve a special time period for Yoga, and these classes consist of these major components:

1. Asana poses which may comprise 70–80% of the total class time.
2. Yoga breathing. While practicing Yoga Asanas, Meditation, and Deep Relaxation, the teacher is constantly bringing the student awareness to the breath, mentioning "breathing in" and "breathing out."
3. Socio-emotional support is facilitated throughout the class in accordance with the ethics of Yama and Niyama. This may include Yoga relationship building games.
4. A short meditation of 2–7 minutes, depending upon students' ages.
5. Deep Relaxation which may be 30 seconds to 10 minutes.

Other Ashtanga Yoga practices that may be included are chanting, Yoga massage, mudra practice, singing, affirmation work, art experiences, and possibly short Yoga ethics dramatizations. These are all Yoga possibilities to choose from and are certainly not mandated for every class. Roll out the creativity, the imagination, and the laughter!! Traditional Yoga asanas were often designed to emulate animal behaviors. This is a great entry point to engage young children with Yoga. "If you could be any animal, who would you be?" Play animal charades. Let them guess who each student is portraying. Include simple animal facts that will bring the experience alive. Use animal metaphors: sleep like a dog, climb like a monkey, stretch like a cat, sing like a bird, sunbathe like a lizard, and leap like a dolphin. These stimulate the student's imagination and connect them with other-than-human nature.

As with all classroom activities, the Yoga teacher is responsible for the safety of the students. Always have your eyes on them. Do not turn your back towards them. Never leave students unsupervised. Eliminate poses like headstands and handstands. If you observe something dangerous, quickly and gently approach the student. Calmly ask the child to come out of the pose. Demonstrate that pose again or another similar pose safely.

If you use background music, consider keeping the volume low so that it does not overtake your voice. Music selections are usually soft and slow. Nature sounds such as birds, jungle sounds, ocean wildlife sounds, water tides, or other natural sounds can be great fun!

Many Yoga teachers remark on the success of utilizing Yoga cards. Some teachers possess huge puppet collections which can also be used. Mats can be useful but may also become a nuisance, if students will be moving. Scarves, streamers, or lengthy pieces of very light cloth are wonderful for movement and dancing. Bean bags, washcloths, socks, or beanie babies can be used as eye bags during Deep Relaxation (Shavasana) if you wish.

Breath–Pranayama

The importance of supporting lung health and full respiratory functioning is gaining in popularity. Nothing is more essential to our overall wellness than proper respiration. Breath is the heart of all Yoga. For children to learn the best practices for healthy breathing early in life, and to have it reinforced throughout their lives, is of special importance to Yoga educators. These practices calm the nervous system, help in developing self-control, and serve as a bridge connecting to the Inner Self.

It is important not to use adult pranayama practices with children under the age of 18. In physical and emotional development, there is some growing and glandular maturing that students must accomplish before engaging in adult pranayamas. The lungs are not fully mature until about third grade and there are physical, emotional, and psychological issues that develop during puberty that need to be "settled into" before upgrading towards adult breath practices.

Introducing the Science of Air

When introducing the element of air, teachers may use props to help young students better understand how this intangible, invisible force works. Some of the explorations can include: (a) Balloons have long been used for fun and learning about how air moves, but we know now that balloons have environmental impacts that outlast the moments of joy they can bring. An alternative experience that has the similar effect of watching something float in the sky is bubble blowing! (b) Construct, decorate, and dance with paper fans. Children can have fun creating airflow by fanning themselves. What do you feel when you fan yourself? Can you make the air touch your face, hands, feet? (c) Take students outside on a windy day and let them observe the effects of the wind on nature (blowing trees, clouds, plants) and feeling it on their skin. (d) Blow a feather and catch it. Watch the wind or an electric fan (or hair dryer) blow it as well. (e) Elementary students can get down on all fours on the floor and blow ping pong balls around the room through straws.

Belly Breathing

The very best breathing practice is "belly breathing" or diaphragmatic abdominal breathing. If you adopt one practice from this Ashtanga Yoga program, this is THE ONE. The belly breath is the one breath that is endorsed by most Yoga practitioners as well as respiratory clinics around the world as the healthiest practice.

On inhaling, the emphasis is placed on getting a healthy movement of the diaphragm to open both the abdominal and thoracic cavities to draw air into the fullness of lungs. For this the abdomen is pushed outward to create a vacuum, bringing the breath into the lower lungs. During the exhalation, the abdomen is pulled in and up towards the spine. Belly breathing can be done while sitting or standing, and can easily be learned in fun ways. You can have young children lie on their backs and place a small stuffed animal or toy on their belly button. Then have them breathe in through their nose and watch the toy rise. *They get big like mountains.* Then have them breathe out, with the teacher making exaggerated "blowing" exhalation sound so children can connect with the concept. *Watch your belly get flat like the valley.* Up and down, slowly, for a minute or so until they get restless. This exercise engages the parasympathetic part of the autonomic nervous system, inviting a feeling of calmness.

Shallow upper chest breathing patterns can be accompanied by symptoms of anxiety, depression, or fear. Upper chest breathing can even trigger these conditions. These emotional states can often be changed merely by initiating the diaphragmatic breathing method. The Yoga teacher highlights and models the diaphragmatic breathing model throughout the day, remembering that breathing is closely aligned with a balanced emotional state.

Unless otherwise specified or unless your nose is stuffed up, breathing through the nose is encouraged for a variety of physiological reasons. The nose moisturizes and warms the breath to the internal body temperature. The nose purifies oxygen intake before it passes through the lungs. Incoming oxygen is better filtered with nasal breathing than through mouth breathing.

Nose breathing has been found to inhibit the "fight or flight" response. So nose breathing can have a more relaxing effect than mouth breathing.

When breathing through the nose, the relaxation response is reinforced which calms the nervous system, lowers respiration and the heart rate.

Benefits of Yoga Breathing

Yoga tells us that there exists a correlation between breath, thought, and many physiological responses. Proper breathing holds the key to a balanced mental state and supports better integration between the physical, mental, and other layers of our being. Deeper, fuller breathing clears out stale air and improves the quantity of oxygen filling the lungs. A harmonious mind is created and sustained by slow, deep, and regular respiration. Oxygen purifies the blood and is good for keeping the nervous system in a state of calmness. Full oxygenation of the blood and organs invigorates the body. A sense of well-being and contentment often follows.

Breathing practices can be woven into the school day for many reasons: Perhaps it is early in the day and the class is overly excited, they need help in calming down. What is your most calming breath? Perhaps they are lethargic, practically falling asleep, they need an energy boost. What breath expression or game is good for this? Breath awareness practice can support the students individually and collectively within and without the Yoga class meditation experience.

Yogic breathing can be closely connected to the abilities of memory and learning. When the breathing is calm, absorbing impressions and learning can be more effectively performed and the power of receptivity may be stronger. The learning capacity can be enhanced with a calm body and calm mind. Best breathing can increase the ability of the mind to concentrate and memory retrieval can be enhanced.

By learning the art of breath awareness, children are reminded of how a calm mind goes hand and hand with proper breathing. Through attention to the breath, we tap into the fullness of who we are. Greater understanding shines through. Yogic breathing is a stressbuster. One feels self-confident, self-aware, and there is more equanimity of mind. Making conscious breathing part of each day has important effects on the classroom climate; it can enhance positive moods and help to cultivate a peaceful environment.

Deep Relaxation–Pratyahara

Deep Relaxation is one of the most significant parts of the Asana class. It is a time of absolute stillness, a time of integrating the deeper layers of the mind. It is when the body absorbs the benefits of the entire Asana practice. The students can dive DEEP. In deep relaxation all body functions are in a state of rest. Children are invited to totally decompress and leave all stress behind. Prior to deep relaxation, the Yoga asana experiences have been energetically winding down into slow motion. To do this, select poses that are relaxing. Having slower and less active asanas will help the students to transition to a successful Deep Relaxation experience. Rest and relaxation do not always come easily to young ones.

Deep Relaxation experiences can be combined with imagery and visualizations, body awareness, breath awareness, stories, and other techniques that bring the mind into a deeper state of inner self-awareness. The teacher's voice is low, soft, slow, and gentle. Emphasis is placed on communicating caring and belonging concepts such as love, joy, peace, beauty. The teacher may choose to play soft calming music or nature sounds to help children focus.

The most popular position for Deep Relaxation is in a supine position. This position, lying on the back with arms on the ground away from the body and the legs a little separated, eyes closed, is known as *Shavasana*. In this position the sensory organs are mostly de-activated. Students can be given the choice to rest in any position that feels comfortable: curled up like a sleeping dog, lying prone on the stomach face down and with hands stacked on top of each other supporting the forehead (like a sleeping crocodile), with legs up the wall (like sleeping bats), or maybe lying on their sides (like sleeping cats). The Deep Relaxation Experiences can even be offered while sitting or bent over a desk with the students' heads resting on the hands.

When at rest, the mind can be particularly receptive. Visualization and imagination activities stimulate certain brain centers that can provide support as students move toward improved emotional and mental balance. Though the "outer senses" are stilled (except for hearing) the "inner senses" (the imaginative sensations of smell, taste, seeing, and touching) are activated, thus stimulating the feeling life of the child. Guided Deep Relaxations should be optimistic and promote unconditional love, caring for all, kindness, and neohumanist expressions showing love for all beings.

Elementary teachers may consider facilitating an open-ended story. This is where the storyteller may pause at certain places and the children (who may be in deep relaxation on the floor) can mentally fill in their own unique details without speaking aloud. Here is an example:

Once upon a time there was a very special place (pause).

In this place you can hear (pause) and see (pause). It was a wonderful secret place.

One day a guide appeared (pause) and took you by the hand.

> The guide led you up to the top of a very high hill.
>
> Once you and the guide arrived there you could very clearly see everything for miles and miles.
>
> It was beautiful. Your guide gave you a piece of paper.
>
> On the paper was a very personal message, it said: (pause). The message was perfect.
>
> It was just for you. When you looked up from reading the message, your guide had disappeared and there was something magical left where your guide had been. (Pause).
>
> You picked up this magic object and carried it with you down the hill. (Pause.)

Breathe in. Breathe out. Let's sit up and whoever wants to can share some details about your journey.

Children may be brought out of deep relaxation with a bell, gentle clapping, a song, a chant, a glockenspiel, a singing bowl, an instrument. But before you close this experience, consider giving a wish, something uplifting and positive. A wish is a heartful gift of hope from teacher to student(s). Words of affirmation and positivity empower one to stay in balance, to acknowledge your inner potential. Affirmations keep the mind anchored in what is important in life. These tools keep individuals from being overwhelmed by fear and perceived inferiorities.

Preschool affirmations are very, very simple. Elementary ones are a bit more complex. Here are some very basic ones:

> May you be happy. May you be at peace. May you be free of troubles. May you be filled with confidence. May you be loving, kind, and understanding with others. May you be a helper to your friends.

When children are sitting up, with eyes open, you may want to introduce Yoga massage (a self-massage). Yoga massage can improve general relaxation and enhance immune function. With the light passing of the fingers over the skin, lymph cell glands are stimulated, nerve cells are relaxed. A light massage increases dopamine (a "feel good" hormone) and decreases cortisol (the stress hormones) in the body. When the stress levels are reduced, anxiety can be diminished and well-being preserved. Massage decreases muscle tension. It has the potential to make children feel a little happier.

To introduce a very simple 1-minute self-massage: Ask the children to give themselves a big hug. They can gently rub their scalp, forehead, face, and neck, waking up that brain. Gently touching the shoulders, underarms, upper arms, elbows, wrists, hands, and fingers. Moving down the chest and tummy, circling around the navel and waist. Finally stroking the hips, upper legs, knees, lower legs, ankles, feet, and toes. A regular body part lesson!

Meditation–Dharana, Dhyana, and Samadhi

These last three "limbs" of Yoga encompass the advanced contemplative practices of Yogis. The many aspects of Yoga explored in this chapter—Yoga Ethics, Yoga postures (Asanas), controlled breathing, and deep relaxation—are all activities designed to prepare the body and mind for meditation. Meditation is the key element in cultivating awareness of the inner world, the balancing factor in an education that has been almost exclusively focused on the outer world. Neohumanist education acknowledges that young people's primary tasks are learning about how the world works, and how to navigate it, how to develop positive relationships, how to form a healthy ego, or sense of self, and so on. Neohumanism also recognizes the evolutionary necessity of cultivating an expanded awareness of affinity with all creation, an awareness that recognizes our deep interconnections in a shared "Ground of Being." For these sentiments to be awakened, attention to the inner world is vital, as it opens access to levels of the mind that house the higher human tendencies of compassion, empathy, creativity, and the desire to serve the common good. Unlike mindfulness practices, which can be very useful but are mostly directed towards awareness of the contents of one's consciousness, neohumanist meditations are more goal directed, seeking this oneness with all, so that the subject/object illusion, the sense of separateness begins to fade.

Neohumanist education is global in scope, and thus, meditation will be differently received depending on whether it is part of a society's cultural traditions. One deep fear that people in societies unfamiliar with meditation may have is a concern about mind control. It is a fact that when the mind is in a state of deep relaxation, it is more receptive to suggestion. Any neohumanist educational project must be absolutely transparent about the aims of this inner work, and the goals of cultivating kindness, compassion, and love for all, and be open to the participation of families. Another concern is that paying quiet attention to the inner world will make a person passive, and vulnerable to control by others. It is important for people to understand that the contemplative activity in a neohumanist school is tempered by a commitment to critical thinking and analysis, to debate and discussion, to exercising judgment and decision-making, and to active involvement in creating a better world, serving human and non-human others to alleviate suffering. It should go without saying that there should never be elements of coercion when it comes to practicing meditation. Students should always be free to choose to participate in contemplative activities and should not be judged or criticized for opting to read or do some other quiet activity.

When a teacher embarks upon the inclusion of meditation in their pedagogy, it is useful to know some supplemental activities that help to prepare the student. A *mantra* is a sound or group of words that are rhythmically repeated over a period of a time. The Yoga science of mantra is based on the idea that sound is a form of energy that has a definite predictable effect on the body-mind. Mantras exist in all languages. Many mantras are in Sanskrit, such as one that is popular with neohumanists: *Baba Nam Kevalam* (loosely translates as "love is all there is"). The difference between concentrating on any object, such as a candle flame or a flower, and a mantra such as this one, is that the phrase carries with it the feeling of benevolent love for all beings on earth. Sanskrit mantras are considered to be extremely powerful because the Sanskrit alphabet evolved from sounds that are linked to vibrations that subtly emanate from particular energy centers of the body. Mantras can be spoken aloud or contemplated internally.

Local chants or affirmations in the native language can also be effective so children can feel the meaning in their hearts. Occasionally, when singing mantras are for some reason culturally inappropriate, the repetition of positive affirmations can be put to a tune and repeated. *I am Love/Peace. I love my Earth Family. Love is everywhere.* The best mantras for children are ones that are simple, embedded with love, and easily repeated. Ideally, mantras, affirmations, and uplifting songs must be fun to sing and engaging.

Chanting is simply the repetitive, rhythmic speaking or singing of words over a period of minutes. Many spiritual traditions consider chanting to be a tool for spiritual development and upliftment, as we discussed in Chapter 12, "The Superpower of Music." Chanting can be accompanied by musical instruments, clapping, and other gestures as well as dancing and movement. Chanting is thought to be an ideal preparation for Yoga and/or meditation practice, as it facilitates deep breathing and centers the mind-heart.

Many cultures have a tradition of *mudras*, sacred hand gestures thought to affect the subtle energy flows in the body/mind and awaken a deeper sense of self-awareness. The word mudra is from the Sanskrit words *mudam* and *drava (mudam* means "bliss" or "happiness" and "*drava*" means "to draw forth"), implying that mudras have the power to bring forth the joy or happiness that lies within us. The traditional practices of mudras vary from culture to culture and are a complex area of study, but there are a few simple ones that children enjoy:

- Grumpy Bear (Arms crossed in front of the chest)
- Namaskar Peace (Palms together close to the heart (prayer position)
- Wise Owl (Hands resting on top of each other in the lap, facing upwards)
- Earth to Sky (Place hand on each knee facing up, joining index finger to thumb)

Openings and Closings

There are many strategies for initiating meditation in a classroom. A neohumanist school may start the day with a school-wide "quiet time" in which children enter the school, stash their belongings and then join their peers sitting together in a large room for a short period of time before starting the busyness of the day. A teacher of young children may start with a story such as this one, demonstrating the sitting position with the hands folded in their lap:

> Once there was a wise child who loved sitting quietly under the apple tree. The child would fold their hands in their lap and close their eyes. Soon the child was so still that a little bird in the tree thought "Oh, this is part of the tree." While the bird was sitting in the child's hands, it thought "This is the perfect place to build my nest." She started bringing little sticks into the child's hands. Flying back and forth gathering sticks, in the blink of an eye, the nest was ready. The little bird sang the sweetest song.
>
> Let's be still and listen. Perhaps the little bird will come to you.

A teacher might experiment with *Walking Meditation* ~ Let's walk very slowly around the room in a circle for 3 minutes. Feel your heels hitting the floor. Feel the ball of your foot stepping down onto the floor. Feel your toes pressing together as they touch the floor. Feel your leg picking the foot up and getting ready to step down once again. Walk as slowly and as quietly as you can. We don't have to be in a single file. You may walk next to another child. *I know I am walking, walking, walking. I know I am breathing, breathing, breathing. I know I am, I am, I am.* Practice this inside or outside in silence.

A beautiful way to end a meditation is with a powerful visualization that connects us to our shared *Ground of Being.* You are surrounded by a beautiful White Light. The Light is peaceful, safe, happy, and loving. Every time you breathe in, the White Light fills you up. Every time you breathe out, the White Light pours out of you and into the world. It touches every child in the room. It touches everything in the room. When everyone inhales, all the love and light comes back to them. When everyone exhales, the light goes somewhere where there is no White Light. The White Light is touching and holding all your friends. They are feeling peaceful, loving and sweet. Exhaling, the White Light continues to fill the room.

Now, the room is completely filled and the White Light goes outside of the room, into the street, into the trees and plants, into all your animal friends, into your neighborhood, into the whole town, into the whole country, and into the entire planet earth. Then it circles back to this room into your heart. We are all connected by this White Light.

In Summary

Meditation has numerous physical, mental, emotional, and spiritual benefits. Many times, these benefits emerge as 'feelings' or 'understandings' that may suddenly bubble up about life. These may sit in the mind for a while. When engaging in meditation, occasionally dilemmas or trauma become resolved a little. Meditation is a way of keeping the inner balance during times when the outer balance has been lost. The child who meditates tries to listen to these whispers of the heart.

Meditation increases positive, creative, and intuitive thinking. This practice redirects the agenda of the self-centered ego in a vastly more expansive way. The practice of entering a contemplative space essentially brings equilibrium to the young child. Meditation connects the child to deeper subconscious layers of the mind.

Such a meditation practice over time can bring a promise of contentment and a greater degree of emotional balance as stress hormones decrease in production. As children regularly practice this inner listening, they will begin to discern the intentions behind the many inner voices. They will (with the teacher's help) detect and identify which thoughts are Sunny Thoughts and which thoughts are Monster Thoughts. With the teacher's patient support, they will eventually launch into aligning themselves with that more benevolent Inner Sunshine.

> Meditation, Yoga, and other mindfulness practices are more popular, and helpful, than ever. Studies have shown that teaching kids mindfulness practices can build students' attentiveness, respect for fellow classmates, self-control, and empathy, all while reducing stress, hyperactive behavior ADHA symptoms, and depression. (Eisler, 2019, para. 2)

Teachers who facilitate these practices notice that there is a marked improvement in social-emotional skills, contentment, overall well-being, and quality of life for their students. The more often that students practice these tools, the closer they come to that portal leading to self-fulfillment.

FOR CONTINUING STUDY

> *Discussion/Reflection:* This chapter highlighted a few concerns neohumanist educators might consider when teaching in a culture that does not have a contemplative tradition at its core. If in a group, share any experiences you have had with this. What are the most important things to think about? What are some strategies you might use in this situation?
>
> *Discussion/Reflection:* What are some ways to keep parents informed about Yoga activities in the school? What kind of events might you sponsor for families?
>
> *Application:* Design a Yoga session for the environment where you live or work. Keep cultural considerations front and center. Identify a specific age group. Be very specific with activity design: What topic might you focus on? How will you begin the session? Will you include a story? What might be an appropriate art project? How much time will each activity take? How will you end the session? Provide as many details as you can.

MahaJyoti Glassman and Nancy Niiti Gannon have written a comprehensive book on teaching Yoga to children, *Come Alive with Yoga,* (2021, Neohumanist College of Asheville Press).

The book *I Love Yoga* by Didi Ananda Rama (2010) contains a varied collection of Yoga poses adapted for children. Available as an e-book at https://www.anandamarga.org/store/ebooks/

References

Eastman, C. A. (2001). *The soul of an Indian and other writings from Ohiyes.* Second Edition. New World Library.

Eisler, M. (2019). 3 kid friendly meditations your children will love. *Chopra.* https://chopra.com/articles/3-kid-friendly-meditations-your-children-will-love

Goleman, D., & Davidson, R. J. (2017). *Altered traits: Science reveals how meditation changes your mind, brain, and body.* Penguin Books.

16

Studying the Social World

Towards a Neohumanist Future

> *Ours is the age of neohumanism—humanism supplying elixir to all, one and all. We are for all, and with everything existent we are to build up a new society, a neohumanistic society.*
>
> —P. R. Sarkar, *A Outline of Prout*, 2018

All educational philosophies are linked to a vision of the good life and of the kind of society that is desired. Educational practices are thus related to the formation of suitable human beings to inhabit these desired conditions. The general stated aim of the social studies in democratic societies is to provide background knowledge in order to cultivate reasoned decision-making and civic competence for purposes of active citizenship. To accomplish this, the multi-disciplinary field of study draws upon core academic disciplines (history, geography, political science, economics) as well as more peripheral ones (anthropology, psychology, sociology, art, and literature).

To study the social world is to study how human beings have evolved and changed over time, how the environment shapes individuals and societies, how humans interact with each other, how economies are developed, how people govern themselves, how conflicts arise, how participation in a society influences and shapes individual identity, and how issues of power, authority, and rights play out in human affairs.

While the term "social studies" emerged in the beginning of the 20th century in Britain and North America, all countries have adopted some form of multi-disciplinary study of the social world. The social studies are most often taught from the perspective of national identity with an interest in preserving narratives that serve dominant national purposes. Common themes, such as those articulated by the National Council of the Social Studies in the United States, can be found, to greater and lesser degree, across the globe. These include:

- *The study of culture* (how cultures develop, adapt, and change, and what explains cultural differences)
- *Time, continuity, and change* (what we can learn from studying the causes and resolutions of past events)
- *People, places, and environments* (the relationships between human populations and the physical environment; the use of geographic tools such as maps, globes, and computer modeling)
- *Individual development and identity* (how this is shaped by various factors, including culture, social class, and lived experience)
- *Individuals, groups, and institutions* (why and how institutions—schools, courts, religions—are formed, what purposes they serve and how they can be influenced and changed)
- *Power, authority, and governance* (political institutions, how they develop, how they have changed over time, what people can do to influence them, and what the rights and responsibilities of citizenship entail)
- *Production, distribution, and consumption* (economics, how goods and services are produced and distributed)
- *Science, technology, and society* (the ways that science and technology have shaped the modern world, and how they have modified the physical world)
- *Global connections* (the ways that the people and nations of the world are interconnected and how actions in one part of the globe have impacts on other parts)
- *Civic ideals and practices* (the skills of democratic participation and citizenship) (https://www.socialstudies.org/standards/national-curriculum-standards-social-studies)

Knowledge Wars

The study of the social world is one of the most contested areas of educational theory and practice. In the United States, for example, fierce battles raged through the 20th and into the 21st century over issues of multiculturalism, the interpretation of history, the biases of economic theories, and issues of gender and sexual identities. These battles are culminating most recently in accusations that teachers are indoctrinating children with "critical race theory" and in the banning and challenges to hundreds of books in the past 2 years alone over issues of race, gender, and sexuality. Contests over the curriculum fall along fairly predictable lines: conservatives seek to maintain the power and privilege of dominant groups by ensuring the continuance of the status quo; liberals and progressives seek a more inclusive, dynamic society with a more equal distribution of power.

Every one of the themes above can serve particular interests: the study of how cultures change, for example, differs when taught from the perspectives of the colonized or the colonizer; economics can be taught from a capitalist perspective or from a Marxist perspective, or from an emergent "degrowth" perspective; science and technology can be celebrated uncritically or they can be shown to have severe environmental consequences; civic ideals can be studied from a privileged point of view or the position of an oppressed or marginalized group. What is important to recognize is *that there is no "single story"*; history, geography, economics, all of the constituent aspects of the social studies, are narratives told from differing perspectives. A rigorous approach to the field recognizes this, and accepts as its mission the exploration and analysis of multiple perspectives, with the aim of growing closer to a truthful understanding of our world.

Philosophies and Perspectives in the Social Studies

This issue of "perspective" can be better understood by recalling the major historic philosophies of education that were introduced in Chapter 1. How do the various schools of educational philosophy approach the study of the social world? For the Perennialists, history is the primary discipline to be studied. It is a conservative approach, valuing past precedent over social change, and believes that the wisdom of the past is the best guide to the future. The Behaviorists disburse rewards and punishments to encourage "right thinking" and so the emphasis is on rote learning and the inculcation of values and perspectives that align with dominant interests. Their "loyalty and patriotism" model of the social studies is a conservative model that resists liberal or progressive change. The Romantics believe that humans are inherently good, and that human nature is corrupted by evil institutions such as governments, schools, cities, and armies, which are thus responsible for social inequalities, sufferings, and injustice. Since Romantic pedagogy concentrates on returning the child to a "state of nature," the study of social issues is student directed, oriented towards the concept of freedom and free expression, and utilizes literature and the arts to foster the aesthetic capacities above rational or technical knowing.

If Romanticism values human freedom above other values, Pragmatism can be said to value social cooperation and cohesion. John Dewey (1916/1966), perhaps the most well-known of the Pragmatists, believed that democracy was more than a form of government; it was, to him, a "mode of associated living, of conjoint communicated experience" (p. 87). Students study real world problems through experiential learning, and engage in cooperative study and rational dialogue in order to cultivate the capacities for democratic living, social problem-solving, and self-governance. If the Pragmatists value social cooperation, more critical thinkers argue that democracy has not been fully actualized due to the oppressive power relations that sustain social hierarchies. Critical pedagogy, grounded in Marxian analysis, claims that unresolved issues related to a capitalist economy and the legacies of enslavement, patriarchy, and the genocide of the original inhabitants of the land that is now the United States (and other countries) have inhibited the full development of a democratic society. In this model, the social studies tend to focus on issues of including more diverse narratives in the curriculum, challenging the "whitewashing" of history textbooks, and studying (and participating in) social movements that increase human rights and freedoms.

Neohumanism and the Holistic Paradigm

Sarkar's discourses place neohumanist education firmly in this philosophical camp, given the importance of laying a foundation for spiritual development. Neohumanist education does draw upon important ideas from Pragmatism and Critical Pedagogy with the aim of tempering spiritual ideology with progressive ideals of justice and equality. A few of the important guiding principles of neohumanist education to consider when deciding how to approach the study of the social world include:

- Focus on the *wholeness* of reality (understanding the interconnections between humans and the rest of the natural world, the systemic nature of all creation, the importance of relation-

ships—between humans, plants, animals, soil, sea and sky—and the subtle ways that changes in anything affect everything else at some level).
- Overcoming limiting sentiments (geo-sentiment, socio-sentiment, species-sentiment) and the extension of identity, love, and connection to all humanity as well as non-human species.
- Acknowledging the embeddedness of the individual in culture, and the important ways that intersectionality (the interconnection of social categories such as race and gender that overlap in people and can heighten discrimination) influences individual identity development.
- Emphasizing multiple ways of knowing (rational-technical, ancestral, traditional ecological knowledge, embodied knowing, etc.).

A Just, Peaceful, and Sustainable Vision for the Future

While many educational theories claim to be "value-neutral" the reality is, as claimed in the first sentence of this chapter, that all educational ideas are linked to a vision of the future and the kind of society that is desired. P. R. Sarkar, the proponent of the philosophy of neohumanism also gave many detailed discourses on social, political and economic theory, outlining principles for the development of a just, peaceful, and cooperative society. The synthesis of his ideas can be found in Prout, the subject of a discourse first presented in 1959. His ideas have important implications for the teaching of the social studies.

Prout is an acronym for PROgressive Utilization Theory, an alternative to the outmoded capitalist and communist socio-economic paradigms, that synthesizes the physical, mental and spiritual dimensions of human nature. The goal of Prout is to provide guidance for the evolution of a truly progressive human society with a harmonious balance between economic growth, social development, environmental sustainability, and between individual and collective interests. Combining the wisdom of spirituality with a universal outlook and the struggle for self-reliance, Proutist thinkers and activists are creating a new civilizational discourse and planting the seeds for a new way of living. (https://prout.info/what-is-prout/ and https://pri.institute)

The principles embodied in Prout provide a clear blueprint for a vision of a neohumanist future. We highlight just a few of them here, alongside principles of neohumanist education that align with them, to provide guidance on the implementation of the social studies. For a complete summary of these ideas, see Kesson et al., 2022.

The Purpose of Education

Prout Perspective

Economic and social institutions are designed to facilitate the attainment of the highest of human potentialities: self-realization, compassion, and love for all beings.

Neohumanist Education Perspective

The nature of what it means to be human is reconceived as one of relationship and interconnection, not as an isolated individual. Non-dogmatic spiritual development is fostered in education, as is the cultivation of empathy, emotional intelligence, and universal love. Cooperation with, rather than mastery over, all species is fostered.

Human Freedom

Prout Perspective

Prout supports the idea of individual freedom to acquire and express ideas, creative potential, and inner aspirations in the belief that such intellectual and spiritual freedom will strengthen the collectivity.

Neohumanist Education Perspective

Students are supported in their choices about what they wish to study and how they wish to learn. Creative thinking is taught and nurtured, as are the arts and aesthetic sensibilities. In the shift away from a standardized curriculum and rote learning, such freedom needs to be thoughtfully nourished in order to understand and maintain the welfare of all.

Preservation of Local Language and Culture

Prout Perspective

Prout encourages the protection and cultivation of local culture, language, history, and tradition. For social justice and a healthy social order, individual and cultural diversity must be accepted and encouraged.

Neohumanist Education Perspective

"Culturally relevant" and "place-based" education need to be at the foundation of the curriculum. Instruction takes place in both the local (Indigenous) language and the "languages of power." Multiple forms of knowing are supported (embodied knowing, ancestral knowing, intuitive and contemplative knowing, narrative knowing and intergenerational knowing) to balance the current emphasis on narrow versions of reason and technical knowing.

Radical Democracy

Prout Perspective

Prout advocates economic and political democracy based on local and cooperative planning.

Neohumanist Education Perspective

Learning is reconceived from an individual act to one of reciprocity, cooperation, and mutuality. Students work together to identify local problems and work on collaborative projects towards their solution. The study of history and economics is not doctrinaire, but looks objectively at systems and their impacts, as well as viable alternatives. School and community attain new levels of partnership and cooperation.

Ethical Leadership

Prout Perspective

Leadership in a Prout society is based on ethical principles, and expressed through collective and cooperative leadership. A Prout society aims for the expansion of democracy to all spheres of life including the economy, the workplace, the community, the school, and the home.

Neohumanist Education Perspective

Students are taught to engage in ethical dialogue and decision-making, and democratic class meetings are an essential component of the curriculum. Social learning, communication skills, critical thinking, and the tools of negotiation and collaborative decision-making are fostered. Service learning is well developed and forms an essential component of the curriculum.

Awakened Rationality

Prout Perspective

Reason, science, and technology form a solid basis for the development of society. These modern Western ways of knowing are but part of an epistemological pluralism that also values traditional, place-based knowing, intergenerational knowing, and embodied, experiential knowing.

Neohumanist Education Perspective

Science is taught in a way that nurtures a reverence for all life and an ecological orientation in which the inherent value of all living things is acknowledged. Ecological ethics are infused across the curriculum in multiple and diverse ways, and students are taught the arts of reflection, deliberation, and discerning judgment so that they might become good ecological citizens with the ability to assess the long term consequences of innovations in technology.

* * *

A neohumanist approach to teaching the social studies is not value-neutral. The values are progressive ones, aligned with the best ideals of Pragmatism and Critical Pedagogy, enhanced and expanded with a deeper understanding of human potential and the evolution of consciousness. The renown curriculum theorist James MacDonald (1995) called this paradigm of education the "transcendental developmental ideology." However, the fact that it is explicit about a set of values does not mean it is doctrinaire. Neohumanism values the free expression and exploration of ideas and the application of rational thinking and discernment, not indoctrination. There is an inherent faith in the capacity of humans, when presented with multiple perspectives and a variety of ways of knowing, to arrive at truths that serve the welfare of all beings.

Neohumanist Principles and Practices in the Social Studies

Identity

Recall from Chapter 1 that an essential element of neohumanist education is the expansion of the feeling of individuality into ever greater circles of connection. The child is first occupied with constructing a sense of self in relation to family or caregivers, then to the land where they live (called, in neohumanism "geo-sentiment"), to one's clan, tribe, community, and to more abstract entities like one's religion, race, caste, nation, or social class (called, in neohumanism "socio-sentiment"), and finally, in a mature humanistic sense, to humanity as a whole. This is not a linear process and it is not a "stage theory" (an inevitable progression through identifiable stages of growth). None of these phases of identity are problematic in themselves: one can hold a great love for the land on which they live, or one's social identity can be a source of strength. Problems arise when a person gets stuck on this "identity chain"—when they come to feel that their race is superior (or inferior) or that their religion is the only correct one. Their expansive flow is then blocked, or reversed.

Neohumanism teaches that it is our destiny to eliminate limiting labels and continue to expand our consciousness into an identity of interconnectedness, of integral unity, rather than separation and superiority. When we remove all the labels we have affixed to ourselves, we find something that precedes all labels, and with that existential awareness lies the connection with the consciousness of everything in the universe—all created beings, animate and inanimate. This is the ontological task of neohumanist educators, to facilitate the movement of young people through this ever-expanding circle of identity and connection, resulting in a *universalist* outlook.

Individual development and identity is one of the main themes in the social studies; the end point of a universal outlook is what is unique to the neohumanist system. A key idea is helping young people become aware of themselves in relationship to other beings, and to locate themselves in time and space.

The contemporary rapidity of change and the constant deluge of information on screens and in the airwaves has created an environment of "presentism" where it seems that only what is happening in the moment is true (or interesting). A paradox presents itself, which is that while many contemplative traditions aim to locate practitioners in the present moment, to release fixations on the past or worries about the future, it is equally true that other contemplative traditions honor ancestral wisdom and believe that there is much to be gained in terms of guidance and healing by attending to our lineages and the collective histories of past societies and cultures. Neohumanism embraces a "both/and" position on this paradox, accepting the importance of being fully present in the moment, while valuing what can be learned from history. It recognizes the maxim that if we fail to learn from events in the past, we risk repeating the same mistakes over and over.

Though the ultimate aim of identity in a neohumanist education is the cultivation of a universalist outlook, the pedagogy is very much a developmental one, beginning in the very early years as teachers work with young children to develop a sense of their personal history, using art, literature, and such social studies strategies as timelines. Children's memories are activated to recall important incidents in their lives—moving to a new place, acquiring a sibling, and so on. They are encouraged to talk with parents or other caregivers for stories that flesh out their memories. These narratives are shared in classrooms, along with "family artifacts" that tell a story.

As children grow, they are taught to inquire into family (or tribe or clan) histories, to ask historical questions and to collect historical data. They learn the about the variety of sources of knowledge about the past (artifacts such as tools, quilts, personal letters, ancient maps, photographs, old newspapers, interviews, cookbooks, fashion magazines, portraits). They learn how to create a "history museum" in their school. Gradually they discover how the past differs from the present, how events in the past shape the present, and how technologies have changed the modern world. They acquire a sense of what history is and come to know it as not just names and dates and facts, but as stories—stories that when gathered together create a collective narrative. In these ways, students meet conventional social studies standards around "inquiry based learning"—how to ask questions and how to collect and analyze data. Perhaps most important, they come to see themselves as *historical actors*—active participants in the making of the world—and with proper guidance, begin to walk the path towards universalism.

Democratic Living

Unlike most other animals, who are largely self-sufficient, humans are dependent on others for food, protection, shelter, comfort, and all of the other goods and services that society provides. We are social animals, born into language, symbol, and cultural systems that orient us to view the world in certain ways and provide the norms and values we are expected to live by.

Democracy as an ideal political system has never been fully realized. In capitalist democracies like the United States, political power can be bought by the highest bidder. Many democracies are rife with corruption. As a political system it has proven inadequate to alleviating poverty, to restraining crime and conflict, and is proving vulnerable to authoritarianism. The second president of the United States, John Adams (1851/2011), a philosopher at heart, is quoted as saying "democracy never lasts long. It soon wastes, exhausts, and murders itself. There never was a democracy yet that did not commit suicide" (XVIII, p. 484).

And yet, the ideal of self-governance persists. Dewey, quoted earlier, held democracy to be the best system yet devised for organizing human society; he believed strongly in the capacities of people to work together to solve the many social problems that confront them. But he cautioned that we need to think of democracy not merely as a political system, but as a way of life (1916). Modern philosophers of democracy differentiate between "weak democracy" which is what schools generally focus on in civics classes (representative voting, majority rule, obeying laws, paying taxes, due process, etc.) and "strong democracy" (characterized by empathy, equity, commitment, and connection, free inquiry and debate, consensus decision making, and people actively engaged in public affairs). But how do we get from our generally weak democracies to the "deep democracy" demanded by a Prout system? (Barber, 1998; Green, 1999).

Dewey believed that such a deep democracy could be nurtured by the educational process. It is not enough, however, for students to be *taught* the principles of democracy, they need to *experience* democracy. In contrast to classrooms organized around competitive self-interest, the democratic classroom must emulate the "loving and just community" required of a deep democracy. To bring this about, certain dispositions and skills need to be developed; a few of these were articulated in Chapter 8, "The Art of Teaching." For a fuller listing of the dispositions and capacities necessary to cultivate democratic living, as well as some of the criteria a school must meet to be a democratic environment, see Appendix at the end of this chapter.

Dispositions and capacities must be nurtured developmentally; it is important to be keenly aware of the moral and cognitive capacities of the students you are working with, as well as of the values and norms of their culture. While skills and habits of mind can all be fostered from the earliest ages, they are designed to come to fruition as students approach adulthood. However, they must be consciously nurtured and supported throughout a student's entire education, from the kindergarten circle where children engage in discussions about fairness, to Socratic seminars where teenagers debate the issues of human impacts on the environment.

A Sense of Place

Place-based education (PBE) is an idea that has begun to attain mainstream status along with the growing awareness that we have exceeded the carrying capacities of our planetary life-support systems and are in the midst of multiple extinction events and potential disruptions due to climate change. Conceptually, its aims and purposes include cultivating ecological awareness of the interconnectedness between human and more-than-human species, increasing young people's knowledge of their environments, getting students out into their communities to pursue authentic investigations, and fostering service and civic engagement. Place-based education is transdisciplinary in that it integrates scientific and social investigations. For the purposes of this chapter, we will focus mainly on the latter.

A place-based curriculum is grounded in the realities of the community in which students live. It is often associated with a "more self-directed, inquiry-based, experiential pedagogy" (Demarest, 2015, p. 5) and with learning activities centered around the solution to local problems. Students experiencing a place-based curriculum might study a local watershed from the perspectives of local history and land use, the biology and botany of the environment, or through interviewing local elders about how life has changed over time in their locale. All of these lenses on a place involve stories: stories about what happened in the past, stories about how flora and fauna evolved in response to the environment, stories of how people have made their livings and made their lives in a particular spot. To have a strong sense of place means to be deeply connected to the stories embodied in the soil, the landmarks, and the built environment of the place, to see oneself as rooted in the place, and to care for the health and well-being of a place and its inhabitants (human and more-than-human).

Given new awakenings to ecological limits, a sense of place is a vital intellectual asset for young people. The current generations are faced with the enormous task of rethinking the various aspects of modernity: how humans live and consume, what they produce, how they spend their time, what they value, how they organize their societies. This rethinking involves facing uncomfortable facts about the places they inhabit.

PBE has tended to be a-historical, in that while *land* is at the center of the pedagogy, few of the models involve historical reckoning with issues of genocide, dislocation, and forced migration that moved Indigenous people off their land to make way for settlers. It has also been relatively silent on the continuing dispossession of Native peoples and the desecration of land and water by national/corporate interests. It thus lacks a larger cultural analysis; contextualization in the critique of modernity, capitalism, and industrial civilization.

One solution that has been proposed is the development of a "critical pedagogy of place," an integration of social justice oriented critical pedagogy and the practices of PBE (Gruenewald, 2003). To accomplish this, neohumanist educators need to acquire complex understandings of the Indigenous peoples, lands, or history in the culture in which they teach. They need to locate themselves in colonial and postcolonial history and develop a deep understanding of the ways that white supremacy has shaped the modern world. A neohumanist approach to the social studies needs to be grounded in anti-racist education, and must center local Indigenous communities by prioritizing relationships and learning contexts with them. In these ways, neohumanism may realize its aims of radical equality, facing history in ways that allow us to heal the wounds generated by centuries of colonization, racism, ethnocentrism, sexism, and environmental plunder.

Understanding Diversity and Celebrating Difference

Culture is a web of meaning—the complex integral whole that constitutes a shared worldview of a group of people. This complex whole comprises the values, beliefs, stories of origin (cosmology), legends, arts, habits of mind, social relationships, social and political structures, and daily practices of a culture. A key principle of neohumanism is the valuing of local culture and local language. Yet, as a global educational movement, teachers do not always come from the culture of the school or educational project. In such cases, teachers need to learn to "think like an anthropologist" and engage in close observation and analysis of the culture, while being keenly aware of how their own subjective cultural lens may impact their interpretation.

The concept of culture is not necessarily defined as a homogenous group of people who appear not to change over time. Culture is no longer regarded as passive, instead it is understood as a complex and on-going series of interactions. At this point in the planet's history, the various cultures of the world are increasingly coming into contact with each other. This is due to a number of factors: five hundred years of European empire building and colonization, technological advances in transportation and communication, and mass migration due to economic dynamics, global conflicts, and environmental factors such as the climate crisis with its droughts, floods, hurricanes, and fires.

Neohumanism values diverse cultural expressions. It also embodies a critical understanding of the ways in which the politics of colonialism, imperialism, racism, consumerism, and ethnocentricity have served to oppress people and destroy the unique cultural expressions of humanity. Neohumanist education seeks to heal the wounds that have been inflicted by the abuses of power and privilege. A starting point in this project is the affirmation of the cultural expressions of the locality in which a neohumanist school exists, or in the case of dislocations, the cultural expressions that people may have unwillingly left behind.

"Culturally relevant pedagogy"—and the interchangeable terms "culturally sensitive" and "culturally responsive" (Ladson-Billings, 1995; 2022; Gay, 2018)—is a way of teaching that works in multiple ways to affirm young people's identities and challenge prevailing injustices in school and society. It also recognizes that there are many "ways of knowing" and values the various expressive means by which children can demonstrate their learning. Related to this is the importance of perspective-taking—working with children to understanding issues from different points-of-view than their own.

Differences abound in our global society, and these are not just differences of cultural origin. Even within cultures, differences exist, and bias, discrimination, and oppression play out around multiple variations: of social class and caste, of ethnicity, of race and skin color, of ability and disability, of age, and of gender and sexual identity. *Intersectionality*, a term coined by Kimberlé Crenshaw (1989), refers to the ways that these social categories of difference intersect, resulting in overlapping systems of discrimination or disadvantage. These intersections can work to deepen oppressions or to produce paradoxical convergences of power, privilege, and disadvantage.

Issues of diversity and oppression constitute fields of study that are vast and ever-changing as new situations and events emerge in society. We cannot begin to do them justice here, and it is recommended that neohumanist teachers engage in continuous study and professional development on the topics. The field of the social studies is a particularly ripe sphere for exploring these issues. There are a few key ideas to keep in mind:

- Issues of representation matter. Children should see themselves and their cultural backgrounds reflected in all aspects of the school curriculum, the textbooks, the décor of the school, and the learning experiences.
- The social studies curriculum should adequately represent the histories, contributions and perspectives of all social groups, especially all of those in the community of the school.
- While awareness of collective experiences is vital, all students need to be treated as individuals, and not as members of groups.
- Social categories such as race should not be swept under the rug, but students should be enabled and equipped to safely explore questions of identity, race equality and racism; and other related issues.
- Controversial topics should not be avoided; rather students need to learn and practice respectful discussion norms, listening skills, perspective-taking, and the art of deliberation.
- Children should have access to teachers and other adults with whom they relate culturally.
- On-going attention needs to be paid to identifying stereotypes in literature, film, and other media that reduce the complexity of individuals and groups.
- Knowledge of issues of social justice should be fostered through readings, inquiry-based learning, and visits from community leaders or outside experts.

- Instances of bias and injustice should be confronted when they occur, and explicit policies designed to combat them.

Issues of language and language difference cannot be easily untangled from issues of culture. Sarkar (2018) was very clear that neohumanist schools in specific locales should offer instruction in the local language, noting that the suppression of local languages leads to the suppression of local culture:

> This in turn leads to psychic demoralization, inferiority complexes and a defeatist mentality. Whenever the sentimental legacy of a group of people is undermined, they become easy prey to the economic, political and psycho-economic exploitation of vested interests. (p. 207)

This does not preclude instruction in a lingua franca (or national or international *link language*), as long as the local, or indigenous languages have full scope to develop. Young people need to cultivate pride in their origins, but they also need access to "languages of power" so that genuine equality of opportunity might be achieved. In diverse communities where numbers of primary languages are spoken, teachers need advanced training in bilingual and multi-lingual education and "trans-languaging," defined as using more than one language in classroom instruction (Espinosa & Ascenzi-Moreno, 2021).

In all of this discussion of the things that divide us, we should not overlook another key idea in neohumanism: the principle of "unity within diversity." P. R. Sarkar noted often that differences in humans were relative factors, but that human society is one and indivisible. A Proutist society, he claimed, with a spirit of selfless service at its core, a guiding psychology of welfare for all, and a dynamic spiritual outlook has the potential to bring about a peaceful and just society. It is up to neohumanist educators to apply their best creative thinking to the questions: *What is meant by universalism? What is the connection between the universal and the particular? Can we have a unified society in which the rights of all are recognized, and in which individuals have maximum freedom? Can we attain the highest social dharma?* (Dharma is a fundamental principle of Yoga that does not lend itself to easy translation, but the idea of a "right way of living" comes close). Again, from P. R. Sarkar (1980):

> Dharma gives inspiration to people in every sphere of their lives. Human life is all-comprehensive. It is not a single flower, but a bouquet... They spread their sweetness, their fragrance, their colour (sic) in all directions. And therein lies their fulfilment, and the meaning of their existence. (para. 2)

Ethics and Critical Thinking

Human beings generally act the way they do because of the values they hold. The study of ethics involves the study of these values, and how we go about making decisions based on what we determine as right and wrong. The moral dimension of democracy emphasizes a particular set of values: the public interest over the private good; the equality of all humans; the importance of human freedom and the concomitant value that one's freedom should not come at the cost of another's. With *deep* democracy, democratic practices are extended to other cultural sites (from the voting booth into the workplace, the community, the school, the home). What do all these conditions have in common? They all signify empowerment—citizens assuming democratic control over aspects of their lives previously deferred to experts and elected representatives. They also signify a democracy that is developmental, one that is devoted to the growth and development of each and every one of its members. These ideals of democracy might be considered the pinnacle of humanist thinking.

However, neohumanism proffers a new dimension to this thinking, in that inherent to its relational ontology is a mandate that the rights of *all* living things be considered in social decision-making. The relational philosophy of neohumanism, the idea that humans are an integral part of the web of nature and that all living beings have inherent worth, requires new thinking about ethics, a new form of ecological citizenship. Ethics expands to become the process by which we navigate and negotiate these wider relationships. While this ethical framework is controversial, neohumanists believe that unless we move from "anthropocentrism" (human centered) to "bio-centrism" (life centered) we will not be capable of creating an environmentally sustainable and regenerative society, one in which all life can thrive. However, this is easier said than done. Many ethical questions remain to be answered. What are the limits of animal rights? Do rivers have moral standing? Should humans interfere in the regulation of animal populations? What are the criteria used to adjudicate the interests, needs, values, and rights of various beings? What level of ecological damage is justified to meet human needs? Do corporations have moral responsibilities to restore damaged land?

The social studies curriculum is the place where students can explore their values and the impact of these beliefs on the world in developmentally meaningful ways. In early childhood, perhaps the most important aspect of the ethics curriculum is the cultivation of love and caring for all—including not only plants and animals, but the water, air, and soil as well through activities such as recycling, gardening, and cleaning up trash. Care for the earth should be fostered through careful choices of children's literature.

As children get older, they become capable of engaging in critical thinking, the art of analyzing and assessing the assumptions and logic of our values and beliefs. To become a critical thinker, one needs to recognize "faulty arguments, hasty generalizations, assertions lacking evidence, truth claims based on unreliable authority, ambiguous or obscure concepts, and so forth" (Burbules & Berk, 1999, para. 4). The adequacy of critical thinking is enriched by the inclusion of critical pedagogy, a tradition informed by its commitments to a more just society. Paulo Freire, perhaps the most well-known of the critical pedagogues, highlighted the importance of students understanding the nature of power and systems of oppressive relationships, and one's place in that system. Critical pedagogy is not merely study, it requires "praxis—both reflection and action, both interpretation and change" (Burbules & Berk, 1999, para. 20).

Critical thinking and critical pedagogy are both very *human* activities; they are grounded in Western theories of cognition and of how people learn. Both have been cited for their epistemological biases, ways of knowing grounded in rational thought. Neohumanist theory values rational thinking, but a sophisticated rationalism tempered by epistemological pluralism (the inclusion of multiple ways of knowing). Our ethical decisions do need to be informed by reason and logic, but there is much to be learned from ancestral wisdom, traditional Indigenous knowledge, embodied knowing, intuition, and so on. In these ways, the narrow, instrumental, human-centered model of rational and ethical thinking can be replaced by a neohumanist model, one that incorporates the aesthetic, sensuous, and spiritual dimensions of human being.

Learning to Serve, Serving to Learn

How can a critical praxis—informed action in the world—best be implemented in a neohumanist school? At the heart of neohumanist development is the idea of service, a necessary adjunct to the spiritual focus of Yoga and meditation. Service is germane to many spiritual traditions, reflecting the theological idea of immanence, that God is present in all of creation. Tapah, one of the cornerstones of Yoga ethics in the framework of Yama-Niyama, presents the idea of service as a selfless act, which can be rendered to ancestors, to family, to plants and animals, or to the human community. Here, we concern ourselves not just with service as a spiritual practice, but with how student learning in the social studies can be amplified by what has come to be called "service learning."

Many schools are requiring community service now, in an effort to get young people more involved in society and to enhance empathy, awareness, and a commitment to making the world a better place. A number of criticisms have been launched at service learning. Some of these relate to more general critiques of philanthropy: that "charity" (such as feeding the poor) may help the recipient of the charity, but does not actually solve the problem (e.g., of hunger); that charity may apply a Band-Aid to a problem, but does not address actual injustice; that charity may actually distract us from finding real solutions to problems; that it can allow governments to escape responsibility for the general welfare. One theorist proposes that the global philanthropic infrastructure, with their stated aim to improve the world and change it for the better, not only preserves the status quo, but also obscures elites' role in creating the problems they propose to solve (Giridharadas, 2018).

Service learning has also been targeted for insensitivity to culture and cultural differences, for viewing recipients of service as "needy" rather than as people caught up in the cogs of an unjust system, for elitism (reinforcing privilege), for fostering pity rather than empathy, and for reinforcing social divides (between the haves and the have-nots). Altruism all too often serves the interests of the provider, above the recipient of the gesture. Young people who do community service have been faulted for advancing their own careers, building their resumes, or developing leadership skills. How can service learning be more than charity? How can it lead to informed action that is more than a Band-Aid?

- First, there must be a recognition that we do not necessarily know what other people need. Therefore communities should be full partners in service learning and be in charge of identifying what they need.
- Empathy, not sympathy or pity, needs to be cultivated. "There but for the grace of God..." is worth remembering, and the act of service approached with genuine humility.
- Students should study the issue related to the service they intend to provide to learn the history of the issue, the root causes of the problem, and relevant policies in place.
- The act of reflection is essential to the act of service becoming a learning experience. Facilitated reflection should include questions about the experience, descriptions of interactions and the analysis of these, how and in what ways the act of service might have changed the students (their assumptions, their biases, their understandings, etc.).

- Students need to have a clear understanding of the differences between generosity, charity, justice, and social change.
- They need to engage in discussions about how society could better address the problems that they have learned about, how society could be more compassionate/informed/involved in the situation, and what they might do with their lives to make a real difference.

The act of selfless service is essential to the spiritual life, and it can also be an important learning experience. When integrated thoughtfully with the social studies curriculum, it can provide opportunities to learn a great deal about how political, social, and economic systems work, what social problems exist, and what the most beneficial solutions might be. Coupled with academic study of the issues, it can provide direction and commitment to students who hope to engage in social justice work. It can certainly foster the neohumanist value of serving the welfare of all, the common good. For young people who are immersed in the development of a self the idea of "selfless service" may be a bit out of reach. But with proper facilitation of the service learning, they may be enabled to grasp the maxim, "Do no harm."

Engaging Students in the Study of the Social World

Real Life Experiences

Students who study the social world in conventional "read the textbook/answer the questions/take the quiz" classrooms often complain of being bored or ask: "Why does this matter?" Textbooks are organized around sound bites—snippets of facts that summarize historical events, generally from the single perspective of historical winners. Young people are more or less told what to think and required to memorize facts. Facts are fine things, but a lively social studies curriculum requires students to do their own thinking. In social studies classes that *do* go beyond the mere acquisition of facts, the emphasis is on analysis and critical thinking, and many excellent lessons involve learning how to assess sources of information, look for evidence in texts, and corroborate information from more than one source. Important as this is, not all students are easily engaged with written text, so teachers must find alternate routes into the construction of knowledge.

Students should know that history is not just about dead people (and wars)—everything in their world has a history, from their smartphone to the shoes they wear. Events that grab headlines in the modern world have a history, from incidents of police brutality to the immigration crisis. The more teachers can link the past to the present, the more engaged students will be. In order to engage students in history, however, they need to *do* history, in the way historians do history—by interviewing elders, by studying artifacts, by visiting historical sites, by reading old letters (Levstik & Barton, 2001). And their thinking needs to be sharpened by engaging in structured protocols, such as debates and Socratic seminars (https://www.facinghistory.org/professional-development/ondemand/socratic-seminar-weimar-republic).

In earlier chapters (see Chapter 4, "The Science of Learning"; Chapter 7, "Curriculum Theory and Design for a Neohumanist Future"; and Chapters 9–14 on integrating the arts), we explored the role of the arts in fostering deep learning. Expert social studies teachers make liberal use of photographs, paintings, literature, songs, and poetry to enhance the study of the social world, recognizing the differing roles that written text and various arts play in learning. Logically constructed texts (as in textbooks, persuasive essays or scientific treatises) are designed to impart information or prove a point. In contrast, the knowledge found in narrative texts or the visual and performing arts communicate dimensions of experience that cannot be easily conveyed through literal language. Interpretations gained from songs, stories, visual images, or poems invoke historical empathy (the ability to reach across time and connect emotionally with the lived experience of historical actors) and create more complex and nuanced understandings of the topic studied. Teachers need to cultivate skill in using such primary sources and practice posing questions:

- What do you see?
- What do you think the creator of this artifact meant to convey?
- What is the "mood" of the piece?
- What do you think is the theme?
- What do you learn from this artifact?; and so forth

Bringing in the arts to the study of the social world can create a more equitable classroom. Think of the multiplicity of "intelligences" that can be enhanced when looking at history through the lenses of music, poems, oral histories, folk tales, historical fiction, or paintings. A curriculum designed for deep learning brings in the arts to convey information (consider what can be learned from facilitated discussions of a photograph of suffragettes marching in a parade or a cartoon of a miner's strike). But the arts also offer students opportunities to demonstrate what they have learned in a variety of ways: through the writing and performing of songs, the design of propaganda posters, or the creation of dramas. When these expressive outcomes are widely shared, all of the students in the class benefit from the breadth and the depth of knowledge presented.

A neohumanist approach that is enlivened by the arts and primary source material, that asks students to *do* history rather than merely memorize dates and facts, that connects their personal histories to our collective histories, that values the lived experiences of their families, that creates and sustains democratic classrooms as model environments for democratic living, and that offers multiple opportunities for community engagement is much more likely to engage students in the study of the social world, and make it more interesting and enjoyable.

Studying the Social World in Transitional Times

Experiments in the implementation of cooperative and just societies, such as that envisioned by Prout, have occurred all through history, in both small ways (such as the Shaker religious societies) and on a global scale (the Soviet and Maoist revolutions that promised to bring about egalitarian societies, but resulted in large scale violence and repression). The enormous failures of these global upheavals are due to factors too numerous to cite here, and are beyond the scope of this chapter. It is sometimes assumed that capitalism has triumphed because it is a superior ideology based on human "nature" (self-interest and greed). However, it has become clear that the capitalist ideology too has failed to bring about a just and equitable society, and is in fact, leading us to the tipping point of ecological destruction.

We are clearly in a period of social transition, in which none of the old ideologies have the capacity to serve us well, or even to ensure the survival of human (and more-than-human) life. We need new ways of thinking, new ways of being, if we are to meet the current challenges facing us now. If the human heart is steeped in geo-sentiment, socio-sentiment, or anthropocentrism (the idea that humans are separate from, and superior to, the rest of nature), people will not respond positively to imperatives to care for the welfare of all. Neohumanist education is dedicated to the evolution of consciousness through the incorporation of meditation, service, and spiritual understanding into academic learning. With the enlargement of the human heart, with new appreciation for the relational nature of life, with the extension of love for all of creation, we have hope that the next generation will discover and create these new ways of thinking and being, and adjust their lives accordingly. The study of the social world in neohumanist education can provide the conceptual and practical tools necessary to implement a more just and egalitarian society, one that is truly committed to the good of the *whole*.

338 ▪ *Becoming One With the World*

FOR CONTINUING STUDY

> *Discussion/Reflection:* This can be an individual or group activity. Choose an illustrated children's book with a social studies theme. Read it through carefully, and consider the following:
>
> - Look for stereotypes (not necessarily "negative" depictions, but oversimplified generalizations).
> - Look for "tokenism" (inadequate symbolic efforts at inclusion).
> - Look for "invisibility" (who's represented, and who is not?).
> - Look for messages about different lifestyles (is one lifestyle represented as normative?).
> - Unpack the moral message of the story (are the characters "agents of change?").
> - Watch for "loaded" words (words with heavy emotional content beyond their literal meaning).
> - How would you describe the quality of the story and illustrations?

For more information about looking for bias in children's books, see: https://socialjusticebooks.org/guide-for-selecting-anti-bias-childrens-books/#:~:text=Books%20containing%20stereotypes%20require%20you,be%20eliminated%20from%20your%20collection.&text=Look%20for%20Tokenism%3A%20This%20is,is%20more%20or%20less%20important

> *Discussion/Reflection:* As a group, decide on a complex social problem in a local community. Think about all of the interests that would be involved (human and more-than-human). Consider all the dimensions of an ethical debate that might be brought in. The aim here is to examine an issue from as many perspectives as possible.
>
> *Application:* Locating yourself in history and culture: Using any format you wish (poster art, written narrative, poem, Powerpoint, song), share the main topics in your personal history. To whatever extent you are comfortable, highlight your origins (birthplace, family of origin, religion, caste/class, lifestyle, (family careers, etc.) schooling, relationship to place.
>
> *Application:* Exploring where you currently reside/work/teach: Describe the geography of the place you live; describe the population of this place; what do you know about the original inhabitants of the place; what do you know of the history of the place; significant conflicts, power struggles; what groups are in power now/what groups are marginalized; how is the class/caste system in place? Any other interesting information related to the study of the social world. What more would you need to know to be an effective teacher?

Appendix

Social Studies Dispositions and Capacities

Dispositions

- Sense of connectedness, understands the importance of relationships and sociability
- Sense of fairness and justice
- Recognition of the fundamental equality of all people
- Care and concern for both friends and strangers
- Acceptance of difference
- Interested in public problem-solving
- Desire to collaborate and work together to solve problems
- Willingness to take the perspective of another
- Open-mindedness—the willingness to incorporate new information into prior conceptual schema
- Capable of modifying beliefs in light of new experience and information
- Self-confidence and the desire for efficacy
- Freedom from fear of conflict
- A sense of humor

Capacities

- Ability to develop logical arguments
- Ability to write and speak coherently and persuasively
- Ability to think critically and utilize the tools of logic (recognizing hasty generalizations and faulty arguments, weighing evidence and evaluating truth claims)
- Ability to question the motivations and interests underlying points of view, and detect bias
- Ability to listen actively and respond empathetically to the varied perspectives and opinions of others
- Ability to deliberate, negotiate, and dialogue across differences
- Ability to think imaginatively and come up with creative solutions
- Ability to work together collaboratively and appreciate the varied skills and talents that others bring to a situation
- Ability to "stand outside" one's own value system, and understand it as socially constructed
- Ability to apply concepts to real life situations
- Ability to make decisions that foster the "common good," not just private gain

Characteristics of Democratic Schools

- an atmosphere in which students feel a sense of belonging or membership in the school community
- a feeling of students' safety, both physical and emotional/psychological
- schoolwork with intrinsic interest for students
- schoolwork that is meaningful not only for school purposes, but also in the real world outside school
- a sense of ownership of their school
- opportunities for students to explore their interdependence with others and with nature
- study of issues of equality and social justice
- discussion, debate, and action on public issues
- critical examination of the lived social reality/exploration of alternatives
- development of students' capacities for public democratic participation
- student participation in school governance

Sehr, D. T. (1997). *Education for public democracy.* SUNY Press.

References

Adams, J. (2011). *The works of John Adams, second president of the United States,* Vol. VI. Cambridge University Press. (Original work published 1851)

Barber, B. (1998). *A place for us: How to make society civil and democracy strong.* Hill and Wang.

Burbules, N. C., & Berk, R. (1999). Critical thinking and critical pedagogy: Relations, differences, and limits. In T. Popkewitz & L. Fendler (Eds.), *Critical theories in education: Changing terrains of knowledge and politics* (pp. 45–66). Routledge.

Crenshaw, K. (1989). Demarginalizing the intersection of race and sex: A Black feminist critique of antidiscrimination doctrine, feminist theory and anti-racist politics. *University of Chicago Legal Forum 1*(8).

Demarest, A. (2015). *Place-based curriculum design: Exceeding standards through local investigation.* Routledge.

Dewey, J. (1966). *Democracy and education.* Free Press. (Original work published 1916)

Espinosa, C., & Ascenzi-Moreno, L. (2021). *Rooted in strength: Using translanguaging to grow multilingual readers and writers.* Scholastic Teaching Resources. https://shop.scholastic.com/teachers-ecommerce/teacher/books/rooted-in-strength-9781338753875.html

Gay, G. (2018). *Culturally responsive teaching: Theory, research, and practice.* Teachers College Press.

Giridharadas, A. (2018). *Winners take all: The elite charade of changing the world.* Alfred A. Knopf.

Green, J. M. (1999). *Deep democracy: Community, diversity, and transformation.* Rowman & Littlefield Publishers.

Gruenewald, D. A. (May, 2003). The best of both worlds: A critical pedagogy of place. *Educational Researcher. 32*(4), 3–12.

Kesson, K., Bussey, M., Oppenheim, M., Maheshvarananda, D., Ananda Devapriya, D., Inayatullah, S., & Russafov, D. (2022, July). Synergy of prout, neo-humanist education, & the spirit of service. *Gurukula Network, 54,* 23–29.

Ladson-Billings, G. (2022). *The dreamkeepers: Successful teachers of African-American children.* Jossey-Bass.

Ladson-Billings, G. (1995). Toward a theory of culturally relevant pedagogy. *American Educational Research Journal, 32*(3), 465–491.

Levstik, L. S., & Barton, K. C. (2001). *Doing history: Investigating with children in elementary and middle schools.* Lawrence Erlbaum Associates.

Macdonald, J. B. (Ed.). (1995). *Theory as a prayerful act: The collected essays of James B. Macdonald.* Peter Lang.

Sarkar, P. R. (1980). Dhritarastra and Sanjaya. In *Discourses on Krsna and the Gitá.* Electronic edition of the works of P. R. Sarkar, version 9.0.

Sarkar, P.R. (2018). *An outline of Prout.* Ananda Marga Pracaraka Samgha.

Note: This chapter paints a very broad picture of teaching the social studies from pre-K through primary and middle school. For more specific guidance on early childhood, consult the website of the National Association for the Education of Young Children at: https://www.naeyc.org/resources/position-statements/dap/contents

They also have extensive resources on creating an anti-bias curriculum:

https://www.naeyc.org/resources/topics/anti-bias

17

Rethinking STEAM for the Anthropocene

I. Science and the Modern World

> *Our human destiny is to become the heart of the universe that embraces the whole of the Earth community. We are just a speck in the universe, but we are beings with the capacity to feel comprehensive compassion in the midst of an ocean of intimacy.*
>
> — Brian Swimme and Mary Tucker, *Journey of the Universe*, 2011

In the early part of the 21st century, a new approach to teaching science emerged in the United States, due largely to the recognition that the country was falling behind other nations in its science and mathematics test scores. STEM (Science, Technology, Engineering, and Math) was the acronym suggested by the National Science Foundation for new science standards for K–12 students that would feature a more integrated pedagogy oriented towards developing analytic thinking, problem-solving, and science competencies. As has generally been the case with revised standards in science and mathematics, the fundamental issue at stake is economic dominance; expertise in research, discovery, and innovation is thought to be the basis of a workforce that can out-compete those in other countries and ensure the United States be at the top of the economic ladder.

STEAM (the inclusion of Arts in the acronym) was an afterthought. Though it serves to foster increased attention to an integrated curriculum, the main focus is on appropriating the kind of creative and innovative thinking employed by artists in the service of more effective science and technology teaching and learning. Rethinking STEAM in the context of neohumanist education is two-fold: First we replace *engineering* (not because engineering isn't important, but because it is a part of technology) with *ethics* (because it is of *vital* importance) in the acronym, second, we ascribe equivalency to all of the elements in the term: *Science, Technology, Ethics, Arts,* and *Math.* The reasons for this will become apparent in this chapter.

Science has become the religion of the modern world. The application of empirical science and precision mathematics through technological virtuosity has achieved unimaginable heights: Machines that fly us across the world (and beyond!), climate controlled environments, awe-inspiring skyscrapers (the latest, in Saudi Arabia, reaching a kilometer into the sky), and devices that allow instant global communication and the transmission of real time images. Scientific exploration enabled by technologies capable of probing the invisible world of the atom and the far reaches of space has expanded our practical and imaginative horizons. Medical science has eradicated diseases and plagues that killed millions of people in the past. It is no wonder that science has come to dominate the modern mind, and many people argue that science is bringing humanity ever closer to perfection.

The application of science has also brought us nuclear disasters, cancer-causing chemicals in our food and water, biological and atomic weapons, and Nazi concentration camps, known for the evil "scientific" experimentation on, torture, and extermination of thousands of human beings. The widespread use of fossil fuels, extracted from the earth in ways that destroy life and landscape, is the primary cause of a dangerous rise in atmospheric, earth, and water temperatures that is already bringing unpredictable weather patterns, treacherous heat waves, sea level rise, disastrous flooding, increasing droughts, intensifying forest fires, widespread species extinction, crop failure and food insecurity, and increasing inequality as the poor and vulnerable suffer the greater part of the burden of global warming. Science has shown us its *shadow*, the ways in which the misapplication of scientific discoveries in the context of a global economic system devoted to profit has brought us a set of interlocking crises that threaten not just the well-being of the bio-system, but the very continuation of life on the planet.

Many scholars, including the authors of numerous United Nations reports on climate change and global warming (Intergovernmental Panel on Climate Change), believe that due to human impacts on the environment related to energy use and other factors, we are shifting the world out of the

Holocene period (GR: *holos,* "whole" + GR: *kainos, cene,* "recent, an epoch or geologic period") into a new geological era, often termed the Anthropocene (GR: ánthrōpos, "man, human" + GR: *kainos, cene,* "recent, an epoch or geologic period"). The Holocene, the most recent Epoch of the Cenozoic Era, began well over 10,000 years ago, and has been characterized by relatively stable climate patterns that have enabled the flourishing of complex human cultures. The Anthropocene is the emerging period in which human activity is the dominant influence on climate and the environment.

Despite the consensus of the world community of scientists that we must reverse course if we are to survive and thrive into the future, the pace of mis-applied science and technology has not subsided: Fossil fuel extraction continues unabated and oil and gas profits are higher than ever, the poisoning of the environment continues, causing the extinction of between 24 to 150 species a day (Djoghlaf, 2007), and with us now or on the near horizon are the cloning of human bodies, the engineering of fake food, widespread applications of artificial intelligence, and increasingly sophisticated weaponry, with little to no public input as to the ethical implications of such "innovations."

Humans have always engaged in empirical science through observation and experimentation, processes that supported human survival and evolution as well as the creation of great civilizations (Meyer, 2013). Many cultures outside of the modern western world developed complex mathematical systems as well as sophisticated medical practices, architecture, and astronomical pursuits. But it is a particular constellation of traditions with their roots in the 15th century that enabled Western science to achieve its current dominance (and which have brought us to the ecological "tipping point" where our earth systems may no longer be able to support life):

- humanism, a philosophy that put man at the center of the world, hence engraining the ideas of human mastery and domination over "nature";
- enlightenment science and the advent of *mechanism* as an organizing principle, replacing the metaphor of *organicism* (Merchant, 1980);
- capitalism, with its limitless pursuit of profit and growth (Foster, 2022);
- centuries of colonialism by European superpowers and the violent global takeover of land and resources from Indigenous populations;
- the marriage of capitalism and missionary Christianity, which provided justification for the abuses of colonialism;

- patriarchy—the persecution and domination of women, and the eradication of female practices of healing and other traditional socio-cultural practices that resisted "colonization" (Federici, 2018);
- enslavement and indentured servitude of thousands of people in the service of economic growth and capital accumulation; and
- rapid industrialization and the devastation of the natural world.

Shrii P. R. Sarkar, propounder of the philosophy of neohumanism, did not disavow the positive impact of science on society; in fact, he emphasized the cultivation of a rational intellect and labor-saving technologies in order to free up humans for intellectual, aesthetic, and spiritual pursuits. However, he also called for the application of ethics across the board, in terms of eliminating "economic exploitation, political suppression, religious indoctrination, cultural imposition, and social subordination" (Sarkar, 1987, para. 16). All forms of imperialism, as noted in the bullets above, run contrary to the spirit of neohumanism and the ethics of human life. Therefore, this chapter analyzes the pursuit of science in the modern context in which it has grown, and proposes a reconceptualization of the pedagogy of science based on neohumanist ideals.

The Power and the Limits of Science

The sciences—physical, geological, chemical, biological, and their many subsets—are powerful but limited approaches to understanding reality. The *objects* of science, the only realms in which it holds out the possibility of truth, are *matter* and *energy*. Matter consists of substances in *space* that have mass and volume, are composed of atomic and subatomic particles, and can exist in various phases (water for example, as ice, liquid, or steam). *Energy* is the ability of a physical system to apply force to another physical system. Matter can be observed directly; energy is observed indirectly, in various forms: heat, calories, gravitation, magnetism, electricity.

Information about matter and energy relies on the senses and their amplification through various technologies such as microscopes and telescopes. Sense data, coupled with precision mathematics aided by measurement tools such as rulers, scales, graduated cylinders, thermometers, compasses, and atomic clocks, enable the processes of experimentation, hypotheses testing, and computer modeling—activities of science that generate new information, and occasionally, groundbreaking discoveries. Assessing the veracity of scientific findings relies upon a number of assumptions about the process of science:

- objectivity—that scientists are free of bias;
- replicability—when independent researchers follow identical experimental processes and arrive at the same conclusions;
- reliability—when results can be reproduced in multiple studies;
- validity—the accuracy of research measures; and
- generalizability—the idea that findings can be generalized to other situations or populations, until new evidence contradicts them.

These assumptions lead people to believe that science is a slow and steady march towards truth with new knowledge bringing us ever closer to an accurate view of reality. However, we now know that the picture is not so clear. We know that *objectivity* is an elusive aim, because scientists are human, and bring conscious and unconscious biases to the identification of problems and the formation of hypotheses. We know that observers have effects on what is observed, both in quantum mechanics and in larger human and animal studies. We know that there can be *selection bias* in the choice of which data to pay attention to, and *confirmation bias* when we gravitate towards findings that concur with our preferred theory or worldview. We know that *consensus bias* exists, in which it is held that the majority of thinkers must be right. And there is *reiteration bias*, in which something takes on the aura of truth because it is so often repeated. It has also become apparent that attempts to *generalize* findings well beyond the experimental sample have resulted in errors, gender bias, racial discrimination, bad outcomes, and unanticipated consequences. An example of this sampling bias is that early medical research on heart disease was mostly done on males; women suffered consequences for decades in terms of treatments, diagnoses, and policy. There probably is no study that is absolutely free of some sort of bias; this should not lead to a mistrust of science and scientists, only a healthy skepticism concerning truth claims.

Of most importance, however, is to understand the nature of the scientific method, because this is the canon taught almost universally in schools. Science pedagogy reinforces the belief that there is a uniform method by which the process of science is carried out; a linear process of hypotheses formation based on inductive reasoning drawn from observation, designing an experiment, predicting outcomes of the testing, gathering data, interpreting and analyzing the data, and developing a conclusion. The reality is that the process is much messier, more complex, and nonlinear, with many dead ends and false turns. Alongside the misunderstanding of method, there is the false impression that scientific findings offer *proof* that something is true. As philosophers of science will tell you, science can offer *evidence* in support of a theory, but is incapable of *proving* anything, due to the unforeseen variables that can emerge to disprove a theory. At best, science can offer partial, contingent truths about limited aspects of reality.

Thanks in large part to Thomas Kuhn (1962) and his groundbreaking book *The Structure of Scientific Revolutions*, we now know that science is a *social* activity, one that takes place in the context of a given paradigm, or worldview, and that is governed by the norms, rules, and taken-for-granted assumptions of the dominant culture in which scientists work. A paradigm is an entire constellation of beliefs, values, methods, expectations, and theories held in common by a scientific community. Kuhn highlighted the ways in which *anomalies*, or findings that do not fit consensus reality, are generally ignored until they amass to a degree that demand attention, and hence the reconstruction of group commitments. Kuhn labeled such events *scientific revolutions*.

One example of a scientific revolution in progress is in the field of conventional agriculture science, which for much of the 20th century was dominated by its reliance on mechanization and the application of inorganic pesticides, herbicides, and fertilizers. A "Green Revolution" mid-century promised to feed an increasing world population. Following the dictates of the dominant science of that time increased short term yields, but had a number of unforeseen consequences: The poisoning of soil and water, the loss of genetic diversity in crops, increased resistance to herbicides and pesticides, and displacement of traditional farmers from their productive land. During this time, organic agriculture was a fringe movement, and held little legitimacy in academic institutions. Now, however, there has been a shift: organic and regenerative farming are increasingly recognized as viable systems for promoting and enhancing the health of entire ecosystems, including their human inhabitants, and of fostering long-term sustainability of the food system. They are finding their way into traditional academic departments, and numerous journals are now devoted to the global spread of related research and practices. We are witnessing a paradigm shift, perhaps even a scientific revolution, in conventional ideas about food, soil, health, and sustainability.

The pursuit of science relies heavily on certain forms of thinking: analyzing evidence based on empirical (sensory) data, inferences, logic, inductive and deductive reasoning. The success of scientific applications rely on mathematical precision. These forms of cognition, coupled with the very real achievements of scientific inquiry and technology, have led to a kind of "scientism," which holds that the scientific method and its related forms of thought are the best, really the *only* legitimate way to understand the world and reality. What follows from this is the doctrine of *materialism*, the notion that nothing exists except matter and energy, and their forms and functions. What lies beyond the pale of a materialist worldview are many of the intangible qualities that make us human: values, meaning, purpose, aesthetics, and spirituality (Sattler, 2021).

The skepticism that has accompanied the demystification of science has had confounding effects—the exponential growth of "pseudo-science" along with conspiracy theories, fake news, and countless modern snake oil salespeople who use social media to sell their useless products and grow wealthy. Pseudo-science is basically science that lacks an empirical basis, and other taken-for-granted aspects of science such as replicability and peer review. It's worth noting, however, that marginal findings, such as information about alternative medicine and healing, or psychic phenomena, are often deemed pseudo-science, though they sometimes make their way into the prevalent paradigm, or even, hypothetically, generate a scientific revolution.

The constellation of knowledge/power that resides in mainstream institutions (professional organizations, schools, bureaucracies) resists deviations from the status quo, and words like pseudo-science and conspiracy theory are sometimes invoked to quash dissenting points of view. We are left with a confusing muddle of truths and half-truths to try and sort through. This situation presents the neohumanist teacher with a challenging task: How to teach the important subjects of science and mathematics in a larger holistic context that fosters rational thinking *and* focuses on the "whole," not just the reductive parts, that understands matter and energy to be but part of a continuum that transcends space and time, and that seamlessly integrates the "intangible qualities that make us human" mentioned above.

Beyond Science

Ethics and Values

Science is very good at generating facts—communicating *what is*. What it cannot do is communicate *what ought to be*. This task falls within the realms of ethics and values, concepts that are related but conceptually different. Values are the principles and ideals by which we live and determine right from wrong. Ethics refer more to guidelines for conduct. It might be said that while values provide our motivations, ethics constrain our actions. In neohumanist education, both are seamlessly integrated into the teaching of science.

If, for example, neohumanists acknowledge the inherent worth of all species, and place a high value on the interconnection and interdependence of humans and other-than-humans, then these values will necessarily permeate the teaching of biology and ecology, as well as many other topics.

And if the overarching ethical question—"Does this contribute to the welfare of all?"—is regularly posed, as well as its sub-questions ("Who benefits?"; "What are the long term consequences?"; "Who or what is harmed?"; "Are there alternatives?") young people will develop the habit of ethical analysis whenever confronted by a socio-scientific issue. Virtually every science topic presents an opportunity to study the ethical dimensions of applied knowledge, whether it be the use of nuclear power, the use of animals in pharmaceutical testing, or the applications of genome research.

Neohumanist education does not present a rigid answer to every ethical question; rather it teaches young people to ask relevant questions and engage in ethical discussions, so that they may arrive at carefully considered conclusions. It is important to create the time and space where these discussions can take place. Ethical decision-making is a skill that takes practice to develop. Role playing, simulations, and reflective debriefing offer opportunities to explore the complexities of ethical issues as well as the potential outcomes and consequences of our decisions. Ethics is not merely a "separate subject"; it needs to be infused across the curriculum in meaningful ways.

Meaning and Purpose

It can be argued that the pursuit of knowledge about the world itself holds great meaning. Indeed, many brilliant scientists are guided by grand passions that fuel their inquiries. But science cannot answer the big questions: "Why does life exist?"; "Is there a God?"; "Is there a point to the cosmic drama?"; "Is it an intelligent universe?" Scientists may indeed be guided by these questions, but science itself cannot answer them.

At the heart of conventional science teaching is a tacit view of the world as matter devoid of purpose or intention, a world in which dead, inert particles are moved about in space by external rather than inherent forces (Merchant, 1980, p. 125), and a view of the natural world as separate from the spiritual world (when a spiritual world is admitted at all). The "how" of phenomena rather than the "why" is of primary importance.

Neohumanist education is designed to aid young people in envisioning a greater purpose in life for themselves than mere survival or the accumulation of wealth, power, or fame. We take for granted that humans evolve in terms of tool use, language and cognitive complexity, and lifestyle changes. Neohumanism also posits the existence of spiritual evolution, a process of increased awareness and function of the more subtle qualities of mind, and the progressive alignment of a society based on peace, connection, justice, and love for all beings.

Aesthetics

How do we determine what is beautiful? How do we know what is true? How is it that certain works of art or music or poetry call up sublime emotions in us? The nature of such experiences and issues of taste and discrimination are all part of aesthetics. Shrii Sarkar spoke extensively of the role of literature and the arts in society, attributing both the sense of subtle aesthetics and the desire to create art to human evolution. Contemporary aesthetic philosopher Ellen Dissanayake, whose ideas we feature in Chapter 9, "Arts-Based Learning at the Center" agrees, suggesting that human beings have a universal, biologically based need for art (Dissanayake, 1988, 1992). From her evolutionary perspective, art is something humans do *because it helps them to survive*.

Though science is too often taught from a dry, reductionist perspective, the world is a place of great beauty and wonder. In much the same way as we are stirred to emotion by the arts, humans derive aesthetic pleasure and emotional enticement from an association with nature. Some researchers argue for the biological basis of such responses, and these ideas are loosely affiliated under the framework of the *biophilia hypothesis*, a term coined by the noted scientist Edward O. Wilson. Biophilia is "the innate need to relate deeply and intimately with the vast spectrum of life around us" (Kellert & Wilson, 1995, p. 42). Proponents claim an evolutionary necessity for such capacities: "Human genetic needs for natural pattern, for natural beauty, for natural harmony are all the results of natural selection over the illimitable vistas of evolutionary time" (p. 51).

Aesthetics is a vast and complex area of study. It is important to keep in mind that issues of taste and discrimination are culturally defined—what is beautiful to people in one culture may be disgusting or scary to another. At best, paying close attention to how we respond to both works of art and the world around us, bringing both reason and emotion to our aesthetic responses, and considering the multiple perspectives that others might bring to the same experience can open our minds and help us appreciate the great diversity of human experience and the forms we create to express that experience. To Shrii Sarkar (1957), the ultimate role of the artist in society is to awaken the desire for transcendent experience, to point our consciousness towards the unknown, to appeal to the intuitional capacities in our minds.

Spirituality

In neohumanist schools, spirituality and religion are welcome topics. While neohumanist philosophy opposes the imposition of dogma or doctrine, it welcomes the discussion of the big questions, advocates knowledge of and appreciation for the great diversity of religions and spiritual practices across the world, and encourages reflective and contemplative practices in order to develop the capacities to access inner wisdom. Neohumanism aims to elevate humanism to universalism, defined by Shrii Sarkar (1982) not as a totalistic shared worldview, but as the "love for all created beings of this universe" (p. 7).

Yoga itself is considered a "spiritual science" by many of its practitioners. Empirical research studies that meet the various tests of scientific validity are increasing on the effects of Yoga practices on mental and physical health (Goleman & Davidson, 2017). However, there are accumulated understandings over the centuries that Yoga has been around that might be better classified as "revealed" knowledge (transmitted by enlightened teachers) or arrived at through shared (hermeneutic) understandings. Concepts such as the existence of the *cakras* (energy centers in the human body that correspond to nerve clusters or major organs) or *microvita* (the revelatory theory introduced by P. R. Sarkar in 1986 that posits particles that exhibit characteristics of both matter and consciousness, thus providing a potential reconciliation of the many body/mind problems that have haunted philosophers for centuries) may not have attained the status of scientific knowledge, but they point the way to empirical investigations that may aid the evolution of human consciousness.

The practice of Yoga can be approached "religiously"—unquestioningly, as a true believer of all revealed knowledge. Or it can be approached in the spirit of inquiry and experimentation, objectively seeking honest results. Yet a third approach is to become comfortable with paradox, the idea that the non-rational qualities of faith, surrender and devotion that are essential to the spiritual mindset can live alongside a healthy skepticism, critical thinking, and rationality.

Cultivating the New Story of Science

In neohumanist education, the study of matter and energy takes place in concert with these larger questions of ethics, values, meaning, purpose, aesthetics, and spirituality. In early chapters, we introduced a number of principles of neohumanist education, threads that have been reiterated throughout the text. In Chapter 1, "Neohumanism: A Philosophy of Education for Our Time," we noted the importance of cultivating new ways of being (ontology). At the heart of neohumanist ontology is a particular understanding of what it means to be human—a shift from perceiving the human as an isolated individual, separate from the rest of creation whose destiny is to manipulate, control, and predict nature to a human who is deeply connected with the "pluriverse" of beings—plants, animals, and animate and inanimate matter. This is a special challenge in the teaching of science, which has proceeded in a reductive way (attention to the parts rather than the whole), which holds "objectivity" in ultimate regard, and which understands emotion as an obstruction to truth.

In that chapter we also addressed the need for "epistemological pluralism"—epistemology being the study of knowledge (where it comes from, and how we can determine what is true). Traditional science pedagogy is concerned exclusively with what Sarkar calls *extroversial knowledge*—what can be seen, heard, felt, touched, tasted by the senses, or logically inferred from the behavior of such phenomena. It discounts subjective knowledge, what Sarkar termed *introversial knowledge*, and relies almost solely on analysis, logic and critical thinking to the exclusion of imagination, insight, and empathy, despite the assertions of well-known scientists such as Albert Einstein, Barbara McClintock, David Bohm, and so many others about the role of these processes in their discoveries. Epistemological pluralism also requires that we look beyond the contributions of modern Western-trained scientists to Indigenous people and others who have lived in harmony with their biosystems, for forms of knowledge such as traditional ecological knowledge, ancestral wisdom, narrative knowing, embodied, and intuitional knowing, a small spectrum of the ways of knowing that have been marginalized under the regime of a modernity governed by capitalism and colonialism.

In that chapter we also explored the role of axiology (ethics and values). In our current global society, the market is the prime arbiter of determining what knowledge is of most worth, and what innovations should be pursued. This has had a huge impact on how science has been applied, and to what ends. In the relational, process philosophy of neohumanism, in which the existential value of all living things is acknowledged, ethics are the principles we must use to regulate these many and varied relationships. In living bodies, which must eat to live and utilize nature's resources to build shelter and warm the body, some harm will be done by humans to other life forms. However, the quest to do as little harm as possible to non-human others should form an ethical foundation for the teaching of science and its applications in human life.

In earlier chapters we noted that the Yogic model of the self conceives of the human as a "multi-dimensional being" constituted of layers of expression ranging from the most dense material structure (the body and the senses) to the more subtle, non-material levels of consciousness. While science relies heavily on sense perception coupled with reasoning, thinking, and calculation, it is the more subtle levels of *being* (the holistic assemblage of mind, heart, and body) that encompasses the realms of aesthetics, imagination, creativity, intuition, discernment, and love. Neohumanist pedagogy is a way of teaching and learning that strives to embrace all of the levels of the mind/heart/body in complex learning activities.

In Chapter 10, "Multiple Literacies: The Role of Language and Story in Neohumanist Education," we explored the role of language in animating the world. Science, as taught in schools, has done a superb job of deadening the world, of rendering it inert to better study its characteristics. The dominant view of nature in the sciences is mechanistic (nature as purely physical and deterministic) and reductionist (defined in terms of its most basic characteristics). With the exception of some of the new ecological sciences and the study of other complex systems, material reality has been reduced to its smallest components and extracted from its living contexts, providing partial bits of information from which theories and concepts have been built to explain the world.

When living reality is reduced to words and numbers, which are reduced to marks on a page, and powerful ideas are reduced to formulae, the sensory world loses its animation. It becomes, as Max Weber told us so long ago, disenchanted, cleansed of feeling and creativity (Labaree, 2019), with the result being "to sanction the uninhibited exploitation of nature for human ends" (Griffin, 1988, p. 11). It is the task of the neohumanist educator to coax the world back to life, to restore the organicism that was replaced by mechanism, and to begin to understand the world holistically, as a living, breathing entity governed by immanent intelligence.

To a community of philosophers and scientists who consider themselves reconstructive postmodernists, much of the degradation of our modern civilizations is due to our failure to tell "cosmic stories." Brian Swimme (1988) frames the fundamental mistake of our era in this way: "All our disasters today are directly related to our having been raised in cultures that ignored the cosmos for an exclusive focus on the human" (p. 49). This happened, according to Swimme, because we threw out our cosmic stories and replaced them with the knowledge that the sciences provide. He reminds us that for millennia, we sat around fires and hearths and told stories—stories of the creation of the world and the genesis of life, of the miracles of creation, of the powers of plants and animals, and of the heroic quests of humans. It must be noted that Swimme uses the term "our" suggesting that humanity as a whole is responsible for this "fundamental mistake," overlooking the fact that many cultural groups have, indeed, preserved their cosmic stories, and sustained ethical ways of life that acknowledge a more holistic universe than Western science portrays.

It is not necessary for people raised in WEIRD cultures (Western, educated, industrialized, rich, democratic) to appropriate the stories of cultures other than their own; there is a new story emerging from science itself, drawn from the descriptions of the cosmos generated by quantum mechanics and astrophysics to the intricacies of the plant world revealed by the electron microscope and time lapse photography. It is this new story of science, one that does not discount reason and logic, but also embraces the more subtle levels of the mind, that neohumanism hopes to convey through its teaching of STEAM. As Swimme (1988) expresses this: "A central desire of scientists in the future will be to explore and celebrate the enveloping Great Mystery—the story of the universe, the journey of the galaxies, the adventure of the planet earth and all its life forms" (p. 51). This new story of science is consistent with neohumanist cosmology as well as its radical proposals for the multi-faceted transformation of modern society. Neohumanist educators will resonate with Swimmes's hopes for the future and his sense of urgency: "As the Great Journey of the Universe breaks into human self-awareness, nothing can dam up our desire to shake off the suffocation of nationalism, anthropocentrism, and exploitation and to plunge instead into the adventure of the cosmos" (pp. 53–54). In Part II, we turn to the very practical applications of this reconceptualized vision of STEAM for a new era, a new cosmic story.

FOR CONTINUING STUDY

> *Discussion/Reflection:* What do you remember about your early exposure to science? Were you attracted to the study of science? Why, or why not? What experiences stand out in your memory?
>
> *Discussion/Reflection:* Think about a current controversial application of scientific knowledge. Either as an individual or as a group, list the pros and cons of applying that knowledge. Have a reasoned debate, either with yourself or with others, about if/how the knowledge should be applied. Give careful consideration to the questions posed in this chapter: (*Who benefits? What are the long term consequences? Who or what is harmed? Are there alternatives?*)
>
> *Application:* As an individual or a group, design an arts-based installation or other expression that illuminates the "intangible dimensions" of a science issue or topic. Use sound, film, photography, illustration, 3-dimensional craft, collage, or any other medium of your choice to communicate your message.

References

Dissanayake, E. (1992). *Homo aestheticus: Where art comes from and why*. The Free Press.

Dissanayake, E. (1988). *What is art for?* University of Washington Press.

Djoghlaf, A. (2007). Speech to the Convention on Biological Diversity. *United Nations Environment Programme*. https://www.cbd.int/doc/speech/2007/sp-2007-05-22-es-en.pdf

Foster, J. B. (2022). *Capitalism in the Anthropocene: Ecological ruin or ecological revolution*. Monthly Review Press.

Federici, S. (2018). *Witches, witch-hunting, and women*. PM Press.

Goleman, D., & Davidson, R. J. (2017). *Altered traits: Science reveals how meditation changes your mind, brain, and body*. Random House.

Griffin, D. (Ed.). (1988). *The reenchantment of science*. SUNY Press.

Kellert, S. R., & Wilson, E. O. (1993). *The biophilia hypothesis*. Island Press.

Kuhn, T. (1962/2012). *The structure of scientific revolutions* (4th ed.). Chicago Distribution Center.

Labaree, D. (2019). Max Weber's "science as a vocation." https://davidlabaree.com/2019/07/29/max-webers-science-as-a-vocation/

Merchant, C. (1980). *The death of nature: Women, ecology, and the scientific revolution*. Harper & Row.

Meyer, M. A. (2013). Holographic epistemology: Native common sense. *China Media Research, 9*(2).

Sarkar, P. R. (1957). The practice of art and literature. In *Discourses on neohumanist education*. Electronic edition of the works of P. R. Sarkar, version 9.0.

Sarkar, P. R. (1982). *The liberation of intellect: Neo-Humanism*. A'nanda Márga Pracáraka Samgha.

Sarkar, P. R. (1987). The neo-ethics of multi-lateral salvation. In *Microvitum in a nutshell* (4th ed.). Electronic edition of the works of P. R. Sarkar, version 9.0.

Sattler, R. (2021). *Science and beyond: Toward greater sanity through science, philosophy, art, and spirituality*. Friesen Press.

Swimme, B. T. (1988). The cosmic creation story. In D. R. Griffin (Ed.), *The reenchantment of science* (pp. 47–56). SUNY Press.

18

Rethinking STEAM for the Anthropocene

Part II: Towards a Neohumanist STEAM Pedagogy

> *One of the primary objectives of the Gurukula system of education is to strive incessantly towards a better understanding of the created world and to fully grasp the... life forces that make up our colorful mysterious world... to help students better understand the mysteries of creations... and live with "awakened consciousness."*
>
> —Ac. (Dr.) Shambushivananda,
> *Thoughts for a New Era: A Neohumanist Perspective*, 2018

In early childhood and elementary school, science is generally given scant attention, a result of pressures to improve literacy and math test scores. When it is taught, perhaps one or two periods a week, it tends to be random, subject to teacher interest and available resources. There is no shortage of science resources online in every area imaginable—biology, anatomy, geology, chemistry, and physics. These include teacher guides, reading selections, ideas for experiments, detailed lesson plans, schedules, assignments and supplementary reading. There is generally no harm in getting ideas from these sources, if they are determined to be reliable. However, in order to realize the aims of a neohumanist education, the creation of a science curriculum needs to be done with great intention. The task is multi-faceted: to cultivate the tools of logic, reason, and critical thinking in young people, to awaken the thirst for knowledge in the sciences, and to ensure that the intangibles—ethics, values, purpose, meaning, spirituality, aesthetics, service, and so on—are incorporated in meaningful ways.

STEAM Themes

As with all subjects in a neohumanist school (see Chapter 7, "Curriculum Theory and Design for a Neohumanist Future") it is important to start with big ideas—concepts that provide a generative framework for understanding reality. There are major themes in science that transcend particular subject matter and disciplinary boundaries, and can provide such frameworks. Some of these include:

Systems

Systems are collections of interacting parts in relationship to each other that form a complex whole. The study of systems can be about any subject matter, natural or human-made: organisms, machines, academic disciplines, ecological niches, natural cycles, organizations. Thinking in terms of systems is a reminder that no one thing can be understood except in relation to the rest of the system. Systems overlap, and boundaries can be drawn according to what is being studied (studying soil, e.g., can be just about the organisms that are present in a sample, or it can interface with studying weather systems to better understand erosion). Studying systems requires understanding inputs, processes, and outputs (e.g., a light bulb requires an input of electricity, which heats a very thin filament, which then puts out light energy). Basic themes across systems include the ideas that:

- changes in one small part may affect the whole (i.e., the Butterfly Effect);
- homeostasis (resilience, or the tendency of systems to maintain their key characteristics);
- feedback loops (how information gets processed in systems);
- emergent properties (the tendency of simple components to develop complex collective behaviors, as in the murmuration of birds).

The study of systems is particularly important in neohumanist education, a pedagogy built on understanding relationships.

Continuity and Change

Our world is a dynamic collection of interacting systems, ever engaged in change at macro and micro levels. The human body ages, tectonic plates shift, weather patterns fluctuate, the planet warms. Change can be incremental (barely noticeable), adaptive (where continuity is enabled in response to external forces), or transformative (the fundamental alteration of a system).

Understanding what causes things to stay stable and what causes things to change is of vital importance in understanding the world, predicting the future, exerting positive human agency, and successful adaptation. Change is driven by a number of processes:

- technological change (inventions such as printing, which changed the speed at which new ideas were adopted, or the steam engine which changed the speed at which people could move from one place to another);
- population change (population growth of any kind affects food, energy and social systems/people migrating to new places bring new language, customs and culture);
- social change (new ways of thinking and legislation [example: equality/civil rights] bring about changes in relationships and institutions); and
- new ideas and beliefs (the discoveries of the unconscious mind, human evolution, gravity, the Copernican revolution) change the way people understand the world and their place in it.

Perhaps the greatest changes we now face are the acceleration of global warming and mass species extinction due to human impacts on the environment. Understanding how these changes have come about, and how they might be mitigated may be the most important learning of this generation.

The Living World

The world, according to Rabindranath Tagore, is "a living thing, intimately close to my life, permeated by the subtle touch of kinship, which enhances the value of my own being" (Taneja & Taneja, 2004, p. 99). In neohumanist education, a matter of key importance is developing a sense of love and kinship for all species, and a deep understanding of the interdependence of humans and non-human others. There are many aspects of this: understanding the characteristics and behaviors of the variety of animal and plant organisms, learning about the history and functions of classification systems, understanding the complex web of food chains and life cycles in ecosystems, and understanding evolution in terms of diversity, adaptation, variation, extinction, and natural selection.

The neohumanist educator strives to not separate the study of "other-than-human" life from human life. It is a great task to undo the anthropocentrism of the modern world, the idea that humans are at the center of things with the mandate to classify, collect, predict, and control all other living beings. Lessons need to be planned and materials intentionally curated to foster a sense of "co-inhabitation" rather than dominance. In considering how to teach about the living world, teachers must ask themselves: "How can I model the moral foundations of Yama and Niyama, such as non-harm, simple living, kindness, responsibility, respect, understanding, and goodness into the study of the living world?"; "How can we begin to transform the power-over relationships between humans and the rest of the world, which have resulted in the tragic consequences of extinction, habitat loss, and unnecessary pain and injury to animals?"; "How can we learn to listen to the wisdom of the plant and animal kingdoms?"

The Human Body

Understanding the human body is an essential science standard in most schools. There are many common concepts to be explored: naming the various parts of the body and their functions, understanding how genetic information is passed along, learning how the body responds to the external environment (microbes, pollution, etc.), and learning about human development and human reproduction.

In a curriculum that includes the practices of Ashtanga Yoga, which seeks all around harmony of mind, emotions, and body, the study of the body is a much deeper and more complex learning experience. Shrii Sarkar has expanded the scientific field of bio-psychology with his integration of Yoga principles with modern Western anatomy and physiology (Jordan, 2010). Care of the body is taught through healthy eating of a plant-based diet, the practice of conscious breathing, the practice of basic asanas (Yoga postures) to increase flexibility, balance, and body awareness, sensitive conversations about feelings and how they affect the body, and an introduction to contemplative practices in order to foster the development of concentration, focus, stillness, calmness, patience, and self-regulation (Gannon, 1999/2018).

Space, Time, Energy, and Matter

The study of energy and matter and their behaviors in space and time are at the heart of the modern science project, and are responsible for the technological achievements of the modern age, positive and negative. Children are naturally curious about the world, and intrepid explorers. The study of matter and energy must start with the very concrete, lived experience of the child, and in the early years of education, there is a focus on becoming familiar with and naming the properties of the material world, their similarities and differences of size, shape, weight, temperature, color, and so on, learning about the various states of matter, studying forces such as inertia, friction, floating, sinking, and motion, learning about common forms of energy (solar, electric, magnetic, etc.), and developing a science vocabulary.

As children get older, their learning should move carefully into increasing abstraction and complexity, observing and recording the behaviors of substances with each other (chemical reactions), the effects of applied force on objects (simple machines), the transformations of energy from one form to another (e.g., water to ice to steam), and the actions of waves and fields (such as the vibration of strings on a guitar). In these areas of study, as in others, it is important to avoid a kind of "presentism." Science is a story with chapters in ancient time, and young people need to understand the development of scientific thought (e.g., how chemistry developed from ancient alchemical explorations or how scientists/philosophers first applied measurements to phenomena such as balls rolling down inclined planes). It is also important for young people to understand the origins of science and applied mathematics in various cultures, and about the many scientific and mathematical discoveries attributed to European scientists and inventors that preceded them in Middle Eastern, Indigenous cultures of the Americas, and Asian cultures, sometimes by centuries.

The story of science has a long past and a compelling present. It also has a future—unknown, uncertain, and unpredictable but deeply connected to what we do in the present. One of the best ways to approach this with older children is through literature, specifically speculative science fiction (Gough, 1993). It is important for young people to cultivate their social imaginations, so that they can participate in the creation of preferred futures; to do this, their aesthetic sensibilities must be cultivated by reading the works of writers who have imagined and created futures very different from the present.

The Universe, Earth, and the Environment

"How did our world begin?"; "How did life emerge?"; "How can we recreate the "cosmic story" in such a way as to cultivate an affinity for scientific investigation in the context of the Great Mystery at the heart of the eternal question: Why is there something rather than nothing?"

This topic might be better named "cosmology"—the branch of physics that deals with the nature of the universe. The study of cosmology takes us to the really big questions about the origins and purpose of the universe. Cosmology has occupied the thoughts of humans for millennia; we have told countless stories about creation. Religions have creation stories at their core, and complex philosophies have developed in a multitude of cultures to explain the existence of life and the universe. Cosmological science has developed with the aid of increasingly effective instrumentation and precision mathematics.

Modern education has primarily concerned itself with what is currently known from scientific exploration: The existence of bodies in the solar system and beyond, the forces that are known to shape and affect them, and current theories about their origin and evolution. As in all other areas of science, this theme has deep connections with other fields of study (systems, matter and energy, the living world). Ideas about the universe and the solar system are abstractions in the mind of the young child, though concepts can be introduced through lived experience that lay the foundation for later understandings of macro-events such as the rotation of the planets, fossilization, sedimentation and other geological processes, seasonal systems, and atmospheric, weather, and related forces that shape life on the planet. Children can explore the contours and characteristics (mountains, rivers, streambeds, etc.) of their unique "place," learn to observe the many layers in rocks and rock formations, gaze at the night sky and wonder about the twinkling stars, and observe the weather, how it changes, and how it makes them feel.

Neohumanism acknowledges an all-encompassing, infinite consciousness as the source of creation, a "first cause" known in Sanskrit as *Brahma*. Brahmacakra (the cycle of creation) is an explanatory principle that is consistent with many mythological views of creation in ancient cultures and many religious ideologies, as well as with theories in modern science, such as evolution. The cycle of creation forms the background of much of science teaching in neohumanist education, as children are presented with increasingly complex ideas about the universe, the earth, the environment, and their identity and place in the scheme of things. In this, as in other areas of science, the neohumanist educator must always keep in mind the importance of *enlivening* the learning, paying close attention to how children think, the questions they have, and how to preserve the wonder and awe that are at the heart of children's exploration of the world through the creative use of art and story.

Integrating the STEAM Curriculum

The modern world is technologically advanced, and most people have limited understanding of how the artifacts they interact with on a daily basis actually work, let alone the theoretical dimensions of nuclear fission or particle accelerators. The consequence of this is that a technological elite has emerged and decisions about how the findings of science and new technologies are implemented are mostly out of the hands of ordinary people. STEAM pedagogy needs to be oriented not only towards young people who will seek careers in research and applied sciences, but to all people concerned with the ethics of scientific endeavors and the consequences they can expect from technological innovations. Every technological "advance" has positive and negative cultural dimensions—whether it is the mass interstate highway system, the use of antibiotics, or digital computing. An integrated curriculum (see Chapter 7, "Curriculum Theory and Design for a Neohumanist Future") assures that technical subjects will not be studied in isolation, but in a larger context that includes the exploration of preferred futures, aesthetics, culture, ethics, and the social implications of scientific discoveries.

STEAM is a multi-faceted field of study, drawing from many academic disciplines; this lends itself easily to curriculum integration. Chapter 7 highlighted the idea that young people don't learn about life in fragmented ways that fit neatly into the boxes of the academic disciplines. It noted that an integrated curriculum incorporates content from multiple sources as well as skills and processes, is of high relevance to the learner, and must prove itself capable of solving real life problems and issues. Also in that chapter, you learned about various possibilities for integrated curriculum design: multidisciplinary, interdisciplinary, and transdisciplinary.

No matter how elegant a curriculum design is, if it does not connect to the students' own questions and concerns, little learning (or integration) is likely to take place. To many young people, science and mathematics seem like rarefied pursuits for a talented few, in part due to alienating pedagogical approaches: rigid, prescriptive processes where formulae, rather than thinking, are valued; memorization rather than understanding is most important; content has been stripped of meaning and wonder; learning is "decontextualized," that is, not connected to the physical world, but merely to symbols on a page; language that is "alien" to a child's ears. As the renown cultural anthropologist Margaret Mead (1959) noted, in her analysis of why so many young people find science alienating:

> Any language taught only by adults to adults—or to children as if they were adults—becomes in certain respects "dead." It fails to enlist recruits, it may lose its productivity, and it serves in the end primarily to separate those who know from those who do not. (pp. 143–144)

Of central importance to neohumanist educators is the importance of knowing each child well, and meeting them where they are in order to better serve them educationally (see Chapter 6, "Contemplative Inquiry: The Art of Knowing the Child"). This art has been developed exceptionally well for STEAM teaching with the practice of "science talks" (Gallas, 1995).

Science Talks

Listening to children talk about science offers a unique window into the questions they have about the world, how they think, how they experience the world, the explanations they have about phenomena, and the misconceptions they hold. It offers a view into classroom dynamics, fostering understanding about how children think and learn together and what each individual brings to the process. A teacher might notice that one child has an expansive collection of facts from reading a lot of nonfiction books. Another child may have the gift of metaphor, enlivening discussions with their figurative language and ability to create vivid mental images. Another child may be extraordinarily imaginative and spark new thinking with their "What if?" questions. Teachers can also notice the children who are comfortable with ambiguity and paradox, and those who strive for certainty and closure.

Science talks are a wonderful way to foster discussions about ethics and values. In one science talk with third graders (between 7 and 9 years of age) that I observed, children are gathered around a terrarium with a snake, to whom the teacher feeds a live mouse. There is great interest (and some revulsion) in observing and describing the processes of coiling, striking, squeezing, swallowing, and the bulging journey of the mouse as the snake takes it in. One child in particular is persistent in his questions: "Why does the mouse have to die?"; "Doesn't it want to live too?"; "Why does the snake have to eat a mouse?"; "Why should we feed the mouse to the snake?"; "Could the snake catch the mouse if they were outside?" His heartfelt questions not only led to a rich discussion about predators and prey in the wild, but an exploration of the ethics of science and the science classroom, the rights of adults to interfere in natural processes, and the morality of holding animals hostage, even for benign reasons.

Science talks take place in every early childhood and primary grade level, and can be catalyzed in different ways:

- Beginning with a focusing question from a teacher, ideally one connected to the children's sense of place and time: In autumn, for example: "Why do the leaves change color?"
- Beginning with a question posed by the children: "Where did the first human come from?"
- Seeking explanations of common phenomena: "How do mirrors work?"; "Where does rain come from?"
- Emerging from a structured classroom experience: "Why do some things sink and some things float?"; "What makes paper clips stick to the magnet?"
- Occurring on an informal expedition: "How do birds chew their food?"; "How are butterflies born?"; "What do they eat?"

The aim of science talks is not for the teacher to spot misconceptions and correct them. It is to value the ways that children are attempting to make sense of their world, and to help a group of children become more effective in their collaborative discussions. Gallas (1995), an expert on science talks, notes the importance of modeling for students "how to use each other's ideas and support new theories, how to ask clarifying questions and apply prior knowledge" (p. 30). Teachers do have important roles in conversations: they can request more details, ensure that everyone is included, ask clarifying questions, model active listening and collaborative talking, and implement protocols that address problems in the conversations such as silencing others or taking more than a fair share of "airtime." But it is of vital importance to allow children's science talks to flow with a minimum of adult interference, in order to allow their thinking to unfold.

In the chapter on curriculum design, we discussed emergent learning. When a teacher follows a rigid, prescriptive curriculum, there is little opportunity for emergence. However, when science talks form an important part of classroom learning, deep interests emerge that can shape future learning experiences. Often, a child will pose a new question that "propels our work forward to new and unexpected levels and refines our dialogue about a subject" (Gallas, 1995, p. 30). Science talks can take place at any point in a learning experience: as a catalyst, as discussed above; in the context of a lesson when perplexing issues arise (in studying the human body, for example, a student may ask "What holds the bones together?"); at the end of a unit of study, when students are discussing what they have learned. The most difficult aspect of science talks, for most teachers, is *staying out of the way*—learning to not interfere or correct when children seem to be seeking an answer. Sometimes, says Gallas (1995), "When teachers intervene in children's interests, they diffuse the children's energy and desire to know, rather than fueling it" (p. 71).

As children work to construct theories that explain the phenomena of the world, they use data from a variety of sources: experiences they have had, observations they have made, non-fiction books they have read; stories told to them by adults, information from movies and television. When a teacher truly understands how children think and where their ideas have come from—ideas about the weather, about the disappearance of the dinosaurs, or about human origins—only then are they capable of designing curriculum and curating resources that respond directly to the interests and concerns of the child. They will be able to discriminate between what films or videos are likely to capture the attention of the class, what fictional stories might add an imaginative dimension to the learning, what materials are needed for further exploration, what art processes could serve to deepen understanding, and what vocabulary is necessary to introduce.

Integrating Mathematics and Technology Into Science Study

Some understanding of the nature of mathematics is essential for scientific literacy, and it is of great importance that teachers of young children have an understanding of both advanced mathematics and how to teach the basics to young learners (pedagogical content knowledge). We recommend the wonderful collection of books and podcasts by math educator Marilyn Burns [https://marilynburnsmath.com/] for an overview and very practical advice about the many dimensions of teaching early and primary math.

Mathematics is essential to the designed world (a bridge could not survive without the accurate application of formulae). But mathematics is also inherent in nature, in the form of patterns and sequences, such as the number of petals on flowers, the hives of bees, the symmetry of veins in a leaf, and the webs of spiders. Given the pervasiveness of mathematics in the everyday world, why is it considered so alien to many people? *I HATE math!* is a statement rarely uttered so vehemently about other academic subjects. It is very likely that the person who utters this statement had an early joyless encounter with endless arithmetic worksheets, corrections, and timed tests rather than a playful set of experiences with concrete materials to develop ideas and vocabulary about size, shape, weight, length, numbers, quantities, patterns, time, duration, speed, and money.

Technology is the designed world, the built world, the knowledge by which science and mathematics have been applied to solve practical problems. Technology includes everything from the simplest tool, such as a hammer, to the most complex machine, such as a particle accelerator. Children in the modern world are born into a highly technical, mechanized society. They have no knowledge of how the products they use every day came into being, the reality that objects have a history, and that the constructed environment is a product of human design. If a child has not had experience with a hammer and nails, they are not likely to appreciate the labor that goes into the construction of a house. If they have not seen the inside of a clock or watch, with its springs and gears and pendulums, they are not likely to understand the evolution of time keeping. In the laboratory school designed by John Dewey and his colleagues in the early 20th century, hands-on activities were the curriculum unifiers:

> When children made things they learned history, science, and mathematics through invention. Science, art, and culture were one. There was thinking involved of the most fundamental kind: continuous observation of materials, planning, and use of the hands. (Tanner, 1997, p. 153)

Dewey recognized that children needed to have the kind of education that would help them understand the impact of various technological innovations on society—the problems as well as the possibilities. Never before has this been as urgent as it is now, as it becomes clear how overconsumption and overproduction, especially of fossil-fuel based products and processes, are poisoning our land and our waters. It is imperative that young people come to appreciate the importance of "appropriate technology"—applications that assist labor without the bells and whistles that have no essential purpose other than to stimulate the desire to acquire them. The well designed neohumanist school setting is a place where children can explore how the modern world has been created by engaging and experimenting with the materials and tools that foster a seamless integration of science concepts, mathematical problem-solving, and technological design. Science talks, as described above, are an essential precursor to more focused explorations and experimentation.

In contemporary classrooms, there is little opportunity to engage in conceptualizing problems and planning experiments. Planning investigations is one of the most important, and most neglected aspects of science learning. Planning is an imaginative activity that encourages children to think through the potential consequences of their actions. But it is time-consuming. To be more efficient, instructions for science activities are generally delineated on instruction sheets or work cards in learning centers.

But providing a set of instructions to follow effectively prevents children from engaging in planning. This approach to science, although better than no science at all, holds little promise of nurturing the "scientist within," for there is little scope for personal interest, extended observation, musing, the twists and turns of genuine exploration, or following a quest until the passion has been exhausted. The structure of the learning is external to the learner, the discovery process already laid out by adults who have predetermined the cognitive outcomes (Kesson, 2018a, pp. 64–71).

An exploration and discovery approach to STEAM learning requires intention, care, and thought in setting up the environment. Reggio Emelia school environments, for example, are not only aesthetically pleasing and intellectually stimulating; they

> convey a respect for the interests, rights, needs, and capacities of those who use that space... the provision of stimulating and provocative displays of objects, whether a careful arrangement of seashells or the positioning of a mirrored surface, serves to educate children's attention to design, detail, or difference; and to contribute to the development of an alert and active response to the world. (Edwards et al., 1998, pp. 266–267)

Learning environments should invite the children to explore and interact with a variety of materials that stimulate cognitive growth. Charles Silberman (1973) documents the importance of unguided exploration in his comprehensive study of the British Infant school model, a progressive set of reforms in England and North America in the 20th century intended to make classrooms joyful places of deep learning. He presents the idea of "messing about," free and unguided exploratory work with concrete materials, during which children test, probe, and experiment without imposed questions or instructions. There needs to be abundant time for the unrestricted encounter with *stuff*, in which a child has the opportunity to touch, taste, feel, see, smell, manipulate, and experiment with the substances and elements, the objects and creatures of the world. Such opportunities are all too circumscribed in formal schooling, where every moment is planned, premeditated, even scripted. Messing about is crucial to the beginnings of things, for it can foster curiosity, guesses, estimations, and speculations.

A fine example of messing about is demonstrated by an experiment begun in 1999 in an extremely poor area of New Delhi. Some innovative business people and educators placed a computer in a hole in a wall, available to passersby in the street. The computer had online access and some programs but no instructions for its use. The children on the street figured out how to use the computer in a minimal amount of time, and within a few hours were surfing the web, opening and closing programs, and downloading games and videos. Over the next few years, this group did the experiment in different places, trying new strategies in self-directed learning, calling the theory they were developing "Minimally Invasive Learning." Not only did the children become adept at using computers, local teachers and field observers noted that "the children demonstrated improvements in enrollment, attendance and performance on school examinations, particularly in subjects that deal with computing skills; English vocabulary and usage; concentration, attention span and problem-solving skills; and working cooperatively and self-regulation" (Mitra, 2012).

For the neohumanist school fortunate to be situated on rural property, or near a forest or woodland, desert, jungle, or beach, the outdoor environment is an extraordinary space to begin explorations. The vastness of the natural world is available for observing, questioning, and interacting, with its soil types, bodies of water, trees, fallen leaves, seashells, pebbles, rock formations, dunes, and of course all creatures great and small, from the fungi and worms in the soil, to the birds and their nests, to the water creatures and the tracks of deer and rabbits. Looking up, young people can gaze at cloud formations and at the night sky, and they can feel the wind patterns on their bodies.

A well-provisioned indoor classroom is also essential to this important first stage of science discovery, as well as for more organized subsequent investigations. Concrete materials—bought, found, and made—can be virtually anything (sand, water, clay, paints, food coloring, paper, glue, duct tape, clipboards, cardboard, food, tools (for sewing, weaving, spinning, wood carving, building, painting, sculpting), and old alarm clocks, radios, and other gadgets that can be taken apart and reassembled. Collections of gathered materials are essential—rocks, shells, feathers, seeds, pinecones. Containers of all sorts are useful—jars, buckets, baskets, bags. String, wire, yarn and rope are often needed, as are the basic office supplies: rubber bands, staples, tape, and paper clips. Materials need to be well organized, tidy and accessible.

Messing about raises questions that require further investigations, and can necessitate the acquisition of new skills such as measuring, for which you need rulers of different kinds, balance scales, stop watches, compasses, measuring cups and beakers and digital scales. Inquiry often requires counting and doing calculations with beads, chips, pencils, paper, coins, or calculators. New tools become necessary in the course of a project: hammers, files, saws, drills, needles, looms, scissors, shovels, rakes. Materials that extend our senses are extremely useful, if often too expensive for all classrooms: microscopes, magnifying glasses, telescopes, small mirrors, binoculars.

Beautifully designed math manipulatives are available for a price—Cuisenaire Rods, Geo-Blocks, Tangrams, Attribute Blocks, Pendulums, Geo-Boards, Fraction Tiles, and so on, though similar materials can be handmade with a bit of imagination, ordinary materials such as popsicle sticks and beans, cardboard, and some design skills. The point is, knowledge about matter and energy in the early grades is best discovered through the playful sensory manipulation of materials, careful attention to the spoken language of children, and sensitive guidance towards concept formation when it is called for.

Literature and the Arts in STEAM

The inclusion of the arts (including literature) in the field of STEAM education highlights the importance of cultivating new ways of thinking in order to bring about imaginative solutions to the many problems faced by our global society. The creative processes so essential to artistic exploration and creation embody habits of mind and dispositions equally important to science learning. Experts in integrated arts in education (Booth & Gambill, 2016) propose four (non-linear/recursive) stages of the creative process:

- generating ideas (identifying key problems; divergent thinking, generating multiple ideas (brainstorming);
- awareness of process (discovering intrinsic motivation, tapping into personal experience, self-assessing, making choices and noting consequences);
- experimenting (testing hypotheses, questioning, risk taking, combining and mixing ideas, synthesizing); and
- engaging multiple perspectives (considering different points of view, perceiving relationships and patterns, attending to both details and the "big picture").

Critical and creative thinking, reasoning and problem-solving are essential in both the arts and the sciences, in mathematical understanding and in the designed and built world.

Details in arts-based educational processes have been elaborated at length in earlier chapters. Arts-based projects in the context of STEAM need to be carefully chosen to deepen and enhance learning, and the relevant academic disciplines need to be thoughtfully aligned (i.e., studying sound waves through musical notes; studying light and color in the context of painting; using creative movement activities to enact concepts of force and motion such as inertia or gravity, studying chemistry through the firing of clay, etc.) There are many excellent children's picture books that bring scientific ideas alive in imaginative ways, such as *If You Find a Leaf* by Aimée Sicuro (2022), *Every Color of Light* by Hiroshi Osada (2020), or the enchanting *Backyard Fairies* by Phoebe Wahl (2018).

Some advocates of a STEAM approach might argue that the arts are to be valued primarily for their utilitarian purposes, their capacity to extend learning in the technical fields. Neohumanist educators counter this with the proposition that art is to be valued for its own sake, for its ability to awaken imaginative processes, to bring beauty into the world, to foster social and emotional development, to bring young people closer to nature and cultivate love for the created world, and to elevate the spirit.

Humanity faces enormous challenges in the years ahead. The many problems-to-be-solved will require new ways of thinking and imaginative solutions. How can we cultivate the vision and the capacities in young people to do the work that must be done? Contrary to conventional thinking, the arts are not mere luxuries, frivolous entertainments, or leisure time pursuits. Creativity and the arts are the *new basics* in education. The role of the imagination, as philosopher Maxine Greene (1995) tells us, is "to awaken, to disclose the ordinarily unseen, unheard and unexpected" (p. 28). There can be no better argument, in times of uncertainty and profound changes, for the integration of creativity and the arts across the curriculum.

Following Up on "Messing About"

In the chapter on Contemplative Inquiry, you learned about the importance of careful observations and reflections in order to further children's learning. In the STEAM classroom, the sensitive teacher recognizes the diversity of interests and attention that children bring to their initial explorations of materials and responds accordingly. One child may need some prompting questions to move their inquiry along, another may need an introduction to new materials or tools. It may become apparent that a child lacks some essential experience such as playing with sand or getting their hands into the dirt. Another child may be at a point where some calculations are required. Or a teacher may notice common interests and suggest a group project. It is important to not be dogmatic about any curriculum design. In a hands-on, experimental environment, it may be necessary to spend some time on a separate subject—even bringing in math problems and worksheets, or vocabulary lists. No problem!

It is tempting to abandon the discovery approach when panic sets in: "Are they learning all the facts they need to know?"; "What about that science exam in their future?" Yes, science is a body of knowledge, a vast reservoir of facts and concepts, a collection of tables to memorize and formulae to learn. But to build genuine interest in the practice of science, it is necessary for young people to explore their world using the methods by which such knowledge is actually acquired, to learn to *think like a scientist.* There is plenty of time in the upper grades to employ more conventional pedagogy, if young children have developed their interests and the joy of learning.

For teachers in a conventional school, it may seem daunting to make the switch to an integrated, discovery approach to STEAM. It is advisable to start small. Set aside one afternoon a week for "exploratory science." Equip a corner of your classroom with math manipulatives and science materials. Set up a learning center that is well stocked with science board games, beautifully illustrated books, and perhaps a science table with a rotating display of interesting natural objects. Take science walks. Try some science talks. See where this leads. You may find a joy in this kind of teaching that you have not experienced when endeavoring to impose adult ideas about how the world works on young people.

The Spiral Curriculum

Out of the multitude of potential STEAM topics, neohumanist teachers need to consider the big ideas and themes that will accomplish the philosophical aims of a neohumanist education. This intentional curriculum development—determining the scope and sequence of particular topics—should be a schoolwide process. The *spiral curriculum* encompasses the notion that a child should revisit concepts they have learned in increasingly complex ways throughout their education. In this process, teachers help them to connect new knowledge to what is already known, thus deepening and reinforcing what is learned. Teachers in a school can make scope and sequence charts by determining what big ideas should be focused on in the school, and then identifying knowledge, skills, and experiences at each level of a child's development to help them attain these concepts. This is called the *vertical integration* of curriculum. With such a school wide framework in place, then teachers can develop the scope and sequence of their classroom curriculum units using the tools of understanding by design (UBD), sometimes referred to as *universal design for learning* as articulated in Chapter 7, "Curriculum Theory and Design for a Neohumanist Future."

Curriculum development is very hard work and creatively rewarding. It should be done collaboratively, bringing the skill and insights of all the teachers in a school together. We sketch here a rough framework of how a spiral curriculum might be developed in an elementary school around a topic of great STEAM importance—Watersheds. A watershed is basically an area of land that channels rainfall and snowmelt into its final destination (a large lake, the sea, or an underground aquifer). Watersheds can be very small—a county, for example—or a huge river basin, such as those of the Mississippi River in the United States, or the Nile River, which crosses the boundaries of many countries.

Every elementary teacher has probably taught the water cycle and its phases: evaporation, condensation, precipitation, deposition. While it is an essential topic, as generally taught this lesson does not begin to address the broader importance of watersheds to human and non-human life, the ways that humans are affecting their watersheds, and the degradation of freshwater sources across the planet. Every topic has a "field of relations"; in studying watersheds, the connections are myriad: land formations, climate, weather, human and non-human inhabitants, food sources, plants and their transpiration, dams (the "built environment"), estuaries, soil health, agriculture, flooding, drainage, acid rain—the list of related topics is endless. In considering a spiral curriculum, it is imperative to think in terms of child development—what dispositions and habits of mind can be cultivated at what levels, how cognitive complexity grows, and when abstractions can be usefully introduced.

Watersheds: PreK-Kindergarten

In the early ages, it is of primary importance to develop a love for nature and a deep appreciation of natural processes. Long walks in the outdoors, observing hills and valleys, streams and rivers, and rock formations is essential to cultivating a "sense of place." Beautifully illustrated and poetic books such as *I Am the Rain: A Science Book for Kids About the Water Cycle and Change of Seasons* (Paterson, 2018) and *Water Is Water: A Book About the Water Cycle* (Paul & Chin, 2015) cultivate children's aesthetic sensibilities and appreciation for nature.

Science talks should be encouraged about children's questions: "What is water?" "Where does it come from?"; "Why is it important?" Water play (indoors and out), a basic activity at preschool levels, serves many purposes, among them developing fine motor skills, encountering early math concepts such as volume and capacity, conservation and displacement, and science ideas about the properties of water. Children at the older end of the age spectrum can make models of a watershed to see how water flows and how it is collected, integrating water play and model-making outdoors with sand and dirt, rocks and sticks (Kesson, 2018b, pp. 125–138).

Games and play can form a solid foundation for appreciating the natural world: kite flying and boat (or leaf) sailing instill principles about wind and water flows, scavenger hunts teach children to find and identify natural objects, follow-the-leader can foster kinesthetic confidence as children experience climbing, crawling, swinging from branches, and clambering over logs and rocks. Dramas and creative movement activities can depict many of the processes of a watershed: the movement of the wind, the cycles of evaporation and precipitation, the hibernation of animals, the metamorphosis of insects. And even very young children can learn the art of "land listening" (closing their eyes, listening to the sounds they hear, and then sharing their perceptions with the group).

Watersheds: Grades 1–2

As children get older, they can take more informative science walks, perhaps with a water conservation expert, to explore storm run-off, what a floodplain is, what marshes and estuaries are and why they are so important to wildlife and water conservation. They can explore a favorite topic: Puddles! to see what lives in them. They can go into more depth with animal studies, exploring the amazing habits and capacities of beavers, the nesting of birds, or other animals in the locale. They can learn about the essential work performed by a multitude of species—plants, animals, insects, fungi, and microbes—and the many benefits to humans of this unappreciated labor. They can begin to study the built environment and how it affects the watershed. In their models, they can explore how pollution travels, and what can be done to counter it. They can study how nature stores and records information, for example in the study of tree rings, fossils, or the layers of rock formations.

They can build pinwheels to study wind patterns, and become acquainted with more sophisticated instrumentation to study the weather: thermometers, barometers, anemometers, wind vanes, and rain gauges. At this age, the child's capacity to draw is developing past the scribbling stage. Introducing them to the careful observation (of bark, leaves, and other phenomena) and accurate botanical drawing leads to a deeper understanding of the structures and functions in the natural world.

It is important to begin the study of the different ways that cultural groups relate to the environment. In the context of the watershed, many Indigenous peoples consider water as sacred, and this enables them to live in balance with the resources of their watersheds (LaPier, 2017). Dramatic enactments and storytelling can feature ways to "make special" the children's relationships to the plants, animals, and landmarks of their watersheds. They can learn how Indigenous people are leading the struggle to save our water systems as illustrated in the children's book *We Are Water Protectors* (Lindstrom & Goade, 2020; Winner of the 2021 Caldecott Medal).

Watersheds: Grades 3–5

At this level, children's reasoning power takes a huge leap forward, and science talks can begin to address more complex questions: "Where does our water supply come from?"; "How do leaves use and lose water?"; "What happens in floods?" Students can begin to gather and examine data about water run-off and water usage in their homes and schools. They can design and build (with adult assistance) a weather station, equipped with basic instruments to study rainfall, wind speed and direction, and air temperature. They can devise plans for conserving water, using arts-based processes such as model making, posters, drawing, board game creation, public service announcements, or song writing to make their case.

They can begin to study the importance of healthy soil to a well-functioning watershed, and explore in more depth how multiple species, seen and unseen, are busy creating healthy soil structure. They can learn how humans can work alongside these non-human laborers, and how our work can complement theirs, through projects like permaculture and agroforestry. Ideally, they have many opportunities to get their hands dirty, and study soil and plants up close! Young people can come to appreciate that the "welfare of all" includes micro-organisms, worms, and beetles as well as people. They can stretch their imaginations by learning what their watershed was like 100 years ago, and what it might be like 100 years from now.

Though older children can become more practical minded and lose some of the imaginative faculties of the very young, it is important to keep alive the sense of wonder, awe, and appreciation for what they are learning from science. Water is one of the four classic elements that humans throughout history defined, along with earth, air, and fire. It is of central importance to our survival. Young people can revisit the idea that many Indigenous cultures hold water as sacred, and learn how their art, ceremonies, stories, and rituals reflect this deep appreciation. In Thailand, for example, many people honor the Water Goddess and the Buddha in a festival called Loy Kratong by floating lighted baskets and lanterns on the water. In this enactment they give thanks for their use of water and apologize for polluting the waters. The creative neohumanist teacher strives to integrate such appreciation for the natural world into their science teaching.

These values of cherishing the water have helped to spark a movement for granting legal rights to nature. In this context, ethical discussions can become more complex and more sophisticated. Questions such as "Who should own the water?" and "Do corporations have the right to build potentially polluting pipelines that endanger the water supply on Indigenous lands?" can initiate interest in important political issues of our time.

When young people reach the pinnacle of an area of study featured in their school's spiral curriculum, a "culminating project" is called for that can synthesize and vitalize their cumulative learning. There are many possibilities that students and teachers might co-create around a study of the local watershed: The restoration of a small plot of damaged land in their area, a drama about how their watershed has changed over time, or a seasonal festival that honors the many species that exist in their watershed.

Ritual, Ceremony, and Festival

In Chapter 9, "Arts-Based Learning at the Center," we introduced the idea of secular rituals, the creation of "cultures of enactment" that involve young people in communal participatory experiences in which they create and recreate the fundamental stories of our existence—our human bonds, our relationships with plants, animals, sea and sky, and the mythic stories that carry forth and transmit the blueprints of a moral universe. These enactments are essential in cultivating an appreciation for the "new cosmic story" as introduced in Part I of this chapter. This new cosmic story has the potential to revitalize the teaching of science, as young people explore and celebrate the enveloping great mystery—the story of the universe, the journey of the galaxies, the adventure of the planet Earth and all its life forms, and their identity and sense of self in this larger context.

In the chapter on arts-based learning, we looked at the historical connections between rituals, ceremonies, and the arts, which bring together music, drama, movement, poetry, light, sound, and costume in ways that "make special" ordinary human experience; that is, heighten the emotional connection with events and stimulate transcendent experiences. It is in this "making special" that we can bring to science learning the awe, wonder, and beauty that animated the early human desire to discover how the world works and how best to live in it. It is how we might awaken the sense of ethics toward the natural world through enhancing appreciation for all life forms. It is how we can establish meaningful links between the past, the present and the future. It is how we can affirm our interdependence with all the creatures of the world. And it can help us create a feeling of unity and sacredness that bonds us, human and other-than-humans.

Bringing It All Together

We have covered a lot of territory in these two chapters on STEAM. We close by aiming for a synthesis—a listing of the principles that should animate the neohumanist approach to STEAM teaching:

- Science and its related disciplines needs to be thought of as compelling stories, rather than dry facts. Albert Einstein emphasized this point when he remarked that scientific explanations are "free creations of the human mind, and are not, however it may seem, uniquely determined by the external world" (Grandy & Bickmore, 2014, p. 4).
- Western science needs to be taught with a healthy balance of appreciation for its power as well as its limits.
- The integration of the intangibles—ethics, values, aesthetics, meaning, purpose, and spirituality—is an important consideration in STEAM teaching.
- Neohumanist education acknowledges the crucial role of "place"—educating the young child about their *surround* (the land, the water, the creatures, and the culture in which they live)—before they are expected to deal with abstractions.
- The importance of *immersion* in the sensory world, outside and inside; ensuring that genuine *experience* is at the root of science learning.
- Implementation of "science talks" at every stage of a new unit of study: the initiation of a topic, the exploration of a topic, and the summary stage (what was learned).
- Consistent incorporation of ethical thinking across the science curriculum through discussion, role play, and debate.
- The incorporation of multiple cultural perspectives into every subject (e.g., how Indigenous people understand plant medicine vs. Western allopathic medicine).
- The arts need to be seamlessly integrated into science study, in terms of:
  - their *experimental use* (e.g., architectural models to test ideas about structure);

- their capacity to *nurture the imagin*ation (e.g., visualizing traveling wind currents on a magic carpet);
- their capacity to *highlight details* (e.g., botanical drawing);
- their capacity to *clarify concepts* (e.g., colorful and vivid mind maps of phenomena studied);
- the *creative expression* of ideas (e.g., dancing the theory of relativity);
- their role in *making special* the ordinary events and processes of life (e.g., creating and celebrating seasonal festivals and ceremonies)

■ The *awakening of rationality*. Reason and logic, key cognitive tools of scientific knowledge, need to be tempered by the cultivation of discernment, intuition, and love—capacities that grow and flourish in an environment where inner knowing and the search for wisdom are fostered through contemplative practices and intersubjective dialogue.

One final point is the importance of community and culture in the teaching of STEAM. Science can exist (and too often does) in the service of global corporate capitalism and elite domination. Or it can exist in the service of the people, all people, and of our non-human kin. Two things are important in this regard: First, there should be deep respect on the part of the teachers and the school for the communities their students come from, the lifeways, customs, and beliefs of the culture. Applied science needs to build on these, not repudiate them. Teachers need to learn what has constituted "science" in the communities where they teach, how people have acquired knowledge and how it has influenced their lives, and bring in the expertise of community members (farmers, weavers, builders, musicians, cooks) in the study of science topics. Second, students need to learn how science can serve authentic needs: By participating in community-based research around technical problem-solving (e.g., water shortages); by exploring how to respond to immediate needs (e.g., invasive crop pests); by introducing technologies that will make lives easier (e.g., experiments with solar power). They need to consider how service can be extended to non-human others. One grade in a neohumanist school in Long Island, New York, studies bats every year as the Halloween holiday approaches. Rather than focus on merely the "scare factor" of bats, they study their ecological significance and their unique characteristics. And, as a special service project they build bat houses to support the local bat population. Other neohumanist schools, in recognition of the importance of bees in our bio-systems, plant pollinator gardens to attract and feed them. At every level of education, service to the community, its people, and its non-human inhabitants should constitute an essential part of STEAM learning.

FOR CONTINUING STUDY

Discussion/Reflection: What do you think Albert Einstein meant by his quote that scientific explanations are "free creations of the human mind, and are not, however it may seem, uniquely determined by the external world?"

Discussion/Reflection: Many people are anti-science, or believe in various pseudo-sciences. What are the most important pedagogical strategies to cultivate "awakened rationality?" How can we ensure that young people use logic and reason carefully, informed by compassion and intuitive wisdom?

Application: This is your chance to play with developing a spiral curriculum. Using the model featured in this chapter (PreK–K, Grades 1–2, Grades 3–5), choose an important science topic that should be revisited every year. Highlight the concepts (big ideas) that you hope to cover. Consider what is most important, developmentally, at each level. Brainstorm possible subjects for science talks and how you would initiate these. Design some inquiry-based science exploration activities that build on what was learned at the prior level (for PreK–K you might talk about the knowledge that children bring with them from the home and how you will build on this). Be sure to integrate math and technology. How will you plan to integrate the arts? How you will include the "intangibles"—ethics, values, purpose, meaning, spirituality, aesthetics, service, and so on?

Drawing upon what you have learned in the arts-based learning section of this book, as well as this STEAM chapter, design a culminating activity for the end of your multi grade spiral curriculum that brings a whole school together in a seasonal festival, a ceremony, or a ritual that highlights what was learned.

Application: If you are a teacher of older children or a special subject science teacher, explore how you might incorporate the "intangibles"—ethics, values, purpose, meaning, spirituality, aesthetics, service, and so on—into a specific science topic.

References

Booth, E., & Gambill, P. (2016). *Creative capacity in Vermont students.* https://www.communityengagementlab.org

Edwards, C., Gandini, L., & Forman, G. (1998). *The hundred languages of children: The Reggio Emilia approach—Advanced reflections.* Ablex.

Gallas, K. (1995). *Talking their way into science: Hearing children's questions and theories, responding with curricula.* Teachers College Press.

Gannon, N. (1999/2018). *Teach me to fly: Insights into early childhood neo-humanist education.* InnerWorld Publications.

Gough, N. (1993). *Laboratories in fiction: Science education and popular media.* Deakin University Press.

Grandy, D. A., & Bickmore, B. R. (2014). Science as storytelling. *BYU Studies Quarterly, 53*(4). https://scholarsarchive.byu.edu/byusq/vol53/iss4/4

Greene, M. (1995). *Releasing the imagination: Essays on education, the arts, and social change.* Jossey-Bass.

Jordan, Ac. S. V. (2010). Biopsychology of dreams. *Gurukula Network*, 31.

Kesson, K. (2018a). Doing good science: On the virtues of simply 'messing about.' In *Unschooling in paradise* (pp. 64–71). InnerWorld Publications.

Kesson, K. (2018b). *The power of play.* In *Unschooling in paradise* (pp. 125–138). InnerWorld Publications.

LaPier, R. R. (2017). "Why is water sacred to Native Americans?" *Open Rivers: Rethinking Water, Place, & Community*, No. 8. https://openrivers.lib.umn.edu/article/why-is-water-sacred-to-native-americans/

Lindstrom, C., & Goade, M. (2020). *We are water protectors.* Roaring Brook Press.

Mead, M. (1959). Closing the gap between the scientists and the others. *Daedalus, 88*(1), 139–146.

Mitra, S. (2012, February 3). The hole-in-the-wall project and the power of self-organized learning. *Edutopia.* https://www.edutopia.org/blog/self-organized-learning-sugata-mitra

Osada, H., & Arai, R. (2020). *Every color of light: A book about the sky.* Enchanted Lion.

Paterson, J. (2018). *I am the rain: A science book for kids about the water cycle and change of seasons.* Dawn Publications.

Paul, M., & Chin, J. (2015). *Water is water: A book about the water cycle.* Roaring Brook Press.

Sicuro, A. (2022). *If you find a leaf: A inspiring nature book for kids and toddlers.* Random House Studio.

Silberman, C. E. (1973). *The open classroom reader.* Random House.

Taneja, V. R., & Taneja, S. (2004). *Educational thinkers.* Atlantic Publishers.

Tanner, L. (1997). *Dewey's laboratory school: Lessons for today.* Teachers College Press.

Wahl, P. (2018). *Backyard fairies.* Knopf Books for Young Readers.

19

Conclusion

Education for a Bright Future

> *Human civilization now faces the final moment of a critical juncture. The dawn of a glorious new era is on its one side and the worn-out skeleton of the past on the other. People have to adopt either of these two.*
> —P. R. Sarkar, *Ánanda Vánii Sam'graha: A Collection of the Spiritual Messages of Shrii Shrii Ánandamúrti* (n.d.)

November 2023

Winter is making its way to the mountains of Vermont, bringing icy storms, deep snow, and long dark nights. The vibrant burst of color in the sugar maples—the deep crimsons, burnished golds, and brilliant oranges—has given way to crumbling brown leaves that quickly fall to nourish the forest floor. It's "stick season" here, bare branches silhouetted against graying skies, a time when it's easy to see the birds that remain foraging for food. The hardy ones, the crows who inhabit my driveway and will eat most anything, the red cardinal sitting on my garden fence, and the tiny black-capped chickadees at my bird feeder are here for the long haul; with me they will do their best to stay warm and cozy. Soon the voles and shrews and mice will make their icy tunnels in the snow, with their nicely laid out rooms for food storage, sleeping, and latrine. I haven't seen any black bears lately, so they may already have found their hollow tree or brush pile to snooze in for the next few months.

Vermont, named *N'dakinna* (the Abenaki word for "Homeland") by the Indigenous people who have inhabited this remote mountainous area for over 10,000 years, is idyllic in many ways. With its incredible natural beauty, stringent environmental regulations, robust organic agriculture system, and traditions of mutual aid and neighborliness, many people thought that Vermont might be a good place to ride out the global chaos we see coming. But we were lulled out of complacency this past year, with first a drought, then a late frost that damaged many crops, then skies filled with smoke from Canadian wildfires, followed by massive amounts of rain and flooding that devastated hundreds of homes and town centers in the period of just a few days. Climate catastrophe descended upon this peaceful corner of the North American continent, making it increasingly clear that there are no safe havens.

We are at a pivotal moment in human history, a "critical juncture" as Shrii Sarkar puts it in the opening quote. The forces of destruction, disintegration, and collapse are gathered to wreak their havoc in the forms of continued extraction of life-destroying fossil fuels, mountains of plastic waste, the manufacture (and use) of armaments, species extinction, and pollution, an assemblage of forces that many are now calling the "predatory capital death cult," with its insatiable appetite for power and profit. That narrative is in seeming control of the world story, as all of our major institutions—schools, media, academia, government, business—seem incapable of imagining a radically different way of doing things.

In the northern winters, stories have long been told of the hungry monsters with gleaming bloody fangs and a carrion stench who traipse the woods and devour humankind. Robin Kimmerer, in her wonderful book *Braiding Sweetgrass* (2013), tells of the Windigo, the monster of Anishinaabe legend, an outsized man with a heart of ice, a "human being who has become a cannibal monster" (p. 304). Here in northern New England, the five Wabanaki tribes talk about a similar creature, known either as the *chenoo*, the *giwakwa*, or the *kiwakwa* (Muise, 2009). These monsters are apt personifications of the unappeasable appetite of the capitalist machine. The native habitat of these creatures is the wintry north woods, but as Ojibwe scholar Basil Johnston says "multinational corporations have spawned a new breed of Windigo that insatiably devours the earth's resources, 'not for need but for greed'" (Kimmerer, 2013, p. 306). Humans seem helpless in the face of such monstrosities, but when we recognize that Windigo nature resides in each of us, as the old stories teach, we can simply refuse to feed it.

Arrayed against the forces of devastation are the revolutionary forces of life, of transition, of transformation. Great numbers of people finally recognize that the climate crisis *is* happening as they experience, close up, their towns and cities flooding and their forests burning. Global social movements for justice proliferate, and are becoming networked, as in the global tapestry of alternatives (GTA), a decentralized movement initiated and sustained by members from the global majority. Experiments in sharing and gift economies, worker's and member's cooperatives, ecological economics, and doughnut economics (Raworth, 2018) are happening, as more young people than ever before question the fundamentals of the rapacious and extractive capitalist economy we live under.

Many people are rethinking the nature of "work" and seeking a deeper understanding of what might constitute human fulfillment. Indigenous people are leading the way to protect the planet with water/energy/food sovereignty movements, and regenerative agriculture, agroforestry, and localization are becoming familiar terms. Mutual aid societies proliferate. We are actually beginning to think about the extension of rights born in the humanist era to non-human others; giving rivers, forests, and oceans standing in the court system. And though church attendance and conventional religion in the West are in decline, the desire for non-affiliated spiritual growth is on the rise, accompanied by a new open-mindedness and curiosity about the transcendent possibilities of human existence. There is a small but growing clamor for a new story, a changing paradigm, a worldview that would center life and the flourishing of the multitudes of human and other-than-human species who share this small and fragile planet.

Worldviews and paradigms are narratives—stories about the world, about human possibility, about relationships, and about meaning. Central to neohumanist education philosophy is the emergence of a new story, what Brian Swimme (1988), an evolutionary cosmologist, calls a "cosmic creation story," conceived to inaugurate a new era of human and planetary health, a "transformation out of a world that is...mechanistic, scientific, dualistic, patriarchal, Eurocentric, anthropocentric, militaristic, and reductionistic" (p. 47). A story that tells us "that the universe is not static; that the universe is expanding each moment into a previously nonexistent space; that the universe is a dynamic developing reality" (p. 50). A story that tells of our "entanglement" in a web of life, one that understands all of creation to be alive, intelligent, and self-organizing, one in which we have been freed from the false sense of separation from the rest of nature, one in which we have awakened from the slumber imposed by capitalism, materialism, consumerism, conflict, spectacle, and all the other distractions devised to convince us we are alive. The great opportunity before us today, say Swimme and Tucker (2011) is

> to tell this new universe story in a way that will serve to orient humans with respect to our pressing questions: Where did we come from? Why are we here? How should we live together? How can the Earth community flourish? (p. 5)

In ordinary terms, a paradigm shift involves a new way of thinking or a new way of doing things (like streaming movies instead of renting DVDs or going to a theater). But according to Thomas Kuhn (1962/2012), who brought the concept of paradigm shifts to an academic audience with the publication of his book *The Structure of Scientific Revolutions*, paradigm shifts are *revolutionary* in nature—overthrowing older constellations of ideas and beliefs that no longer have the explanatory power of the new paradigm. Some shifts have proven to be world historical, driven by events that shake the very foundations of the way that humans understand themselves and their place in the world. One important example is the major shift in the concept of the person that occurred as a result of a number of events at the dawn of humanist thinking: the Copernican Revolution that overturned the geocentric understanding of the planet and brought about the heliocentric worldview, the black death which killed off most of the European population, the decentering of the dogma of the Medieval religious regime as empirical science advanced, and new philosophies of human rights, freedom of inquiry, justice, and the dignity of human life. All of these things supported the emergence of the concept of the *individual*, a category to which only a privileged few had aspired (priests, emperors, kings, etc.) since ancient times.

The new view of persons as individuals took centuries to include not just elite (mostly white) men of property, and for much of the humanist era women, people of color, children, and people with disabilities were not regarded as full human beings, and in fact were often considered as property of men. With the advent of individualism has come a number of positive outcomes; on the one hand, the moral worth of persons has come to be recognized, people have the freedom to identify their own objectives and obtain them, they can acquire property and do with it what they will, and the political concept of the individual (one person, one vote) has led us on a path towards more inclusive democracy.

On the other hand, with this notion that "man is the measure of all things" has come the sense of human mastery and control over all of nature, the idea that humans can possess and exploit the resources of the planet without concern for consequences, and the determination that individual interests supersede the interests of the collective. It has become clear that not only has this notion of the autonomous individual brought about a decline in community and solidarity, it has brought us to an ecological tipping point at which planetary life systems are deteriorating, and even continued human survival can no longer be taken for granted.

From chaos and complexity theories, we know that when systems move into "far from equilibrium states," change is both inevitable and unpredictable. At certain bifurcation points, a system may *devolve* into an even more chaotic state, or things may *evolve*—reorganize themselves into a new order, a more productive place that might not have been reached through incremental change. If we draw an analogy from the historical period described earlier, the time during the shift to humanism in which many systems (social systems, governmental, cognitive, religious) were in far-from-equilibrium states, we can see a parallel to the current moment in time. We are living through a period of great conflicts across the globe, devastating climate effects, a global pandemic, mass migrations, unprecedented wildfires, shifting social mores, and mass extinction events. In my most optimistic moments, I theorize that the chaotic state we are in right now could prove to be a portal, an opening inviting us into a radically new way of being in the world (Kesson, 2020). Perhaps our bifurcation point is the "critical juncture" we find ourselves at: with the glorious new era on its one side and the worn-out skeleton of the past on the other.

In 1982, Fritjof Capra published a book called *The Turning Point*, in which he elaborated on the revolutionary/evolutionary possibilities evident in the many small shifts occurring in the academic worlds of science, economics, psychology, ecology, and health, shifts which he believed represented a new vision of reality, a fundamental change in our thoughts, perceptions, and values. These academic shifts paralleled "a whole series of social movements that all seem to go in the same direction, emphasizing different aspects of this new vision of reality" (p. 16). The story that seems so dominant now, says Capra, the decaying structures and institutions that refuse to give way to the new, will inevitably collapse, making way for the "turning point"—the advent of "a transformation of unprecedented dimensions, a turning point for the planet as a whole" (p. 16). While many of us who were inspired by Capra's thinking were perhaps disappointed when decades passed without experiencing much of a turning point, it is possible that "Though the mills of God grind slowly; Yet they grind exceedingly small" (Henry Wadsworth Longfellow's version of a well-known aphorism). Cosmic time differs from Earth time—things may move slowly from our limited points of view, but they *do* move, and we can take heart from knowing this. It is to these transformative possibilities that this book is devoted.

Neohumanist education, in theory and practice, is dedicated to the idea that humans can choose this "bright new era" on the other side of the abyss that we face; that we can choose to build a life-affirming ecological civilization, that we can bring about a society of radical equality, that we can co-create a world grounded in ecological ethics and natural abundance, and that the sense of deep interconnectedness is the place from which all right action grows. These values and commitments form the core of a curriculum designed to prepare young people for the challenges of the Anthropocene, to provide hope, and enable them to survive and thrive into the future.

We need to honor what we have learned from the collective mistakes of the past, bring with us the ancient wisdom that can still serve the interests of humans and non-human others, hold onto what is useful, good, and true from the modern era of science and rationalism, but gather and bury the bones of the "worn out skeleton of the past," the remains of the isms that divide, conquer, and destroy us: predatory capital*ism*, ego-centric individual*ism*, rampant material*ism*, anthropocentr*ism*, sex*ism*, rac*ism*, ethnocentr*ism*, age*ism*, class*ism*, able*ism*. We need to root out the Windigo that lies within us all, by refusing to feed it, and opt instead to feed that which gives us a sense of connectedness, of care for the Earth, of kinship with all species, of empathy and compassion for other humans, of appreciation for the natural abundance and the simple life, and a desire to live a life of purpose and meaning.

It is a mistake to title this closing chapter a "Conclusion," conventional as it is to end a book in this way. There is no way to write a conclusion to a book on neohumanist education, as it is, by its own dynamic definition, a work-in-progress. I hope the book serves as a conversation starter—a place from which to jump off into exploration of what neohumanism looks like in different times, in different places, and in different circumstances. If human beings actually do survive this perfect storm of disasters facing us, and manage the quantum leap into a holistic paradigm that centers life, justice, equality, joy, beauty, and spiritual upliftment, neohumanist education could become the norm, with its explicit, and absolutely necessary commitment to *becoming One with the world*.

References

Capra, F. (1982). *The turning point: Science, society, and the rising culture*. Random House, Bantam Books.

Kesson, K. (2020, April 12). Three scenarios for the future of education in the Anthropocene. *Journal of Futures Studies.* https://jfsdigital.org/2020/04/12/three-scenarios-for-the-future-of-education-in-the-anthropocene/

Kimmerer, R. (2015). *Braiding sweetgrass: Indigenous wisdom, scientific knowledge and the teachings of plants.* Milkweed Editions.

Kuhn, T. (2012). *The structure of scientific revolutions,* 4th edition. Chicago Distribution Center. (Original work published 1962)

Muise, P. (2009). *Cannibal giants of the snowy northern forest.* http://newenglandfolklore.blogspot.com/2009/01/cannibal-giants-of-snowy-northern.html

Raworth, K. (2018). *Doughnut economics.* Chelsea Green Publishing.

Swimme, B. T. (1988). The cosmic creation story. In D. R. Griffin (Ed.), *The reenchantment of science* (pp. 47–56). SUNY Press.

Swimme, B. T., & Tucker, M. E. (2011). *Journey of the universe.* Yale University Press.

Further Resources

If you are interested in learning more about neohumanism and neohumanist Education, we recommend the following resources:

Neohumanist Education
   https://neohumanisteducation.org/

GANE—Global Association of Neohumanist Educators
   https://gane-educators.org/

Ananda Marga Gurukula
   https://gurukul.edu/

NHCA—Neohumanist College of Asheville
   https://nhca.gurukul.edu/

Research, development and outreach of P.R. Sarkar's teachings and related ideas
   https://prsinstitute.org/

Publications

Books
   https://neohumanisteducation.org/materials/
   http://gurukul.edu

Gurukula Network Newsletter
    https://gurukul.edu/newsletter/about-amgk-newsletter/

Neohumanist Review
    https://theneohumanist.com/

Neohumanist Education Resources
    https://nheresources.gurukul.edu/

About the Author

Kathleen Kesson is professor emeritus of teaching, learning, and leadership, LIU-Brooklyn. She is the former director of teacher education at Goddard College in Vermont, and was the founding director of the John Dewey Project on Progressive Education at the University of Vermont, a research and policy organization. She has authored and co-authored numerous books (6), book chapters (20), and articles in peer reviewed journals (33) and taught graduate and undergraduate courses in educational philosophy, aesthetics, the social foundations of education, spirituality and education, curriculum studies, educational futures, and qualitative research for 30+ years. She is currently a global affiliate with the GUND Institute for Environment at the University of Vermont, and is a contributing member of the Great Transition Initiative, a project of the Tellus Institute in Cambridge, MA. She first wrote about neohumanist education in 1988, and has studied the work of P. R. Sarkar for over 50 years. She is currently program director and faculty in a global program she designed for preparing neohumanist teachers, under the auspices of Gurukula (based in India), through the new Neohumanist College of Asheville, in North Carolina.

About the Contributors

Alieta Belle is a passionate advocate for integrating creativity with learning, and promoting quality arts, media, and environmental education for young people. She is currently the arts and cultural studies teacher at the Neohumanist Primary School, The River School; teaching visual arts and media arts to students across the grades. She works with networks of professionals in environmental and arts fields to enrich student learning, offer real-world hands-on experiences to students, and promote active citizenship in the area of sustainability.

MJ "MahaJyoti" Glassman lives in Denver, Colorado and has spent over 30 years working in a yoga-based preschool. MJ teaches multi-generational adults and facilitates yoga teacher trainings. A registered 500 hour yoga teacher, she is an avid yoga enthusiast and community service advocate who occasionally instructs others on how to teach Ashtanga Yoga to kids of all ages.

Ron Miller founded the journal *Holistic Education Review* in 1988 and was publisher/editor of many other periodicals and books, and author or editor of nine of his own books, on the history and philosophy of educational alternatives. He has been a teacher from Montessori preschool through adult education.

Leeza Stratford, with over 30 years experience working with infants, children and families in healthcare, education and expressive arts therapy, believes in the power of curiosity and connection with all around us as the foundations for learning, health and healing. The core from which she supports others is a reflexive space of creative curiosity, about what another is experiencing and coming to know—always wondering what the child is noticing in their heart, mind, and body.

Index

A

Abram, David, 190, 194
Anthropocene, xxv, xxvi, 3, 23, 345, 359, 386
    extinctions, 327, 345, 359, 360
Arts, 12, 168, 351
    approaches to arts education, 170
    evolution and, 165–167, 188–189, 242, 351
    as experience, 171–172
    creative thinking, 174–175, 370
    cultural appropriation, 169
    enactment, 177, 189–190
    expressive therapies and, 211–213
    multi-arts integration, 170
    multiple intelligences and, 61, 174, 189
    neuroaesthetics, 205, 232
    participatory ritual, 189, 376–377
    pseudo-culture, 167
    spiritual development and, 176–177, 218–220
    in STEAM education, 344, 370–371, 377–378
Assessment, 126–127
    authentic, 197–198
    eugenics, 127–128
    formative, 129
    in literacy, 197–198
    portfolios, 107
    rubrics, 130–131
    summative, 129–130
    testing, 127
Ashtanga Yoga, xxix, xxxiii–xxxv, 37–38, 288, 291, 305, 360
    meditation, science of, xxxiv, 56, 158, 289–290
    meditation, teaching of, 311–314
    Yama and Niyama, xxxiv–xxxv, 33, 302
    Yoga Sutras, 37, 288

B

Behaviorism, 13, 62–63
Behavior management
    restorative practices and, 160–161
Bettleheim, Bruno, 187–188
Bildung, 10
Brahmacakra, xxxviii, 5–6, 185, 283, 362
Biophilia hypothesis, 351
Biopsychology, 27, 68–69

C

Child Development
  ends-in-view, 43–44
  the individual, 49–50
  neohumanism and, 52–53
  norms and, 48, 83–84, 93, 115–116
  social construction of, 42–43
  stage theories, 44–48
Community-based learning, 86, 151–152
Cosmology, xxxviii–xxxix, 5–6, 32, 355, 362
Creative drama
  choral reading, 279
  debriefing, 280–281
  definition of, 270
  dialogue exercises, 273–274
  eco-theater, 282–283
  fantasy play, 270–272
  improvisation, 273–274, 278, 281
  pantomime, 273, 278
  puppetry, 275–276
  reader's theater, 279–280
  role play, 157–158, 274–275
  storymaking, 194–195, 271–272
  warm-ups, 272–274
Creative movement
  curricular applications, 262–264
  definition of, 250–251
  elements of, 253–254
  environmental space, 252
  language development and, 196, 254–255, 265–266
  materials, 252–253
  movement stories, 255–258
  movement vocabulary, 254–255
  pantomime, 262
  rules, 253
Critical Pedagogy, 14, 17, 64–65, 117, 320, 328, 333
Critical thinking, xxxiii, xxxviii, 8, 14, 65, 147, 198–199, 218, 266, 311, 323, 333, 335, 352, 358
Csikszentmihalyi, Mihaly, 172
Curriculum
  aims, 118–119
  Common Core standards, 114–115
  content, 24, 120–122
  control of, 114–115
  culminating activities, 123–124
  definitions of, 113–114
  design, 117–118, 122–126, 132–136
  emergent, 132–136, 161–162
  experiences, 58–60, 64, 114, 124–126, 171–172, 335–336
  hidden curriculum, 115–116
  horizontal integration, 131
  integrated, 131–132
  interdisciplinary, 132
  multidisciplinary, 131–132
  null curriculum, 116
  objectives, 119–120
  pedagogical content knowledge, 122–123, 146, 366
  scope and sequence, 118, 122–123, 372
  sources of, 116–117
  spiral curriculum, 372–376
  transdisciplinary, 132
  Universal Design for Learning, 122–124
  vertical integration, 122, 372
Davidson, Richard, 158, 287
Decolonization, xxxvii, 80, 81, 85
  in the U.S., 78
  in India, 78
Dewey, John, 63, 171–172, 216, 320, 367
Dharma, 331
Discipline, 160–161
Dissanayake, Ellen, 165–167, 188–189, 232, 238, 351
Doll, William, 135

E

Egan, Kieran, 185
Einstein, Albert, 7, 233, 254, 353, 377
Eisner, Elliot, 206, 210, 217
Epistemology, 8, 32–33
  ancestral knowledge, 117, 322, 325, 333, 353
  epistemological pluralism, xxxix, 9, 30, 32, 72, 80, 226, 323, 353
  embodied knowledge, xxxix, 72, 94, 250, 322, 323, 333, 353
  extroversial knowledge, xxxiii, 8, 66, 353

intergenerational knowing, xxxix, 9, 73, 117, 183, 322–323
introversial knowledge, xxxiii, 8, 66, 353
intuitional knowledge, xxxix, 9, 32, 66–67, 69, 72, 351, 353
non-rational knowing, 73, 352
Ethics, 10–11, 33, 72, 85, 282, 291–302, 324, 332–333, 344, 346, 349–350, 364, 376

F

Forest schooling, 152
Franck, Frederick, 206
Freire, Paulo,14, 64, 175, 180, 198, 333

G

Gallas, Karen, 364–366
Gardner, Howard, 49, 60, 174
Goleman, Daniel, 158, 287
Growth mindset, 129–130

H

Holism, 15–16
Holistic education, xxxiii, 16, 65–66, 132
Holocene, xxv, 345
Humanism, xxvi–xxviii, xxix, 11, 14–15, 19, 385
    post humanisms, xxviii

I

Individualism, 115, 384–385
Inquiry, 8, 13, 17, 24, 29–30, 64, 92
    contemplative inquiry, 92
    descriptive inquiry, 94–105
    phenomenology, 105–106
    school-based, 106–108, 326, 327, 369
Intersectionality, 321, 330
Interspecies intersubjectivity, xxxii

J

Jacobson, Arun, 191

Johnston, Basil, 382
Jung, Carl, 25, 56, 208, 221

K

Kimmerer, Robin Wall, 183, 382
Koshas, 26–27, 38, 67–68, 106
Kuhn, Thomas, 348, 384

L

Learning
    active learning, 124, 146, 155, 157–158, 250
    brain-based learning, 58–60
    cooperative learning, 43, 64, 146, 157
    multiple intelligences and, 60–62, 174–175
Literacy
    assessment and evaluation of, 197–198
    creative movement and, 265–266
    critical thinking and, 198–199
    definition of, 180–181
    enactment, 188–190
    fantasy and fairy tale, 187–188
    language and place, 182–184
    media literacy, 198–199, 218
    neohumanist principles of, 199–200
    pictorial approach, 194–195
    preservation of local language, 83, 179–180, 322, 331
    pre-text societies, 181–182
    pseudo-culture and, 191–192
    the reading wars, 193–197
    social media, 87, 114, 198, 349
    storytelling, 184–185, 280
    whole language, 193
London, Peter, 223–224

M

Macdonald, James, 16, 65–66, 92, 106, 324
Mental images, 206, 243, 252, 265, 364
Microvita, 283, 352
Moffett, James, xxxv–xxxvi, 150
Montessori, Maria, 15, 45, 46, 65

Music
  composition, 233
  culture and, 237–239
  elements of, 234
  language and, 235–236
  math and, 235
  neuroaesthetics and, 232–234
  purposes of, 231–232
  social-emotional learning and, 236–237
  spirituality and, 241–245
  therapy, 233, 243,

N

Neohumanism, xxviii–xxx, xxxv, 5, 238, 244, 292, 311, 320–321, 324–325, 329, 331–332, 346, 350, 362

O

Ontology, xxx, xxxix, 6–8, 32, 250, 332, 352–353
Orbach, Nona, 219–220

P

Perennialism, 13, 62, 147
Piaget, Jean, 45, 254
Pragmatism, 13, 63–64, 147, 320
Presence, 161–162

R

Restorative practices, 161
Romanticism, 13, 63, 147

S

Schooling, 85–87, 114, 148–150
  democratic classrooms, 327, 337
  democratic dispositions, 159
  deschooling/unschooling, 149–151
  design of the environment, 153–154
  metaphors of, 150–152
Service learning, 333–335

Sheldrake, Rupert, 208–209
Silberman, Charles, 368
Sloan, Douglas, 187
Smithwhite, Marguerite, 221–223
Social-Emotional Learning, 11, 86, 93, 158–160, 176, 190, 287
  creative movement and, 250
  educational drama and, 270, 272, 281
  multiple intelligences and, 61
  music and, 236–237
  Yoga ethics and, 293, 296, 314–315
Social Reconstructionism, 64
Social Studies
  aim of, 317
  controversial topics in, 330
  democratic living, 320, 326–327, 337
  diversity, 329–331
  ethics, 332–333
  experiential learning in, 335–337
  identity, 324–326, 330
  knowledge wars in, 319
  neohumanist principles of, 320–321
  place-based learning, 86, 327–328
  Prout perspectives in, 321–324
  service learning in, 333–335
  themes in, 318
Spitzer, Michael, 232
Spolin, Viola, 274
STEAM
  aesthetics in, 351
  arts-based STEAM learning, 370–371
  assumptions of, 347
  bias in science, 347
  community and, 378–379
  definition of, 343–344
  ethics and values in, 349–350
  Green Revolution, 348
  integrating mathematics, 366, 370
  integrating technology, 366–367
  limits of science, 348–349
  materialism, 348–349
  meaning and purpose in, 350
  mechanism, advent of, 345, 354
  messing about, 368–369, 371
  neohumanist principles of STEAM teaching, 377–378

new story of science, xxxviii, 5, 352–355, 383–384
organicism in, 345, 354
planning in, 367–368
power of science, 346
pseudo-science, 349
ritual, ceremony, and festival in, 376–377
science talks, 364–366, 367, 373, 375
scientific method, 347–348
scientific revolutions, 348–349
spirituality in, 351–352
themes in, 358–362
watersheds, study of, 373–376
Steiner, Rudolph, 45, 65
Swimme, Brian, 354, 383

T

Taminga, Tang, 191
Teacher development
balanced emotions, 29
care of the self, 28
dimensions of the self, 26–28
moral development, 30–31
pedagogical arts, 24
self-knowledge, 25–26
social competence, 29
subject matter knowledge, 24
Teaching
cooperative learning, 157
discussion, 156
gallery walks, 157
instructional methods, 146
lecture, 155, 184

pedagogical arts, 24, 122, 146
philosophies of, 147
modeling, 155, 295, 365
neohumanist teaching principles, 148
participation structures, 155, 158
project-based learning, 157
rhythm of the day, 154–155
role play, 157–158, 274–275
self-paced learning, 155–156
teacher presence, 161–162

V

Visual art
child development and, 210–214
cognitive skills in, 211
elements of, 207–210
Expressive Therapies Continuum, 211–213
mandalas, 220–223
media literacy, 218
meditation and, 221–223
modeling and sculpture, 214–216
nature and, 223–225
neuroaesthetics, 205
Prospect School archives, 220
spiritual dimension of, 218–220
viewing and responding to, 216–218

W

Waldorf schools, 45, 189, 194, 195, 208
Wisdom, 70, 72, 325, 333, 352, 360, 378, 386

Printed in the USA
CPSIA information can be obtained
at www.ICGtesting.com
LVHW021731041124
795688LV00039B/1172